ECONOMIC ORGANIZATION, CAPABILITIES AND CO-ORDINATION

G.B. Richardson is often thought of as one of the 'founding fathers' of the theory of the firm and the market. His work has given insights into key issues and debates such as markets versus hierarchies, the antitrust implications of price agreements, the economics of information and the concept of competition based upon differentiated firms. Yet whilst he is often quoted, few people are familiar with his original work.

Drawn from a recent colloquium held in his honour, the papers in this volume tie in with the themes central in G.B. Richardson's work, addressing their significance, their relationship to the work of other economists and their potential for further development. The first few chapters cover themes related to the comparative neglect of Richardson's work, the links with the Marshallian school and Austrian economics. Later chapters go on to discuss modern thinking on the theory of the firm, connections between economic and management approaches, as well as applications of the 'Richardson model' to collaborative arrangements, the growth of the firm and innovation policy. Crucially, the book also includes a recent essay by G.B. Richardson himself, which clearly shows the continuing development of his ideas.

This collection aims to encourage further development of Richardson's themes. It will make excellent reading for students looking at the capability/competence approach to the firm, and for all those wishing to get to know the work of this important economist.

Nicolai J. Foss is Associate Professor in the Department of Industrial Economics and Strategy at the Copenhagen Business School in Denmark. **Brian J. Loasby** is Emeritus Professor in the Department of Economics, University of Stirling.

ROUTLEDGE STUDIES IN BUSINESS ORGANIZATION AND NETWORKS

1. DEMOCRACY AND EFFICIENCY IN THE ECONOMIC ENTERPRISE
Edited by Ugo Pagano and Robert Rowthorn

2. TOWARDS A COMPETENCE THEORY OF THE FIRM
Edited by Nicolai J. Foss and Christian Knudsen

3. UNCERTAINTY AND ECONOMIC EVOLUTION
Essays in Honour of Armen A. Alchian
Edited by John R. Lott Jr.

4. THE END OF THE PROFESSIONS?
The Restructuring of Professional Work
Edited by Jane Broadbent, Michael Bietrick and Jennifer Roberts

5. SHOPFLOOR MATTERS
Labor-management relations in 20th century American manufacturing
David Fairris

6. THE ORGANISATION OF THE FIRM
International Business Perspecives
Edited by Ram Mudambi and Martin Ricketts

7. ORGANIZING INDUSTRIAL ACTIVITIES ACROSS BORDERS
Anna Dubois

8. ECONOMIC ORGANIZATION, CAPABILITIES AND CO-ORDINATION
Edited by Nicolai J. Foss and Brian J. Loasby

ECONOMIC ORGANIZATION, CAPABILITIES AND CO-ORDINATION

Essays in Honour of G. B. Richardson

Edited by Nicolai J. Foss and Brian J. Loasby

London and New York

First published 1998
by Routledge
11 New Fetter Lane, London EC4P 4EE

Simultaneously published in the USA and Canada
by Routledge
29 West 35th Street, New York, NY 10001

© 1998 Nicolai J. Foss and Brian J. Loasby, selection and editorial matter; individual chapters, the contributors

Typeset in Garamond by Routledge
Printed and bound in Great Britain by
Redwood Books, Trowbridge, Wiltshire

All rights reserved. No part of this book may be reprinted or reproduced or utilised in any form or by any electronic, mechanical, or other means, now known or hereafter invented, including photocopying and recording, or in any information storage or retrieval system, without permission in writing from the publishers.

British Library Cataloguing in Publication Data
A catalogue record for this book is available from the British Library

Library of Congress Cataloging in Publication Data
Economic organization, capabilities and co-ordination/edited by Nicolai J. Foss and Brian J. Loasby.
'Drawn from a recent colloquium held in his honour, the papers in this volume tie in with the themes central in G. B. Richardson's work.'
Includes bibliographical references and index.
1. Competition – Congresses. 2. Investments – Congresses.
3. Uncertainty – Congresses. 4. Equilibrium (Economics) – Congresses. 5. Prices – Congresses. 6. Capitalism – Congresses. 7. Richardson, G. B. I. Foss, Nicolai, J.
II. Loasby, Brian J. III. Richardson, G. B.
HD41.E29 1998
338.5–dc21
97–39553
CIP

ISBN 0–415–18390–1

CONTENTS

List of illustrations ix
Notes on contributors x

1 Introduction: co-ordination and capabilities 1
  NICOLAI J. FOSS AND BRIAN J. LOASBY

2 George Richardson's career and the literature of economics 14
  PETER E. EARL

  Introduction 14
  Richardson's path to economics 15
  The research co-ordination problem 18
  The limited impact of Richardson's work 20
  Was Debreu the cause of Information and Investment's *failure to take off in the 1960s? 24*
  Networks, institutions and academic search processes 30
  Conclusion 34

3 Some principles of economic organisation 44
  GEORGE B. RICHARDSON

  The need for co-ordination 44
  The invisible hand 45
  A cardinal principle of economic organisation 46
  The need for co-operation 47
  The need for direction 48
  Direction: its scope and limits 50
  The firm as a microeconomy 51
  Pricing within a firm 52
  Communications, scale and structure 54

A summary of the argument so far 55
The costs of consolidation 57
Other functions of the firm 58

4 **Co-operation and competition paradoxes in the theory of the organisation of industry**   63
JACQUES-LAURENT RAVIX

Introduction 63
Information, knowledge and industrial co-ordination 64
The nature of the firm and the paradox of co-operation 70
The nature of industry and the paradox of competition 75
Conclusion 79

5 **Marshall, Andrews and Richardson on markets: an interpretation**   83
RICHARD ARENA AND CLAIRE CHARBIT

Introduction 83
General Economic Equilibrium: agents and markets 84
Agents and markets in a Marshallian perspective 86
Individual agents in Andrews and Richardson 92
Global markets in Andrews and Richardson 97
Conclusion 101

6 **Information and investment in a wider context**   104
DENIS O'BRIEN

Introduction 104
Richardson's criticism of general equilibrium 106
The origins of the problem of knowledge 107
Attempts to mend the model: the Marshallian elements 109
The defence of cartelisation 113
The planned economy 115
Considerations from the wider literature 116
Conclusion 117

CONTENTS

7 Information and co-ordination in an effective competitive process: Downie's evolutionary model as a means of resolving Richardson's problem with competition in the context of post-Marshallian economics   121
JOHN NIGHTINGALE

Introduction 121
Downie's population ecology of the industry 122
Richardson's competitive process 127
An alternative welfare economics 132
Conclusion 134

8 Austrian and post-Marshallian economics: the bridging work of George Richardson   138
NICOLAI J. FOSS

Introduction 138
Marshall, the post-Marshallians and Austrian economics 140
George Richardson: Marshallian answers to Austrian problems 144
Austrian and post-Marshallian economics: the theory of the firm 152
Conclusion 156

9 The concept of capabilities   163
BRIAN J. LOASBY

Introduction 163
The division of labour and the organisation of knowledge 164
Direct 'knowledge how' 167
Indirect 'knowledge how' 170
Competitive advantage 171
Capabilities in decision-making 178
The evolution of capabilities 179

10 Capabilities and the theory of the firm   183
RICHARD N. LANGLOIS

Introduction 183
Production costs I: Pigovian price theory 184
Transaction costs 185
Modern transaction-cost theory 188
Production costs redux: capabilities 193

CONTENTS

11 Information costs and the organisational structure of the multinational enterprise   204
MARK CASSON

*Introduction 204
General principles 206
Meta-rationality: minimising the risk of mistakes 209
Decisiveness, consultation and the internal balance of power 211
The quality of information 213
Applications to the multinational enterprise 216*

12 Clusters of collaboration: the firm, join ventures, alliances and clubs   222
NEIL M. KAY

*Introduction 222
The evolution of collaborative activity 223
The evolution of collaboration in the diversified firm 226
The evolution of strategic business alliances 230
Conclusions 240*

13 Limits to a firm's rate of growth: the Richardsonian view and its contemporary empirical significance   243
GAVIN C. REID

*Introduction 243
Richardson's view on restraints to growth 244
Contemporary evidence on limits to a firm's growth 246
Limits to small-firm growth: the trade-off relationship 252
Conclusion 256*

14 Information, similar and complementary assets, and innovation policy   261
PAUL L. ROBERTSON

*Introduction 261
Information and innovation 262
Information, similarity and complementarity 275
Innovation and industry maturity 278
Conclusion 282*

Index   *289*

ILLUSTRATIONS

Figures

11.1	Maximisation of expected profit net of information cost	209
11.2	Optimising the collection of costly information	211
11.3	Basic model of intermediate product flow in a multinational enterprise	217
12.1	Joint venture strategy and structure	223
12.2	New venture opportunity for large diversified firms	227
12.3	Merger and joint venture options for diversified firms	228
12.4	Main nodes of the networked knowledge-based oligopoly in the biotech-based pharmaceutical industry	231
12.5	Collaboration	233
12.6	Alliance	234
12.7	Club or network	236
12.8	Small-firm involvement in collaboration	239
12.9	Club and extra-club linkages	240
13.1	Possible organisational forms for three small-firm types	249
14.1	Existing and potentially useful relationships between problem holders and solution holders	266
14.2	A model of the communication process	267
14.3	Performance of an established and an invading product: burst of improvement in established product	281

Tables

2.1	Citations of Richardson's work in widely used industrial economics texts	23
13.1	Size and business type	248
13.2	Performance and business type	251
13.3	Profitability equation (dependent variable: *ProfRate*)	253
13.4	Two iteration 3SLS estimates of growth and profitability equations	255
13.5	Three iteration estimates of growth and profitability equations	256

NOTES ON CONTRIBUTORS

Richard Arena, Département Economie, Université de Nice-Sophia Antipolis LATAPSES-CNRS.

Mark Casson, Department of Economics, University of Reading.

Claire Charbit, Département Economie, Ecole Nationale Supérieure des Télécommunications, Paris.

Peter E. Earl, Department of Economics, Lincoln University.

Nicolai J. Foss, Department of Industrial Economics and Strategy, Copenhagen Business School.

Neil M. Kay, Department of Economics, University of Strathclyde.

Richard N. Langlois, Department of Economics, University of Connecticut.

Brian J. Loasby, Department of Economics, University of Stirling.

John Nightingale, Senior Lecturer in Economics, University of New England, NSW.

Denis O'Brien, Department of Economics, University of Durham.

Jacques-Laurent Ravix, University of Nice-Sophia Antipolis and LATAPSES-CNRS .

Gavin C. Reid, CRIEFF, University of St Andrews.

George B. Richardson, Oxford.

Paul L. Robertson, Department of Economics and Management, University College, University of New South Wales.

1

INTRODUCTION

Co-ordination and capabilities

Nicolai J. Foss and Brian J. Loasby

In 1974 George B. Richardson, who had been a Reader at Oxford University and a Fellow of St John's College, became Chief Executive of Oxford University Press. In doing so he consciously abandoned his career in economics, because of an apparent lack of interest in his work by fellow economists and his own dissatisfaction with the trend of economic thinking. After managing Oxford University Press for fifteen years, he became Warden of Keble College, Oxford, and retired from that position in September 1994. In January 1995 two dozen economists met in St John's College for a colloquium which was designed not only to mark his formal retirement but also to welcome him back to economics. (The colloquium was organised by the editors, but Professor John Kay, then with the London Business School and Chairman of London Economics, and now Director of Oxford University Business School, offered to handle the practical arrangements with St John's College, for which the editors are extremely grateful.) The participants were representative of a growing number of economists who have developed an interest in, and appreciation of, Richardson's work, which has been marked by the publication of a second edition of his *Information and Investment*, incorporating reprints of two articles, a new Introduction and a foreword by David Teece. The chapters which follow constitute a selection from the papers presented at the colloquium, all of which received comments from Richardson himself, together with a paper from Denis O'Brien, who was not able to attend. In this Introduction, we wish to introduce these chapters and identify the themes in them which correspond to the themes in his work and are of contemporary relevance.

In a letter to one of the editors, Richardson said of himself that 'Perhaps we each of us have only one song to sing – with variations' (Richardson 1993). On the other hand, as Stan Metcalfe states in his entry in the *The Elgar Companion to Institutional and Evolutionary Economics*:

> In Richardson's work are found clear insights into modern debates on markets v. hierarchies, the stability of prices, the economics of information, the basis for rational expectations, and the economic reform of socialist economies. More significantly, by emphasizing competition as a process based upon differentiated firms, Richardson anticipated many of the questions credited to modern evolutionary economic theory.
>
> (Metcalfe 1994: 241)

We may add to Metcalfe's list recent writing on networks, on the capabilities view of the firm, industrial policy and much else. How can one theme, one song, relate to all this?

The paradox vanishes on the realisation that Richardson's theme is the co-ordination of specialised activities, each requiring distinctive capabilities, in complex systems. He seeks to explain how real economies are able to achieve some measure of successful co-ordination given the dispersion of knowledge which is represented by the distinctiveness of capabilities: hence the title of this book. Since co-ordination, sometimes presented in the form of allocative efficiency, is at the heart of economic theory, and since Richardson challenges the prevalent theoretical treatment of these issues, his work has profound implications both for the substance of economics and for the ways in which economists proceed.

As already indicated, almost all of Richardson's papers went largely unnoticed by the economics profession at the time they were produced. The reason for this neglect, which is considered more fully in Chapter 2, lies in their combination of strong originality, inspiration from non-Walrasian sources (notably Marshall and Hayek) and unwelcome subversive potential.

It is in *Information and Investment* (1960) that we find the fullest statement of Richardson's song. It is composed in a rather standard way: build up tension and release this tension. On the whole, however, the composition is performed *sotto voce*; like his one-time thesis adviser, John Hicks, Richardson speaks to the reader in a soft, persuasive style, and is always careful to explain what he is doing and why he is doing it.

He begins by criticising the superficial way in which economists have traditionally treated the process of co-ordination, pointing out that the attainment of equilibrium depends on expectations. However, expectations are based on information, but how much information economic agents are able to acquire and how reliable that information is depends on the structure of the markets in which they operate. Thus Richardson is diagnosing a problem – the co-ordination of dispersed and incomplete knowledge – which is of crucial interest to Austrian economists, and he is anticipating a Marshallian answer by pointing to the role of markets as information structures.

Richardson demonstrates in a long-run Walrasian setting that general equilibrium cannot be a configuration that a perfectly competitive economy could be expected to approach. Producers are unable to co-ordinate their investment decisions because they lack the necessary knowledge of other producers' plans; consequently there is no logical basis for the long-run supply curve in this setting. Like Sraffa (1926) more than three decades earlier, in directing his attack towards the supply curve Richardson is identifying a theoretical anomaly in price theory; however, his attack is far more fundamental and cannot be met by Sraffa's proposals. For Richardson is criticising the neoclassical idea of the atomistic individual producer or consumer existing in a complete institutional vacuum. His targets are not rationality or individualism as foundational concepts, but the very special interpretation that has come to be imposed on them by economic theorists; he is arguing that rationality, understood as the ability to make informed decisions, has to be embedded in a supporting and stability-providing network of institutions. Real economies are stabilised by the presence of numerous phenomena that represent imperfections relative to the Walrasian ideal, but which are necessary for the effective working of the economy. Richardson is thus anticipating the concerns of modern neo-institutionalist economists (Langlois 1986).

The stabilising mechanisms in question incorporate vertical integration, credit market imperfections, the Penrose effect, covert collusion, price notification schemes and much else, including sheer ignorance. Their overall effect is to stabilise producers' plans by making adjustment to a co-ordinated state somewhat sluggish – and therefore possible. The well-known stability problem of Walrasian economics is thus solved as a result of being restated in non-Walrasian terms.

During the 1960s Richardson applied the theoretical reasoning of *Information and Investment* to policy issues, such as the problems on which he worked as a member of the British Monopolies Commission, including price notification schemes (Richardson 1967) and restrictive trade practices in general (1965a). He also applied it to problems of socialist allocation (Richardson 1971) and to consultancy work for the British Electrical and Allied Manufacturers' Association (Richardson 1969).

A notable feature of Richardson's analysis of the co-ordination problem is his emphasis on the need to co-ordinate complementary investments. In his 1972 paper he draws on Penrose's (1959) analysis of distinctive capabilities to provide a rationale for vertical inter-firm arrangements, arguing that these arrangements allow the qualitative co-ordination of capabilities which, though *closely complementary*, are also *dissimilar* and therefore, in accordance with the principles of specialisation, best managed within separate organisations. However, the analysis has much wider implications: to paraphrase Hayek (1945) with a bow to Richardson, 'the marvel' is precisely that competition *and co-operation* together ensure that effective use is made of capabilities that are not possessed by any single firm.

Richardson's final publication before his recent return to economics was a paper on 'Adam Smith on competition and increasing returns' (1975). Although concerned with doctrinal history, this is a systematic and radical statement of Richardson's own economics, in which he both demonstrates the affinities of his own thought to that of Smith and explores a number of themes that were not fully developed in his earlier work. The stance taken is evolutionary and disequilibrium-oriented, emphasising path-dependence and increasing returns. Kaldor's paper on 'The irrelevance of equilibrium economics' (1972) is approvingly quoted.

Like his anticipation of the concerns of neo-institutional economists, this evolutionary formulation clearly suggests the contemporary relevance of Richardson's thought. It is also relevant to firm strategy and growth theory. Richardson's ideas and insights have not been fully incorporated in contemporary work on such issues and their implications have not been fully developed. Our objective in presenting the chapters which follow is to encourage further development of his ideas, not least through rereading his works.

In Chapter 2 Peter Earl relates Richardson's work and methods to the corpus of economics and seeks to explain the general lack of response within the profession. In the process he offers insights into questions which may be asked of any discipline, and which recur in several subsequent chapters. Why do some problems become a focus of attention at the expense of others which may seem to disinterested observers no less important? How do particular people try to deal with particular problems, and why? What explains the reception which their work receives?

Earl has no difficulty in demonstrating that the market for economic ideas cannot be characterised as an equilibrium of optimising agents – unless the crucial analysis is buried in the definitions of equilibrium and optimisation. Market processes, in academia as well as in the economy, depend on information and institutions, and those wishing to trade in the marketplace of economics face co-ordination problems of the kind that Richardson analysed in *Information and Investment*.

In seeking to explain why Richardson's fundamental criticism of the perfectly competitive model was neither refuted nor accepted but simply ignored, Earl takes issue with an explanation put forward some years ago by one of the editors (Loasby 1989: 99). That editor is now inclined to agree with Earl that the principal reason was probably a widespread feeling that since actual competition seemed to work fairly well the model of perfect competition, which combined the merits of familiarity and apparent rigour, could be safely, and comfortably, retained. 'The argument in favour of competition does not rest on the conditions that would exist if it were perfect', as Hayek (1949: 104) observed; but that argument is ignored in favour of the familiar analysis. Ronald Coase's notable failure to persuade economists to accept the message of 'The problem of social cost' (Coase

INTRODUCTION: CO-ORDINATION AND CAPABILITIES

1960), which was published in the same year as *Information and Investment*, is certainly consistent with that explanation; for Richardson and Coase were both arguing that 'current economic analysis is incapable of handling many of the problems to which it purports to give answers' (Coase 1988: 15). This is a sad commentary on the standards of conceptual, as distinct from technical, rigour within economics.

In Chapter 3 George Richardson revisits his 1972 article on 'The organisation of industry'. By focusing on the need to co-ordinate specialised activities, each of which requires specific capabilities, he links it with the theme of *Information and Investment*; and by setting this co-ordination problem within the context of endogenous growth, which entails changes in the structure of both industries and individual firms, he invokes the argument of the last article that he wrote before abandoning economics – 'Adam Smith on competition and increasing returns'. His principal subject in this chapter is the management of a business as a microeconomy, and it is illuminated by his own experience as Chief Executive of Oxford University Press. Management is not adequately represented by the selection of production plans from a well-defined production set; and though access to information is important, Richardson believes that patterns of experience and skills – capabilities – are more important than transaction costs, as these are normally defined, in explaining the scope of each firm, its internal organisation, which relies on authority, incentives and internal prices, and its relationships with other firms (what Marshall called its 'external organisation'). He disagrees with Oliver Williamson's emphasis on combating opportunism: like Edith Penrose, he believes that the primary reason for firms is the co-ordination of the growth and use of knowledge, including knowledge of performance skills.

Jacques-Laurent Ravix focuses explicitly on the relationship between the work of Richardson and that of Coase, and examines this relationship within a methodological perspective. He points out that 'methodology matters because of its real effects on analytical developments' (Chapter 4) – in this particular instance because a focus on allocative efficiency leads to a very restricted view of information and to the neglect of productive capabilities, thereby encouraging the conception of economics as a tautological rather than an empirical science. It is not, therefore, surprising that, as Coase observed in 1972, economists have so little to say 'about what firms actually do' (Coase 1988: 65). Coase challenged marginalist theory by pointing to the costs of using the price mechanism, and demonstrated that a recognition of these costs could explain the scope of a firm in a way that resolved an old dilemma of perfect competition (and of imperfect competition too, as he pointed out). As Langlois observes in Chapter 10, the scope of the firm in price theory is a matter of assumption.

However, Coase's own theoretical system did not deal satisfactorily with inter-firm transactions, which are far more important than one would expect from Coase's (or Williamson's) writings, and it was precisely this theoretical deficiency that provided the focus of Richardson's 'The organisation of industry'. Whereas Coase had replaced the product as the unit of analysis by the individual transaction, Richardson selected the specific productive activity as his unit. Though Coase had recognised that '[a] given set of activities will facilitate the carrying out of some activities but hinder the performance of others' (1988: 63), he was unable to theorise about the relationship; but Richardson employed the concepts of similarity and complementarity to explain how the co-ordination of economic activities is distributed between firms, markets and inter-firm networks — and to provide the ingredients for an analysis of innovation. Competition, as a process, is preserved because the irreducible ambiguity of information encourages firms repeatedly to draw different conclusions about their prospects from the same data.

Ravix's juxtaposition of Richardson and Coase is followed, in Chapter 5, by Richard Arena and Claire Charbit's juxtaposition of Richardson and Philip Andrews as interpreters and developers of Marshall's economics. Marshall's treatment of markets was ambiguous: he offered general principles which he intended to apply in his second volume; and in the absence of this second volume the ambiguity has been resolved in accordance with methodological preconceptions (and with little regard by some interpreters for those elements of that volume which appeared in *Industry and Trade*, 1923). Arena and Charbit draw attention to Andrews's concern for the particularities of specific markets, each of which is constituted by those with the relevant knowledge needed to use it (as Menger had included knowledge of use in his definition of a good), and match this with Richardson's citation of Marshall's warning against 'plain and simple doctrine' and his extensive discussion of particular arrangements in *Information and Investment*. They then go on to consider Marshall's treatment of human behaviour within society, which is reflected in market behaviour, and of the influences of convention and adaptation on that behaviour, emphasising his preference for free choice rather than competition as the fundamental principle of modern economies, and conclude by examining the reflections of this treatment in the work of Andrews and Richardson.

Denis O'Brien was among the first economists to appreciate the force of the 'profound and entirely valid criticism of general equilibrium' (Chapter 6) in *Information and Investment*, but he has always been uneasy about what he considers to be Richardson's unjustifiably favourable attitude in that book towards cartels and planning. His chapter (Chapter 6) examines the source of this unease, which is methodological. As Earl notes in Chapter 2, Richardson adopted Hicks's method of thinking through problems without attempting systematically to confront his conclusions with evidence, either from econometric analysis or, as Andrews did, by visiting firms. (As is now well known, Hicks had a poor opinion of Andrews's work.) But this might not have mattered had Richardson appreciated the difficulty of remedying the fundamental incoherence of perfectly competitive general equilibrium by introducing Marshallian and Austrian elements which were incompatible with it. (The Austrian criticism of central planning is, equally, a criticism of the perfectly competitive equilibrium model on which the case for planning is based.) O'Brien argues that Richardson fails to make a consistent distinction between perfect competition, which excludes all competitive activity, and competition in real-world markets, which provide much of the information which is needed for co-ordination. In particular, Richardson fails, in O'Brien's view, to appreciate the full implications of Marshall's treatment of time, both for the practical solution of the co-ordination problem and for the relevance of that problem as defined within a purely axiomatic system.

In Chapter 7 John Nightingale provides another perspective on *Information and Investment* by comparing it with Jack Downie's *The Competitive Process*. Whereas Richardson had tried to supply a missing theory of equilibration, Downie simply dismissed the notion of equilibration as irrelevant to explaining economic progress. (Richardson came close to echoing this judgement in his 1975 article on Adam Smith.) This freed him to develop an analysis of historical causation, which takes the form of an evolutionary theory. The selection pressures in competitive – not, of course, perfectly competitive – markets, and their financial consequences, lead to a convergence on best practice technology (the transfer mechanism); but they also provide a strong incentive for the laggards to develop improvements which will arrest, and sometimes even reverse, their decline (the innovation mechanism). Thus variety is continually renewed, providing a changing menu for continuing selection; and in contrast to biological evolution, the generation and reduction of variety are joint products of a competitive system. Downie's theory of progress depends (like Marshall's) on the tendency to variation among firms, whereas Richardson's search for means of equilibration and the theoretical context in which he defined his problem (to which O'Brien draws attention) led him to focus in *Information and Investment* on a typical firm. His later articles of 1972 and 1975 and his chapter in this book mark a change in emphasis in both problem definition and analytical method.

Whereas O'Brien argues that in 1960 Richardson, though drawing on the Marshallian and Austrian traditions, did not make full use of them, Nicolai Foss (Chapter 8) argues that the full range of his work provides an excellent basis for a productive combination of those traditions. He begins by outlining the main features of each, notably their concern with change and with institutions and organisations as means of adapting to and promoting change, and seeks to demonstrate that the apparent disjunction between them is the result of differences in focus which are not conflicting but complementary. He then identifies Marshallian and Austrian (especially Hayekian) themes in Richardson's work, all of which is related to the organisation of knowledge in a production economy; and in his final section he proposes a common theme for Austrians and Marshallians which draws directly on Richardson's ideas: a theory of the firm in the market, which emphasises capabilities, institutions, flexibility and innovation.

Capabilities provide the theme of Brian Loasby's chapter (Chapter 9). He begins with Adam Smith's theory of endogenous growth through the division of labour, which promotes the discovery of differentiated knowledge, and then offers a two-dimensional categorisation of knowledge: knowing that v. knowing how (citing Gilbert Ryle's *Concept of Mind*, 1949); and direct v. indirect knowledge. The Austro-Marshallian theme of Chapter 8 is continued in a review of Marshall's and Hayek's early ventures into evolutionary psychology, which suggest that performance skills are much more important relative to ratiocination than one would suspect from economic models. Decision-making itself is not an unambiguously logical process, but depends on situationally relevant capabilities. As Smith recognised, everyone faces a problem of co-ordination in the form of knowing how to get things done by other people; and the solution is not to be found in rational choice theory. It is often found in organisations such as firms and in inter-firm relationships which embody structures of complementary knowledge. Firms may find competitive advantage in distinctive capabilities, direct and indirect – as Drucker told us many years ago; but capabilities, like other kinds of knowledge, are never static but always conjectural. A variety of capabilities provides diversity within a system and therefore reserves against unforeseeable contingencies – which may stimulate the development of new capabilities.

Richard Langlois argues in Chapter 10 that because of his focus on the co-ordination of capabilities Richardson is 'as much a critic as an ally' of modern theorists of the firm. Since the firm in price theory is defined as a supplier of an identifiable product, its boundaries are subject to assumption, not explanation. Modern transaction cost theory seeks to supplement price theory by combining cognitive limitations and a specific behavioural assumption of opportunism in order to generate an additional category of incentive problems, which are resolved by the design of efficient organisations, or, in property rights and moral hazard theories, by efficient contracts. But this theoretical system bypasses Coase's concern for qualitative co-ordination. Richardson shares this concern, both in his 1960 study of co-ordination (though this is independent of Coase's writing) and in 'The organisation of industry'; and his distinctive contribution, already discernible in 1960 but central in 1972, is to bring production costs back into the theory of the firm, not as a device to explain prices and output but to provide a realistic explanation of industrial structure. In Langlois's terms, the organisation of industry, and above all the changing organisation of industry, requires the co-ordination both of commitments and of production; and this dual requirement entails a fine balance between stability and flexibility in economic systems.

INTRODUCTION: CO-ORDINATION AND CAPABILITIES

Richardson's argument that co-ordination depends on information has been a primary inspiration of Mark Casson's conceptualisation of firms as information-handling systems, which is the theme of Chapter 11. Because change is continuous, co-ordination requires a sequence of decisions; and information is valuable to a firm only if it can affect decisions. The value of each specific item of information, which is the product of the cost of being wrong and the reduction in the probablility of being wrong which results from obtaining that particular information, should be balanced against its cost. The sources of information are dispersed because of the division of labour, for managers will acquire much relevant information (for example about markets or production costs) in the performance of their specialised activities. Dealing with interdependencies requires information to be synthesised; when its tacit content is significant interpretation may be problematic and best handled within a relatively flat and informal structure. Some kinds of information may affect decisions only if other kinds falls within a particular range; then information sources may be ordered in a sequence which generates a well-defined hierarchy. Casson suggests that the typical example is the priority of market information over information about production costs. He then considers the quality of information, which depends on both the capabilities – discussed in the two preceding chapters – and the honesty of the sources. Honesty may be encouraged both by cultural norms and by competition, which may be internal or external. By applying this analysis to the multinational enterprise, Casson concludes that the reduction in trade barriers has increased both the interdependence of market-related decisions and the substitution possibilities in production; we therefore observe the global management of markets coupled with a dispersion of production, both within the organisation and, increasingly, through outsourcing.

In Chapter 12 Neil Kay draws on Richardson's analysis of 'dense networks of co-operation' to explain the recent popularity of joint ventures. He notes that complementary activities can be co-ordinated by contract when the requirements can be clearly specified in advance, but that ambiguity, uncertainty and the prospect of novelty create a need for continuing management. Kay argues that the governance costs of a single project will normally be higher when it is managed as a joint venture, which involves joint control, a mixture of direction and contract, and overlapping ownership rights, than when it is subject to unitary control. But if this project is one of many, then the local advantages of unified management for each business unit may be outweighed by the systematic difficulties of managing within a single firm a variety of complementary assets many of which will not be at all similar. Kay is not comparing equilibria but explaining a historical sequence: in the early stages of a firm's growth internalisation is likely to be most efficient, but as the number and range of activities grows, the additional costs for the existing complex business of incorporating yet another complementarity begin to outweigh the additional costs of handling this particular complementarity as a joint venture. This explanation accounts for the common pattern of large firms turning to joint ventures after a sequence of mergers, and Kay extends it to explain the frequency of multiple collaboration between pairs of firms and the emergence of clusters of firms which share partners.

Gavin Reid's chapter (Chapter 13) is related to Richardson's work by both method and topic. Reid begins by recalling Richardson's (1964b) discussion of the limits to a firm's rate of growth, which was grounded on evidence collected by an Oxford research group, and his conclusion that the principal obstacle is the difficulty of expanding the management team. Bidding up the price is not an adequate remedy, for the task of management, as noted in other chapters, is qualitative co-ordination. A particular problem for the more adventurous entrepreneur is the limited flexibility of both organisations and individuals, which is not adequately represented by the rising cost curves of the textbooks but is fully consistent with Richardson's, and Penrose's, analysis. Reid then uses the evidence collected from his fieldwork with seventy-three small firms to test Richardson's conclusion that there is a trade-off between efficiency and growth, and therefore between profitability and growth. He divides these firms into three organisational categories – sole proprietors, partnerships and private companies – which match their ranges of size and also their organisational histories; and he finds both that growth rates decline across the categories and that within each category the smaller firms tend to grow faster. The implication that increasing business complexity retards growth is supported by a simultaneous equation model, which also shows a trade-off between growth and profitability.

In the final chapter Paul Robertson uses Richardson's ideas, and follows Richardson's methodological recommendation of tolerance and eclecticism, to examine the scope for government innovation policy. He begins by distinguishing between uncertainty about future events or the actions of other people (the co-ordination problem posed by Richardson in the opening chapter of *Information and Investment*) and ignorance, which itself may be subdivided into ignorance of what already exists and the absence of solutions to problems that seem potentially soluble. Robertson's main emphasis is on the communication of knowledge, the fundamental problem of which is to match sources with appropriate recipients. Since the need for communication is likely to arise only because the two parties interpret knowledge in different contexts, there is no simple means of identifying relevant matches; and so the principles on which any piece of knowledge should be codified in order to create a specific link can be sensibly decided only when the link has already been made. Thus, though governments may be able to help, especially in defining standards, they may also frustrate potentially valuable communications. Governments may, however, improve absorptive capacity by appropriate education. Robertson discusses the relationships between innovation and industrial form, and, using Richardson's categories of similar and complementary capabilities, questions the value of general prescriptions, suggesting instead that appropriate policy should be context-specific. The inherent tendency to inflexibility in mature industries, which tend to constrict the range of their absorptive capacity in the process of strengthening their existing capabilities, pose particular problems for governments. A successful policy for innovation is likely to be neither simple nor easy to work out.

The recurrent themes in this collection are those of Richardson's own work. Because that work has been generally neglected but highly valued by a minority, it is natural that several authors are much concerned with the ways in which the enterprise of economics is conducted – in a word, methodology; and because Richardson has written so incisively about the co-ordination of economic activities, it seems natural to enquire into the causes of co-ordination failure within the community of economists. In fact, the problems of economists and those of the economy have a common foundation in the characteristics of the human brain, which has great potential – provided that the development of this potential is restricted to a small segment of the possibilities that are initially open. The knowledge available to a community can be greatly increased if it is divided among members of that community: that is why the division of labour is the foundation of both productive and academic knowledge. It allows workers, managers, consumers and academics to develop particular ways of framing problems which facilitate the development of particular kinds of specialised knowledge.

There is a consequent need for co-ordination of knowledge; however, that knowledge is not only dispersed but differently framed. It is therefore not well represented by the conventional definition of the co-ordination problem. (It is not surprising that the codification systems favoured by economists often baffle or amaze outsiders.) Also ignored in most economic theory is the possibility – indeed the virtual certainty – that the way in which each of us frames problems will prevent us from recognising significant opportunities or major threats. The organisation of knowledge is therefore a pervasive problem for firms, governments and members of an academic discipline, and a failure of vision within any field is a methodological failure. However, no universally correct method is available. This is the real argument for competition and against unified planning. Opportunism is an important complication, but it is a supplement to more fundamental analysis, as our authors explicitly or implicitly agree. Since knowledge is never complete but always capable of improvement, these authors share a preference for process rather than equilibrium as an organising principle; and that leads them to favour economists who have, in varying degrees, shared this preference: that means, notably, Adam Smith, Marshall and (some of) the Austrians. But their only dogma is to avoid being dogmatic.

APPENDIX

The published work of George B. Richardson

Richardson, G. B. (1953) 'Imperfect knowledge and economic efficiency', *Oxford Economic Papers* 5: 136–56.

—— (1955) 'Schumpeter's history of economic analysis', *Oxford Economic Papers* 7: 136–50.

—— (1956) 'Demand and supply reconsidered', *Oxford Economic Papers* 8: 113–26.

—— (1959) 'Equilibrium, expectations and information', *The Economic Journal* 69: 223–37.

—— (1960/1990) *Information and Investment: A Study in the Working of the Competitive Economy*, Oxford: Oxford University Press.

—— (1964a) *Economic Theory*, London: Hutchinson.

—— (1964b) 'The limits to a firm's rate of growth,' *Oxford Economic Papers* 16: 9–23.

—— (1965a) 'The theory of restrictive trade practices', *Oxford Economic Papers* 17: 432–49.

—— (1965b) 'Les Relations entre firmes', *Economie Appliquée* 18: 407–30.

—— (1995c) 'Ideal and Reality in the choice of techniques,' *Oxford Economic Papers* 17: 291–298.

—— (1966) 'The pricing of heavy electrical equipment: competition or agreement?', *Bulletin of the Oxford University of Economics and Statistics* 28: 73–92.

—— (1967) 'Price notification schemes', *Oxford Economic Papers* 19: 359–69.

—— (1969) *The Future of the Heavy Electrical Plant Industry*, London: British Electrical and Allied Manufacturers' Association Ltd.

—— (1971) 'Planning versus competition', Annex to G. B. Richardson (1960/1990) *Information and Investment*, Oxford: Oxford University Press.

—— (1972) 'The organisation of industry', *Economic Journal* 82: 883–96.

—— and Brown, B. C. (1974) 'Economic Implications of Popular Growth in the United Kingdom', in Parry, H. B. (ed.) *Population and Its Problems*, Oxford: Oxford University Press.

—— (1975) 'Adam Smith on competition and increasing returns', in A. S. Skinner and T. Wilson (eds) *Essays on Adam Smith*, Oxford: Clarendon Press.

—— (1990) *Information and Investment*, 2nd edn, Oxford: Oxford University Press.

—— (1995) 'The Theory of the Market Economy,' *Revue Économique* 46: 1487–1496.

—— (1996) 'Competition, innovation, and increasing returns', *Working Paper 96–10*, Danish Research Unit of Industrial Dynamics.

—— (1997) 'Economic analysis, public policy, and the software industry', *Working Paper 97–4*, Danish Research Unit of Industrial Dynamics.

—— (1998a) 'Some principles of economic organisation', in this volume.

—— (1988b) 'What can an economist learn from managing a business?', in P.E. Earl and S. Don (eds) *Economic Knowledge and Economic Coordination: Essays in Honour of Brian J. Loasby*, Aldershot: Edward Elgar.

—— (forthcoming) 'Autobiographical Introduction,' in N.J. Foss (ed) *The Economics of Imperfect Knowledge: Collected Papers by G.B. Richardson*, Aldershot: Edward Elgar.

REFERENCES

Coase, R. H. (1960) 'The problem of social cost', *Journal of Law and Economics* 3: 1–44.

—— (1988) *The Firm, the Market, and the Law*, Chicago: University of Chicago Press.

Hayek, F. A. von (1945) 'The use of knowledge in society', *American Economic Review* 35: 519–30; reprinted in *Individualism and Economic Order*, Chicago: University of Chicago Press, 1948.

—— (1946) 'The meaning of competition'; reprinted in *Individualism and Economic Order*, Chicago: University of Chicago Press, 1948.

Kaldor, N. (1972) 'The irrelevance of equilibrium economics', *Economic Journal* 82: 1237–55.

Langlois, R. N. (ed.) (1986) *Economics as a Process: Essays in the New Institutional Economics*, Cambridge: Cambridge University Press.

Loasby, B. J. (1989) *The Mind and Method of the Economist*, Aldershot: Edward Elgar.

Marshall, A. (1923) *Industry and Trade*, London: Macmillan.

Metcalfe, J. S. (1994) 'Richardson, George B.', in G. M. Hodgson, W. J. Samuels and M. R. Tool (eds) (1994) *The Elgar Companion to Institutional and Evolutionary Economics, L–Z*, Aldershot: Edward Elgar.

Penrose, E. T. (1959) *The Theory of the Growth of the Firm*, Oxford: Basil Blackwell.

Richardson, G. B. (1993) Letter to Nicolai Foss, 14 May.

Ryle, G. (1949) *The Concept of Mind*, Oxford: Oxford University Press.

Sraffa, P. (1926) 'The laws of return under competitive conditions', *Economic Journal* 36: 535–50.

2

GEORGE RICHARDSON'S CAREER AND THE LITERATURE OF ECONOMICS

Peter E. Earl[1]

INTRODUCTION

George Richardson's academic career is full of the kinds of achievements of which most academics can merely dream. His entry in *International Who's Who* reveals that, after teaching economics as a fellow of St John's College, Oxford, from 1951, he was promoted in 1969 to University Reader in Economics, a post he held until 1973. Between 1974 and 1988 he was Chief Executive of Oxford University Press and from 1989 until his retirement he was Warden of Keble College, Oxford. His expertise as an industrial economist was recognised in his appointments as a member of the Monopolies Commission and as a Member of the Economic Development Committee for the Electrical Engineering Industry. He was also a member of the Royal Commission on Environmental Pollution (1973–4). His citation record, discussed later in this paper, shows his work to have been used by scholars in many countries and many disciplines. Yet, despite this, the impact of his work has been far smaller than he might justifiably have expected and, indeed, he records his disappointment in his introduction to the second edition of *Information and Investment* (1990: xvii). Interest in his work is growing, but his contributions remain unused by most economists and unknown to their students. This chapter is an attempt to clarify and explain the place of Richardson's writings within the literature of economics. It has something of a reflexive dimension, for George Richardson's contributions to economics are helpful for making sense of co-ordination problems and processes in the market for scholarly ideas.

The chapter extends some of the ideas that I first outlined over a decade ago in a paper on the behaviour of economists (Earl 1983a). In that paper I considered the roles that career aspirations and academic search processes play in shaping the kinds of works that economists prefer to produce and whether particular contributions to economics are accorded high status or are marginalised. Richardson's contributions were grouped with those of P. W. S. Andrews, Jack Downie and Edith Penrose as being of a modern-day Marshallian variety, whose neglect by the mainstream of the economics profession is on a par with that accorded to the Carnegie–Mellon behaviouralists Richard Cyert, James March and Herbert Simon. In recent years key contributions from all of these deviant scholars (with the exception of Downie) have been reprinted in new editions. This must be very gratifying for those deviants such as Richardson who, unlike Andrews and Downie, have lived long enough to see a belated growth of interest in their work. Even so, the fates of their contributions continue to call into question the dynamic efficiency of markets for economic ideas, challenging the sanguine views of Stigler (1982).

The rest of the chapter is divided into five main sections, followed by a brief conclusion and a lengthy appendix listing citations of Richardson's work in scholarly journals. In the first section I provide an account of Richardson's path into economics and his method of operating as a scholar; this turns out to be significant in terms of shaping his outputs and their marketability. Second, I examine the research co-ordination problem: the need for scholars to ensure that they are not engaged in mere reinvention or simultaneous invention of ideas. Third, I present citations evidence of the patchy impact of Richardson's work. Fourth, I examine critically Loasby's (1989) claims about the role of unfortunate timing in the initial reception of *Information and Investment*. Finally, I consider the role of networks as key determinants of the fates of contributions to knowledge.

RICHARDSON'S PATH TO ECONOMICS

Richardson's early career is both intriguing and paradoxical in relation to his contribution to economics. Since he was born in 1924, his university education was affected by the Second World War, as were his initial periods of employment. During the 1940s he completed a pair of two-year degrees, following each with periods of government service. His education could very easily have led him to become a physical scientist rather than an economist, for in 1942 he commenced studies at Aberdeen University and read mathematics and physics. This left him far better equipped in mathematical terms than most of his fellow economics students when he took up a scholarship to Oxford in 1947 and switched from science to Philosophy, Politics and Economics (PPE). At Oxford, his economics papers were in Economic Organisation, Economic Principles, Economic Theory and Statistics. Though the Oxford BPhil in PPE had been newly established in 1946, Oxford teaching was for the most part conservative rather than contemporary in its coverage (Young and Lee 1993: 167). However, this was the period in which Hicks was very much in the ascendant at Oxford, and in 1952 Hicks was ranked ahead of both Robbins and Harrod for the Drummond Chair of Political Economy. By that time Hicks had became Richardson's mentor.

It was Richardson's mathematical training that led to his links with Hicks. His regular tutor in economics was Neville Ward-Perkins, an economic historian who had been taught by Andrews. When Richardson came to take the theory paper, Ward-Perkins initially arranged for him to be tutored by Frank Burchardt. However, after Richardson showed off his mathematical skills in presenting a paper on Keynes's theory of employment, Burchardt asked Hicks to tutor Richardson instead. This rather immature display of mathematical prowess is recalled by Richardson with some shame – one of his classmates remarking on leaving the seminar that if this was economics, then he wanted none of it – but he notes that without it he would not have become an economist. The irony, of course, is that much of what he was subsequently to write points away from analysing economic problems with the aid of mathematics and leads instead to a recognition of the need to become familiar with institutional details of devices that firms use to assist co-ordination.

Richardson's publications nevertheless have a distinctly Hicksian look to them: despite the paucity of diagrams and the absence of mathematical notation, Richardson's *Information and Investment* closely resembles Hicks's (1939) *Value and Capital* (Hicks 1945), with its absence of section headings and only the use of occasional footnote references, mainly to classic writings. Unlike today's scholars, who sometimes err in the direction of citation overkill when setting their works in the context of existing literature, Richardson and his mentor wrote about theoretical issues as if applying logic in their armchairs. Richardson's experience of being taught by Hicks was conducive to this, for the latter's method involved getting his students to read the work of great figures such as Marshall, Menger and Walras rather than mastering a list of recent articles. Unlike Andrews, who followed in Marshall's approach of writing from a firm base in practical knowledge of business, Richardson's scholarship was driven by curiosity and an eye for (what seemed to him to be) 'the obvious'; it involved much time thinking about problems in his college room or whilst walking round the college garden. When he came to write *Information and Investment*, Hicks read the book in draft but provided few comments and did not discuss its central themes.

Though Hicks seemed rather distant from Richardson's own contributions, apparently regarding him as having focused too narrowly, too soon (so Richardson discovered after Hicks had died), he did much to help Richardson to get started as an academic. He was initially unsuccessful in convincing Richardson to stay in academic economics rather than pursue a diplomatic career but a year later, when Richardson had second thoughts and wrote to his mentor, Hicks managed to secure him a doctoral studentship at Nuffield College. Richardson was not particularly enamoured with his initial DPhil thesis research under Hicks and was thus happy to abandon it after only two terms, when he obtained a Fellowship at St John's on the basis of the promise he had shown. (The Senior Tutor at St John's advised him that it was no longer appropriate to read for a doctorate!) The ease with which Richardson got established at Oxford in the early 1950s is to be contrasted with the difficulties that Andrews had in retaining his Fellowship at Nuffield College in 1953: Hicks actively sought to prevent this, having a very low opinion of Andrews's capabilities as an economist (Lee 1993: 22).

Differences between Richardson and Andrews in terms of background and relations with Hicks are perhaps significant in helping us to understand why they had almost no discussion together despite feeling they had something in common in doctrinal terms: in the 1950s Richardson would have seemed an abstract theorist to Andrews, who had become suspicious of theoreticians and was immersing himself in empirical studies. The latter's uneasiness in the company of theoreticians at least meant that there was little danger of links developing between these two post-Marshallians that could harm Richardson's standing in the eyes of those in positions of influence. Even so, having been introduced to full cost pricing as an Oxford undergraduate, Richardson did take from Andrews the idea that spare capacity facilitates the avoidance of co-ordination problems since it permits firms to satisfy new demand without losing the goodwill of regular customers (Richardson 1960: 127).

During the 1960s Richardson's style of research increasingly came to resemble Andrews's post Marshallian/behavioural mode. He became involved with applied studies, beginning with the heavy electrical plant industry, which led to his membership of the Monopolies Commission and provided the knowledge that eventually inspired his most influential work – his (1972) article 'The organisation of industry'. This change of research style arose by chance but built on insights from his armchair theorising: at a dinner in Sidney Sussex College he happened to sit next to Sebastian de Ferranti, an electrical engineering industrialist, who mentioned that the Restrictive Practices Court was about to consider a price agreement on transformers. Though Richardson knew nothing about the case, he immediately grasped the relevance of his work on co-ordination and remarked that there were arguments in favour of such restraints on trade, which most economists wrongly ignored (see further Richardson 1965, 1966, 1967, 1969).

To conclude this commentary on how Richardson became an economist and how he operated as a scholar, I want to suggest that Richardson's early spells of work outside economics may have affected the contribution he made. Richardson himself reports that *Information and Investment* originated in a long struggle with a theoretical conundrum, his awareness of which emerged from uneasiness he felt even as an undergraduate about economists' accounts of how equilibrium states might be achieved. A modern industrial economist presented with the Richardson Problem would tend to recognise that it can be framed in terms of the theory of games. However, Richardson's writings about the problem of investment co-ordination do not presume that entrepreneurs place their bets without first trying to improve the information they have about the plans of others whose actions may impinge on the outcomes of their own ventures. Another way of putting this is to say that entrepreneurs seek to gather *intelligence* by observing what rivals are up to or by exchanging information by mingling together or deliberately sending signals. That Richardson should have come to view the mitigation of the problem in this way is hardly surprising when we note that Richardson's spells of government service in the 1940s included intelligence work. Just before the end of the war and soon after graduating from Aberdeen, he was sent, as a temporary naval officer, to Germany for intelligence work on radar. Subsequently he was employed as a civilian at the British Army of the Rhine headquarters, on political intelligence work, and immediately after his PPE studies he went into the Foreign Service, having taken the entrance examination before taking his Oxford Finals.

THE RESEARCH CO-ORDINATION PROBLEM

Academics have to grapple on a daily basis with a co-ordination problem every bit as complex as that upon which Richardson focused in *Information and Investment*: rewards will go to those who succeed in staking claims to authorship of pioneering contributions valued highly by their peers, or whose contributions succeed in capturing the attention of their peers because of the way that they have been marketed, despite not being the first in which the ideas were developed. Physical scientists are not shy about debating in public their claims for primacy as discovers of particular phenomena: a recent case in point is the battle between French and American AIDS researchers over the initial discovery of HIV. Economists tend to be rather more reticent, or simply ignorant of potential for disputes, so that it is left to historians of economic thought to explore possible instances of simultaneous invention or of credit going to reinventors who, whether out of ignorance or opportunism, did not give credit where credit was due (cf. Earl 1993).

Here is a touch of irony: George Richardson's own career as an academic illustrates well the potential for simultaneous invention of ideas and for an academic to be in the right place at the wrong time. In respect of the former we can note two examples. First, Richardson's (1972) article on the co-ordination of complementary investment and the subtle methods for co-ordinating vertical production and distribution processes appeared around the same time as a paper on a similar theme by Blois (1972), from which the term 'quasi-integration' seems to have come into the language of economics and strategic management. Richardson had the greater richness of vision, but Blois had the buzz-phrase. Second, there is Richardson's (1975) awareness that he and Kaldor (1972) were thinking on similar lines about the significance of increasing returns; he notes that 'This paper was already in draft before the publication of Professor Kaldor's article "The Irrelevance of Equilibrium Economics" in the *Economic Journal* . . . and I did not try to adapt it to take account of what he said. The arguments I put forward here are similar in important respects to those of Professor Kaldor' (Richardson 1975: 351). Like Kaldor, he acknowledged the significance of Allyn Young's (1928) 'justly celebrated article' as a source of inspiration (Richardson 1975: 352). To date, Kaldor's paper has attracted much more attention, probably due to its location in a core journal and Kaldor's fame, but the profession would benefit from being familiar with Richardson's paper too, and from seeking to pull together links between the different points of focus of the two contributions: unlike Richardson, Kaldor has nothing to say on the relationship between specialisation and diversification in the growth strategies of firms. Both works deserve to receive more attention from those who work in the emerging literature on strategic international trade theory.

In respect of the question of primacy, we should note that, although the profession at large may ultimately follow Brian Loasby and myself (Earl 1983a), and label the investment co-ordination problem in his honour as the Richardson Problem, he was by no means the first to recognise it. Nor was Richardson the first to write about the potentially beneficial role of market 'imperfections'. For example, discussions of interlinked expectations and the importance of frictions for the practical workings of the competitive system are to be found in the work of Clark (1923: 417, 460) and Dobb (1937: 206–7), though in relation to the process by which prices are changed. More noteworthy is a neglected article by Williams which is concerned with the economics of structural change: its main theme is that 'dynamic competition cannot be "perfect" ' (1949: 124). The closeness of Williams's thinking to that of Richardson may be gauged from the following extracts:

> The fact that there are fixed factors means that capital losses inevitably follow a change in demand. Furthermore, these fixed factors, or frictions, are a pre-condition of the operation of the pricing mechanism. For if there were perfect mobility the emergence of a difference between price and cost in one sector would cause such a flood of resources there as to ensure losses for all. Nor could the flow back to the now prosperous deserted sectors be orderly, for with static expectations and perfect mobility (which implies that no producer has a preference or special competence for

one industry rather than another) there would be nothing within the price mechanism as such to make it possible for producers to choose a profitable transfer.

. . . he cannot rely on the law of large numbers to bring it about that too many firms will not go to one industry or another, for it is likely that industries will have need for widely varying numbers of firms.

(Williams 1949: 126 and footnote)

The avoidance of such a breakdown of the pricing mechanism is due to lack of mobility, and to firms having, at any one point of time, differing degrees of mobility.

(Williams 1949: 127)

The difficulty of co-ordinating structural change and cyclical demand patterns was also considered by Joan Robinson (1954), but she did not raise the possibility that less than perfect flexibility of response might be a desirable feature. That she did not do so is perhaps surprising given both her closeness to Keynes and the latter's (1936: 239, 269) macro-level realisation that stickiness in the wage unit was essential to provide an anchor for the price level because in the event of a shortfall in or excess of effective demand changes in money wages would not necessarily change the level of real effective demand and hence the demand for labour. The greater overall farsightedness of Williams's paper obviously includes the role he assigned in passing to special competences as limiting the industries in which firms will wish to participate: this theme not only resurfaces in Richardson's work (including his 1975 paper) but is also, of course, central to recent work on the resource-based view of the firm that takes its lead from Penrose (1959).

Though scholars such as Williams and Robinson came to see the essence of the Richardson Problem before Richardson did, the case for naming it after him is that they focused on it briefly, without also highlighting complementary investment as a problem area and without his subtle appreciation of what might be included on the list of beneficial imperfections.

THE LIMITED IMPACT OF RICHARDSON'S WORK

Economists who read Loasby (1989) or my (Earl 1983a) paper on economists' behaviour may infer from comments therein about the neglect of Richardson that his publications were almost completely ignored. This inference would be somewhat mistaken but would certainly be correct in respect of research and teaching in the core microeconomic theory area of the discipline. His work challenged the wisdom expressed in the textbooks that were available as he developed his thinking, and it provided a basis for studying economics as a co-ordination problem, with a novel focus on institutional arrangements that facilitate co-ordination. But after three decades it had not become incorporated into standard textbooks.

Richardson's own textbook *Economic Theory* (1964a) was commissioned by Roy Harrod, general editor of the Huchinson University Library economics series, shortly after the publication of *Information and Investment*. It was hardly the ideal package to become a standard tool in a revamped economics paradigm. It began, like its rivals, with the logic of choice, Richardson's strategy being a very Hayekian one of going on to show that the dispersion of knowledge made it necessary to have decentralised decision-making. Unfortunately, it was too dense for the typical student and lacked the more lavish attention to matters of layout that was beginning to characterise the bloated conventional texts at the time it appeared; it was a book of intricate continuous argument in the style of the introductory philosophy texts by Russell and G. E. Moore that Richardson had himself enjoyed and was not at all the type of work to appeal to those with short attention spans.

Richardson's textbook was not a complete sales disaster, despite not taking off into multiple editions, and was translated into Spanish and Portuguese. Between it and my recent treatment (Earl 1995: ch. 10), the only textbook on microeconomics to offer a taste of Richardson's perspective was the readings collection by Wagner and Baltazzis (1973) which reprinted his (1971) article 'Planning versus competition'. Given that this article first appeared in *Soviet Studies* and given also the recent interest in the relevance of Richardson's work for countries undergoing the transition from communism to more market-based methods of economic organisation, it is interesting to note that at the time of the Prague Spring he was approached by an economist from Bratislava, Madame Sestokova, about the possibility of translating *Economic Theory* into Slovak. The book was seen in what was then Czechoslovakia as addressing the problem of how to move towards decentralised decision-making. Madame Sestokova visited Richardson in Oxford and, a few weeks before the Russian invasion, Richardson visited Prague and Bratislava. With Dubcek out of power it seemed to Richardson unwise to write to those who had warmly hosted his visit to Czechoslovakia – letters from the West might put their positions in jeopardy. After the fall of communism, Richardson did try to resume contact and was greatly saddened to discover that Madame Sestokova and her family had fared badly in the interim and that she was seriously ill in hospital.

Though the central ideas in George Richardson's work imply the need for a major reworking of textbooks, they are not fundamentally difficult to grasp. He expressed them in plain English and, particularly in his post-*Economic Theory* work, with plenty of memorable real-world examples. My experience over many years is that students find Richardson's ideas easy to assimilate compared with many of the concepts of neoclassical theory: a teacher who wishes to inspire an intermediate microeconomics class will find it far easier to do so by beginning with the economics of information and co-ordination than with the axioms of mainstream choice theory.

To see his ideas being discussed in textbooks it is generally necessary to move from the core of economics, which any student will cover, to industrial economics and business strategy. There, Richardson might have more of a feeling of success, but still considerable grounds for feeling that the profession has not made as much of his work as it might have done. The most widely read discussion of the entry co-ordination problem is doubtless the chapter on capacity expansion decisions in the bestseller by Porter (1980), but Porter seems engaged in reinvention, for he makes no reference to Richardson as he examines the problem and considers various pre-emptive signalling approaches for dealing with it. Richardson's vision of the significance of corporate capabilities and relational contracting is going to be absorbed by many managers via John Kay's strong-selling *Foundations of Corporate Success*, which refers to Richardson (1972) very briefly as 'an early contribution' (Kay 1993: 85), in a guide to the literature; Richardson's way of thinking will thus spread but probably without his name attached to it and with Kay's readers being oblivious of his personal links with Richardson.

It would certainly be incorrect to say that Richardson is ignored in industrial economics. He is cited in the leading British undergraduate-level texts, and occasionally in American ones, though generally without his contributions being made central to the analysis – there is a big difference between being merely footnoted and being discussed at length (as in Earl 1995) as an important contributor whose focus can be summed up as the Richardson Problem. (At present, anyone who uses this shorthand term with students has to be careful to remind them of its limited currency.) Table 2.1 shows the extent to which Richardson's contributions are discussed or noted in some of the widely used texts.

If economists were as well informed as their hypothetical decision-makers it would be natural to expect to see Richardson's work on co-ordination receiving more attention as industrial economics texts at the advanced level have become dominated by an interest in game theory, but it is not mentioned in the market-leading texts by Tirole (1988) and Martin (1993). Though Richardson had originally wanted to call his 1960 book *The Economics of Imperfect Knowledge*, anyone who hopes to see his ideas being discussed in Phlips's *The Economics of Imperfect Information* (1988) will be disappointed. One might even be so bold as to suggest that the more industrial economics texts incorporate modern microeconomic theory focused on incomplete information, the less likelihood there is of Richardson receiving attention. Even so, there are still some occasions on which Richardson is cited in modern survey discussions at exactly the point where he might expect to be: for example, *Information and Investment* is cited in R. J. Gilbert's

Table 2.1 Citations of Richardson's work in widely used industrial economics texts

Richardson reference	1960	1964b	1965	1966	1967	1972
Cited in (with page no.):						
Pickering 1973	295/324	115/309	278/323		295/324	
Devine *et al.* 1976	407, 436, 445		436, 445	436, 445		
Hay and Morris 1979	412	303, 393–4	173, 593	173		57, 593
George and Joll 1981				173		
Reid 1987	65, 69, 213					
Scherer and Ross 1990	299			295, 309	311	
Greer 1992				408		

chapter on mobility barriers in the *Handbook of Industrial Organization* (Schmalensee and Willig 1989: 534) and 'The organisation of industry' is quoted by Steve Davies in his chapter on vertical integration in *The Economics of the Firm* (Clarke and McGuinness 1987: 84). To some extent, then, Richardson's ideas have been received into the normal science textbooks of industrial economics, but they certainly have not had a revolutionary impact on the hard core of this subdiscipline. However, to the extent that modern advanced-level texts are concentrating on surveying *recent* contributions to the field, it is somewhat surprising that Richardson receives attention at all in these works.

Whereas a Kuhnian historian of science would look to textbooks for evidence of a scholar's revolutionary impact, present-day academic audits of research productivity focus on success in being published in 'core' journals, on the basis that it is much more difficult to have works accepted in these journals and that articles published in them are likely to be cited in subsequent work. All of Richardson's English-language articles were in high-ranking journals but that did not guarantee that they would be rapidly picked up and frequently cited. It is somewhat difficult to study the citation pattern of Richardson's work before 1969, for it was not until that year that the *Social Sciences Citation Index* (*SSCI*) commenced publication in its present form. In the Appendix to this chapter is a complete listing of citations of Richardson's works recorded in the first quarter-century of the *SSCI*.

Richardson is cited around seven times per year, on average, 186 times in all (including only two self-citations), with the lion's share of the citations being *Information and Investment* (fifty times) and 'The organisation of industry' (eighty-three times). The *SSCI* listings provide a fascinating picture of how his work has been used.

Richardson has been cited in most major economics journals and by many eminent economists, including Nelson, Scherer, Scitovsky, Teece and Williamson, but these 'core' citations, most of which are of *Information and Investment*, account for only a small fraction of the total. Many citations are not in English-language journals or are in journals outside economics, in disciplines such as marketing, strategic management, geography and sociology. This is particularly the case with his 1972 paper. Richardson's work is not yet famous in the sense that most teachers and students of economics have heard of it, but that has not prevented it from being discovered and used by scholars working outside the core of economics. So far, I have only been able briefly to examine the lists of works cited by some of the articles that cite Richardson and which I had not previously seen. The initial impression is that these papers tend to cite not only Richardson but also relatively underused works by other scholars such as Malmgren and Hirschman that I stumbled across myself in the late 1970s when first searching for contributions that might augment the Richardson perspective. But there were many works listed with intriguing titles that were unfamiliar to me. A major reason for appending the *SSCI* listings is to encourage readers to explore these works further and develop a clearer picture of the extent of thinking by other neglected authors, completing the augmentation process.

WAS DEBREU THE CAUSE OF *INFORMATION AND INVESTMENT*'S FAILURE TO TAKE OFF IN THE 1960s?

It seems worthwhile, as a source of lessons to academic economists writing today and wondering how their work will fare with its intended audience, to examine likely reasons for Richardson's failure so far to have a major impact on the core of economics despite being surprisingly successful in being noticed in an interdisciplinary sense. According to Loasby (1989: 99), Richardson's great misfortune was that his critique of general equilibrium analysis appeared just after Debreu's exposition of an abstract economic model in which complete contingent claims markets 'solved' the co-ordination problem, for Richardson's prose lacked the hard scientific appeal of Debreu's mathematics. This view can be challenged.

For Loasby's view to be correct, it would seem to require that economists in the early 1960s were actually worried about the co-ordination problem, and that Debreu was indeed praised for his solution to the problem around the time that Richardson's work appeared. This being so, mainstream scholars would have no need to search for alternative perspectives that might remove their uneasiness. Contemporary reactions to both Debreu and Richardson provide evidence to the contrary and may indicate how the profession at large has tended to construe particular contributions and choose between theories. Before we consider the content of the reviews it is worth noting that book reviews in professional journals can be seen as the academic equivalent of quality signalling devices in other markets, such as reports of restaurants in good food guides, credit ratings by agencies such as Standard and Poor's, and admission to trade association membership – in other words, they are devices of the kind that Richardson has sought to emphasise in his work on co-ordination.

Debreu's book was not widely reviewed beyond the American journals. There were no reviews in *Economica*, the *Economic Journal* or the *Economic Record*, while the review in *Econometrica* is in quite difficult French and so would have been relatively insignificant in the English-speaking world. In the four reviews that I have unearthed Debreu was generally praised for his innovative technical exposition but the reviewers did not appear to be cheering him for showing how general equilibrium and uncertainty could be made compatible. On the contrary: either the issue was not highlighted or he came in for criticism for his abstractions and failure to use examples. In the *American Economic Review* Hurwicz correctly predicted that the book would have a major long-term impact but commented that, in relation to Debreu's fifth and sixth chapters (on existence and optimality of competitive equilibria, respectively), 'One's understanding of the problem would have been greatly deepened by examples lacking equilibrium due to the failure of one or another of the assumptions' (Hurwicz 1961: 416). Hurwicz had little to say, however, about Debreu's treatment of uncertainty, merely mentioning that this was introduced in the seventh chapter. Harrell hardly went further, simply ending his purely descriptive review in the *Southern Economic Journal* by saying that 'In the last chapter a revised definition of a commodity leads to a theory of uncertainty which is normally identical with the previously elaborated theory of certainty' (1960: 150). Much more critical is Baudier (1961), in *Econometrica*, who noted that the cost of Debreu's concern to state his purpose precisely is that he gives readers no indications of implications of the theory about which they must themselves form judgements. Baudier then commented that:

> The consequences are, however, to my way of thinking, too important to pass by in silence and too numerous to be counted. Let's mention this one: the last chapter introduces the possibility of 'commodities' of a new type for which there is no market (at least in general) and therefore the prices of those 'commodities' could not be

held as given by economic agents who don't even know them. Thus one of the conditions of applying the theory of equilibrium to the real world collapses.

(Baudier 1961: 259–60; my translation,
with assistance from Pascal Tremblay)

Similarly, in the *Journal of Political Economy* the young Frank Hahn (1961) praised the *Theory of Value* as a technical achievement but criticised it for proceeding implicitly as if the non-existence of contingent commodity markets does not matter; for leaving no role for money; and for having nothing to say about what happens in an economy when conditions are insufficient to produce an equilibrium. That Hahn should have reacted in this way is ironic given his later spirited defences of the Arrow–Debreu approach as a benchmarking tool for policy diagnosis – arguments that Richardson (1990: xxi–xxii) finds utterly unacceptable.

None of the reviewers of the first edition of *Information and Investment* made any reference to Debreu's contribution, and none noted another point that would be obvious to modern-day economists, namely that Richardson might have done well to relate his work to the literature that, by the late 1950s, had appeared on the theory of games: Morgenstern, one of the co-founders of game theory, recognised as long ago as 1928 that the attainment of economic equilibrium could not be explained in terms of existing theory in cases where an agent's choice of a plan of action required knowledge of plans of other agents (see Borch 1973: 67). Rather, the reviewers focused on the *overly theoretical* nature of the book. In other words, Richardson's marketing problem seemed to be one of getting economists to agree that there was *actually* a problem of co-ordination worth worrying about. It seems unlikely that, in 1960, he would have better satisfied his reviewers if he had made the most of his mathematical training and set out the co-ordination problem in Debreu's style. His reviewers appear merely to have wanted the kinds of down-to-earth examples that he was to use so effectively in his later writings.

Potential readers of the book can hardly have been encouraged by the observation by Power in an otherwise perceptive and favourable review in the *American Economic Review* that:

> The method of the book is essentially armchair reasoning with only occasional reference to empirical studies. . . . Readers may find the concluding section of the volume disappointing in the light of earlier bold statements about the omissions of conventional theory.
>
> (Power 1961: 761)

The first comment is an accurate characterisation of how Richardson had worked, but the second is somewhat unfair: its intended implication seems to be that the book does not offer much to fill the gap that it exposes.

Lesley Cook begins her *Economic Journal* review by suggesting that the title *Information and Investment* is 'slightly misleading' and that the book is a 'theoretical examination of the effects on investment of uncertainty resulting from inadequate information' (Cook 1964: 168). The book is surely better characterised as a critique of conventional theories of the workings of the price mechanism and an alternative analysis of how allocation mechanisms work in the face of incomplete knowledge; however, Richardson may well have been wiser than his publisher in wanting to call the book *The Economics of Imperfect Knowledge*. (Hicks, as one of the Delegates of Oxford University Press, had been unwilling to accept that title, remarking to Richardson that it would demonstrate an imperfect knowledge of economics.) While also broadly favourable, Cook's review can only have damaged the book's impact by suggesting that 'He is largely concerned with problems related to the cobweb theorem' (Cook 1964: 168). Conventional theorists seem to be predisposed to view the cobweb theorem as affecting only agriculture and the construction industries. Thus, they would have been inclined to agree with Cook when she argued that Richardson was probably exaggerating the importance of the co-ordination problem when he applied it to investment decisions in general. (Such an inclination would have been particularly likely if they had just read Muth's (1961: 330–4) now-famous work on rational expectations, which highlights the empirical limitations of cobweb models and tentatively argues that the rational expectations hypothesis has superior predictive capabilities – even though Richardson (1959: 233) had already called into question any notion of rational expectations.) The fact that Richardson's book was four years old before this review appeared could hardly have helped its chances with, particularly, British economists who had not noticed it on its publication if they had in the meantime tuned into the message of Debreu. (I could find no review of it in *Economica*, merely one by Laurence Harris (1965) of Richardson's (1964a) textbook. Harris does note Richardson's focus on the restrictive nature of the perfect knowledge assumption but gives no clue to the problem Richardson has in mind; instead he goes on to criticise the text for being too brief and superficial and for lacking any discussion of method or suggestions for further readings.)

Cook argued that an orderly process of market adjustment through sequential market entry would have seemed much more plausible, especially if he had chosen to analyse the problem in disequilibrium terms rather than with comparative statics. In fact, Richardson (1960: 51–2) had presented an examination of sequential entry but noted difficulties for entrepreneurs in assessing precisely how much capacity rivals had already commissioned, the more so the larger the number of firms participating in the market. Cook further failed to explain to potential readers that Richardson's aim was not to demonstrate, as Joan Robinson wished to do, that the co-ordination problems cause chaos and 'the impossibility of profits' (Robinson 1954); rather, he was more concerned to show how such problems may be avoided in practice and thereby to put readers in a better position to appraise the implications of competition policies based on conventional theories which neglect the information structures that help markets to function.

The reception given for Australian audiences by John Grant in the *Economic Record* echoes the sentiments of both Power and Cook. He claimed that:

> the book is not wholly satisfying, because the argument remains on a purely theoretical plane throughout. The reader cannot fail to wonder about the magnitude of the problem under discussion in the real world. Some empirical research would not only have made the book more interesting but may also have increased the author's contribution to economic analysis.
>
> (Grant 1962: 125)

The line of thinking here seem to be that the price mechanism in practice does not seem to produce chaos, so Richardson is worrying about a problem that does not really matter and therefore it is safe to continue with conventional theoretical analysis. The reviewers seem blind to Richardson's key point: the traditional theory has a logical flaw and chaos is avoided, insofar as it is avoided, because supply decisions are reached in ways fundamentally different from those posited by traditional theory. This being so, it is conceivable that attempts to make the world resemble the traditional theoretical world more closely in terms of the competitive rules of the game may result in inferior patterns of resource allocation, due to the world then functioning in a more chaotic manner or entrepreneurs in general becoming more hesitant about investing. Thus, even without any buttressing from Debreu's make-believe world of complete contingent commodity markets, the traditional theory seemed to have been quite acceptable to Richardson's reviewers as an 'as-if' approximation of how the world works.

In taking issue with Loasby here on the impact of Debreu's success on the reception of *Information and Investment* I am not denying that the timing of its release might have been more fortuitous. Indeed, there are several reasons to believe that the market for Richardson's message has ripened steadily since 1960 and that the book would have fared far better had it been published around 1972, with Richardson's originally intended title and including material from his 1972 article, which is logically linked with it (see Foss 1994, on the relationship between Richardson 1960 and 1972):

1   One might expect traditional theory to look less good as an approximation when the 'golden age' of economic growth came to an end and excess capacity creation would no longer rapidly tend to be rendered non-problematic by ongoing demand growth. During the golden age interest in investment co-ordination problems tended to centre on the question of which firms should exit from markets suffering from chronic

excess capacity due to changes in global competitive conditions – for example traditional staple industries such as cotton textiles (see Miles 1968) and wool textiles (see Wool Textile EDC 1969) – and on the possibility of dysfunctional defensive investment (Lamfalussy 1961). Richardson, however, had not focused on exit games under conditions of gross immobility of capital and human resources. Nowadays, with frequent periods of recession and new investment occurring despite chronic overcapacity in many modern industries (for example the motor vehicles industry), it is not easy to dismiss Richardson's work as empirically insignificant.

2   Those who were less enamoured with the price mechanism doubtless learnt a lot more about the nature of the co-ordination problem in the decade after *Information and Investment* appeared. Attempts at indicative planning, such as those of the UK Labour Government in the late 1960s, and the 'balanced versus unbalanced growth' debate in development economics may have aroused a greater recognition of complementary aspects of investment, as well as of the difficulty of ensuring the right amount of investment in any one sector if directives were not to be given to individual firms and communication between them was not allowed. It is easy to see why Richardson's (1971) timely article 'Planning versus competition' was so swiftly reprinted in Wagner and Baltazzis (1973). Had his 1960 book not already been published, Richardson's (1969) report on collusive tendering in the UK's heavy electrical engineering industry would have made a powerful empirical addition to it, since it embraces both the complementarity problem (a capacity problem due to the electricity industry expanding rapidly in keeping with the National Plan, only to find that most of the rest of the UK economy did not) and the question of whether market imperfections might enhance dynamic efficiency.

3   It was around 1972 that the so-called Crisis in Economic Theory really seemed to break out, with widespread criticism (for example Kaldor 1972) of the kind of abstract and institutionally implausible research that Debreu's work had helped to foster.

Had Richardson's work attracted wide attention during the early 1970s, it is conceivable that a good deal of subsequent work on industrial economics would have been done differently. In particular, those involved with the development of contestability theory would have had reason to be rather more cautious in advocating the removal of entry barriers in industries such as passenger aviation and financial services that have since suffered from severe adjustment problems (see further Earl 1995: 305–9).

PETER E. EARL

NETWORKS, INSTITUTIONS AND ACADEMIC SEARCH PROCESSES

The sheer volume of potentially relevant material that academics might find worth reading makes it seem inappropriate to try to make sense of the fate of particular contributions to knowledge in terms of a perspective which sees academics as if they know not merely which kinds of ideas they like but also where to find them. Though some economists in the 1960s may have been deterred from reading Richardson (and even Debreu) by contemporary reviews, and though some of them may have seen his work and decided not to read it because it did not fit with their growing taste for technical rigour, it is unlikely to be the case that most economists currently working have sized up Richardson's work with the aid of such reviews and have decided not to read it in detail, or, like his reviewers, have read it and decided not to take his ideas on board. A more plausible hypothesis is that most economists are simply unaware of his contributions and use search processes or move in social circles that are not conducive to discovering what Richardson has had to say.

In the analysis of product life-cycles of consumer products it is commonly recognised that social factors play a major role in determining how much attention potential buyers pay to new products and whether or not they experiment with them. The same seems to hold in academia and, as with consumer markets, some people may have more influence than others. Networks of personal contacts would have had a far smaller role to play in shaping the esteem attached to particular contributions to knowledge if: (1) researchers habitually searched for relevant materials with the aid of indexing and abstracting systems in the manner that libraries nowadays try to inculcate among students; and (2) such systems covered older works as well as recent contributions. In some cases, the confidence of modern librarians in their information systems is such that they see lecturing staff not as experts in their subject areas who point students speedily to pertinent contributions but, rather, as dangerous individuals whose use of reading lists and inclination to place favoured material in restricted loan sections is liable 'to bias students' reading' (to quote the words of the Librarian of Lincoln University). However, I suspect that until recently very few academics made great use of such potential as existed for systematic search, with the result that networks were of vital significance.

When the bulk of Richardson's work appeared there were relatively few economics journals with which to keep up to date. However, this was also a period in which indexing systems were poorly developed and economists were not accustomed to making extensive use of abstracts (the *Journal of Economic Abstracts* commenced publication as late as 1963 and only turned into the more extensive *Journal of Economic Literature* in 1969). It is also probably fair to say that it was only in the 1970s that the Harvard system of referencing really caught on and made it far easier for potential readers to get a flavour of a work by examining its bibliography. In terms of presentation and layout, the reprint of *Information and Investment* is remarkably uninviting to the casual browser of the 1990s, for, as already noted, Richardson's works were typical of their time – the world of infrequent references scattered around in footnotes and of a notable absence of the use of section headings in chapters and papers.

Prior to the age of information and the development of sophisticated indexing systems, scholars who became aware of Richardson typically either would have done so by serendipity (for example, stumbling across his books or articles whilst looking purposively for something else that happens to be physically adjacent) or would have discovered them to a greater or lesser extent with the aid of networks. Seven main types of connections promote the discovery of contribution to knowledge, and some of them can be illustrated by reference to tales of 'routes to Richardson' reported to me by contributors to the Richardson colloquium held in Oxford in January 1995:

1 *Being a pupil or colleague of the author in question, or a student with an intellectual lineage traceable back to the author.* For example, given their associations with St John's College, Oxford, it should be no surprise that John Kay and Leslie Hannah have been influenced by Richardson. John Nightingale's lineage, by contrast, links Oxford and Australia: he recalls that Richardson was one of a number of authors (including Penrose, Downie and Andrews) whose recent works were discussed by Don Lamberton in a final-year undergraduate unit at the university of New South Wales in the mid-1960s – Lamberton had recently returned to Australia after meeting Richardson when working on his DPhil at Oxford.

2 *Seeing a work that cites the author, or at least cites a work that cites the author.* For example, the writings of Loasby (particularly his 1976 book) introduced the name of Richardson to myself, Nicolai Foss (who discovered Richardson around the same time also from the citation in Leijonhufvud (1968: 69–70)) and Richard Langlois. In turn, Richard Arena reports that he first saw Richardson mentioned in Earl (1983b). It is, of course, common for academics to prime their markets (or assert their property rights) via preliminary publications, such as articles and discussion papers, that foreshadow their major works whilst pre-emptively staking their claims as market leaders in particular areas of research. Richardson's articles from the 1950s pave the way directly to his (1960) book in intellectual terms. He also certainly helped his readers discover his earlier work by his own citations (oddly enough, in his 1972 paper his footnote reference (p. 891) to *Information and Investment* lists it as published in 1961, not 1960!). Though he did not engage in forward citation, his work was helpfully discussed by his Oxford colleague

Malmgren (1961) in the *Quarterly Journal of Economics* at a very early stage. This should have helped stir up interest among potential readers in America who were not regular readers of *Oxford Economic Papers* or the *Economic Journal*. Malmgren's work, unfortunately, seemed to suffer much the same initial fate as Richardson's.

3   *Being taught by someone familiar with the author's work despite not being a direct or indirect pupil of the author.* For example, Mark Casson commented that 'I think Richardson (as well as Coase, Penrose, etc.) was on the undergraduate reading list at Bristol, and I used to read the things on the list. So I never "discovered" any of these writers – I was simply directed to them. Hence I never regarded them as particularly unorthodox.' Neil Kay was introduced to Richardson's work as a pupil of Loasby at Stirling University. Gavin Reid used a Richardson (1964a) text as a second-year undergraduate at Aberdeen University in 1966–7 when looking for a short, clear conspectus of basic economics, but thinks that J. N. Wolfe, a close friend of Richardson, introduced him to *Information and Investment* in the early 1970s when he was a graduate student at Edinburgh University.

4   *Meeting with the author, or with other scholars familiar with the author's work, at conferences and/or meetings of professional societies or during the author's periods of sabbatical travel.* In this connection we might note that Richardson's impact in North America ought to have been greater given that *Information and Investment* was in part written whilst he was on a Rockefeller Foundation fellowship that left him free to 'indulge in stimulating conversations with colleagues at Harvard and the University of California at Berkeley' (Richardson 1960: xv).

5   *Receiving a word-of-mouth recommendation from a colleague.* For example, Paul Robertson believes that he first heard of Richardson's 1972 paper around 1986, from Dick Merrett, a fellow business historian in Melbourne, who in turn had just read it for the first time himself.

6   For academics in the future, the *Internet* is likely to become the ultimate networking device for affecting the spread of new ideas (see further MacKie-Mason and Varian 1994; Goffe 1994 – references to which my own attention was drawn via an e-mail from Don Lamberton).

7   *Publishers' mailing lists and catalogues, and their use of particular 'names' to endorse their products.* For the second edition of *Information and Investment*, David Teece and Oliver Williamson provided supportive comments: the fate of the first edition might have been very different had it come with a foreword from, say, Hicks (who had read it in draft) or Shackle. In future, online indexes of books and contents listings (such as Bridges to Blackwell/New Titles On-Line) may have a major role to play in enabling academics to decide what to order without being overwhelmed by printed catalogues, so choices of titles and contents designs will become even more important: we should all take note of Richardson's

view that his publisher's favoured title *Information and Investment* was unfortunate, since it led to the work being catalogued in libraries alongside books on the Stock Exchange (see his preface to the 1990 edition, p. xvii).

The existence of so many potential linkages is significant given the danger that any single aid will be of limited effectiveness. If academics are working under pressure they may not register signals as they encounter them, or may not bother to act upon them. My own route to Richardson illustrates this graphically. When, as a postgraduate student in 1977, I read Richardson (1972), inspired by the discussion in Loasby (1976), I realised that I had encountered it before, at high school in 1972 – the trouble was that, in giving us such memorable examples from 'the latest *Economic Journal* that has arrived from the town library', my teacher had not mentioned Richardson by name as the author. Later, on rereading Leijonhufvud (1968), a work which had played a crucial role in getting me hooked on the economics of uncertainty, I noticed for the first time the footnote references to Richardson (1959), in precisely the part of the book that had made such an impact. Later still, when collating old subject outlines I discovered that my final-year industrial economics reading list from Alan Hughes's lectures at Cambridge included *Information and Investment*, but somehow I had not followed it up at the time.

Whether or not recommendations or citations *are* followed up may depend considerably on the availability and anticipated quality of the work in question. Certainly, in using the *SSCI* to compile the Appendix to this chapter I was struck by the obscurity of many of the journals in which Richardson has been cited (Assistance from librarians is required even to track down the full names of some of them, let alone access copies). Richardson's articles, being in major English-language journals, are relatively easy to obtain at a moment's notice in older libraries, as are his books, but all could easily be dismissed on account of their age by current scholars unless they have been discovered by more modern secondary sources of note in which their virtues have been extolled at length.

To conclude this section I would like to emphasise that when a scholar has to go to some trouble to obtain a work – for example, an interlibrary loan to a recently established institution – learned societies have a major role to play in determining whether it will look sufficiently attractive in prospect to seem worth chasing, as well as whether it gets discovered in the first place. Although it is rare for such societies to insist that members conduct their research in a particular manner – unlike trade associations, who may debar from membership those whose standards of work do not meet with association norms – their ability to control what gets presented at their conferences or what gets published in their official journals means they have a major gatekeeping role in respect of the marketing of contributions to knowledge. A further aspect of this professional control is the ability to determine which journals are abstracted in the society's abstracting publications. This is important not merely because articles published in unlisted journals have a smaller chance of being discovered but also because librarians, concerned to see that their investments are thoroughly used, may refer to the places in which a journal is abstracted as criteria for deciding whether or not to agree to take out a subscription – so, woe betide the economics journal which is not abstracted in *ABI-Inform* and the *Journal of Economic Literature*.

Mere publication of an article signals to the academic community that it has been through a pretty stiff competitive refereeing process if it is published in a dominant professional grouping's generalist journal, or signals the height of refereeing hurdles and the likely style and content if it is published in a subdisciplinary or heterodox journal. (It is probably fair to suggest that when Richardson published frequently in *Oxford Economic Papers* in the 1950s and 1960s, this journal was much less of an international organ than it is today.) Commercially published journals serve a similar signalling role, and, of course, many of these are associated with academic societies or networks. Firms that publish a large number of journals of high quality have a incentive to maintain their standards as they add new journals to their catalogues, for fear of damaging their overall image and hence the subscriptions they can command. Editorial boards of reputable academics signal the standards that are being targeted even if no learned society sponsors the journal. Likewise, in respect of book publishing, catalogue branding is extensively used to signal the type of book to potential purchasers: most publishers run a variety of imprints and under any particular imprint may also include a number of series of books of particular kinds.

CONCLUSION

Richardson's work on economic organisation and co-ordination has been widely used despite so far failing to become part of the core of microeconomic theory. It also provides valuable perspectives for viewing the operations of academia, encouraging us to look for networks and other institutional devices that assist academics to reduce co-ordination difficulties. The risk that academics will unwittingly reinvent each other's ideas or pursue dysfunctional lines of inquiry owing to their ignorance of particular contributions is reduced to the extent they can search systematically with the aid of subject and citation indexes, abstracts and book reviews or contents listings. In the past, haphazard methods of research and weaker networking/indexing made it all too easy for scholars to to be unaware of works that they would have welcomed or that would have forced them to rethink their ideas. It was not wise to presume that if a contribution to knowledge was of a high standard this would necessarily be swiftly reflected in its rate of citation or the number of copies in circulation. Now, as the twentieth century comes to an end, we are entering a new world where information technology will permit scholars to operate in a far less haphazard manner as they attempt to discover and screen contributions for their likely usefulness. Much screening will take place on-screen and ideas will be able to spread far more rapidly so long as they have been judiciously titled and summarised. Even so, older contributions or contributions in obscure journals may remain at risk of being neglected. The Appendix that follows is offered not merely by way of documenting some of the use made of Richardson's work but also to concentrate readers' minds on just how narrow are their normal ranges of reading compared with the range required if one is to be able truthfully to say 'I know the literature'.

APPENDIX

Citations of G. B. Richardson recorded in the *Social Sciences Citation Index*, 1969–94

Note: Each entry is listed in terms of the author making the citation (longer names may be truncated and only the first author is shown in the case of joint works), the name of the journal in which the citation occurs (which may be abbreviated), and by the volume number, the number of the first page of the article and the year of publication.

'Imperfect knowledge and economic efficiency', *Oxford Economic Papers*, 1953
C. S. W. Torr	*South African Journal of Economics*	48	115	80
J. High	*Contemporary Policy Issues*	3	21	84

'Demand and supply reconsidered', *Oxford Economic Papers*, 1956
C. S. W. Torr	*South African Journal of Economics*	48	115	80
J. High	*Contemporary Policy Issues*	3	21	84

'Equilibrium, expectations and information', *Economic Journal*, 1959
H. Abele	*Zeitschrift für Nationalökonomie*	31	45	71
G. B. Richardson	*Soviet Studies*	22	433	71
R. Huler	*Zeitschrift für Nationalökonomie*	31	229	71
F. M. Scherer	*Journal of Industrial Economics*	22	157	73
F. F. Esposito	*Review of Economic Studies*	56	188	74
H. Albert	*Law State*	13	129	76
N. Shapiro	*Australian Economic Papers*	17	207	78
R. R. Keller	*Nebraska Journal of Economics and Business*	19	30	80
J. A. Kregel	*History of Political Economy*	12	97	80
W. Fuhrmann	*Jahrbuch für Sozialwissenschaft*	33	269	82
N. Ferretti	*Giovnale degli Eco-nomisti e Annali di Economia*	42	191	84
J. High	*Contemporary Policy Issues*	3	21	84
D. E. Allen	*South African Journal of Economics*	54	18	86
M. Dietrich	*Cambridge Journal of Economics*	10	318	86

(*Note*: the citation by H. Albert is listed as 'Keynesian Economics, 1968', which corresponds to none of Richardson's works but is probably based on a reference to the citation of Richardson (1959) by A. Leijonhufvud (1968: 69–70).)

Information and Investment, 1960/1990
F. M. Scherer	*American Economic Review*	59	72	69
J. S. Fleming	*Review of Economic Studies*	36	52	69
K. W. Lemke	*Journal of Accounting*	8	47	70
A. Beacham	*Journal of Industrial Economics*	19	97	71
O. E. Williamson	*American Economic Review*	61	112	71

F. R. Kaen	*Rivista internationale di economia*	18	353	71
G. B. Richardson	*Soviet Studies*	22	433	71
F. F. Esposito	*Review of Economic Studies*	56	188	74
A. Longhi	*Analyse et Prévision*	18	541	74
J. B. Nugent	*Journal of Common Market Studies*	14	198	75
A. Cukierman	*Bell Journal of Economics*	7	132	76
D. A. Hay	*Oxford Economic Papers*	28	240	76
J. Scouller	*Journal of Economic Studies*	3	156	76
B. J. Loasby	*Scottish Journal of Political Economy*	25	1	78
N. C. Sarantis	*Kyklos*	31	437	78
B. Smith	*World Economy*	2	65	79
R. E. Smith	*Journal of Economic Issues*	13	629	79
M. Lipton	*World Development*	8	1	80
C. S. W. Torr	*South African Journal of Economics*	48	115	80
S. C. Littlechild	*Economic Journal*	91	348	81
R. R. Nelson	*Bell Journal of Economics*	12	93	81
S. C. Dow	*Australian Economic Papers*	22	30	83
M. S. Addleson	*South African Journal of Economics*	52	156	84
W. S. Bishop	*Journal of Marketing*	48	95	84
R. J. Gilbert	*Rand Journal of Economics*	15	197	84
B. J. Loasby	*Journal of Economic Studies*	11	75	84
D. J. Teece	*California Management Review*	26	87	84
C. S. W. Torr	*Economic Journal*	94	936	84
T. Cowen	*American Economic Review*	75	866	85
B. J. Loasby	*Journal of Economic Studies*	12	21	85
A. Nove	*Dissent*	32	357	85
D. E. Allen	*South African Journal of Economics*	54	18	86
C. Foster	*Journal of Transport Economics*	20	191	86
B. J. Loasby	*Scottish Journal of Political Economy*	33	145	86
D. J. Teece	*Journal of Economic Behavior and Organization*	7	21	86
M. Dietrich	*Cambridge Journal of Economics*	10	318	86
R. J. Gilbert	*Rand Journal of Economics*	18	17	87
T. M. Jorde	*California Management Review*	31	25	89
C. P. Hallwood	*Journal of Institutional and Theoretical Economics*	146	576	90
T. Scitovsky	*Journal of Economic Perspectives*	4	135	90
J. A. Kay	*Economic Journal*	101	57	91
D. Paraskevopoulos	*Management Science*	37	787	91
J. T. Mahoney	*Strategic Management Journal*	13	363	92
D. J. Teece	*Journal of Economic Behavior and Organization*	18	1	92
P. A. O'Brien	*Business History*	34	128	92
L. M. B. Cabral	*Journal of Economic Theory*	59	403	93
D. M. Higgins	*Economic History Review*	46	342	93
A. Nove	*Problems of Economic Transition*	35	20	93
J. Khazam	*Research Policy*	23	89	94
J. S. Metcalfe	*Economic Journal*	104	931	94

Economic Theory, 1964
J. D. House	*Canadian Review of Sociology and Anthropology*	11	111	74
A. Beacham	*South African Journal of Economics*	42	118	74
J. D. House	*Canadian Review of Sociology and Anthropology*	14	1	77

'The limits to a firm's rate of growth', *Oxford Economic Papers*, 1964
G. M. Heal	*Oxford Economic Papers*	24	137	72
L. Hannah	*Economic History Review*	27	252	74
S. Lofthouse	*Rivista internationale di economia*	21	1014	74
M. Slater	*Economic Journal*	90	520	80
K. Brockhof	*Zeitschrift Betriebswirtschaft*	50	475	80
P. N. O'Farrell	*Environment and Planning*	20	1365	88
J. T. Mahoney	*Strategic Management Journal*	13	363	92
D. Hay	*Oxford Review of Economic Policy*	9	1	93

'The theory of restrictive trade practices', *Oxford Economic Papers*, 1965
D. Dewey	*American Economic Review*	69	587	79
F. S. Lee	*Australian Economic Papers*	23	151	84
T. J. Dilorenzo	*Journal of Institutional and Theoretical Economics*	144	318	88
A. H. Amsden	*European Economic Review*	38	941	94
R. W. Bethlehem	*South African Journal of Economics*	62	280	94
D. F. Leach	*South African Journal of Economics*	62	254	94

'The pricing of heavy electrical equipment: competition or agreement', *Bulletin of the Oxford University Institute of Economics and Statistics*, 1966
A. G. Fraas	*Journal of Industrial Economics*	26	21	77
B. Epstein	*Cambridge Journal of Economics*	6	33	82
F. S. Lee	*Australian Economic Papers*	23	151	84

'Price notification schemes', *Oxford Economic Papers*, 1967
K. Imai	*Japanese Economic Studies*	3	3	74
F. S. Lee	*Australian Economic Papers*	23	151	84

'Planning versus competition', *Soviet Studies*, 1971
M. J. C. Surrey	*Bulletin of the Oxford University Institute of Economics and Statistics*	34	249	72
A. Cairncross	*Economic Journal*	82	311	72
M. S. Addleson	*South African Journal of Economics*	52	156	84
M. S. Addleson	*South African Journal of Economics*	58	173	90

'The organisation of industry', *Economic Journal*, 1972
J. Lemuet	*Analyse et Prévision*	16	107	73
P. Rubin	*Journal of Political Economy*	81	936	73
T. P. Hogarty	*Journal of Economic Literature*	13	89	75
J. B. Nugent	*Journal of Common Market Studies*	14	198	75
F. E. Hamilton	*Tijdschrift voor Economische en Sociale Geografie*	67	258	76
V. P. Goldberg	*Bell Journal of Economics*	7	426	76

V. P. Goldberg	*Bell Journal of Economics*	8	250	77
G. Paquet	*Revue d'économie politique*	87	607	77
J. Arndt	*Journal of Marketing*	43	69	79
J. Arndt	*Michigan State University Business Topics*	27	5	79
K. Blois	*Management Decision*	18	55	80
S. Globerman	*Journal of Economics Issues*	14	977	80
S. Lall	*Bulletin of the Oxford University Institute of Economics and Statistics*	42	207	80
C. S. W. Torr	*South African Journal of Economics*	48	115	80
N. T. Flaherty	*Bell Journal of Economics*	12	507	81
C. S. W. Torr	*South African Journal of Economics*	49	334	81
P. Zusman	*Management Science*	27	284	81
R. Hardin	*Social Science Information*	21	251	82
H. Leblibic	*Administrative Science Quarterly*	27	227	82
J. Arndt	*Journal of Marketing*	47	44	83
S. N. S. Cheung	*Journal of Law and Economics*	28	1	83
E. G. Jones	*R & D Management*	13	155	83
P. Mariti	*Journal of Industrial Economics*	31	437	83
P. Sheard	*Australian Geographical Studies*	21	49	83
D. C. Mead	*World Development*	12	1095	84
P. J. Buckley	*Hitosubashi Journal of Economics*	26	117	85
K. Kojima	*Hitosubashi Journal of Economics*	26	135	85
H. Gunz	*Organizational Studies*	6	247	85
B. J. Loasby	*Journal of Economic Studies*	12	21	85
A. J. Scott	*Environment and Planning*	17	479	85
S. Globerman	*Journal of Economic Behavior and Organization*	7	199	86
R. F. Imre	*Environment and Planning*	18	949	86
S. Paba	*Cambridge Journal of Economics*	10	305	86
A. J. Scott	*Annals of the Association of American Geographers*	76	25	86
A. J. Scott	*Economic Geography*	62	216	86
O. E. Williamson	*American Economic Review*	76	114	86
J. Child	*Journal of Management Strategy*	24	565	87
J. Child	*California Management Review*	30	33	87
G. K. Dow	*Journal of Economic Behavior and Organization*	8	13	87
A. Friedman	*British Journal of Industrial Relations*	25	353	87
D. Klein	*Harvard Journal of Law*	10	451	87
W. W. Powell	*California Management Review*	30	67	87
J. Davies	*Journal of Post Keynesian Economics*	11	3	88
P. Enderwick	*Managerial and Decision Economics*	9	35	88
H. F. Gospel	*Business History*	30	104	88
R. N. Langlois	*Journal of Institutional and Theoretical Economics*	144	635	88
G. Lorenzon	*Journal of Business Venturing*	3	41	88
W. G. Ouchi	*California Management Review*	30	9	88
K. Sekkat	*Cahiers économiques bruxelles*	–	181	88
J. L. Bradach	*Annual Review of Sociology*	15	97	89
A. Delmonte	*Regional Studies*	23	219	89
J. Gronewegan	*Journal of Economic Issues*	23	1059	89
E. Kieland	*Tijdschrift for Samfunforskining*	30	263	89

K. Kojima	*Hitosubashi Journal of Economics*	30	65	89
L. Suarezvi	*Tijdschrift voor Economische en Sociale Geographie*	80	194	89
W. W. Powell	*Research in Organisational Behaviour*	12	295	90
R. D. Whitley	*Organizational Studies*	11	47	90
C. Debresso	*Research Policy*	10	363	91
M. Dietrich	*Scottish Journal of Political Economy*	38	41	91
R. Florida	*American Sociological Review*	56	381	91
D. Foray	*Research Policy*	20	393	91
J. H. Mulherin	*Journal of Law and Economics*	34	591	91
N. Nohria	*Strategic Management Journal*	121	105	91
R. D. Whitley	*Organizational Studies*	12	1	91
P. Y. Badillo	*Revue économique*	43	615	92
R. H. Dossanto	*Desarrollo economico – revista de ciencias sociales*	32	198	92
G. C. Cainarca	*Research Policy*	21	45	92
J. L. Badaracc	*California Management Review*	34	64	92
B. Baudry	*Revue économique*	43	871	92
K. Brockhof	*Management Science*	38	514	92
T. Cowen	*Economics and Philosophy*	8	249	92
R. N. Langlois	*Research Policy*	21	297	92
J. Lincoln	*American Sociological Review*	57	561	92
J. T. Mahoney	*Strategic Management Journal*	13	363	92
M. Sorper	*Economic Geography*	64	60	92
D. Courpasson	*Revue française de sociologie*	35	698	93
A. Mody	*Journal of Economic Behavior and Organization*	20	151	93
N. Leiper	*Annals of Tourism Research*	20	221	93
G. White	*Institute of Development Studies Bulletin*	24	4	93
R. M. Buxbaum	*Journal of Institutional and Theoretical Economics*	145	698	93
M. Fransman	*Telecommunications Policy*	18	137	94
R. Garud	*Research Policy*	22	385	94
S. K. Majumdar	*Journal of Institutional and Theoretical Economics*	150	375	94

'Adam Smith on competition and increasing returns', in A. Skinner and T. Wilson (eds) *Essays on Adam Smith*, 1975

E. G. West	*Southern Economic Journal*	45	343	78
H.C. Recklenwald	*Journal of Economic Literature*	16	56	78
C.P. Blitch	*Journal of Post Keynesian Economics*	5	359	83
R. Prendergast	*Cambridge Journal of Economics*	16	447	92
I. Steedman	*Manchester School*	52	123	84
K. Aftab	*Journal of Development Studies*	23	60	86
J.P. Henderson	*History of Political Economy*	18	111	86

Private Communications, 1981 and 1986

F. S. Lee	*History of Political Economy*	24	373	92

Review of 1990 edition of *Information and Investment*

B. J. Loasby	*Manchester School*	59	348	91

NOTES

1 I would like to thank Michael Brooks for many useful comments on an earlier version of this paper, which has also benefited from comments by the editors and the publisher's referee, and from correspondence with George Richardson (who provided some very useful autobiographical notes) and Fred Lee.

REFERENCES

Baudier, E. (1961) 'Review of G. Debreu's *Theory of Value*', *Econometrica* 29: 259–60.

Blois, K. J. (1972) 'Vertical quasi-integration', *Journal of Industrial Economics* 20: 253–71.

Borch, K. (1973) 'The place of uncertainty in the theories of the Austrian school', in J. R. Hicks and W. Weber (eds) (1973) *Carl Menger and the Austrian School of Economics*, Oxford: Oxford University Press.

Clark, J. M. (1923) *Studies in the Economics of Overhead Costs*, Chicago: University of Chicago Press.

Clarke, R. and McGuinness, T. (eds) (1987) *The Economics of the Firm*, Oxford: Basil Blackwell.

Cook, P. L. (1964) 'Review of G.B. Richardson's *Information and Investment*', *Economic Journal* 74: 168–9.

Debreu, G. (1959) *Theory of Value*, New York: Wiley.

Devine, P. J., Jones, R. M., Lee, N. and Tyson, W. J. (1976) *An Introduction to Industrial Economics*, 2nd edn, London: George Allen & Unwin.

Dobb, M. H. (1937) *Political Economy and Capitalism*, London: Routledge.

Earl, P. E. (1983a) 'A behavioral theory of economists' behavior', in A. S. Eichner (ed.) *Why Economics is Not Yet a Science*, Armonk, NY: M. E. Sharpe, Inc.

—— (1983b) *The Economic Imagination*, Brighton: Wheatsheaf.

—— (1993) 'Epilogue: whatever happened to P. W. S. Andrews's industrial economics?', in F. S. Lee and P. E. Earl (eds) *The Economics of Competitive Enterprise: Selected Essays of P.W.S. Andrews*, Aldershot: Edward Elgar.

—— (1995) *Microeconomics for Business and Marketing*, Aldershot: Edward Elgar.

Foss, N. (1994) 'Cooperation is competition: George Richardson on coordination and interfirm relations', *British Review of Economic Issues* 16: 25–49.

George, K. D. and Joll, C. (1981) *Industrial Organisation*, 3rd edn, London: George Allen & Unwin.

Goffe, W. L. (1994) 'Computer network resources for economists', *Journal of Economic Perspectives* 8: 97–119.

Grant, J. McB. (1962) 'Review of G. B. Richardson's *Information and Investment*', *Economic Record* 38: 125.

Greer, D. F. (1992) *Industrial Organization and Public Policy*, 3rd edn, New York: Maxwell-Macmillan.

Hahn, F. H. (1961) 'Review of G. Debreu's *Theory of Value*', *Journal of Political Economy* 69: 204–5.

Harrell, C. (1960) 'Review of G. Debreu's *Theory of Value*', *Southern Economic Journal* 27: 149–50.

Harris, L. (1965) 'Review of G. B. Richardson's *Economic Theory*', *Economica* 32: 236–7.

Hay, D. A. and Morris, D. J. (1979) *Industrial Economics: Theory and Evidence* Oxford: Oxford University Press.
Hicks, J. R. (1945) *Value and Capital*, Oxford: Oxford University Press.
Hurwicz, L. (1961) 'Review of G. Debreu's *Theory of Value*', *American Economic Review* 51: 414–17.
Kaldor, N. (1972) 'The irrelevance of equilibrium economics', *Economic Journal*, 82: 1237–55.
Kay, J. A. (1993) *Foundations of Corporate Success*, Oxford: Oxford University Press.
Keynes, J. M. (1936) *The General Theory of Employment, Interest and Money*, London: Macmillan.
Lamfalussy, A. (1961) *Investment and Growth in Mature Economies: The Case of Belgium*, London: Macmillan.
Lee, F. S. (1993) 'Philip Walter Sawford Andrews, 1914–1971', in F. S. Lee and P. E. Earl (eds) *The Economics of Competitive Enterprise: Selected Essays of P. W. S. Andrews*, Aldershot: Edward Elgar.
Leijonhufvud, A. (1968) *On Keynesian Economics and the Economics of Keynes*, New York: Oxford University Press.
Loasby, B. J. (1976) *Choice, Complexity and Ignorance*, Cambridge: Cambridge University Press.
—— (1989) *The Mind and the Method of the Economist*, Aldershot: Edward Elgar.
MacKie-Mason J. K. and Varian, H. (1994) 'Economic FAQs about the Internet', *Journal of Economic Perspectives* 8: 75–96.
Malmgren, H. B. (1961) 'Information, expectations and the theory of the firm', *Quarterly Journal of Economics* 75: 399–421.
Martin, S. (1993) *Advanced Industrial Economics*, Oxford: Basil Blackwell.
Miles, C. (1968) *Lancashire Textiles: A Case Study of Industrial Change*, Cambridge: Cambridge University Press/NIESR.
Muth, R. F. (1961) 'Rational expectations and the theory of price movements', *Econometrica* 29: 315–35.
Penrose, E. T. (1959) *The Theory of the Growth of the Firm*, Oxford: Basil Blackwell.
Phlips, L. (1988) *The Economics of Imperfect Information*, Cambridge: Cambridge University Press.
Pickering, J. F. (1973) *Industrial Structure and Market Conduct*, London: Martin Robertson.
Porter, M. E. (1980) *Competitive Strategy*, New York: Free Press.
Power, J. H. (1961) 'Review of G. B. Richardson's *Information and Investment*', *American Economic Review* 51: 761–2.
Reid, G. C. (1987) *Theories of Industrial Organization*, Oxford: Basil Blackwell.
Richardson, G. B. (1959) 'Equilibrium, expectations and information', *Economic Journal* 69: 223–37.
—— (1960) *Information and Investment: A Study in the Working of the Competitive Economy*, Oxford: Clarendon Press.
—— (1964a) *Economic Theory*, London: Hutchinson.
—— (1964b) 'The limits to a firm's rate of growth', *Oxford Economic Papers* 16: 9–23.
—— (1965) 'The theory of restrictive trade practices', *Oxford Economic Papers* 17: 432–49.

—— (1966) 'The pricing of heavy electrical equipment: competition or agreement?', *Bulletin of the Oxford University Institute of Economics and Statistics* 28: 7392.
—— (1967) 'Price notification schemes', *Oxford Economics Papers* 19: 355–65.
—— (1969) *The Future of the Heavy Electrical Plant Industry*, London: BEEMA.
—— (1971) 'Planning versus competition', *Soviet Studies* 22: 433–47.
—— (1972) 'The organisation of industry', *Economic Journal* 82: 883–96.
—— (1975) 'Adam Smith on competition and increasing returns', in A. S. Skinner and T. Wilson (eds) *Essays on Adam Smith*, Oxford: Oxford University Press.
—— (1990) *Information and Investment: A Study in the Working of the Competitive Economy*, 2nd edn, Oxford: Clarendon Press.
Robinson, J. V. (1954) 'The impossibility of profits', in E. H. Chamberlin (ed.) *Monopoly and Competition and their Regulation*, London: Macmillan.
Scherer, F. M. and Ross, D. (1990) *Industrial Market Structure and Economic Performance*, 3rd edn, Boston: Houghton Mifflin.
Schmalensee, R. and Willig (eds) (1989) *Handbook of Industrial Organization*, vol. 1, Amsterdam: North-Holland.
Stigler, G. J. (1982) *The Economist as Preacher*, Oxford: Basil Blackwell.
Tirole, J. (1988) *The Theory of Industrial Organization*, Cambridge, MA: MIT Press.
Wagner, L. and Baltazzis, N. (eds) (1973) *Readings in Applied Microeconomics*, Oxford: Oxford University Press.
Williams, B. R. (1949) 'Types of competition and the theory of employment', *Oxford Economic Papers* 1 (new series): 121–44.
Wool Textile EDC (1969) *The Strategic Future of the Wool Textile Industry*, London: HMSO.
Young, A. (1928) 'Increasing returns and economic progress', *Economic Journal*, 38: 527–42.
Young, W. and Lee, F. S. (1993) *Oxford Economics and Oxford Economists*, London: Macmillan.

3

SOME PRINCIPLES OF ECONOMIC ORGANISATION

George B. Richardson[1]

THE NEED FOR CO-ORDINATION

The division of labour, upon which the wealth of nations depends, requires the existence of means by which specialised activities can be properly co-ordinated. The different means of co-ordination available and the different purposes to which they are suited, which have long been a central concern of economists, are the subject of this paper.

I addressed these issues in an article entitled 'The organisation of industry', which was published in the *Economic Journal* in 1972. It maintained that we should think of firms not as making products, but as undertaking *activities*, the nature of which would be in accordance with their particular *capabilities*, as determined by their skills, experience and market connections. I observed that these activities could be co-ordinated in three basic ways: though *market transactions*, through *co-operation* and by *direction*. Using these ideas, the article sought to explain the existence, within real-world economies, of 'the dense network of cooperation and affiliation by which firms are related' (Richardson 1972: 883). This phenomenon did not, at that time, much attract the attention of economists, although it has done so since.

I hope now to take this analysis further and to remedy at least some of its deficiencies. In particular, I shall in due course shift the focus of attention from relationships between firms to what happens within them. In the 1972 article I mentioned how when I began to teach economics I told pupils that firms were islands of central planning in a sea of market transactions; I admitted in that article to having been wrong about the sea, which cannot be properly described in terms of pure market transactions, and have to admit now to being wrong about the islands, co-ordination within which is not merely a matter of direction, at least in any simple sense. Ample opportunity to appreciate this latter fact was provided for me when, in 1972, I gave up economics to become Chief Executive of Oxford University Press.

SOME PRINCIPLES OF ECONOMIC ORGANISATION

THE INVISIBLE HAND

In seeking to explain how economic activities are co-ordinated, it is upon the role of *market transactions* that economists have overwhelming concentrated. Their functioning was described famously by Adam Smith in terms of an 'invisible hand', and modern general equilibrium theory is seen, by some, as the culmination of his line of thinking. I do not myself see it that way. Smith took account of the pervasive existence of increasing returns to scale, and envisaged free competition as increasing the wealth of nations by engendering continuous structural change. His theory of the working of markets is also therefore a theory of endogenous economic growth.[2] All this was largely lost sight of in the development of the more formalised models that now hold the stage. And this may account for the neglect of the process of continuous morphological change which I shall later discuss in this article.[3] It seems to me significant that both Smith and Marshall are concerned to explain the advantages of a regime of *economic freedom*, rather than of *competition* narrowly conceived; freedom enables businesses to co-operate as well as to compete, to merge or to separate, to take on activities or to give them up. Smith and Marshall allowed, in other words, for the continuous reshaping of industry, the process of constant mutation and selection that takes place under capitalism.

I do not wish to question the central role played by co-ordination through competitive market transactions, which are individually subject to, and which collectively determine, a system of prices. I have argued, however, that decisions taken by individual firms independently can achieve co-ordination only if certain conditions are met, and I have maintained that unless we understand the nature of these conditions, we shall be unable to explain why, in their absence, recourse to co-operation and direction is sometimes essential. One key condition, paradoxically, is that competition be not 'perfect'. The reasons for this assertion were set out in my book *Information and Investment*, first published in 1960, and I shall not try to rehearse them properly here. A summary statement is needed, however, to put what will follow it into context.

Economists have never been able to explain how, in perfectly competitive conditions, equilibrium could come about other than by fictitious and implausible arrangements, such as Edgeworth's system of re-contracting or the activity of Walras's auctioneer. Some have endeavoured to cut the Gordian knot simply by assuming that entrepreneurs somehow foresee equilibrium prices, presuming, for no good reason, that this foresight would lead to actions which would cause these prices to be realised. The reason for the failure to explain how equilibrium could be reached is in fact simple; for it to be possible for the equilibrium configuration to be attained through independently taken investment decisions, conditions must exist that are incompatible with the assumptions of the perfect competition model.

If a producer is to invest so as to supply an expected future demand, he must have some assurance that the profit opportunity to which he wishes to respond will not be open equally to everyone else. In the real world this condition can be met naturally; the number of those likely to respond may be limited by the fact that only some are aware of the opportunity, and, of these, only some have the capability appropriate to respond to it. There exist, in other words, both *imperfect information* and *imperfect mobility*, which provide a natural restraint on the likely volume of *competitive* production. The incentive to invest depends, therefore, on the existence of circumstances which are deemed absent, by assumption, in the perfect competition model. A whole host of phenomena, the existence of which may, in certain circumstances, be necessary for informed decision-making to be possible, are either ignored or condemned as 'restraints on trade', with no attempt to analyse their essential function.

The firm contemplating investment will need also be reasonably confident that products *complementary* to its own will be available, that it will be able, for example, to purchase on the market the necessary inputs. If these inputs are currently available, then the firm will have to be confident that they will continue to be so. If they are not currently available, then the firm, if it does not have good reason to expect their future availability, will have to take steps itself to ensure it. Much will depend here upon the *closeness* of the complementarity in question, whether, that is to say, there will be a need for inputs that are highly specific to the process of production envisaged. And much will depend also on whether the producers of the needed inputs, assuming these are available, will be able to accommodate the additional demand.

A CARDINAL PRINCIPLE OF ECONOMIC ORGANISATION

Perfect competition theory ignores what we may call a *cardinal principle of economic organisation*, a principle which applies to any group in which there exists interdependence, in the sense that the action that any member would choose to adopt will depend on what that member expects other members to do.[4] If the members of this group have complete freedom of action, being subject to no constraints, whether external or self-imposed, then there can be no informed decision-making within it. Members of an interdependent group, that is to say, cannot entertain informed expectations as to what other members will do unless there are restrictions on their freedom of action.

This is true irrespective of the numbers within the group. On the reasonable assumption that their activities will be more productive if co-ordinated, what Robinson Crusoe would choose to do will depend on what Man Friday chooses to do, Man Friday, however, being in the same situation with regard to his fellow islander. The possibility of informed choice in this context depends upon the existence of constraints that narrow down freedom of action, either in the form of external circumstances that preclude some actions for either party, or through reciprocal undertakings, habits or conventions. In the case of a large group, the same is true. The co-ordination of economic activities can result from independent market transactions only in appropriate circumstances, in the absence of which co-operative behaviour, in one or more of its many forms, is required.

To put the matter somewhat over-simply, for co-ordination to result from decisions taken independently there has to be a certain stability in the economic environment. Such co-ordination can ensure adaptation to change, but only within a context where, in the short run, most things remain substantially the same. If a manufacturer perceives a profit opportunity, he or she will be prepared to commit resources in response to it, on the assumption, which may not be consciously entertained, that the prices and availability of relevant *competitive activities* (i.e. those which would reduce the profitability of the investment) and of the relevant *complementary activities* (i.e. those which are necessary for, or would enhance, the profitability of the investment) do not change overmuch. Very often these conditions are sufficiently met – as each new dawn does not bring a completely new configuration of prices and outputs. In that sense, *natura non facit saltum*, to employ the observation with which Marshall (with a different implication) prefaces his *Principles* (1890).

THE NEED FOR CO-OPERATION

It is, however, perfectly possible that the existing pattern of output in the economy does not provide a firm contemplating investment with the complementary inputs it requires. It has then the choice between itself making the input or entering into a co-operative arrangement with an outside supplier. The balance of advantage between these options will depend, in part, upon whether producing this input requires a *capability* different from those the firm itself possesses.[5]

If the firm chooses to turn to an outside supplier, a framework of co-operation will have to be devised which offers an acceptable degree of security to both parties. The purchaser of the special input will wish to be able to depend on a continuing and reliable supply; the producer of the input will want assurance of continuing demand. The ways in which such arrangements can be put together are well known, as is the difficulty of making them completely satisfactory to both parties. 'The dense network of cooperation and affiliation', discussed and exemplified in my 1972 article referred to above, is composed of arrangements of this kind, and the co-ordination of economic activity in the real world would be impossible without it.[6]

Co-ordination can therefore come about through market transactions, as a result of independent decision-making, given an adequately predictable environment, or through co-operation, which provides predictability by means of reciprocal undertakings. In either case, of course, decisions will both be influenced by and collectively determine a system of competitively determined prices, so that the relative scarcity of different resources and the relative preferences of consumers come to influence the resultant allocation of resources.

THE NEED FOR DIRECTION

What then is the function of *direction* as I defined it in my 1972 article? Or what, to pose a related question, to which Ronald Coase notably drew attention, is the role of the firm?

I recall, when first reading Coase's 1937 article, now some fifty years ago, being puzzled by the following passage.

> Within a firm, ... market transactions are eliminated and in place of ... exchange transactions is substituted the entrepreneur-co-ordinator, who directs production. It is clear that these are alternative methods of co-ordinating production. Yet, having regard to the fact that if production is regulated by price movements, production could be carried on without any organisation at all, well might we ask, why is there any organisation?
>
> (Coase 1937: 19)

Having posed this question, Coase then proceeds to answer it by maintaining that 'the main reason why it is profitable to establish a firm would seem to be that there is a cost of using the price mechanism' (Coase 1937: 20).

Implicit in this reasoning appears to be the belief that 'the price mechanism' could somehow spontaneously bring into existence any required combination of human and material resources, if only the cost of using it were acceptable. But, by what sorcery is this to come about? In order to produce a good, a firm has to identify and assemble, and then properly deploy, an appropriate set of human and material resources; prices enter into the process by influencing the combinations chosen. This conscious ordering is certainly mediated by prices, but prices do not make it possible to dispense with it. There is no magic by which prices can by themselves lead people to assemble themselves spontaneously and simultaneously in appropriate groupings, and to work with each other and the non-human resources similarly assembled for a particular process of production. This requires planning, and the prime purpose of a firm is to plan and execute, on a continuing basis, the processes that make and sell a product or service.

There are, as we have seen, circumstances in which independent decision-making can lead to spontaneous co-ordination; such co-ordination takes the form of incremental changes which can, over time, change the economic landscape. But where, as in a production process, *a complex set of closely complementary activities has to be put in place simultaneously*, conscious co-ordination is required. Were these activities each under, as it were, separate management, none would be undertaken without the assurance that the others would be undertaken; each activity would be effective only as a member of the set, and there would be no way in which the set could somehow, without conscious planning, be identified and brought simultaneously into being.

I cannot therefore agree with Coase that the existence of firms has to be attributed to the cost of using the price mechanism. As we shall see, a cost of this kind may be a consideration, even if not a principal one, in a firm's decision to 'make or buy' a necessary input, but to say that transaction costs explain the *existence* of firms is to reduce the role of conscious business planning to vanishing point. The term 'price mechanism' may perhaps too readily lead us to think that resources are somehow allocated without human agency. The reality, as we know, is that things happen because people do things; in this context, firms and consumers do things on the basis of plans that they consciously make, but plans which by interacting in their execution are so modified as to become woven into an overarching economic order.

Where ordering can be built up through incremental adjustment it can come about spontaneously, as a result, that is to say, of decisions taken by firms independently, without any consideration being given to their necessary integration. But where ordering relates to a set of closely complementary activities that must fit together in a specific way there must be conscious design and planned execution. And it is the function of management, at different levels within the organisation, to provide this.

Any one firm is concerned with only some stages in the process of producing final output; the physical inputs which they purchase are the outputs of other concerns and the labour they employ embodies some prior education and training. The question therefore arises as to what particular stages a firm will itself undertake. Adam Smith, as noted above, showed how the gains from the division of labour would lead to the emergence of specialist producers, enjoying economies of scale, who concentrate on particular activities, thus becoming the suppliers to a number of firms which previously would have undertaken the corresponding activities themselves. Firms therefore find that it is best for them to buy certain inputs, general-purpose inputs, we may say, on the market; special-purpose inputs, which they alone need, will either be obtained from other firms on the basis of a special contract or made by the firm itself.

The so-called 'make or buy' decision has been subject to intensive examination in the literature. If the *closely complementary* activities are *dissimilar*, in that undertaking them requires different skills, experience and market connections, there will be an advantage in seeking to achieve their co-ordination by means of an agreement between firms with the appropriate – and, by assumption, different – capabilities. But there are well-known obstacles in the way of such agreement. It may not be possible to provide the supplier of the needed input, the making of which might require substantial fixed investment, with sufficient assurance of continuing demand for it. And it may be impracticable to draw up an agreement which allows for necessary unpredictable changes in what each party has to do. In such cases the closely complementary activities may have to be consolidated within one firm, despite their dissimilarity, in order to achieve a coherent production plan.

A firm is a system of organised co-operation. Where only a few complementary activities have to be fitted together, this can be achieved by co-operation between the relevant parties, each of them having a more or less equivalent say. It is possible for a handful of people to work out together a concerted plan of action and then to be jointly responsible for its execution. But even then it will prove at best laborious to agree whatever modifications in the plan will from time to time be required in order to meet changing circumstances. A leader is likely to emerge, or be chosen, and members of the group will tend usually to follow that leader, without having to be convinced at each and every stage that he or she is on the right road. Where the number of closely complementary activities or investments is large, where they have to be put into a precise relationship in respect of their character, magnitudes and timing, I have said, for want of a better term, that *systematic close complementarity* exists. In such circumstances, co-ordination requires *direction*.[7]

DIRECTION: ITS SCOPE AND LIMITS

Let us now consider the notion of direction and its modus operandi more closely. Direction, of a kind, is to be found on the parade ground, as men move like automata under the commands of the drill sergeant. Those directed decide nothing for themselves and respond to the will of the director as would his arms and legs. Clearly, in the economic sphere – and, indeed, also in the military one – little can be achieved by direction of this kind. There can be, say, within a factory operation conditions that require workers to act very precisely according to a set of detailed instructions, but rarely will there be no need for them to exercise discretion in response to circumstances that cannot in every particular be foreseen. Indeed, if they were expected to behave as automata, then machines could do their work.

Direction, of the kind that concerns us, does indeed mean telling people what to do, but in the sense of allotting them roles and providing associated job descriptions. Management's function is to establish an appropriately related set of roles and rules – an appropriate organisation – and not to seek to prescribe what people should, in every foreseeable set of circumstances, seek to do. Management will change the organisation from time to time as circumstances change and to take account of personalities within a business, but will not routinely intervene to instruct a particular job holder to take this or that particular action at a particular time.

Co-ordination through direction is not, therefore, what it might at first seem. It does not mean that those who undertake the activities to be co-ordinated are being continuously told how to carry them out. It implies, rather, the setting up, for a chosen purpose, of an organisation in which people with appropriate skills, aided by appropriate fixed equipment, are given appropriate roles. The roles established, and the relationships between them, are designed to be such that if all the members of the organisation further the particular aims set for them the aim of the organisation will itself be realised. But how, we may ask, can this come about?

THE FIRM AS A MICROECONOMY

The mode of co-ordination which I have referred to as direction requires, as a necessary condition for its fulfilment, the creation of a particular system or organisation within which the relevant activities are carried out. Each organisation of this kind will comprise men and equipment working within a specifically designed set of relationships and for designated purposes, the 'operating software', as it were, being the roles and rules established. A firm, we may say, is a *microeconomy* both similar to and different from the *macroeconomy* within which it functions.

It is interesting to compare the microeconomy of the firm with the macroeconomy of which it is part. The former is the product of design, in a sense that the latter is not. Governments do not manage economies in the way that directors manage companies; they are responsible chiefly for the legal framework and the provision of central services, but they do not – at any rate in peace time – prescribe what pattern of goods should be produced (except in response to their own requirements) any more than they set up the organisations that will produce them. It is firms that take decisions about what will be produced, and although governments have essential economic functions to perform, it is competition and co-operation between firms that we expect to produce the co-ordination needed to ensure that resources are used efficiently and in accordance with consumer demand.

Between the two kinds of economy there are, however, similarities, which derive fundamentally from the fact that the knowledge and the capability of any individual are limited, as must therefore be the tasks they can undertake. The consolidation of activities within an enterprise does not change this circumstance. The division of labour continues to be practised, and the need for integration remains. The organisation of a firm will have been devised to put in place the jobs and equipment necessary for the co-ordination of a set of systematically complementary activities, but co-ordination will not result from that fact alone. A firm's external transactions are guided by market prices reflecting demand and scarcity, and it is necessary that decisions taken within the microeconomy are guided similarly. Within the contrived system of relationships which constitute a firm there may have to be a contrived system of prices.

PRICING WITHIN A FIRM

In our so-called 'theory of the firm', as featured in elementary textbooks, only market prices come into consideration, those of the 'inputs' purchased and the 'outputs' sold. The efficient deployment of inputs to produce outputs is seen, in this context, as a problem in the logic of choice, to be solved by one mind, that of the entrepreneur. In firms as they exist in reality, of course, the work is done by many people, perhaps a handful, perhaps many thousands, each with a specified role, and in order that they act in conformity with the firm's aim of profit maximisation ways have to be found of causing their decisions to take account of the cost of inputs or the prices of outputs, even although they do not themselves buy or sell on the market. Most subdivisions within a business will enter into transactions with other subdivisions, whether profit centres or cost centres, and, as these transactions will generally have an effect the costs and revenues of the firm as a whole, a way has to be found of guiding them accordingly. Ronald Coase has remarked that 'the distinguishing mark of the firm is the supersession of the price mechanism' (Coase 1937: 20). This is true in the sense that external market prices affect directly only the external transactions of the firm, but is false if interpreted to mean that decisions within a firm are not guided by prices of a kind, by prices, that is, which the management of the business has contrived to introduce, by means of the whole apparatus of profit centres, transfer pricing, cost accounting and so on. As Voltaire said of God, if prices did not exist, we should have to invent them, and in the design of the internal arrangements of a firm, this is what we in fact do.

Paradoxically, the creation of profit centres within a business may appear at once necessary for and incompatible with the maximisation of profits for the business as a whole. This situation arises where one profit centre sells to another a good or service, the unit cost of which falls with the volume produced. The example is sometimes taken from the oil industry, where, within an integrated operation, the division selling crude, if it is free to choose its own trading terms, will charge the refining division more than is consistent with maximising profits for the combined business. The same issue arises in publishing, where, say, an Oxford University Press (OUP) publishing division in Oxford sells books to the OUP publishing division in New York for onward sale in the United States. In both cases, if the parties each seek to maximise their own profits, the outcome is that the volume of oil or books sold is less than that for which the profits of the business as a whole would be maximised; the marginal cost of increased output, for the business as a whole, remains below the marginal revenue that could be expected from its sale. In these circumstances, group management may intervene to secure a more satisfactory arrangement, but will inevitably find it hard to reconcile group profit maximisation with divisional accountability.

For the chief executive struggling with these problems, two consolations offer themselves. First, he or she should have in mind that the dilemmas posed are not characteristic only of internal price systems, but are also present where, in the macroeconomy, co-ordination takes place through real price movements. If activities have shared overheads and exhibit increasing returns they do so irrespective of whether they are consolidated within firms. One simply has to accept that there can be circumstances in which no system of price signals, whether those developing spontaneously in the macroeconomy or those specially contrived for a microeconomy, can ensure that firms within the one or profit centres within the other will, by seeking to maximise their own profits, automatically maximise the general welfare or group profits. The result obtained, in other words, will be inferior to those which could be obtained if the combined resources were deployed centrally to maximum advantage.

This comparison, however, provides no clear presumption, in the case of either the macro- or the microeconomy, that centralised deployment should be attempted. Against the disadvantages of the decentralised approach have to be set the difficulties, which complexity soon make insurmountable, inherent in the timely and continuous collection of, processing of, and acting upon information that centralised deployment would require. Decentralisation has advantages, of course, in terms of motivating and developing those taking the decisions, but recourse to it is essential, most fundamentally, because complex tasks requiring much detailed and 'local' information have to being broken down into parts, each of which becomes the responsibility of particular persons or group. It is interesting for us to know where decentralisation will give an outcome which is second best relative to the available practical alternatives, but less interesting to know when it is second best only in the sense that a preferable outcome would prevail were we, by being able to call upon the services of an omniscient, omnipotent and beneficent Supreme Being, to live in a different world.

COMMUNICATIONS, SCALE AND STRUCTURE

In discussing earlier the relations between firms, we reviewed considerations which would influence management in its choice of the range of activities to undertake. By undertaking closely complementary activities in-house, where there can be rapid communication between those undertaking them, a firm may sometimes be able to secure co-ordination that is quicker and more effective than that which could be arranged through complex co-operative arrangement with outside suppliers, but, being unable to enjoy the economies of scale and specialisation available to these suppliers, have to accept a cost penalty for doing so. The issue faces a publishing business, for example, in deciding whether to undertake its own warehousing or its own marketing in a particular country.

The same issue arises, however, in designing a firm's internal organisation. At one time, for example, OUP had, in the United Kingdom, a central services division, separate from the editorial divisions, which was responsible for the design of books, for arranging their printing, and for their marketing, warehousing, distribution and sale. This arrangement appeared to offer advantages. It permitted a finer division of labour within each service activity. By combining the variable demands from different publishing departments, the load on the design department could be made more steady; by combining printing requirements, it was hoped, greater bargaining power could be obtained in dealing with printers; and there seemed everything to be said, on the face of it, for having a single sales and marketing force.

In fact the arrangement worked badly. The editing and design of, say, an English Language Teaching textbook with copious illustration are very closely complementary activities which have to be undertaken by people with different skills but in close touch. The marketing of such a book, moreover, requires those who do it to know a good deal about both its content and the needs which it would meet. When the central services division was in place, disputes frequently arose between the editors, designers and marketing people associated with particular titles, each expressing dissatisfaction with the work of the others. This would be in no way surprising, the reader will conclude, particularly if these people did not see themselves as members of a team. But it was not so much the disputes that gave most concern, but the difficulty in settling them. Had those undertaking the complementary activities been members of a team, there would certainly have been fewer disputes, and, importantly, such as did arise could be settled by rapid arbitration by the head of the team.

With the organisation OUP had in the UK at that time the issue became a matter for the heads of the editorial and services divisions, who, if they could not themselves resolve it by agreement, had to refer it to the head of the business for decision.

Where hundreds of people are involved, as was the case with OUP's UK publishing divisions, an organisation of the kind described soon ceases properly to work. In any organisation there must be co-operation between its members and the means of speedy and informed arbitration when this co-operation fails or falters. The centralisation characteristic of the arrangements in OUP, as I have described them, both prevented the development of the team spirit which, in small groups, fosters co-operation, and provided arbitration that was slow, remote, relatively uninformed and, in both the kind and the quantity required, beyond the capacity of those whose time and attention needed to be devoted to the strategy of the business as a whole. As the reader will surmise, the organisation of OUP was altered to provide greater decentralisation, large editorial departments being made responsible for their own design, marketing, etc. Of course, it is always a matter of balance; there was no question, for example, of giving these departments responsibility for their own warehousing, in which scale economies are particularly great.

I have chosen to illustrate my argument by an example, but it applies quite generally within industry. Ease of communication, the fostering of a team spirit, and the availability of informed and rapid arbitration are advantages just as much as are the economies of scale and specialisation, and there are trade-offs between them. Thus we have in the microeconomy effectively the same issue as concerned us earlier in discussing the macroeconomy. It appears in the former in terms of choosing a balance between centralisation and decentralisation; in the latter, in terms of where and when to consolidate activities within firms. Perhaps the beginning of wisdom, in the understanding of either system, is to appreciate human limitation.

A SUMMARY OF THE ARGUMENT SO FAR

Let us now pause to consider where the argument has taken us. The division of labour, upon which the creation of wealth depends, creates the need for co-ordination, which is achieved, in a regime of competitive free enterprise, through market transactions involving independent decision-making, through co-operation and by direction within firms. The first of these three mechanisms, in terms of which explanation of the working of the economy is normally provided, depends for its success on a certain stability in the relevant environment, on the ability of a firm contemplating investment to take for granted that the volume of competitive investment will not be excessive and that necessary complementary investments will be in place.

Where these conditions are not met, firms will exchange undertakings in order to remedy the deficiency. Co-operation is usually required, in particular, through long-term contracts or similar forms of association, where the activities to be co-ordinated are closely complementary, as when a firm needs an input of a specialised, non-standard kind.

Such co-operation fails to work well when the co-ordination of *systematically and closely complementary* activities is required. It then becomes impracticable to devise – and, as need be, revise – the complex set of agreements that simple co-ordination would require. An organised form of co-operation, which I have called *direction*, is then needed to design and execute a particular pattern of investment, or to ensure that a particular set of activities is properly matched in kind, quantity and timing.

Having identified what seemed to be the essential rationale of a firm, we then turned to consider more closely how intra-firm co-ordination was achieved. We recognised the firm as a contrived system, as a microeconomy similar in many ways to the macroeconomy within which it operates. Such a microeconomy has to be large enough to ensure the scope of the co-ordination required, but the number of activities it undertakes will be limited by the fact that these will generally exhibit economies of scale and require different appropriate capabilities for their successful execution. Nevertheless, a firm may be willing to sacrifice some economies of scale and specialisation, which it could have obtained by relying on outside suppliers, in order to be able itself, through direction, to co-ordinate complementary activities better, and it may choose again to make the same sacrifice, by creating a decentralised internal organisation able to facilitate co-ordination through closer communications and rapid arbitration.

The essential rationale of the firm is indeed to permit direction, but the direction is normally limited to ensuring that a set of related investments and appointments is put in place and kept in adjustment, thus to provide a context within which co-ordination is carried on by internal transactions and co-operation, guided by prices, in a way that mimics the processes at work in the larger economy of which the firm is part. In the macroeconomy, governments do not generally set the terms on which firms trade or co-operate; the presumption is that competition will do so appropriately, intervention being called for only where monopoly is present. Within the microeconomy, however, no such presumption can be made and central management will typically either set or supervise the internal pricing arrangements to which subdivisions are subject.

Within a firm, it is often remarked, hierarchy prevails. It does, but one should not imagine that, for this reason, the firm works by means of commands which originate from the top and are filled in with appropriate detail at each operational level. It is doubtful that even armies and navies function in this manner, far less so-called 'command economies'. Management does not consist just in giving orders from the bridge, though this is part of it, but, rather, in creating, monitoring and, when need be, modifying a system of working relationships designed to ensure that each person employed by the organisation, by doing the specified job allotted to him, will further an overarching purpose. A chief executive can scarcely do more harm than by spending all his time telling people what to do.

THE COSTS OF CONSOLIDATION

I have sought to identify the essential *raison d'être* of the firm, but have said nothing about the determinants of its size. Nor have I mentioned the functions, other than this essential one, that a firm can perform. These are the matters to which I wish now to turn.

If I am correct, direction can achieve co-ordination in circumstances in which both market transactions and unorganised co-operation cannot. It might then seem, on the face of it, that direction should be the preferred mode of securing co-ordination, given that it can work both where the other methods cannot and, presumably, where they can. But such a conclusion would, of course, be false, and for two reasons. The first, and most important, relates to the economies of scale and specialisation; the second, to the costs of designing and supervising a microeconomy.

I have already had a good deal to say about the cost of consolidation in terms of economies forgone. There is no presumption that the activities which are to be co-ordinated by direction within a firm will relate to the same or similar capabilities, or that the scale on which they would be carried out would be large enough to exploit potential economies. It might be maintained that the firm could carry out any activity on the required scale and offer the balance not required on the market; this argument was used to urge the retention by OUP of a printing business and a paper mill. But if it is possible to sell the unrequired balance of printing or paper on the market, then it is probably possible to buy it on the market. And the advantage of the latter course is that of not being obliged to possess and maintain disparate capabilities.

Thus in circumstances in which it may at first seem that co-ordination can most perfectly be achieved by direction, the cost of the consolidation required to do so may be prohibitive. It might be technically better, for example, to produce a good from parts each specially developed in-house, but economically better to produce it from more standard parts obtainable from others.[8]

The second disadvantage of consolidation lies in the cost of arranging and supervising it. Ronald Coase attracted our attention to the need to compare the costs of making transactions on the market and the costs of organising them within a firm. I appear to differ from him in believing that a certain kind of co-ordination, that of systematically complementary activities, can be achieved only by direction, irrespective of cost. But where market transactions, co-operation and direction are real alternatives, costs then obviously do matter. The order that is achieved through market forces, as a result of the interaction of many independent decisions, comes with no general design cost, whereas a planned configuration, a systematically related set of investments in manpower and equipment, clearly does. And that is not the only cost of direction. Within the designed microeconomy, as we have seen, there will exist market-type transactions, on the basis of terms that have to be prescribed, and co-operation, for which supervision will have to be provided. All these arrangements cost something to put in place, and, as they are difficult to make successfully, the people able so to make them are relatively scarce and therefore expensive. To be set against this, of course, are the costs associated with market transactions, but, in terms of the attention of senior management, internal transactions and co-operation may well exert the greater claim. Bureaucracy, everyone knows, is endemic in large organisations, but it is less well appreciated that once co-ordination is sought by direction rather than markets the costs of supervision are unavoidable. Given also that the span of effective control within an organisation is limited, complex hierarchical layers are equally inevitable, unless the business is broken up into small, quasi-independent profit centres, at the possible cost of potential economies of scale.

These circumstances go some way to explain why, in the economic field, victory does not always go the big battalions. And it is not hard to find examples of where large firms, relying on co-ordination by direction, have lost ground to smaller ones less burdened by the cost of doing so and more able to take advantage of specialisation by others. Commercial freedom provides competition not only between firms, but also between different forms of economic organisation; the appropriateness of each of these forms will depend on the circumstances in which they have to operate, and which will not for long remain the same.

OTHER FUNCTIONS OF THE FIRM

I have been concerned with the firm in its role of arranging for the co-ordination, through direction, of systematically complementary activities. But it is worth mentioning, for the sake of perspective, that although this seems to me to be the prime function of firms it is not their only one. Indeed, firms may exist which do not perform this function; management consultants or window cleaners could, for example, associate together under some central authority in order to arrange for the distribution of their aggregate earnings in a particular manner. And the more typical limited liability company, the prime purpose of which is co-ordination through direction, and which has workers, managers and shareholders, also performs a distributive function of this kind, particularly by taking account of differential willingness or ability to assume risk.

Firms also provide a system of incentives, of which the distribution of their gross revenues is a key part. This article has been concerned with the co-ordination of activities, and not with the motivation of those who have to carry them out. The two issues, though distinct, are obviously related. I have been considering how, if people pursue limited and specific aims – in plain terms, do particular jobs – there may result a pattern of resource allocation that is efficient overall. But the question arises as to how people can be induced to pursue these particular aims, when doing so does not in itself answer to their own private interests.

In praising the work of the 'invisible hand', attention is often focused on how this latter alignment is achieved; there is mention of how private greed can be harnessed in the service of the public interest, and of course Adam Smith himself famously observed that 'it is not from the benevolence of the butcher, the brewer or the baker, that we expect their dinner, but from their regard to their own interest'. This is true, but it is also true that, even were people guided only by altruism, arrangements of the kind we have been discussing would still be required, whether at the level of the macro- or the microeconomy. Each individual person would still have to be assigned, somehow or other, tasks specific and limited enough to be within his or her competence, and ways would have to be found to achieve subsequent co-ordination. If a person were moved only to serve the public interest, it would usually still be best for that person to find a job where his or her talents were in demand and do it well.[9]

In addition to their co-ordinating, distributing and motivating functions, firms may also replace the market in its selective function. Independent enterprises have mandates to deploy resources which will wax or wane according to their earnings and their credit with wealth-owners generally. In this sense, automatic selection prevails; the units within a firm, on the other hand, have mandates that are determined by the central authority, which is not obliged to determine them on the basis of achieved earnings.

I have not considered, in this article, what determines the amount of resources that firms, or economic agents generally, can command. In a regime of private property this is determined by their wealth and their credit. Those responsible for direction within a conventional firm exercise authority derived from, and on behalf of, owners of wealth. Of course, the directors may be given great discretion, though they are rarely inattentive to their share price. Of course, the directors are also subject to important constraints, legal, moral and practical, to the extent that they will often claim that they have a triple responsibility, to consumers, workers and shareholders. Nevertheless, the authority to deploy resources depends, under capitalism, on their ownership. And, despite the inequality of wealth in capitalist economies, this ownership is sufficiently dispersed to produce a plurality of free and independent decision-making.

NOTES

1 Brian Loasby and Nicolai Foss provided helpful comments on an earlier draft of this paper. I am very grateful to them for doing so and for encouraging me to return to economics after a break of over twenty years.
2 This is discussed in my article 'Adam Smith on competition and increasing returns', published in *Essays on Adam Smith*, edited by Andrew Skinner and Thomas Wilson and published by OUP in 1975.
3 Keynes, in a letter written in 1934 to Hicks, who incidentally was writing *Value and Capital* at the time, expressed the opinion that 'Walras's theory and all others along those lines are little better than nonsense' (Skidelsky 1992: 615). Schumpeter, on the other hand, maintained that:

> as far as pure theory is concerned, Walras is in my opinion the greatest of all economists. His system of economic equilibrium ... is the only work by an economist that will stand comparison with the achievements of theoretical physics. Compared with it, most of the theoretical writings of that period – and beyond – however valuable in themselves and however original subjectively, look like boats beside a liner, like inadequate attempts to catch some particular aspect of Walrasian truth.
>
> (Schumpeter 1954: 827)

What are we to make of a subject on which two such very eminent practitioners take such divergent views?

4 Game theory has provided us with insight into the logic of choice given interdependence, but is not concerned with the question that has engaged me. That prior question is about how, in the real world, circumstances may exist, or may fail to exist, or may be deliberately contrived that sufficiently reduce our area of ignorance to permit tolerably informed decisions. Put otherwise, my concern has been with the availability of information to the participants in a market seen as a function of that market's structure.
5 The decision whether to buy in a good or service is sometimes represented as likely to turn on transactions costs, on the costs of making and monitoring a contract with another firm as compared with managing the activity in-house. But this is usually a minor consideration; most businesses use a lot of paper, but refrain from acquiring paper mills, far less a forest. The reasons are easy to see; they lack experience of this manufacture and are unlikely to use sufficient paper to employ a mill of optimum size. Transaction costs are real enough, and are incurred both between firms and within them, but they are not normally critical for the decision in question.
6 My experience in publishing introduced me to a particularly luxuriant variety of such arrangements. Publishing firms exist, to a remarkable degree, by taking in each other's washing. OUP was exceptional in the number of distinct activities it undertook; when I joined it, some 3,000 people were employed, some in printing and paper-making. At the other end of the spectrum, the Marvell Press, with which Philip Larkin published his first poems, was staffed by George and Jean Hartley, and by them alone. Of course the two businesses were doing different things, whether or not they find they are included in the same standard industrial classification. Book publishing comprises many different activities – commissioning, editing, designing, warehousing, marketing and so

on. And even these categories need breaking down; firms that market in the United States will commonly not market in India, and marketing school books is an activity significantly different from marketing novels. Typically, therefore, publishing businesses find themselves linked with each other in both competitive and co-operative relationships.

7   It is worth observing that direction may become necessary in response not only to the complexity of co-ordination, but also to the speed with which it has to be carried through. It is noteworthy that planning is often introduced in wartime, when a radical and rapid reconfiguration of activity is required. So long as change can proceed fairly gradually, or at any rate does not need to take place on many different fronts at the same time, normal market mechanisms, we have seen, may be able to effect the adjustment required. But if change has to be radical, rapid and widespread, then individual businesses, being unable to assume that the presence and prices of relevant complementary and competitive activities will remain the same, may lack the informational basis on which to make the needed investment decisions. In these circumstances, governments may assume special powers of direction; 'manpower budgets' may replace or supplement financial ones, and investments, prices, profits and the movement of labour may all be brought under control. These measures promote the required co-ordination, but at a price. Market disciplines are undermined, so that the pressures to control costs are diminished and the fate of individual businesses is no longer automatically linked to their performance.

8   The microcomputer industry developed very much in the latter way, as is described by Professor R. N. Langlois in his interesting article 'External economies and economic progress; the case of the microcomputer industry', *Business History Review* 66: 1–50.

9   It is worth observing, at the risk of modest digression, that the principles of economic organisation, some of which this article has sought to address, are unlikely to be correctly elucidated on the assumption that people are moved only by selfishness. Certainly Smith himself, so often selectively quoted, did not think so. It is in his *Theory of Moral Sentiments* that Smith argues that, were we not moved by a sense of justice, 'a man would enter an assembly of men as he would enter a den of lions' (Smith 1976: 86). He did not consider beneficence, unlike justice, essential to the subsistence of society, but observed that society would however be 'not in the most comfortable state' (Smith 1976: 86) without it. A too close alignment of a manager's remuneration with the profits of the department with which he is responsible may often work against the interests of the business as a whole. It may sharpen distracting argument about the allocation of overheads, always to some extent arbitrary, upon which the determination of departmental profits depends. It may also cause departmental management to resist changes which, although in the interests of the business as a whole, happen to reduce the earnings attributed to a part of it. A chief executive is likely to value a manager whose keenness to make profits for his department is balanced by loyalty to the business of which it is part.

REFERENCES

Coase, R. (1937) 'The nature of the firm', *Economica*, N.S. 4: 386–405; reprinted in O.E. Williamson and S.G. Winter, (eds) (1991) *The Nature of the Firm*, New York: Oxford University Press.

Marshall, A. (1890) *Principles of Economics*, London: Macmillan.

Richardson, G. B. (1960) *Information and Investment: A Study in the Working of the Competitive Economy*, Oxford: Oxford University Press; 2nd edn 1990.

—— (1972) 'The organisation of industry', *Economic Journal* 82: 883–96.

Schumpeter, J.A. (1954) *History of Economic Analysis*, New York: Oxford University Press.

Skidelsky, R. (1992) *John Maynard Keynes: The Economist as Saviour*, London: MacMillan.

Smith, A. (1976) *Theory of Moral Sentiments*, Oxford: Clarendon Press.

4

CO-OPERATION AND COMPETITION PARADOXES IN THE THEORY OF THE ORGANISATION OF INDUSTRY

Jacques-Laurent Ravix[1]

INTRODUCTION

'The organisation of industry' (Richardson 1972) describes an industrial system that consists of direction within firms, inter-firm co-operations and market transactions. Such an organisation may be considered as a framework for the analysis of what has been called the 'institutional structure of production' (Coase 1992), i.e. the division of productive co-ordination among different kinds of institutional arrangements. The theory of industrial co-ordination proposed by Richardson is not simply another criticism of the theory of industrial organisation to be inserted in a transactional framework; this criticism proposes a new explanation of the organisation of industry, an explanation endowed with a greater empirical content. Indeed, the last footnote in Richardson's article tells us that the theory provided in this paper 'might be taken as giving content' (Richardson 1972: 896, fn 1) to the Coasian theory of the boundaries of the firm, this being revealed by introducing an explicit distinction between inter-firm co-operation and market transactions as modes of co-ordination.

The purpose of our paper is to inquire about what is meant by 'giving content'. This question is mainly a methodological problem that concerns the relationships between theoretical and empirical aspects regarding the functioning of industrial organisation. In fact, in such evolutive areas as the theory of the firm and that of industry, methodology matters because of its real effects on analytical developments. Such effects are related to the analysis of information, which is the core question of modern theories of the firm and industrial organisation. In particular, methodological choices made by economists have caused them to consider the economic problem as one of allocative efficiency, i.e. almost entirely in relation to price signals. This has had the effect of developing a very narrow view of 'information', conceived as the construction of incentives and information patterns on contractual bases. The focus on contract and transactions has been made at the cost of almost completely neglecting production problems. When Coase complained, in his NBER (National Bureau for Economic Research) address (Coase 1972), that Industrial Organisation had nothing to tell us about the organisation of industry, because it is only applied price theory, a new way of considering the co-ordination problem was opened. The switch to activities and to the capabilities which support them, proposed in the same year by Richardson in his article, can be considered as a methodological development in this new context, which also has real effects on the topics which are discussed by economists, undermining in the process the central notion of economic rationality, and with it the standard concept of information. This is precisely how Richardson gives a deeper empirical content to Coase's theory, as we shall discuss it in our first section.

However, this way of giving content to the theory of the boundaries of the firm is not simply a more realistic method of coping with the 'nature' of both the firm and industry. In fact, the search for realism in economics is often based on weak methodological grounds. This is why the precision and coherence obtained with abstract theories founded on the 'primacy of exchange' and allocative efficiency have long superseded the theory of production and that of the firm (McNulty 1984). Our contention is that the connection between Coase and Richardson is interesting because it reveals the 'progressive' aspect of the theory of industrial co-ordination. This means that the study of the organisation of industry reaches at the same time a better empirical foundation and a new coherence.[2] To explain this, we shall study the methodological structures of Coase's theory (see 'The nature of the firm and the paradox of co-operation', pp. 70–4) and Richardson's theory (see 'The nature of industry and the paradox of competition', pp. 75–8), and try to show that they share common features based on refutational requirements (Popper 1959, 1963, 1972). The notions of co-operation and competition 'paradoxes' will play a central role in this argument as 'potential falsifiers' of these theories.

INFORMATION, KNOWLEDGE AND INDUSTRIAL CO-ORDINATION

An interesting aspect of the papers published in the same year (1972) by Coase and Richardson is that they explain and complement the real content of the research programme opened up thirty-five years earlier by Coase (1937), and which can be appropriately defined as a study of industrial co-ordination. Coase's 1972 paper was a contribution to a roundtable organised by the NBER on the subject of policy issues and research opportunities in industrial organisation. The topic seemed very urgent at that time because, in the opinion of V. R. Fuchs, the editor of the book published after this roundtable, the 'once flourishing field' of Industrial Organisation was dramatically losing its audience. Coase's NBER address, although less celebrated than the article of 1937, deserves attention especially because of its critical treatment of industrial economics.

The author first distinguishes between industrial organisation as a field and industrial organisation as an object of analysis. Indeed, as he writes it: 'Very little work is done on the subject of industrial organisation at the present time, as I see the subject, since what is commonly dealt with under this heading tells us almost nothing about the organisation of industry' (Coase 1972: 59). What the author criticises is a theory of industrial organisation without any element that could explain the co-ordination of industrial activities. However, as he adds:

> We all know what is meant by the organisation of industry. It describes the way in which the activities undertaken within the economic system are divided up between firms. As we know, some firms embrace many different activities; while for others the range is narrowly circumscribed. Some firms are large; others, small. Some firms are vertically integrated; others are not. This is the organisation of industry or – as it used to be called – the structure of industry.
>
> (Coase 1972: 60)

At that time, the prevailing state of the art in the field of industrial economics can be explained by the fact that this field was mainly considered as applied microeconomics. As Stigler writes, Industrial Organisation took on the 'chores' of 'empirical measurements of cost curves, concentration and so forth', and 'public policies questions, particularly antitrust and regulation' (quoted by Coase 1972: 61). Therefore industrial economics lies between two difficulties: the absence of a theory of its own, and the overdetermination of normative studies of monopoly and antitrust policy. But this was not always the case, as Coase argues, signalling a number of studies dealing in detail with the organisation of particular industries, or more general books on the subject of industrial organisation, among which Alfred Marshall's *Industry and Trade* and Austin Robinson's *The Structure of Competitive Industry* are the most famous.

But, as Coase puts it, 'if we are to tackle the problems of industrial organisation seriously, a theory is needed' (1972: 63), and that is why he wrote 'The nature of the firm'. Obviously, the theory needed is something other than the price theory to be applied in the field of industrial organisation in

Stigler's sense. Besides the allocation of resources co-ordinated by the pricing system, there is the allocation of resources as a result of an administrative decision within the firm. The reason for this is that resorting to the market is costly, and the costs that have to be incurred can be avoided by the use of an administrative structure.

> But, of course, the author adds, the firm has to carry out its task at a lower cost than the cost of carrying out the market transactions it supersedes, because it is always possible to revert to the market if the firm fails to do so.
>
> (Coase 1972: 64)

All this line of argument is well known. It only replicates Coase's earlier argument (1937). The interesting thing is that by treating these questions in an explicit industrial framework and as a means of criticising the standard analysis of industrial organisation, the author reaches a new argument which was not so clearly stated in the previous paper:

> the cost of organising an activity within any given firm *depends on what other activities it is engaged in*. A given set of activities will facilitate the carrying out of some activities, but hinder the performance of others. It is these relationships, the author adds, which determine the actual organisation of industry.
>
> (Coase 1972: 64; our emphasis)

By asserting the importance of industrial activities carried on by firms, and suggesting that relationships between firms have something to do with these activities being similar or not, Coase is on the way of a positive theory of the organisation of industry. He is not yet in a position to construct this theory, but he can already infer from the absence of interest for 'what firms actually do' (1972: 65) the reasons for the incapacity of standard Industrial Organisation to treat the organisation of industry, that is, to explain 'why General Motors [is] not a dominant factor in the coal industry, or why A & P [does] not manufacture airplanes' (*ibid.*: 67).

In a recent comment, Coase has pointed out the methodological background of his theory (Coase 1993a: 52–4), claiming again, as he did in 1937, that his concept of the firm is intended to be both 'realistic and manageable', i.e. both devoid of unrealistic assumptions concerning production and nevertheless capable of being analysed by the ordinary technique of equilibrium analysis. This procedure is of course opposed to Robbins's dismissal of the 'incredible banalities of much of the so-called theory of production' which 'necessarily precludes precision', in favour of the 'modern treatment of organisation of production' where it is shown 'how factors of production are distributed between the production of different goods by the mechanism of prices and costs' (Robbins 1932; quoted by Coase 1993a: 53). Nowadays, the 'modern treatment' of industrial organisation and production has become a matter of incentives and information. But to examine 'what firms actually do' is still beneath the notice of professional economists, and to affirm that the cost of organising an activity within a firm depends upon the other activities it is engaged in implies going beyond incentives and information.

Even if Coase himself did not suggest how to proceed, albeit along these lines, his attempt to explain 'the institutional structure of production in the system as a whole' (Coase 1993b: 73) cannot be reduced to principal-agent theories and game-theoretic treatments of the firm as proposed by new industrial economics. Nor can it be subsumed by Williamson's transaction cost theory in terms of comparative efficiency analysis of different forms of governance structures. Now it is precisely here that Richardson's 1972 article provides the methodological development that gives content to Coase's theory.

Indeed, the questions raised by Coase's NBER address take their full analytical meaning with the paper published by Richardson in the same year (1972). As we have already noticed, this paper must also be considered mainly as a criticism of standard Industrial Organisation. What is new is that this criticism is made by referring more directly to the productive characteristics of industrial co-ordination. The empirical observation that the dense network of inter-firm co-operation is absent from the crude firm–market dichotomy carries with it the necessity of developing the productive content of industrial organisation. Even the simplest form of inter-firm co-operation – a trading relationship between a number of parties which is stable enough to make demand expectations more reliable – is intended to 'facilitate production planning' (Richardson 1972: 884).

The treatment of production planning as oriented to an uncertain future must be linked to the developments Richardson made on this subject in his book *Information and Investment* (Richardson 1960), and especially in Chapter IV, about the co-ordination of complementary investments. The formulation of an investment programme consisting of a set of planned activities is to be analysed as a trade-off between uncertainty and flexibility based on reciprocal – and more or less fixed – commitments, depending on the length of the period and the nature of uncertainty and available information (*ibid.*: 79–83). This analysis leads to 'an untidy conclusion', as the writer recognises it, about the multiplicity of ways in which complementary investments come to be co-ordinated – this co-ordination occurring spontaneously or by means of different kinds of agreements, or else requiring deliberate planning under unified control (*ibid.*: 84).

'The organisation of industry' can then be considered as an attempt to formulate a more well-ordered description of the division of labour among these different ways of co-ordinating production. This is done by referring more directly to productive co-ordination as a notion.[3] This productive rationale differs from a pure exchange one, inter-firm co-operation being first of all opposed to pure market transactions which are 'a limiting case' in the *continuum* of institutional forms of industrial co-ordination (Richardson 1972: 886). The productive co-ordination of such an industry is then analysed from a qualitative perspective, referring to an indefinite number of activities, 'these being understood to denote not only manufacturing processes but to relate equally to research, development and marketing' (*ibid.*: 895), carried out by organisations endowed with appropriate capabilities.

To refer to activities rather than products makes an important change of methodological perspective. Assuredly, as the author writes (Richardson 1972: 887–8), to define 'products' as what firms make is to transform the statement that 'firms make products' into a mere tautology. This representation is useful for the formal theory of the firm and its pure logic of choice formulated into a given set of productive possibilities, as the author says, but it leaves out important elements: 'the roles of organisation, knowledge, experience and skills' (*ibid.*: 888). The formal theory of the firm which abstracts totally from these elements 'thereby makes it the more difficult to bring these back into the theoretical foreground in the way needed to construct a theory of industrial organisation' (*ibid.*: 888).

Two fundamentally different conceptions of economics as a science are implicitly opposed in these statements. The first one, subsumed here in the 'formal theory of the firm', is the conception of economics as a 'tautological science', in the sense of Hutchison (1938) or, according to Georgescu-Roegen, a 'theoretical science' in which one has operated 'a logical filing of all extant knowledge in some particular domain such that every known proposition be either contained in the logical foundation or deducible from it' (Georgescu-Roegen 1966: 108). The second one, represented by the 'theory of industrial organisation', is the conception of economics as the 'empirical science' Hutchison was trying to define on purely methodological lines.

The role of knowledge in this conception of economics as an empirical science has been put forward by Hayek (1937). Knowledge is not to be assimilated to the rationality of pure theory of choice; it explains the tendency towards equilibrium obtained along a discovery procedure which secures the co-ordination of plans of dispersed agents. This challenge to knowledge assumptions underlying perfect competition is also present in *Information and Investment* (Richardson 1960), where ignorance and unequal distribution of knowledge among individuals are supposed to facilitate the working of the whole system (*ibid.*: 57–8); it is such also for the process of manufacturing, which is not to be considered as a 'chemical reaction', but more properly as a process of 'trial and error', the co-ordination of complementary investments being largely subject to 'dispersed information' (*ibid.*:

83).[4] Vertical integration and co-operation then become more proper ways to cope with uncertainty than long-term contracts, for gaining control on complementary investments (*ibid.*: 83–4). In the same way, for Coase the relationship termed a firm is obtained in place of a detailed long-term contract, 'owing to the difficulty of forecasting' (Coase 1937: 337). Taking notice also that '[t]he most obvious cost of "organising" production through the price mechanism is that of discovering what the relevant prices are' (*ibid.*: 336), one may conclude that transaction costs as specified by Coase are 'knowledge costs: the costs of discovering the relevant prices, the costs of negotiating contracts, and the costs of discovering the relevant future contingencies which need to be provided for' (Loasby 1994: 251).

Knowledge, being something different from pure information, cannot be treated by the ordinary techniques used to study allocative efficiency in the formal theory of the firm. Paraphrasing Richardson, we could say that the formal theory of industrial organisation, because it neglects knowledge, makes it all the more difficult to bring this notion back into the foreground of a theory of industrial co-ordination. Then, the construction of such a theory must be founded on another form of coherence, empirical rather than formal, which can be drawn from methodological prescriptions. What is remarkable in Hayek's case is that the theoretical assumptions regarding the co-ordination of agents' dispersed knowledge and the epistemological definition of the empirical method for economics are set on the same level; they are both founded on the functioning of a discovery procedure. This implies a homology between economic knowledge of the agent proceeding by trial and error, and scientific knowledge of the economist doing the same by looking for evidence which refutes his or her propositions.[5] In his definition of economics as an empirical science, Hayek refers to Popper's 'falsificationism', albeit in a very loose way.[6] What we intend to do in the next sections is to take this methodological stance more seriously into account and to analyse on Popperian lines the *empirical approach* implemented by Coase and Richardson. The formal approach is 'tautological' in the sense that it is self-contained; the notion of knowledge cannot be reinserted into a theory which has been constructed on its dismissal without utterly modifying the theory or the notion. The empirical approach, on the contrary, tries progressively to insert new elements. This process is not, however, a cumulative, but a critical one, each new empirical element being first used as a 'potential falsifier' of the theory. We shall see that this role can be played by the notions of co-operation and competition in Coase's and Richardson's treatments of the institutional co-ordination of industry.

JACQUES-LAURENT RAVIX

THE NATURE OF THE FIRM AND THE PARADOX OF CO-OPERATION

In spite of its title, Coase's 1937 contribution is not properly a study of the very 'nature' of the firm. It can be better understood as an analysis of its 'emergence' and its boundaries in a specialised exchange economy. This contribution is not simply, as it is sometimes said (e.g. Archibald 1987), to bring to light the hierarchical co-ordination internal to the firm, nor is it to differentiate co-ordination by conscious planning within firms and spontaneous relations on the market. The fact that alternative methods of co-ordinating production exist was already well known and had been introduced by a number of authors, among whom Marshall, Clark, Knight and especially Robertson and his famous metaphor of 'islands of conscious power in this ocean of unconscious co-operation' (quoted by Coase 1937: 333).

The problem Coase is mainly preoccupied with is 'to enquire why co-ordination is the work of the price mechanism in one case and of the entrepreneur in another' (Coase 1937: 334); it is 'to explain the basis on which, in practice, this choice between alternatives is effected' (*ibid.*: 335). The research programme is therefore to provide a unified theory of the simultaneous interventions of firms and markets in the co-ordination of productive activities. As Coase strongly reaffirms it: 'Our task is to attempt to discover why a firm *emerges at all* in a specialised exchange economy' (*ibid.*: 335; our emphasis), i.e. in an economy where there already exists a division of labour among producers and where there is theoretically no need for the notion of enterprise.

The core of Coase's theory can be found in the second paragraph of his article. We will propose an analysis of the methodological structure of this paragraph and try to make clear on what ground are constructed its novelty and its critical power over the current standard theory of economic co-ordination. This is done in three successive stages, as we shall argue in a more detailed fashion: (1) the proposal of a new conjecture concerning the functioning of the market, (2) a test of the theory built on this conjecture and (3) the appearance and resolution of a particular problem concerning the coherence of this theory.

1 Coase's argument is developed in a theoretical environment – the marginalist theory of value – of which it constitutes a criticism. This criticism is based on an initial hypothesis which comes almost from scratch. A relation called the firm emerges because 'there is a cost of using the price mechanism' (Coase 1937: 336). This criticism is obviously empirical in nature, as Loasby (1976: 64) argued; the only objection Coase makes to the hypothesis of given prices in the static theory is that 'this is clearly not true in the real world' (Coase 1937: 336, fn. 18). But the hypothesis of costly transactions sounds also like a

Popperian 'bold conjecture', especially in the marginalist theoretical environment. The argument based on transaction costs which follows from this hypothesis is summarised in this way by the author:

> the operation of a market costs something and by forming an organisation and allowing some authority (an 'entrepreneur') to direct the resources, certain marketing costs are saved. The entrepreneur has to carry out his function at less cost . . . than the market transactions he supersedes, because it is always possible to revert to the open market if he fails to do this.
>
> (Coase 1937: 338)

Therefore, Coase's hypothesis allows definition of the simplest among possible institutional divisions of productive co-ordination: a bipolar and reversible one.

2 The Coasian hypothesis, however, gives a superior content to his theory of the firm as compared to others in the special context of co-ordination. This hypothesis gives, as the author writes:

> a scientific meaning to what is meant by saying that a firm gets larger or smaller. A firm becomes larger as additional transactions (which could be exchange transactions co-ordinated through the price mechanism) are organised by the entrepreneur and becomes smaller as he abandons the organisation of such transactions.
>
> (Coase 1937: 339)

This advantage constitutes, in Coase's own words, a real progress of his theory as compared with previous theories of the firm in the sense that Knight himself, in his celebrated Preface to the 1933 reissue of *Risk Uncertainty and Profit*, 'would appear to consider that it is impossible to treat scientifically the determinants of the size of the firm' (*ibid.*: 339).

By treating the problem of the size of the firm and explaining its growth, Coase gives an answer to an old dilemma: the problem of the optimal size of the firm in a world of perfect competition. In fact, the critical role of internal costs of co-ordination in limiting the size of the firm had already been studied a few years before by Kaldor (1934) and Robinson (1934).[7] This literature identifies a particular form of indivisibility represented by a specific competence of the entrepreneur in co-ordinating the activities of the firm, which can play the role of an opposing force, making for decreased efficiency with growth in size, thus offsetting the expansion of the firm. There is, however, a marked difference between Kaldor, on the one hand, and Robinson and

Williamson on the other. For the first, the co-ordinating function of the entrepreneur is essentially a dynamic function which plays its part only in adjustment processes, i.e. in disequilibrium, and disappears under static assumptions, which makes the assumptions of long-period static equilibrium and perfect competition incompatible. For the others, even in a deterministic situation of perfect foresight (Robinson 1934) or in stochastic quasi-static conditions of bounded rationality (Williamson, 1967) there still exist obstacles to be surmounted and new circumstances to adapt to by co-ordinated efforts, thus limiting the size of the firm, contrary to what they call the Nirvana-like long-period equilibrium described by Kaldor.

The position held by Coase (1937) in this discussion is usually described as following the Robinson–Williamson line of argument; but this paper makes an important qualitative jump, such as to represent the point of inflexion from the 'technological' to the 'neo-institutionalist' concept of the firm. Indeed, on the one hand, Coase uses *internal* costs of co-ordination in the same way as Robinson (to which he assimilates Kaldor) uses it. But, on the other hand, he gives birth to transaction-cost economics by supplying the hypothesis of costly *external* co-ordination. It is the conjunction of these two empirical criticisms that allows him to propose an analysis of the nature of the firm, i.e. of its role in industrial co-ordination. This analysis should be, as he puts it, at the same time 'realistic' and 'tractable' by the ordinary technique of equilibrium analysis (Coase 1937: 331). The problem of the size and growth of the firm then becomes something new. After being a paradigmatic *dilemma* (Shackle 1967) in the theory of the competitive structure of industry, it becomes the paradigmatic *test* of the scientific meaning of this theory.[8]

The question asked by Knight in 1933 is why could not a firm, producing with increasing returns to scale, experience a continuous and unlimited expansion because of the possibility of monopoly gains. In the case of costly market transactions, the advantages of internal co-ordination lead Coase to ask an equivalent question: 'why, if by organising one can eliminate certain costs and in fact reduce the cost of production, are there any market transactions at all?' (Coase 1937: 340). Apart from the monopoly considerations raised by Knight, should costly market transactions not lead all production to be carried out by *One Big Firm*? The answer given by Coase to this problem consists mainly in adopting the idea of decreasing returns to management proposed by Kaldor and Robinson. The association of internal costs of using direction and external costs of using markets allows him, by applying a simple rule of substitution, to affirm that:

> Naturally, a point must be reached where the costs of organising an extra transaction within the firm are equal to the costs involved in carrying out the transaction in the open market, or, to the costs of organising by another entrepreneur.
>
> (Coase 1937: 340)

We reach here an undeniable analytical progress. To be sure, Coase exploits Robinson's argument; but the principle of internal co-ordination is not called upon to explain that the cost curve turns upward, thus limiting the size of the firm in perfect competition.[9] By passing the test of the size of the firm that the author imposes on his theory, Coase's conjecture offers a theory of the firm, the 'truth-content' of which is superior not only to the post-Marshallian and Knightian theories of the firm but also to the price theory they dwell upon.[10]

3   This result is obtained in the particular conditions of a bipolar institutional structure which allows an argument in terms of substitution at the margin to be developed easily. Coase's formulation of the test of the boundaries of the firm, however, involves an ambiguity. Let us consider again the terms of this formulation, as repeated twice by the author:

> a firm will tend to expand until the costs of organising an extra transaction within the firm become equal to the costs of carrying out the same transaction by means of an exchange on the open market *or the costs of organising in another firm*.
>
> (Coase 1937: 341; our emphasis)

The author must therefore treat the case where the firm will stop its expansion at a point where the extra transaction will have a cost inferior to the one of the 'open market' but equal to the cost of organising it in another firm. This implies that there exist transactions between producers organised at costs below the 'actual marketing costs' (Coase 1937: 341). 'How is the paradox to be resolved?', the author asks (*ibid.*: 341).

This paradox is indeed very troublesome in the bipolar institutional structure of the theory. It involves a type of transaction which is organised neither by the direction within a single firm, nor by exchange in the 'open market', but results from a particular relation between two firms. The only relation left is the one Richardson (1972) designates under the general term of 'co-operation'. The *paradox of co-operation*, as we may call it then, jeopardises Coase's theory founded on the duality of the division of productive co-ordination between the firm and the market, the only one to allow a smooth functioning of the marginal substitution principle.

To protect his theory, the author must therefore find an answer to this paradox in terms of substitution, i.e. by the technique of analysis he made use of up to this point of his argument. He then extends the principles of decreasing returns to management to these inter-firm transactions, by asserting, first, that they take place between firms that share different stages of a production process, and, second, that the additional costs of organising an extra stage for one firm will be greater than the other firm's cost of performing the same activity. Thus, it pays to 'divide production in such a way that the cost of organising an extra transaction in each firm is the same' (Coase 1937: 342), a decision, we may add, which is difficult to take *ex ante* without any minimum co-operation between the parties. Coase can then affirm that his definition of a firm can be used to give more precise meaning to the terms 'combination' and 'integration', and conclude his argument by asserting that 'The whole of the "structure of competitive industry" becomes tractable by the ordinary technique of economic analysis' (*ibid.*: 344).

The ad hoc solution given by Coase to the paradox of co-operation has the advantage of maintaining his marginalist analytical background untouched. It is nevertheless unsatisfying on two main points (Ravix 1990). First, the definition of these new forms of transactions in addition to pure market transactions and internal direction remains necessarily ambiguous: these transactions are neither of the one type nor of the other, but they are artificially reduced to one or to the other, depending on how the process is divided up. Second, the paradox has been solved by resorting to a notion of the production process organised in a series of stages bound together whose logic of organisation has little to do with an analysis in terms of substitution. We reach here the vanishing line between the comparative institutional approach to transaction-cost economics *à la* Williamson and a more empirical and evolutionary approach to the organisation of productive activities.

Besides its intuitions about the institutional structure of industry, Coase's article is also interesting because of its analytical rigour and fairness. This facilitates a precise study of its method and a clearing of its contribution to the analysis of industrial co-ordination. On the one hand, the adoption of the test of the boundaries of the firm as a precondition of the determination of its empirical content shows that an institutional theory of productive organisation is actually superior to a technological theory of the firm which is the background of standard Industrial Organisation described in terms of market structures. On the other hand, the stating of inter-firm co-operation as a paradox to be solved aids the tracing of the limits of the theory and suggests the way of going beyond them. In fact, the paradox of co-operation puts to the fore two dimensions that cannot be easily eliminated from the analysis of productive co-ordination: co-operative relations between firms, and the structure of production as a sequential process in time.

THE NATURE OF INDUSTRY AND THE PARADOX OF COMPETITION

These dimensions of industry are present in Richardson's theory of industrial co-ordination, which results from the conjunction of two criticisms addressed to the standard theory of industrial organisation: first, a theoretical criticism of the division of labour between the firm and the market, considered as given in the previous theory; second, an empirical criticism of this dichotomy, which does not take into account 'the dense network of co-operation and affiliation by which firms are inter-related' (Richardson 1972: 883). Like Coase's (and Williamson's), Richardson's theory is intended to be a criticism of the standard theory of industrial organisation based upon given market structures where the frontier between the firm and the market is not explained (see Coase 1972; Williamson 1975). Like Coase (and Williamson again), Richardson considers that the theory of the firm must be conceived within the framework of a theory of institutional division of labour.

The original and interesting aspect of Richardson's 1972 article is that it shows three other characteristics: (1) it proposes an approach to industrial organisation founded on the necessity of co-ordinating production plans; (2) this approach is grounded upon a theory which combines the concepts of 'activities' and 'capabilities' – activities are distinct from products to which they are ordinarily assimilated in the standard industrial analysis and may represent different stages of a production process; capabilities allow a relationship between the activities carried on and the institutions endowed with these competencies to be established; (3) inter-firm co-operation is considered, in the *continuum* of available co-ordination methods, as an institutional arrangement conceptually distinct from the market and the firm.

These characteristics play an important role in the analysis. The main criticism of the standard theory is that it leaves unexplained the principles of the division of labour between consolidation (within the firm), co-operation and market transactions. The answer to this major theoretical problem is built on 'conceptual distinctions' which state a principle of strict separability between the 'similarity' and 'complementarity' of industrial activities. The combination of these separable elements then becomes the basis of the proof of the division of labour of industrial co-ordination between different possible institutional arrangements. This theory leans, in fact, on the two following main hypotheses:

- *Hypothesis H1: the activities grouped within a firm have a strong tendency to be similar* (Richardson 1972: 889). Firms indeed tend to develop in areas where their competencies offer 'some comparative advantage' (*ibid.*: 888), as the author writes it, referring to Penrose (1959), who showed that companies exhibit two different rhythms of evolution: the slow

evolution of their competencies and the faster expansion of their activities in the direction set by the former.
- *Hypothesis H2: complementary activities must be co-ordinated both qualitatively and quantitatively* (Richardson 1972: 890). E.g. 'Polymer production has to be matched, for example, with spinning capacity, both in terms of output volume and product characteristics, and investment in heavy electrical equipment has likewise to be appropriate, in scale and type, to the planned construction of power stations' (*ibid.*: 890).

By the operation of these two hypotheses, the 'appropriate division of labour' between consolidation, co-operation and market transactions can be demonstrated. The conclusions we may draw from the confrontation of the two separated principles of similarity and complementarity, and concerning the division of labour of industrial co-ordination, are the following:

- *First conclusion*: where activities are 'both similar and complementary' (Richardson 1972: 895) they are co-ordinated by the direction within an individual business.
- *Second conclusion*: 'closely complementary but dissimilar' activities (Richardson 1972: 892) have to be co-ordinated *ex ante* by inter-firm co-operative arrangements.
- *Third conclusion*: the other activities (which are not closely complementary) are co-ordinated *ex post* by market transactions.

Then the result obtained is double.

First, it provides an explanation of the boundaries of the firm. If the firm did not tend to be limited to the operation of a single capability, or bordering capabilities (contrary to H1), the hypothesis concerning complementarity (H2) would induce all production processes of the economy to integrate into One Big Firm. The conjunction of H1 and H2 implies, then, that a fraction of industrial co-ordination be imparted to the other forms of institutions. Therefore there exists an appropriate division of labour between firms, on the one hand, and co-operation and market on the other hand (QED).

Second, this result explains the reason why there exist 'complex networks of co-operation and association', the necessity of which has been put forward, as an empirical intuition, from the beginning of the analysis. The 'prime reason' for its existence is that:

> [t]his co-ordination cannot be left entirely to direction within firms because the activities are dissimilar [H1], and cannot be left to the market forces in that it requires not the balancing of the aggregate supply of something with the aggregate demand for it but rather

the matching, both qualitative and quantitative, of individual enterprise plans [H2].

(Richardson 1972: 892)

The *ex ante* co-ordination is thus highlighted by this approach, which has enlarged the scope of the analysis of industrial organisation by choosing 'to refer to activities rather than goods' (Richardson 1972: 892).

In the terms of Popper's critical method, this theory exhibits a 'truth-content' which is superior to the one of transaction-costs economics (based on the hypothesis of costly transactions), for it allows a positive answer to be given to the test of the boundaries of the firm with an empirical foundation which integrates the phenomenon of inter-firm co-operation. In fact, there is no longer any paradox of co-operation in Richardson's theory.[11]

These advantages notwithstanding, we have not for all that reached the 'absolute' theory telling us 'the truth' about the organisation of industry. The very principle of Popper's 'fallibilism' should immunise us against such an idea. Richardson himself remains very modest in his conclusions. He warns us against trying to do too much with theories of industrial organisation and advises us to apply 'with discretion' his distinction between the different forms of co-ordination (Richardson 1972: 896). But there is another observation with which the author wishes to end his paper. It is the fact that by seeking to stress the co-operative element in business relations he 'by no means (takes) the view that where there is co-operation competition is no more' (*ibid.*: 895). After all, '[f]irms form partners for the dance but, when the music stops, they can change them' (*ibid.*: 896). Thus, 'competition is still at work even if it has changed its mode of operation' (*ibid.*: 896).

These considerations are more than simple conclusive sentences. They bring to light that there is a real problem in the theory due to the fact that market transactions are only provided with a residual analytical role. The analytical separation between co-operation and pure market transactions is realised only on the basis of the definition of more or less 'closely complementary' activities. This characteristic, associated with the intentional *ex ante* co-ordination of plans, makes out a conception of industry as a purely pragmatic system,[12] a kind of *One Big Co-operation*. But this, after all, is no more than a healthy fallibilist attitude. Richardson's theory has found its own potential falsifier, which takes the form of what we may call a *paradox of competition*.

From this point of view, the author's subsequent article (Richardson 1975), which comments upon the notions of competition and increasing returns in *The Wealth of Nations*, besides the penetrating observations made on the notion of economic development, may be seen as complementing the theory of industrial organisation developed in the previous paper. After having considered why monopoly would not necessarily be produced by increasing returns, Richardson grapples with the question of what we could call the *boundaries of co-operation*. 'It may be instructive', as he writes it, 'to ask why monopoly should not emerge in any case simply because firms choose to come together' (1975: 358). Firms would gain from doing so, as the author explains: 'Even if the merger of all the firms in an industry was expected to leave the profits no higher than before, at least the firms would be relieved of uncertainty about the likely size of their share' (*ibid*: 358). And if there were any unexploited opportunities, 'then profits could be increased and everyone made better off than they would have been in competitive conditions' (*ibid.*: 358).

Even if this combination is assuredly a minimum form of co-operation, there exists a force which opposes this tendency. This force is competition, but competition as a process, 'competition in terms of activity rather than structure' (Richardson 1975: 359), by which each firm searches for a profit share superior to the one it would obtain in the sharing of monopoly profit. As Richardson puts it, 'Surely it is of the essence of competition that the participants hold uncertain and divergent beliefs about their chances of success' (*ibid.*: 359). And we must 'recognise that rivals will in general hold inconsistent views of their competitive chances' (*ibid.*: 359). This appears all the more pertinent today when one refers to Fransman's study of the Japanese information and communication industry, where the author repeatedly demonstrates the divergence of beliefs between firms which have access to approximately the same information (Fransman 1995).

The analysis of competition as a process of uncertainty and of knowledge then appears to be the directions towards which the analysis of industrial organisation – as a theory as well as an empirical approach – should tend, so as to improve what Popper would have called its 'verisimilitude'. This method is effectively illustrated by Fransman's 1995 essay on Japanese firms. This essay, though empirical in nature, is firmly grounded on theories of industrial co-ordination referring to the notions of knowledge, competencies and beliefs (Fransman 1994). Even in more standard Industrial Organisation, authors are becoming conscious of the necessity of taking into consideration the dynamic aspects of competition (Baumol 1992; Geroski 1992; Jacquemin 1994; Vickers 1995). These aspects can justify not only the existence of inter-firm co-operation, but also their welfare effects to be accounted for in competition policies. The problem in this case is that because the concept of institutional division of labour is lacking, this literature is not prepared to delimit the frontiers of co-operation and give an effective account of the collusive outcomes that could, notwithstanding, be generated by such institutional forms.[13]

CONCLUSION

The method applied in this paper to examine the 'growth of knowledge' within the field of the economic analysis of industry has shown a close connection between Coase's and Richardson's research programmes. In fact, to 'give content' to the transaction-cost hypothesis, as Richardson does, is not the same thing as to 'operationalise' this hypothesis in the way Williamson does. The difference lies in the notions of 'paradoxes' to be solved by the theory of the organisation of industry. We have seen in this paper how a common refutational line of thought can be thus defined between Coase and Richardson. This can be opposed to the traditional regrouping of Coase and Williamson under the head of transaction-cost economics. Indeed, contrary to Coase's paradox of co-operation, Williamson's notion of the 'hybrid' form of governance is not paradoxical. Smoothly inserted by Williamson (1985) into the bipolar structure of the transaction-cost theory as an element of confirmation of the latter, this notion does not play the role of the potential falsifier that would be necessary to implement a progressive theory of the organisation of industry.[14] Thus, the Coase–Williamson connection leads to a *contractualist* vision of the organisation of industry, as Alchian and Woodward (1988) rightly – and approvingly – notice, underlining that the boundaries of the firm then become 'fuzzy'. The comparative institutional analysis of transaction-cost economics is thereby driven into a closure. First intended to propose a critical approach to the organisation of industry, it becomes compatible with – and a subset of – the incentives and information apparatus of *New* Industrial Organisation. Showing the existence of a Coase–Richardson connection makes clear that the critical programme for the analysis of the institutional structure of production remains open. Each new institutional form, far from being a 'confirmation' of the coherence of a definitely self-contained theory, is a new challenge to an evolving approach. Contrary to Alchian and Woodward's statement, 'the firm is dead, long live the firm' ('as a nexus of contracts', they might add), in the Coase–Richardson legacy the firm is well alive and still remains the central institution for organising the co-ordination of industrial activities.

NOTES

1 The author would like to thank Cécile Dangel and Brian Loasby for helpful comments and suggestions.
2 Such notions as 'progressiveness' or 'empirical content' refer to the conceptions of scientific progress put forward by the *Growth of Knowledge* literature, i.e. authors like Popper, Lakatos or Kuhn. We will use, however, a somewhat prescriptive method *à la* Popper rather than the descriptive approaches of Lakatos or Kuhn.

3 In this volume, R. N. Langlois distinguishes between the *co-ordination of production* and the *co-ordination of commitments*, Richardson's 1972 article being more centrally about the first and Richardson's 1960 book about the second.
4 The influence of Hayek on these developments has been studied in details by Foss (1995).
5 This is close to an argument used by Loasby (1991).
6 See Hayek (1937: 33, fn. 1).
7 Their conclusions had been summed up and developed by Williamson (1967).
8 More generally, the boundaries of the firm are the paradigmatic problem of the field called 'New Institutional Economics' (Langlois 1986). This field is larger than – and incorporates – the 'neo-institutionalist' school defined by Williamson.
9 In his fourth paragraph, Coase shows in fact that when products are diversified the upward sloping of the cost curve does not give a limitation to the size of the firm. The same is true for imperfect competition, where it is not sufficient that the marginal cost is inferior to marginal revenue.
10 We use the term 'truth-content' in a simple intuitive way. For a more technical definition, see Popper (1963: ch. X; 1972).
11 That is the reason why this theory can be usefully developed as an analysis of innovation (Richardson 1972: 892–5). The recent development of the 'capability view' or the 'competence perspective' of the firm (Langlois 1992; Foss 1993) shows that this approach is still promising in that by adopting a process of production logic it gives a good account of the institutional arrangements depending on the type of innovation involved, which can be 'autonomous', i.e. involving only one stage, or 'systemic', i.e. involving many stages of the chain of production.
12 In the sense of Menger (1883), that is, intentionally implemented, as opposed to spontaneous orders unintentionally resulting from individual actions.
13 The fact that 'co-operation is competition' in the Richardsonian system (Foss 1994) still needs to be confronted to case studies. An interesting attempt in this sense is made by Krafft (1996).
14 According to Williamson, the 'operationalization efforts' have spawned a growing empirical literature which is 'broadly corroborative' (Williamson 1993: 90). This confirmationist stance is assuredly not the critical method proposed by Popper (see, for instance, Popper 1963: 95–7; Boland 1982: 23–5), to which Coase's and Richardson's way of thinking better corresponds.

REFERENCES

Alchian, A. A. and Woodward, S. (1988) 'The firm is dead; long live the firm: a review of Oliver E. Williamson's book *The Institutions of Capitalism*', *Journal of Economic Literature* 26(1), 65–79.

Archibald, G. C. (1987) 'Firm, theory of the', in J. Eatwell, M. Milgate and P. Newman (eds) *The New Palgrave: A Dictionary of Economics*, vol. 2, London: Macmillan.

Baumol, W. (1992) 'Horizontal collusion and innovation', *Economic Journal* 102(410), 129–37.

Boland, L. (1982) *The Foundations of Economic Method*, London: Allen & Unwin.

Coase, R. H. (1937) 'The nature of the firm', *Economica* (NS) 4; reprinted in G. Stigler and K. Boulding (eds) *Readings in Price Theory*, London: Allen & Unwin, 1953.
—— (1972) 'Industrial organisation: a proposal for research', in V. R. Fuchs (ed.) *Policy Issues and Research Opportunities in Industrial Organization*, New York: NBER/Columbia University Press.
—— (1992) 'The institutional structure of production', *American Economic Review* 82(4), 713–19.
—— (1993a) 'The nature of the firm: meaning', in O. E. Williamson and S. G. Winter (eds) *The Nature of the Firm: Origins, Evolution, and Development*, Oxford: Oxford University Press.
—— (1993b) 'The nature of the firm: influence', in O. E. Williamson and S. G. Winter (eds) *The Nature of the Firm: Origins, Evolution, and Development*, Oxford: Oxford University Press.
Foss, N. J. (1993) 'Theories of the firm: contractual and competence perspectives', *Journal of Evolutionary Economics* 3(2), 127–44.
—— (1994) 'Cooperation is competition: George Richardson on coordination and interfirm relations', *British Review of Economic Issues* 16(40), 25–49.
—— (1995) 'The economic thought of an Austrian Marshallian: George Barklay Richardson', *Journal of Economic Studies* 22(1), 23–44.
Fransman, M. (1994) 'Information, knowledge, vision and theories of the firm', *Industrial and Corporate Change* 3(3), 713–57.
—— (1995) *Japan's Computer and Communications Industry: The Evolution of Industrial Giants and Global Competitiveness*, Oxford: Oxford University Press.
Georgescu-Roegen, N. (1966) *Analytical Economics: Issues and Problems*, Cambridge: Cambridge University Press.
Geroski, P. (1992) 'Vertical integration between firms and industrial policy', *Economic Journal* 102(410), 138–47.
Hayek, F. (1937) 'Economics and knowledge', *Economica* (NS); reprinted in F. Hayek *Individualism and Economic Order*, Chicago: University of Chicago Press, 1948.
Hutchison, T. W. (1938) *The Significance and Basic Postulates of Economic Theory*, Reprint of Economic Classics, New York: A. M. Kelley, 1965.
Jacquemin, A. (1994) 'Capitalisme, compétition et coopération', *Revue d'économie politique*, July–August, 501–15.
Kaldor, N. (1934) 'The equilibrium of the firm', *Economic Journal* 44(173), 60–76.
Knight, F. R. (1921) *Risk, Uncertainty, and Profit*; reprinted 1965, New York: Augustus M. Kelley.
Krafft, J. (1996) 'Le Processus de concurrence: une proposition de critères d'évaluation', *Revue d'économie industrielle* 76 (2ème trimestre), 49–66.
Langlois, R.,N. (1986) 'The New Institutional Economics: an introductory essay', in R. N. Langlois (ed.) *Economics as a Process: Essays in the New Institutional Economics*, Cambridge: Cambridge University Press.
—— (1992) 'Transaction-cost economics in real time', *Industrial and Corporate Change* 1(1), 99–127.
Loasby, B. J. (1976) *Choice, Complexity and Ignorance: An Enquiry into Economic Theory and the Practice of Decision Making*, Cambridge: Cambridge University Press.
—— (1991) *Equilibrium and Evolution: An Exploration of Connecting Principles in Economics*, Manchester: Manchester University Press.

—— (1994) 'Organisational capabilities and interfirm relations', *Metroeconomica* 45(3), 248–65.
McNulty, P. (1984) 'The nature and theory of economic organisation: the role of the firm reconsidered', *History of Political Economy* 16(2), 233–53.
Menger, C. (1883/1985) *Investigations into the Methods of the Social Sciences*, New York: New York University Press.
Penrose, E. (1959) *The Theory of Growth of the Firm*, New York: John Wiley & Sons.
Popper, K. (1959) *La Logique de la découverte scientifique*, French trans. 1982, Paris: Payot.
—— (1963) *Conjectures et réfutations*, French trans. 1985, Paris: Payot.
—— (1972) *La Connaissance objective*, French trans. 1978, Paris: Editions Complexe, Presses Universitaires de France.
Ravix, J.-L. (1990) 'L'Emergence de la firme et des coopérations interfirmes dans la théorie de l'organisation industrielle: Coase et Richardson', *Revue d'économie industrielle* 51, 27–50.
Richardson, G. B. (1960) *Information and Investment: A Study in the Working of the Competitive Economy*, Cambridge: Cambridge University Press.
—— (1972) 'The organisation of industry', *Economic Journal*, 82(327), 883–96.
—— (1975) 'Adam Smith on competition and increasing returns', in A. Skinner and T. Wilson (eds) *Essays on Adam Smith*, Oxford: Clarendon Press.
Robbins, L. (1932) *An Essay on the Nature and Significance of Economic Science*, 3rd issue, London: Macmillan.
Robinson, A. (1934) 'The problem of management and the size of the firm', *Economic Journal* 44 (June), 242–57.
Shackle, G. L. S. (1967) *The Years of High Theory*, Cambridge: Cambridge University Press.
Vickers, J. (1995) 'Concepts of competition', *Oxford Economic Papers* 47(1), 1–23.
Williamson, O. E. (1967) 'Hierarchical control and optimal firm size', *Journal of Political Economy* 75, 123–38.
—— (1975) *Markets and Hierarchy*, New York: Free Press.
—— (1985) *The Economic Institutions of Capitalism: Firms, Markets, Relational Contracting*, New York: Free Press.
—— (1993) 'The logic of economic organization', in O. E. Williamson and S. G. Winter (eds) *The Nature of the Firm: Origins, Evolution, and Development*, Oxford: Oxford University Press.

5

MARSHALL, ANDREWS AND RICHARDSON ON MARKETS

An interpretation

Richard Arena and Claire Charbit

INTRODUCTION

The present period is characterised by a substantial change in the contents of microeconomics. At the end of the 1970s the General Economic Equilibrium (GEE) approach was predominant, even if its research programme had not been entirely implemented. The various existing versions of the *tâtonnement* theory indeed proved unable to capture the main features of the working of actual competitive economics (Fisher 1972). The introduction of imperfect competition in the GEE framework forbade obtaining the results already reached within a competitive economy (Roberts and Sonnenschein 1977; Guesnerie and Laffont 1978). Finally, the extension of the Arrow–Debreu model to an uncertain world turned out to be disappointing (Radner 1982).

This Pyrrhic victory did not last. In the 1980s and the 1990s 'new microeconomics' appeared, which took seriously imperfect information and competition into account but which, in return, renounced the concept of general economic interdependency and the explanation of the economy tendency towards a general equilibrium. Today, these 'new microeconomics' tend to replace progressively the GEE old view, but the problem of the construction of a model of the working of actual market economies still remains.

It may therefore be useful to recall the existence of this problem and to come back to it from a different perspective. From this point of view, the contribution of George Richardson is an unavoidable cornerstone. As early as 1960, in his *Information and Investment*, this author indeed pointed out that:

> there is, in fact, a genuine gap in our theoretical presentation of the working of the competitive economy. The theory of the maintenance

or the attainment of equilibrium under perfectly competitive conditions fails to account for the process of adjustment in terms of investment decisions by individual entrepreneurs, who have expectations which they could reasonably be presumed to form, on the basis of information which can reasonably be presumed to be available.

(Richardson 1960: 28)

This critique of the GEE perspective was not, however, purely destructive. It also tried to offer an alternative conception of economic activity founded on non-Walrasian traditions, such as the Marshallian or the Austrian ones.

Now, this is also the general prospect of our contribution. After having recalling briefly the GEE view on markets and its shortcomings (see the next section), we shall try to find in Alfred Marshall's analysis a source of inspiration for the purpose of rediscovering a different approach to markets. This attempt will exhibit two different dimensions, the one connected to individual behaviour and rationality, the other considering the interaction of those behaviours on markets (see 'Agents and markets in a Marshallian perspective', pp. 86–92). We shall investigate successively those dimensions in Andrew's and Richardson's contributions which revived the Marshallian tradition and detached it from the interpretation that Pigou and Viner developed (Pigou 1912, 1928, 1953; Viner 1941, 1958). We shall first cope with the level of individual agents (see 'Individual agents in Andrews and Richardson', pp. 92–7). We shall then consider the problem of market interactions in an uncertain world (see 'Global markets in Andrews and Richarson', pp. 97–101). We hope some materials will finally be available to incite modern economists to think again of markets in a fresh and innovative way.

GENERAL ECONOMIC EQUILIBRIUM: AGENTS AND MARKETS

The success of the GEE theory is obviously related to its capacity to offer an analysis of the interaction among *markets* in a global competitive economy. This capacity is founded upon an axiomatic conception of agents and exchanges which can be characterised in a clear-cut way. This conception was described by Richardson (1964: ch. 2) as the 'logic of choice', which is not so far from the expression 'exchange paradigm' (Kaldor 1972; Pasinetti 1981; Baranzini and Scazzieri 1986). It implies five elements. The first three refer to the Walrasian contents of the GEE approach, while the last two are related to the hypothesis of perfect competition:

1 *Perfect rationality.* Global economic phenomena are the aggregate results of individual rational behaviour. Rationality presents two dimensions.

One is 'instrumental rationality' (Walliser 1985): agents are optimisers; they are supposed to use the scarce resources they own as well as possible. The other dimension is 'cognitive rationality' (*ibid.*): individual knowledge is perfect; agents use relative prices as true 'signals' which reveal all the existing information on markets.

2   *Independent agents.* On any given market, buyers and sellers are supposed to be perfectly independent. Indeed, they establish their individual supply and demand functions before they meet on markets, according to the knowledge they have of the state of techniques, their own preferences and their budget constraints. They have no inter-individual contact before exchanges on markets.

3   *Logical time.* All *effective* market transactions are supposed to be held simultaneously, even if some goods or services are delivered later.

4   *Free entry.* No potential supplier of demander can be excluded a priori if he or she owns resources and desires to participate to market transactions. To use Marshall's own words, demands and supplies are 'universal' (1916: 326).

5   *Homogeneous products.* Products are standardised and therefore perfectly identical. Agents are able to define and distinguish them unambiguously.

As we know, John Hicks strongly contributed to popularising this approach in the English-speaking world, presenting *Value and Capital* as an explicitly Walrasian contribution:

> What we mainly need is a technique for studying the interrelations of markets.
>
> When looking for such a technique we are naturally impelled to turn to the works of those writers who have specially studied such interrelations – that is to say, the economists of the Lausanne School, Walras and Pareto, to whom, I think, Wicksell should be added. The method of General Equilibrium, which these writers elaborated, was specially designed to exhibit the economic system as a whole, in the form of a complex pattern of interrelations of markets. Our own work is bound to be in their tradition, and to be a continuation of theirs.
>
> (Hicks 1939: 2)

However, *Value and Capital* was not just a tribute paid to the Walrasian tradition. Trying to build within this tradition real 'dynamic economics', Hicks quickly met *the problem of uncertainty*.

This problem already appears when tastes, productive techniques and resources are given. Hicks first raised the problem of the existence of price expectations. He stressed the fact that agents were able to define expectations of markets conditions, that is, supply or demand schedules, but not price expectations as such (Hicks 1939: 125). Hicks then raised some doubts about the degree of precision of expectations (*ibid.*). He also mentioned agents' mistakes in foreseeing what Richardson will call later 'technical conditions' (Richardson 1960: 28), that is, conditions relative to tastes and productive techniques (Hicks 1939: 134).

Hicks also referred to the increasing complexity of those problems when dynamics implied changes in those 'conditions':

> Even when we have mastered the 'working' of the temporary equilibrium system, we are even yet not in a position to give an account of the process of price-change, nor to examine the ulterior consequences of changes in data. These are the ultimate things we want to know about, though we may have to face the disappointing conclusion that there is not much which can be said about them in general.
>
> (Hicks 1939: 246)

Finally, Hicks also foresaw the problem of the *inter-individual consistency* of agents' expectations or plans (Hicks 1939: 133), but he did not point out with sufficient precision the theoretical consequences of the inclusion of expectations in the data of a GEE (*ibid.*: 246).

As we know, Hicks tried to find some partial solutions to these various problems (Hicks 1939: chs XXI and XXII) but his conclusion was that there is an 'imperfect stability' of general temporary equilibria (*ibid.*: 248).

AGENTS AND MARKETS IN A MARSHALLIAN PERSPECTIVE

Marshall is sometimes credited for having built a non-*tâtonnement* theory which would contrast with the contents of a Walrasian process but lead to the same kind of final equilibrium (for instance, Negishi 1985: 155, 178). Things are, however, far more complex.

First, the Marshallian conception of economic rationality is very different from Walras's:

> In all this [economists] deal with man as he is: not with an abstract or 'economic' man: but a man of flesh and blood. They deal with a man who is largely influenced by egoistic motives in his business life to a great extent with reference to them; but who is also neither above vanity and recklessness, nor below delight in doing his work well for its own sake, or in sacrificing himself for the good of his family, his neighbours or his country.
>
> (Marshall 1916: 27)

In other words, individual agents lay down and then respect rules which serve as guides in their practical lives (Marshall 1916: xiii). Some of those agents are able to found their actions 'on deliberate and far-reaching calculations' and to execute them 'with vigour and ability' (*ibid.*: xiv); they correspond to 'economic men', to 'normal actions' (*ibid.*: xiv–xv) and to 'selfishness' (*ibid.*: 6). But, men can also be 'unselfish':

> Everyone who is worth anything carries his higher nature with him into business; and, there as elsewhere, he is influenced by his personal affections, by his conceptions of duty and his reverence for high ideas. And it is true that the best energies of the ablest inventors and organizers of improved methods and appliances are stimulated by a noble emulation more than by any love of wealth for its own sake.
> (Marshall 1916: 14)

The reasons for this 'unselfishness' are numerous: the nature of men, the 'instincts of emulation and of power'; 'the hope of victory over his rivals, [more] than the desire to add something to his fortune'; 'the desire to earn the approval' of colleagues; etc. (Marshall 1916: 23). It is easy to understand their common origin.

On the one hand, Marshall tries to show that human beings must be considered in their totality and not only as money-marker agents. We can therefore see that their main motivations are not necessarily wealth or the maximisation of income. For instance, in a text dedicated to the possibilities of economic chivalry, Marshall showed that businessmen as well as scientific men, have in common the same 'instincts of the chase'. And, if they wish to earn money, it is not so much because of the desire in itself, but rather because, 'in business, a man's money-earning power, though not an accurate test of the real value to the world of what he has done, is yet often the best available' (Marshall 1966a: 282).

On the other hand, Marshall's conception of agents gives an essential part to conventions or custom:

> The present indeed never reproduces the past: even stagnant people gradually modify their habits and their industrial techniques. But, the past lives on for ages after it has been lost for memory; and the most progressive peoples retain much of the substance of earlier habits of associated action, industry and trade; even when the forms of those habits have been so changed under new conditions, that they are no longer represented by their old names.
> (Marshall 1919: 6)

The acquisition of conventions or habits by economic agents is the result of a real learning process. Using time and experience, decision-makers adapt themselves progressively to the market they are considering, until they reach the point where they act as if they optimised:

> At the beginning of his undertaking, and at every successive stage, the alert business man strives so to modify his arrangements as to obtain better results with a given expenditure, or equal results with a less expenditure. In other words, he easily applies the principle of substitution with the purpose of increasing his profits; and in so doing, he seldom fails to increase the total efficiency of work, the total power over nature which man derives from organization and knowledge.
> (Marshall 1952: 295)

Finally, as Marshall (1966b) carefully stressed in his description of the human environment of industrial organisation, people are also motivated by collective purposes:

> Chivalry in business includes public spirit. . . . But it includes also a delight in doing noble and difficult things because they are noble and difficult.
> (Marshall 1966b: 330)

> This kind of behaviour is the result of collective life, i.e., of the fact that men belong to social organisms which give them the sense of serving their human companions or, at least, their 'neighbours'.
> (Marshall 1952: 5)

For all these reasons, it is easy to understand why Marshall hesitated to characterise a modern economic system as a *competitive* system. He preferred to define it as a system founded on *free choice* (Marshall 1952: 5):

> It is often said that the modern forms of industrial life are distinguished from the earlier by being more competitive. But this account is not quite satisfactory. . . .
>
> There is no one term that will express these characteristics adequately. They are, as we shall presently see, a certain independence and habit of choosing one's own course for oneself, a self-reliance; a deliberation and yet a promptness of choice and judgement, and a habit of forecasting the future and of shaping one's cause with reference to distant aims. They may and often do cause people to compete with one another; but on the other hand they may tend, and just now indeed, they are tending, in the direction of cooperation and combination of all kinds of good and evil.
> (Marshall 1952: 4)

Therefore, according to Marshallian rationality, co-operative behaviours are not impossible. They can occur to the same extent that competitive ones do.

This Marshallian conception of rationality could not, however, be understood exhaustively if we did not relate it also to its cognitive dimension and, therefore, to the notion of uncertainty. One of the authors tried elsewhere (Arena 1993) to characterise the main dimensions of this notion in the works of Alfred Marshall. This attempt showed a strong diversity, and many different meanings or conceptions of uncertainty are present in Marshall, according to the part of economic analysis one is considering. However, even if the notion is not yet completely elaborated, its importance is far from being negligible, especially in the respective realms of the theories of the determination of the levels of output and of the formation of investment decisions. In the present framework, one of the main dimensions of uncertainty which is worth emphasising in Marshall is the fact that organisational or institutional arrangements appeared to Marshall as privileged means to struggle against uncertainty. This feature of Marshall's analysis clearly appears when he tackles the problems related to industrial localisation. Some forms of organisation of work (especially primitive forms of subcontracting) are mentioned, to describe how they can contribute to limiting the risks taken by the firms which decided to encourage them.

Marshallian and Walrasian conceptions differ not only according to their views on economic agents. They might also be contrasted in relation to their characterisation of markets. Thus, in *Industry and Trade* Alfred Marshall opposed two meanings of the word 'market':

> Everyone buys, and nearly every producer sells, to some extent in a 'general' market, in which he is on about the same footing with others around him. But nearly everyone has also some 'particular' markets; that is some people or groups of people with whom he is somewhat in close touch: mutual knowledge and trust to approach them, and them to approach him, in preference to strangers.
>
> (Marshall 1919: 182)

It seems that Marshall reserved the term 'general market' for 'the markets of a more advanced state of civilization' (Marshall 1952: 276–7). In other words, Marshall assimilated 'general' markets to purely competitive ones. Indeed, only this kind of market corresponds to 'the simple cases of a true equilibrium value' (*ibid*.: 277).

Now, if we consider the 'particular' markets described by Marshall at the beginning of Book V of the *Principles*, we can verify that the 'general' market corresponds in fact to two specific ones, i.e. the markets for 'Stock Exchange securities' and for 'the more valuable metals' (*ibid*.: 272). Indeed these markets 'satisfy in an exceptional way these conditions of being in general demand, cognizable and portable' (*ibid*.).

The reference to 'general demand' corresponds to the notion of 'free entry' we mentioned earlier. In other words, it ensures that nobody is a priori excluded from the market. Therefore, the number of demanders is large and all of them are anonymous. The case of the basic raw materials (wool, cotton, wheat, etc.) is particularly significant if we consider it at the international level. As Marshall stressed, this type of market is international and 'buyers from all parts of the Western world [compete] with one another for the same supplies' (Marshall 1952: 271).

The reference to 'cognisable' goods is partly a consequence of the universal dimension of the market. Goods which can be sold everywhere in the world must be easy to describe. In other terms, they are supposed to be standardised and, if possible, measurable. Therefore, a priori, the reference to 'cognisable' goods excludes the existence of a differentiation process, coming from the producer or being the fact of the consumer. But it also eliminates what modern economics would call quality definition problems. If goods are cognisable, there cannot be any asymmetric information among individuals agents. Here we meet our previous assumption of product homogeneity.

Finally, the reference to 'portable' commodities means that the market must not be confined to the near neighbourhood of specific demanders and tradesmen, but rather to a more universal part of those agents. It is therefore easy to understand why, defining a market, Marshall quoted Cournot, who denied that a market could be a particular place or location. This last reference also corresponds to the assumption of perfect competition. Thanks to the portable dimension of goods, there are no barriers for producers of consumers and no differentiation among individual agents.

Marshall, then, refers to the markets he defines as 'at the opposite extremity to international Stock Exchange securities and the more valuable metals' (Marshall 1952: 273). We could characterise them as markets in which competition is less free.

There are first 'things which must be made to order to suit particular individuals, such as well-fitting clothes' (Marshall 1952: 273). In this case, we can verify that suppliers and demanders are necessarily specific and not universal at all. Moreover, it is doubtful that, within a given industry – here the clothes industry – the good appears to be standardised or homogeneous: the conditions of perfect competition are clearly violated. We might also raise the problem of the validity of the assumption of independent agents: demanders and suppliers indeed enter into *goodwill* relations and therefore they are no longer independent.

'At the opposite' of competitive markets, Marshall also refers to 'perishable or bulky goods' (Marshall 1952: 273). They are not easily portable ones, therefore they do not correspond to competitive markets' goods.

Then comes 'the great majority of the markets which the economist and the business man have to study' (Marshall 1952: 274). They are located between the two extremes just referred to. Marshall seems to include commodities markets amongst this last category:

> Manufactured goods of textile materials, leather, metals, wood, etc. . . . , not being perishable, can often be maintained in constant supply at no very great cost; especially if they are not bulky; are not in uncertain demand, through changes of fashion or otherwise; and are so far standardized at all events relatively to the needs of the locality, that the demand for them is not greatly affected by varieties of individual need or taste.
>
> (Marshall 1919: 281)

Other types of markets are also being considered by Marshall. We shall only mention here the markets 'which cater for individual idiosyncrasies and not merely for the stable requirements of various classes and sub-classes of customers' (Marshall 1919: 282). They correspond to markets 'for unique or rare things' (Marshall 1952: 276), like old pictures. They are mentioned both in *Principles* (1916: 276) and *Industry and Trade* (1919: 282), and their working is obviously very different from that of the competitive markets.

The apparatus of supply and demand therefore only applies in Marshall to the competitive 'specific' markets, even if it is characterised by our author as the regulator of a 'general' market. The cases of 'specific' markets, however, violate either the microeconomic GEE framework or the perfect competition assumptions. The problem is, therefore, to analyse what happens on those markets, in which competition is weaker.

Little is told by Marshall in this framework. However, Marshall stresses the importance of what he calls the 'organization of markets' (Marshall 1952: 270). This organisation includes two different activities. The *bargaining* activity concerns the use of the rules of price changes and implies speculation, while the *marketing* activity refers to 'the whole of the effective organization of the trade side of a business' (Marshall 1966a: 278). More generally, in *Industry and Trade* Marshall characterises markets through their organisational and institutional specificities and not as 'imperfections' or 'frictions' which will remove us far from a 'pure' model. He shows the role played by intermediaries in the process of marketing and in the circulation of information between buyers and sellers.

Therefore it seems rather inadequate to use the analytical tools offered by the theory of the 'general' market in order to understand what is going on in 'specific' markets, where competition is limited. It is clear that the working of *specific* markets can be explained only by a set of *specific* models. In other words, the Marshallian distinction between a general and several specific markets has nothing in common with the Walrasian opposition between the pure exchange model and models of imperfect competition. Therefore, far from being founded on a theory of a simple barter between two commodities, the Marshallian analysis of specific markets requires the construction of a family of models, each of them corresponding to a particular organisation of the market and a particular system of information circulation.

INDIVIDUAL AGENTS IN ANDREWS AND RICHARDSON

Andrews and Richardson extended Marshall's theoretical approach and continued to stress why it differed so much from Walras's. Andrews certainly contributed strongly to revising what he called 'the theory of the individual business' (Andrews 1949). His point of view consisted in trying to reconcile economic theory with the normal practice of business. This is why in a letter to Andrews, D. Robertson recalled a lecture in which he taught that 'the Hall–Hitch model'

> has affinity rather with the work of Marshall, who, at the cost of some laziness of language, interlards his mathematical marginalism with frequent reminders of the way in which, under what is ordinarily thought of as competition, the individual producer is preoccupied with the calculation and covering of average full cost of production – thus short-circuiting as it were the results of the competitive process as foretold by the more logical but less realistic theory.
> (Robertson, quoted in Andrews 1993: 116)

Andrews thanked Robertson for these quotations, which were taken from his lectures, and answered significantly:

> I do argue that, whenever in my field one gets shown to realistic thinking, there is Marshall already. I wish that I had been trained to use the representative firm – by Marshall – I am sure that it was an important tool in his thinking, and that great book *Industry and Trade* – completely and undeservedly neglected here, how is it in Cambridge? – shows how good his thinking was.
> (Andrews 1993: 119)

This deliberate attitude of replacing the normative by a realistic interpretation of Marshall is also present in a passage where Andrews refers to Pigou: 'It seems to me now that Professor Pigou played a special part in the subsequent development of Cambridge doctrine, which was marked by the avoidance of any detailed contact with the actual world' (Andrews 1952: 185).

This 'realistic' attitude is perfectly illustrated when the usual theory of value is modified in order to reflect the daily behaviour of entrepreneurs. As Lee accurately noted:

> Andrews argued that the works of Pigou, the Cambridge economists, and E. H. Chamberlin were misdirected when they applied their version of Marshall's deductive system to industrial and retail or consumers markets. In addition, he directly challenged marginalist equilibrium methodology, dismissing not only demand curves for the firm but also reversible cost curves, the independence of cost and demand functions, and the *equilibrium of the firm*, which he considered to be the fundamental principle of marginalism. Thus, Andrews argued, manufacturing and retailing business neither maximized profits along marginalist lives, nor could be captured by models based on equilibrium of the firm.
>
> (Lee 1993: 20)

The abandonment of 'instrumental' standard rationality through the reflection of profit maximisation has been justified by Andrews's reference to normal price policy. The idea is the existence, at any moment of time and in any given activity, of a normative long-run profit margin per output which permits the survival of the firm. To put it briefly, 'a certain minimum of profits may be required for the comfortable continuance of a business; beyond that lies the "quiet life", both for it and for its managers' (Andrews and Brunner 1962: 365–6).

Now, this profit minimum is a compromise between a higher price which will attract competitors on the market and a lower price which will be unprofitable because the rightness of the price results from its representing normal costs. The 'normal' profit therefore corresponds to a kind of 'right price', and satisfying replaces optimising in this view of entrepreneurial behaviours.

On the demand side, Andrews first introduced the possible assumption of irrational consumer preferences: if there exist price differentials for two identical goods supplied by two different firms, the cheapest commodity will not necessarily be chosen. Irrational preferences can lead consumers to choose the most expensive one if they are strongly fond of one of the goods. Such behaviour is, however, sometimes easier to understand when facing a producers' market: buyers try 'not [having] all [their] eggs in one basket' (Andrews 1959: 152). The relation of consumers to a specific trademark thus appears to be a first exception to the usual supply and demand analysis.

The kind of shop used for buying can also be referred to. 'General' shops, which contain all kinds of commodities, make rational consumer behaviour easier (in particular, goods ordered according to preferences). 'Specific' shops imply less rationality (Andrews 1959: 103–4). The existence of 'impulsive buyings' (*ibid.*: 105) or of 'stocks' may also be in contrast to the prescriptions of standard consumer theory. Finally, goodwill relations between consumers and producers also play their role.

All these devices, however, violate the assumptions of the marginal theory of prices. Some deny the independence of consumers and producers. Others contradict the rationality assumptions of consumer theory. The last are incompatible with the assumption of product homogeneity.

Andrews also contributed to a revision of the cognitive dimension of economic rationality. His theory of the determination of prices indeed offers a clear illustration of the importance of uncertainty and of its effects on producers' rationality. More precisely, Andrews refers to a specific dimension of uncertainty, which we have called elsewhere 'systemic uncertainty' (see Arena and Charbit 1994). This dimension derives from the very organisation of our modern economic system. In this system, production and investment decisions must indeed be taken in a moment, when it is often uneasy to foresee how the market will react to them. This feature is the mere consequence of the existence of the division of labour at the social level. If they wish to enter into a new circle of production, entrepreneurs must indeed be able to sell their outputs in order to repay banks or credit institutions and, therefore, to be allowed to buy new inputs for the subsequent circle. This division of labour, in its turn, implies a 'division of knowledge' – stressed by Hayek (1945) or, more recently, by Malmgren (1961) – according to which the results of production and investment activities are only visible after the implementation of expected corresponding projects. These remarks confirm why, in this theory of the determination of normal prices, Andrews does not accept the usual short-term marginal theory of prices under imperfect competition. We know that, according to this theory, the equilibrium price will be chosen at the point of equalisation between marginal cost and revenue. Now, when they are at this level of output, firms do not supply demanders, exploiting economies of scale sufficiently. In other terms, they obtain extra profits by decreasing the level of output and increasing prices more than would be necessary to permit firms to go on to further production. For Andrews, such behaviour is implausible, unless firms are short-sighted or protected against any potential entry into their industries. If that were not the case, firms would enter into a price war and therefore achieve exactly the opposite of what they were trying to achieve.

It is thus necessary to fix long-run normal prices, referring to a longer temporal horizon. Therefore, the short run is abandoned. The firm creates its own productive capacities in order to be able to satisfy the possible demand fluctuations in the normal level of output.

Now, this existence of reserve capacities prevails in the short run, at least. That means that, in order to avoid uncertainty related to demand behaviours, entrepreneurs build their equipment with a certain volume of output in mind, but they leave some degree of freedom in response to possible demand variations. The capital equipment can then produce a larger output than it is normally expected to produce, so that average costs fall when the rate of utilisation of this equipment is increased. This analysis might be extended to the long period. If we indeed assume that a firm constructs a plant that includes many identical plants segments:

> then its short-period average direct cost curve would be horizontal not upward sloping as depicted in neo-classical theory. In addition, Andrews adopted MacGregor's position that managerial organization was a technique which could be altered as the firm's scale of production increased.... Thus, the firm's average managerial costs would decline not only in the short period when the managerial technique was given, but also in the long period when it could be altered. Therefore Andrews concluded that the firm's short- and long-period average total cost curves declined instead of being U-shaped as in neo-classical theory.
>
> (Lee 1993: 15)

Richardson also shares the assumption of a permanent excess capacity implemented by entrepreneurs. On one side, this excess plays the same part as it played in Andrews's theory. It helps to reduce the uncertainty implied by demand fluctuations. Richardson certainly took it into account, stressing the difficulties related to the use of probabilistic calculus to evaluate entrepreneurial expectations; and emphasising the necessity of expectations on the technical conditions of markets (Richardson 1960: 75, 82, 83).

However, excess capacity can also provide a means of reducing strategic uncertainty. This form of uncertainty also derives from the organisational and institutional form of modern market economies. The problem here comes from the multitude and the decentralisation of decision-makers. To understand this feature, let us reread Richardson:

> The problem arises ... from the fact that the activities of the members of the system, though inter-related, are taken independently. No individual member, it is clear, can decide what to do on the basis of primary information only, of information, that is, about such factors as production functions and consumers' preferences. He could not, for example, judge whether to invest in any particular direction without a minimum of knowledge about the supply plans of his competitors. In other words, it is the essence of the competitive system that the profit opportunities open to one seller depend on the actions proposed by others, so that, for example, if A, B, C ... are all equally well placed to supply a given market, then A cannot rationally decide upon a particular level of output without some knowledge of what B, C, ... *et al.* may do, while each of these similarly need some prior secondary knowledge of the intentions of

A and others. This mutual interdependence clearly presents, for entrepreneurs, a barrier to obtaining the necessary secondary information, and, if we are to hope to show how a system can work, we cannot escape the obligation to explain how the barrier is overcome.
(Richardson 1959: 230)

The solutions to this problem are, above all, organisational or institutional. They correspond to all forms of co-operation which can contribute to the reduction of risks for the producers: the implementation of an *ex ante* co-ordination of investments (Richardson 1960) or the introduction of a market or a non-market co-operation (Richardson 1965, 1972) are two main examples of what could be done. Richardsonian solutions are not, however, only organisational. They might also exert effects on individual attitudes and therefore be considered as 'behavioural'. The solution is then the acceptance by the community of entrepreneurs of 'behavioural rules':

Les codes de comportement qui atténuent les risques de gaspillage dans la concurrence ont ceci de commun que chaque firme s'engage à faire quelque chose ou à s'abstenir de faire quelque chose sous la condition implicite que les autres firmes en feront autant. Il s'agit donc pour l'essentiel d'un comportement de coopération. Les accords réciproques qui en sont l'expression peuvent être ou bien exprimés de façon explicite, ou bien former les prémisses tacites du comportement réel. La motivation est l'intérêt de chacun, éclairé par les sentiments que les intérêts de tous les membres du groupe coïncident, au moins partiellement avec l'intérêt du groupe dans son ensemble.
(Richardson 1965: 411)

It is in relation to those rules – organisational or behavioural – that Richardson introduced the concept of strategic uncertainty.

This introduction appears to he crucial, especially today, when we have in mind the space new microeconomics afforded to it.

First, strategic uncertainty is a direct consequence of the organisational setting up of a market economy. This type of uncertainty does not come from ignorance of the future or from the multiplicity of the possible states of the world. It is directly related to the decentralisation of individual decisions and to the type of division of labour which prevails in a market economy. The simultaneous behaviours of my neighbours create uncertainty because I cannot forecast them.

No improvement of predictive techniques is possible here and the only conceivable solutions suppose organisational or institutional changes able to reduce the areas over which agents exercise decision-making responsibility. Therefore, strategic uncertainty cannot be eliminated from the very structure of a market economy and the GEE tradition has to face a very serious problem:

> Equilibrium is not secured merely by the existence of a particular set of economic activities in themselves, but by their co-existence with a particular set of beliefs. Therefore, we have to discover what beliefs must be associated with the configuration we have described in order that it can be regarded as self-perpetuating.
>
> (Richardson 1960: 8)

Now, we know that the inclusion of expectations in the GEE data makes the problem of stability still more complex if we continue to consider it from a Walrasian point of view.

We have examined Andrew's and Richardson's contributions from the angle of individual economic rationality, either instrumental or cognitive. It is now time to enter into the problem of market interactions seen at the global level.

GLOBAL MARKETS IN ANDREWS AND RICHARDSON

Andrews commented carefully on the distinction between 'general' and 'specific' markets, which we have already considered in the context of Book V of Marshall's *Principles*. Referring to the usual post-Marshallian interpretations, Andrews raised three main objections.

On the one hand, coping with the concept of demand, Andrews considered the possibility of defining 'specific markets' as deviations from an abstract 'general' one:

> Where an industry is normally competitive, in this sense of heirs open the entry of new producers, Marshall's analysis runs in terms of industrial demand and supply schedules. On the demand side, later theorists have persisted in interpreting the analysis in terms of a perfectly competitive market, on the lines of the simple markets discussed by Marshall at the beginning of Book V. This seems to me to be a mistake. It is quite true that Marshall does start his analysis of the markets for competitive industry by an examination of the type of market which has provided the model for post-Marshallian analyses of pure competition – the great primary markets of the world, the large stock exchanges, etc. . . . In these, with their completely undifferentiated products, not only is there but one price at any one time, but each seller provides so small a part of the

> total supply that he may be presumed to meet an infinitely elastic demand at the prevailing level of price.
>
> (Andrews 1951: 142–3)

On the other hand, Andrews contested the fact that manufacturing industries markets had to be considered as competitive ones. He insisted upon the possibility of different goods within one single industry:

> Marshall analysed ordinary manufacturing industries as if an identical commodity were produced throughout the industry. He must have known this for the abstraction it was: otherwise, with his knowledge of world, he could not have referred, for example, to the boot and shoe industry, or to the woollen industry. A number of realistic asides would justify our assuming him to have known that the typical products of individual producers would quite frequently differ in their technical specifications, their producers thus specializing to meet the demands in different sections of the 'broad' market with which Marshall was concerned.
>
> (Andrews 1951: 143)

This conception obviously implies that there is no direct relation between a given industry and its own market. In other words, in compliance with this perspective, an industry can be associated with various sub-markets.

Finally, Andrews also emphasised the fact that Marshall considered competitive markets as consumers' markets. The author of the *Principles* analysed those markets as if their commodities were always intended to supply the final consumer. Now, it is not clear at all that traditional demand functions can be used when the exchanged commodity is a capital good. In this case, it is doubtful that the only arguments of the demand function will be the prices of all other goods. The demand for a capital good is not independent of the present orientation of production or from present and future investment decisions. Therefore, here again the use of a 'general' market model for the explanation of the working of specific competitive markets has proved to be misleading.

In order to correct the usual view on Marshallian 'general' and 'specific' markets, Andrews introduced two main elements.

First, he stressed the importance of information in the very definition of a market: 'The sales-market of an individual business consists of all the people who are sufficiently aware of its product to consider buying it' (Andrews 1959: 145). Second, he showed how, to avoid uncertainty, agents were led to abandon the anonymous social relations of a pure 'competitive' market and to replace them by more familiar ones:

> At any given time, the market will consist of a fairly definite group of people. Indeed, at the very start of a business, the business man has to make up his mind what classes of customer he will try to reach, and his decisions will result in his getting into touch with particular individuals. Once his business has been established, the people who will at all regularly consider the purchase of the product will be a quite definite group, so much so that in many cases it would be possible to list by name nearly all the buyers or potential buyers and these will usually be a smaller group than all the buyers of that particular kind of product.
>
> (Andrews 1959: 146)

Important space is therefore afforded to notions like custom, experience or goodwill in the characterisation of market relations. Custom or routine means that producers or consumers generally adopt extrapolative behaviours, seeing that they worked during the past. Experience is the source of custom or routine. Finally, *goodwill* permits the introduction of stable relations between and among consumers and producers.

Richardson also considers the problem of 'specific' markets. However, the existence of specific markets is not seen as a means of avoiding the dimension of competition which is related to prices. To put it briefly, the advantages of 'specific markets' must be preserved by firms but they are not sufficient weapons within the competitive struggle:

> Marshall himself, it will be remembered, held that a producer with a particular market 'does not expect to get better prices . . . but he expects to sell more easily'. A firm may enjoy the attachment of this customers through goodwill or reputation; but these are benefits to be preserved rather than exploited. They give to existing firms a measure of advantage which affords them an assured market, but only on condition that they continue to offer a product which is no more expensive than comparable alternatives.
>
> (Richardson 1990: 126–7)

This view of 'specific' markets comes from two aspects of Richardson's analysis. On one side, it derives from his point of view on Marshallian competition. Andrews considered that Marshall's conception of competition was incompletely elaborated and even, in some cases, misleading. Richardson emphasises the ambiguity of the complexity of Marshall's message on competition. He quotes a passage of the *Principles* in which the author considered that in a dynamic context 'every plain and simple doctrine as to the relations between cost of production, demand and value is necessarily false; and the greater the appearance of lucidity which is given to it by skilful exposition, the more mischievous it is' (Marshall 1916; quoted by Richardson 1990: 15).

Now, Richardson's personal answer to the problem he discovered in Marshall is clear and it derives from one of the main theoretical advances included in his work. It is located in his conception of information and in the role he gives to this notion within his own analysis of the working of market economies.

As we know, in the realm of information Richardson made distinct two types of 'conditions' which participate in the characterisation of a given economic system, as 'fundamentals' can do. On one side, he defined 'primary' (Richardson 1959: 225) or 'technical' (Richardson 1960: 29) conditions, i.e. the technical possibilities of production and the existing state of consumer preferences. On the other side, he refereed to 'secondary' (Richardson 1959: 225) or 'market' (Richardson 1960: 29) conditions, i.e., the relevant projected activities of the agents of the system-customers, competitors and suppliers. Now, in compliance with the GEE theory tradition, primary conditions are always assumed to be given and known; secondary conditions also, provided an explicit assumption of perfect and complete information is formulated. However, this formulation is clearly unacceptable if we wish to describe a real market economy. Therefore, in general, secondary conditions are not known by individual agents and must be expected by them.

Now, the amount of information on secondary conditions available to agents and, especially, to entrepreneurs crucially depends on 'the nature of the economic arrangements or system postulated' (Richardson 1959: 223). In other words, the search for information implies organisational or institutional devices able to reduce uncertainty. This is the point of view we must therefore privilege when we consider the different forms of 'organisation of markets' or 'of the industry'. Some institutional arrangements will offer less or more information than others. We shall consider them later. Yet, as this stage, it is essential to stress the importance of Richardson's view. Emphasising the fact that the behaviour of information search implies new forms of organisation on markets and in industries, Richardson gives an implicit answer to Marshall's problem. Specific markets are, in fact, associated with specific organisational arrangements, and therefore their relative performances greatly depend on the nature of these arrangements. In other terms, according to the privileged social device, one specific market can be more informative than another.

More generally, the existence of specific markets does not offer in itself a sufficient solution to the problem of the 'informational requirements for competitive equilibrium', according to Richardson's expression (Richardson 1960: vi):

> Thus although I shall have occasion to refer to cooperation and market transactions as distinct and alternative modes of coordinating economic activity, one must not imagine that reality exhibits a sharp line of distinction; what confronts us is a continuum passing from transactions, such as those on organized commodity markets where the cooperative element is minimal, through intermediate areas in which there are linkages of traditional connection and goodwill and finally to those complex and interlocking clusters, groups and alliances which represent cooperation fully and formally developed.
>
> (Richardson 1972: 229)

This whole 'continuum' of modes of co-ordination shows that a market economy can no longer be defined as an interrelated system of clones of a universal market but rather as an organised set-up of behavioural and institutional arrangements which is permanently changing.

CONCLUSION

Although both belonged to the Marshallian tradition, Andrews and Richardson, however, developed very different research programmes. Richardson tried to understand the role of the informational requirements which may allow the working of a competitive market economy. His preoccupations were therefore highly theoretical and his argumentation was predominantly rooted in economic logical analysis. Andrews focused on the characterisation of individual businesses in a market economy and of their behaviours. These behaviours had to conform to the practice of real-world businessmen and Andrews' framework was, therefore, predominantly 'realistic', that is, based on observed industrial reality. In spite of these fundamental differences – which still remain – Andrews and Richardson found a common source of inspiration in Alfred Marshall's works and they developed analogous as well as complementary elements. Those materials gave valuable elements to economists interested in offering a scheme of the working of a market economy in which ignorance or imperfect knowledge is the rule. They are not sufficient but they pointed out new directions of research. Much work is still to be done but there is now some hope of solving, in the future, one of the main problems of economic analysis.

REFERENCES

Andrew, P. W. S. (1949) 'A reconsideration of the theory of the individual business', *Oxford Economic Papers*, I: 54–89.

—— (1951) 'Industrial analysis in economics – with especial reference to Marshallian Doctrine', in T. Wilson and P. W. S. Andrews (eds) *Oxford Studies in the Price Mechanism*, Oxford: Clarendon Press.
—— (1956) 'Limites économiques à la dimension et à la croissance des entreprises individuelles', *Revue économique* 1: 39–67.
—— (1959) *Manufacturing Business*, London: Macmillan.
—— (1964) *On Competition in Economic Theory*, London: Macmillan.
—— (1993) *The Economics of Competitive Enterprise – Selected Essays of P. W. S. Andrews*, ed. F. Lee and P. Earl, London: Edward Elgar.
Andrew, P. W. S. and Brunner, E. (1962) 'Business profits and the quiet life', in F. Lee and P. Earl (eds) *The Economics of Competitive Enterprise – Selected Essays of P. W. S. Andrews*, London: Edward Elgar.
Arena, R. (1993) 'Le Traitement de l'incertitude chez Alfred Marshall', Contribution au Colloque Charles Gide, Paris Dauphine, September.
Arena, R. and Charbit, C. (1994) 'Frontières de la firme, frontière des firmes: un point de vue néo-marshallien', Contribution au séminaire Frontières de la firme, Université Lumière-Lyon II, January.
Baranzini, M. and Scazzieri, R. (eds) (1986) *Foundations of Economics, Structure of Inquiry and Economic Theory*, Oxford: Basil Blackwell.
Fisher, F. (1972) *Microfoundations of Disequilibrium Economic Analysis*, Cambridge: Cambridge University Press.
Guesnerie, R. and Laffont, J. J. (1978) 'Advantageous reallocations of initial resources', *Econometrica* 48: 835–41.
Hayek, F. A. (1945) 'The use of knowledge in society', *American Economic Review* 35(4): 519–30.
Hicks, J. (1939) *Value and Capital*, Oxford: Oxford University Press.
Kaldor, N. (1972) 'The irrelevance of equilibrium economics', *Economic Journal* 82: 1237–55.
Lee, F. (1993) 'Introduction: Philip Walter Sawford Andrews – 1914–1971', in F. Lee and P. Earl (eds) *The Economics of Competitive Enterprise – Selected Essays of P. W. S. Andrews*, London: Edward Elgar.
Malmgren, H. B. (1961) 'Information, expectations, and the theory of the firm', *Quarterly Journal of Economics* 75: 401–421.
Marshall, A. (1916) *Principles of Economics*, 7th edn, first published in 1890, London: Macmillan.
—— (1919) *Industry and Trade*, London: Macmillan.
—— (1952) *Principles of Economics*, 8th edn, first published in 1890, London: MacMillan
—— (1966a) 'Some aspects of competition', Presidential address to the Economic Science and Statistics Section of the British Association, Leeds, 1890; reprinted in A. C. Pigou (ed.) *Memorials of A. Marshall*, London: Macmillan, 1st edn, 1925. Reprints of Economic Classics, New York: A. M. Kelley.
—— (1966b) 'Social possibilities of economic chivalry', *Economic Journal*, XVII, 1907; reprinted in A. C. Pigou (ed.) *Memorials of A. Marshall*, London: Macmillan, 1st edn, 1925. Reprints of Economic Classics, New York: A. M. Kelley.
Negishi, T. (1985) *Economic Theories in a Non-Walrasian Tradition* Cambridge: Cambridge University Press.

Pasinetti, L. L. (1981) *Structural Change and Economic Growth: A Theoretical Essay on the Dynamics of the Wealth of Nations*, Cambridge: Cambridge University Press.

Pigou, A. C. (1912) *Wealth and Welfare*, London: Macmillan.

—— (1928) 'An analysis of supply', *Economic Journal*.

—— (1953) *A. Marshall and Current Thought*, London: Macmillan.

Radner, R. (1982) 'Equilibrium under uncertainty', in K. J. Arrow and M. D. Intriligator (eds) *Handbook of Mathematical Economics*, vol. II.

Richardson, G. B. (1959) 'Equilibrium expectations and information', *Economic Journal* 274, vol. LXIX: 223–237.

—— (1960) *Information and Investment: A Study in the Working of the Competitive Economy*, Oxford: Oxford University Press.

—— (1964) *Economic Theory*, London: Hutchinson University Library.

—— (1965) 'Les Relations entre firmes', *Economie appliquée* XVIII: 407–430.

—— (1972) 'The organization of industry', *Economic Journal* 82: 883–896.

—— (1990) *Information and Investment: A Study in the Working of the Competitive Economy*, 2nd edn, Oxford: Oxford University Press.

Roberts, J. and Sonnenschein, H. (1977) 'On the foundations of the theory of monopolistic competition', *Econometrica* 45: 101–13.

Robertson, D. H. and Dennison, S. (1960) *The Control of Industry*, first published 1923, Cambridge: Cambridge Economic Handbooks, Nisbet, Cambridge University Press.

Viner, J. (1941) 'Marshall's economics in relation to the man and his times', *American Economic Review* (June).

—— (1958) *The Long View and the Short*, Glencoe, IL: Free Press.

Walliser, B. (1985) *Anticipations, équilibres et rationalité économique*, Paris: Calmann Levy.

Whitaker, J. K. (1977) 'Some neglected aspects of Alfred Marshall's economic and social thought', *History of Political Economy* 9: 161–197.

6

INFORMATION AND INVESTMENT IN A WIDER CONTEXT[1]

Denis O'Brien

INTRODUCTION

It can fall to few authors to succeed in generating, with a single work, a subculture in which professionals, familiar with the work, all acknowledge both its importance and its neglect by the wider intellectual community. Yet this is precisely what George Richardson achieved with *Information and Investment* (1960). Nonetheless, precisely because it is a subculture that is involved, the real nature of the book's importance and influence remains shadowy, and it may well be that for others, as for me, the matter has required some further reflection. It is with gratitude that I recognise that the invitation from Brian Loasby has enabled me to engage in such further reflection.

I first read George Richardson's classic *Information and Investment* in the 1960s when working with Dennis Swann on information agreements (O'Brien and Swann 1966, 1968). The argument of the book has continued to nag away at me over the years. On the one hand, as Dennis Swann and I made clear in a number of publications (O'Brien and Swann 1966, 1968; Swann and O'Brien 1967; Swann *et al.* 1974), it was hard to accept Richardson's favourable attitude towards cartels (1960; see also Richardson 1965, 1966, 1967), an attitude which we believed – increasingly, as we studied these organisations – was fundamentally misconceived. On the other hand, it was clear that Richardson had identified a fundamental problem with conventional analysis. It is only with the writing of this chapter that I *think* that I have finally identified the nature of the difficulties which have been nagging away at me over these years.

One problem, I shall argue, which relates to Richardson's profound and entirely valid criticism of general equilibrium, is the fact that his critique failed to include *time*, a neglect of which is, I believe, at the heart of the incoherence of attempts to employ general equilibrium in the analysis of concrete competitive situations.

This neglect of the role of time in turn led Richardson to fail to allow sufficiently for time, except as a possibly beneficial friction in permitting adjustment to take place, when he came to consider *actual* competition – as distinct from *perfect* competition, which I once heard Leijonhufvud call a perfect contradiction in terms. For it is time which, in real competition, solves many of the problems which Richardson believed cartels might be needed to solve.

To avoid both misunderstanding and accusations of nihilism I should say that general equilibrium does have a valid role to play, as a *critical* device designed to show the limitations of conclusions – especially welfare conclusions, most especially those relating to taxation – drawn from a partial equilibrium framework, and in this form it was employed successfully by authors as disparate as Edgeworth and Robbins. Richardson's criticisms seem to me much more damaging to the idea of general *equilibrium* than to that of analysing the interactions within the economy in a general equilibrium framework.

It was in considering genuine competition that a second very real difficulty arose. For Richardson seems to have allowed himself to be bemused by what might be called the 'Perfect Competition Shuffle'. This requires some explanation. In the debates over competition in the 1930s, and especially in the 1930 exchanges between Sraffa, Shove and Robertson, one group consistently took propositions from *perfect* competition and then argued as if they were the concomitants of *all* competition. This 'shuffle' was performed with particular virtuosity by Sraffa; and although it did not fool the acute Gerald Shove, Dennis Robertson does seem to have been taken in (O'Brien 1984: 253). But one cannot draw *any* conclusions about how *industrial* competition may or may not work from *perfect* competition – in which competition does not exist. It is the word 'competition' which permits the verbal trick. Interwar economists were by no means universally deceived – a notable exception is Chamberlin (1933: 6, 25–9). Moreover Richardson himself at various points, like P. W. S. Andrews, agrees that there is no actual competition in perfect competition (Andrews 1949, 1964). Yet throughout the book he slips repeatedly, at least as it seems to me, between perfect competition and actual competition; and it is this which leads to his endorsement of cartels and cartelisation.

The order of the discussion is as follows. After considering Richardson's criticism of general equilibrium, I go on to consider his attempts to graft elements of Marshall's analysis on to the general equilibrium model in order to remedy the defects that he had correctly identified. I then discuss the way in which Richardson proceeded from this to endorsement of both cartels and national planning. Finally, I note contributions from the wider literature which Richardson did not discuss but which were, and still are, relevant to his argument. But let us begin by looking at Richardson's very real achievement.

RICHARDSON'S CRITICISM OF GENERAL EQUILIBRIUM

Richardson's key insight was that general equilibrium is impossible because perfect competition could not provide enough information (1960: 1–2; a preliminary statement is in Richardson 1959). As Richardson elegantly put it:

> [Perfect competition] shows that a particular economic configuration, if associated with a particular set of beliefs, can be regarded as self-perpetuating so long as the ultimate determining conditions remain unchanged. No explanation was given, however, of how these beliefs could come to be established, no account was offered of the information upon which, if rationally held, they would have to be based, and no proof was given that this information would, under the conditions which define the model, be available. The analysis cannot therefore be regarded as offering sufficient grounds for the conclusion that, if once the general equilibrium were attained, it would persist. Far less ... does it entitle us to claim that, under perfectly competitive conditions prices and outputs would actually tend to their equilibrium values.
>
> (Richardson 1960: 9)

As Richardson argues, equilibrium cannot be defined without reference to knowledge (1960: 5); and, paradoxically, 'there is clearly no presumption that the general equilibrium of production and exchange would be reached provided that all the members of the system had full information about its ultimate determinants' (*ibid.*: 6). The identification of a perfectly competitive equilibrium 'represents a system in which entrepreneurs would be unable to obtain the minimum necessary information' (*ibid.*: 2). Thus identification is a long way from the prospect of attainment. In turn, as Richardson argues, there is little point in having a perfectly competitive equilibrium as an ideal if there is no indication that it could ever be reached (*ibid.*: 89).

Richardson also correctly identifies the device which Leontief (1937) had discerned, notably in Cambridge theorising, as 'implicit theorising' – what Richardson refers to as a procedure which 'merely presumes the existence of functional relationships between different variables in the system and then proceeds to work out the consequences' (Richardson 1960: 24).

Building on these perceptions, Richardson is able to show that the problem of circularity, which is widely recognised to dog oligopoly theory, extends also to perfect competition and is simply evaded therein by assuming it away. The form of the evasion, as he explained in the Preface to *Information and Investment*, is the assumption of perfect knowledge. Yet in actual competition the acquisition and processing of knowledge are all-important. Beliefs and plans are central to economic activity. Entrepreneurial expectations are the pivot of economic decisions. There is a vital need for horizontal information (about competitors at the same stage of production) and, as Richardson recognises later on in the book (1960: 75–9), for vertical information (about suppliers and customers).

Richardson focuses his critique upon the key problem of the way in which firms, under perfect competition, would respond to a product market demand shift (1960: 13–14). Richardson's argument, brought into stark relief both by his neglect of time and by his decision to ignore all adjustments which do not involve investment (*ibid.*: 15), is that, under perfect competition, the volume of extra investment in response to a demand increase is *infinite*. Those familiar with the perfectly competitive model will immediately recognise that in using and expounding the model they themselves implicitly assume that extra investment will, initially at least, be made by those firms already in the industry and that, in so far as supernormal profits give rise to entry, this will take time. But these are implicit assumptions which have to be tacked on to the perfectly competitive model to hide its central incoherence; and Richardson recognised their inadequacy. At a later stage he extends his critique to the idea that the increase in output under perfect competition might be infinitely large as well (*ibid.*: 33–4).

Not content with identifying the central problem in the perfectly competitive model, Richardson also identified similar difficulties existing in the imperfect competition variant (Richardson 1960: 108–12); and, as Lancaster (1972) pointed out when reviewing Arrow and Hahn, general equilibrium analysis has failed to deal, even on its own terms, with genuine imperfect competition.

THE ORIGINS OF THE PROBLEM OF KNOWLEDGE

The acceptance of perfect competition as an ideal really only dates from the 1930s. Although Richardson referred to the origins of this idea in the work of the Lausanne school, it was only in the 1930s that Pareto Optimality entered the mainstream of economics with Robbins's attempt at LSE to encourage an alternative to Pigovian welfare economics, leading to the development of the 'New Welfare Economics'. Joan Robinson, indeed, initially believed that equality of price and *average* cost was the key welfare criterion, until corrected by Lerner (1933–4; O'Brien 1983: 285); and in the 1930s debates there were important dissidents from the idealisation of perfect competition, notably (again) Chamberlin (1933: 25–9). I have documented elsewhere the process whereby the abandonment of Marshallian economics was involved in the welfare economics programme of which Joan Robinson's *The Economics of Imperfect Competition* was the outstanding example (O'Brien 1983); but it is worth emphasising this point because it was the 1930s writers who drew welfare implications from a model which, as Richardson showed, could never have a real-world counterpart.

Earlier writers on general equilibrium, especially Walras and Edgeworth, both knew – and made some attempt to rectify the matter through '*tâtonnement*' and 're-contracting', respectively – that there was a fundamental problem about the attainment of equilibrium, as Richardson recognises (1960: 10–13). He is perhaps less appreciative of the fact that Edgeworth's attitude towards general equilibrium was more than a little detached; as Stigler (1941: 228) has noted, Walras devoted a book to general equilibrium, and Edgeworth did general equilibrium in a footnote (Marshall devoted an appendix to it). But nonetheless it was clear to Richardson that the founders of general equilibrium were less culpable than their successors (and one could argue that this is a trend which has continued beyond the 1930s) in an apparent willingness to avert their eyes from a fundamental flaw in the whole construction.[2]

Although the driving force behind Joan Robinson's work was, in the last resort, ideological – the inherent misallocation of capitalism as she saw it – there were other forces at work which helped to ensure the widespread acceptance in the 1930s of exchanging the real world for a model (as Shackle (1967: 47) has put it). Richardson himself refers to 'scientism'; and this is a perfectly valid point (Richardson 1960: 40–1; Hayek 1942–4). It perhaps arises because economists feel that what they are doing is in some sense scientific – it deals with relationships between observable phenomena – but then feel unease when confronted by the disdain of natural scientists. This striving after 'scientific status' is very evident in the work of Pigou, to parts of whose welfare economics Edgeworth's jibe about 'an exuberance of algebraic foliage' (Edgeworth 1889: 435), originally directed at Walras, could well apply. It was Pigou who, in 1928, introduced the concept of the 'equilibrium firm' (Pigou 1928), replacing Marshall's very different Representative Firm, and clearing the way for the assumption of uniformity of firms which was an essential part of Joan Robinson's model of industry equilibrium (Robinson 1933: 98).

It was in the 1930s that the most blatantly unreal assumptions about knowledge – the centre of Richardson's concern – were introduced into economics. In particular, Joan Robinson felt able to draw average revenue curves which incorporated the reactions of all other firms (Robinson 1933: 21). Although the circularity of such a procedure is blatant, it seems to have taken economists a long time to realise the difficulty (Triffin 1941: 68–70).

ATTEMPTS TO MEND THE MODEL: THE MARSHALLIAN ELEMENTS

Having established his central thesis, Richardson went on to explore other aspects of the working of competition. Unfortunately he then encountered the very real difficulty that different parts of competing 'paradigms' (to borrow Kuhn's term, which, in this context at least, is most helpful) do not fit together – the concepts, even where they have similar labels, do not match.

This was pointed out with particular clarity, in discussing the case of general equilibrium, by Alan Coddington. In a paper dissecting some of the more ambitious modern claims for general equilibrium, Coddington discussed the difficulties of *translating* other theoretical approaches into general equilibrium (Coddington 1975). Although the criticism was directed, with accuracy, at one particular writer (Hahn), Coddington's point is more general – and it is precisely this difficulty which dogged Richardson. For Richardson tried – and failed – to use elements of Marshall's analysis to supply the deficiencies in general equilibrium; and he failed because he did not appreciate the fundamental difference between a theoretical structure *grounded in* time, real as well as logical, and a definitional ('axiomatic', as Coddington has it) approach, which is general equilibrium.

Time

Time is central to Marshall's analysis of competition. Time is required both for the firm and the industry to adjust, and for the entrepreneur to gather, assimilate and act upon knowledge. The central role of time in Marshall's analysis has long been recognised (Opie 1931). Yet, despite the attempt to remedy the shortcomings of perfect competition analysis by the importation of Marshallian elements, the most fundamental difficulty which a reader of Richardson's book encounters is that the matter of time is unresolved. Yet the absence of time is a central difficulty with both perfect and imperfect competition analysis. As George Shackle pointed out, perfect competition has no time, whether logical or historical, but entry and exit take time (Shackle 1967: 59).

It is true that Richardson does make the occasional brief reference to time (e.g. Richardson 1960: 36). There is also an implicit recognition of time in the reference to 'restraints on competitive activity which are essentially short lived' (*ibid.*: 125); and at other points in the book there is arguably a confusion of time with what Richardson considers to be 'imperfections' (*ibid.*: 68–71). Of Marshall's perception that the expansion of output takes time – and thus that cost curves have a time dimension – there is no sign. Nor is there any sign of the recognition that the need for management to 'digest' phases in the growth of the firm, to which Richardson refers (*ibid.*: 59–60), is an aspect of time.

The perfect competition shuffle

It is the neglect of time which makes possible the 'perfect competition shuffle' noted above. For time is entirely absent from perfect competition, and if we neglect its importance in genuine competition we enable elements of perfect competition to be smuggled in to a discussion of the latter. Thus, limitations on the expansion of an industry resulting from the economic history of that industry are of course inconsistent with *perfect* competition (Richardson 1960: 58–9); but they are certainly not inconsistent with genuine competition, and thus it is not necessary to argue that, because such limitations are inconsistent with (perfect) competition, there is some need for cartelisation.

Markets as information mechanisms

Following from the failure to distinguish genuine competition from a series of axioms going under that name is an apparent failure in Richardson's work to perceive that genuine markets – and there are no genuine markets in perfect competition – are information mechanisms. Active competition involves the gathering and assimilation of information. At an academic level this lack of appreciation may be traceable to lack of familiarity with the Austrian tradition as embodied recently in the work of Kirzner (1973) and, earlier, in that of Mises (1932) and Hayek (1949).

Yet even those unfamiliar with the Austrian literature can gain such insights from Marshall. The Representative Firm in Marshall's work is an information device – it gives an idea of the supply response of an industry to a change in demand, and it tells potential entrants whether entry is worthwhile.

However, there are particular aspects of the Austrian literature of which we do need to take particular account in the context of the present discussion, and Richardson's reliance on Marshall's work as a source of remedies for the ills of perfect competition may have led to neglect of this. Firstly, the Austrians stressed that a price *contains* a good deal of information. This is the very reason that markets work (and planning does not). Now it was open to Richardson to argue that the information could be misleading; but the initial point needs to be recognised, particularly as Richardson showed apparent enthusiasm for planning. Secondly, some of the Austrians stressed *general* rather than *equilibrium*; and it could be argued that Richardson's critique was really directed at the idea of equilibrium, not at the objections to going outside the context of partial analysis to understand the transmission of economic information.

At a more practical level, Richardsons's neglect of the role of markets as information mechanisms may reflect the ignorance of many academic economists of the operation of informal means of transmitting information which may be generally classified as 'gossip'. (I once worked for a firm which employed an economics department – of which I was a member – one of whose tasks was to distil the economic significance of such 'gossip'.) It is this same academic innocence of the way in which industry operates which could lead to the belief that in genuine (as distinct from perfect) competition there is likely to be a recurrent problem of over-investment. Here the role of the capital goods industry is vital: firstly, it is through the suppliers of capital goods that firms learn of investment plans by other firms and, secondly, capacity in the capital goods industries is itself limited and the strength of demand is reflected in the variability of quoted delivery times.

The entrepreneur

The (unconscious) importation into discussions of actual competition of aspects of perfect 'competition' leads also to a neglect of the role of the entrepreneur. An understanding of this role is present in the Austrian tradition (as recently manifested by Kirzner) and it is *central* to Marshall's work. It is true that halfway through Richardson's book we find a Marshallian kind of entrepreneur searching for technological best practice (Richardson 1960: 105); but, for the most part, the entrepreneur is conspicuous in this discussion only by absence.

The emphasis on investment

Richardson ignored, apparently deliberately, Marshall's 'time-period' solution to a change in demand – the celebrated fishing industry example (Marshall 1920: 369–80; cf. pp. 331–6; see also Opie 1931). The whole thrust of the book is on the expansion of output as a result of increasing capacity rather than of working capacity harder. It is thus easy to respond – as indeed Swann and I did – to the thesis of this book, as applied to actual competitive situations, in the following way: firms initially expand along their marginal cost curves and the process of expanding in this way gives them some feel for the desirability or otherwise of extra investment (O'Brien and Swann 1968: 118–19). The neglect of this form of response by firms to an increase in demand leads not merely to an overstatement of the problem which concerns Richardson – at least it is an overstatement once we step outside perfect competition – but also to the introduction of investment variations into situations where they do not take place. An example is Richardson's discussion of the cobweb theorem, which in truth involves acreage variation not investment (Richardson 1960: 27–8). The significance of the distinction is that acreage variation can be reversed without writing off fixed capital.

Richardson's interpretation of Marshallian competition

Richardson recognised that Marshall was not concerned with perfect competition (Richardson 1960: 14–15) – how could he be indeed, given his obsessive concern with industrial realities? He recognised too that Marshall had been misapplied (it might be more accurate to say that his name had been misappropriated) by later generations. Richardson acknowledged that Marshall 'far more than either Walras or Edgeworth, was deeply concerned with the problems of adjustment and of time, and his treatment of them is much more profound' (*ibid.*: 14–15). He recognised the role which Marshall saw for buyers' preferences (because firms sold both in a general and in their own particular market) in limiting over-entry into an industry (*ibid.*: 62–4).

Yet in developing his analysis he failed to appreciate the content of what Marshall had to say. The reader is left with the impression that Richardson himself had been deeply affected by the programme of perfect competition which he was criticising – to the point where he defined uncertainty as a result of incomplete information about preferences and production functions (Richardson 1960: 81–2), even though knowledge of preferences is, by definition, unobtainable and production functions were, in Marshall's view, not fixed. On the matter of preferences the Austrian tradition is quite clear; preferences are non-observable. On the second matter, Marshall was, as always, instructive; in his view, factor combinations were the result of the continuing knowledge-assimilation process. But both these sources of insight do not seem to have affected Richardson as deeply as the perfect competition he was criticising. It is true that, having stated the problem in terms of preferences and production functions, Richardson then retreated some way from it (*ibid.*: 82–3); yet the initial statement is itself instructive. It explains why Marshall's careful discussion of the way in which firms respond to increases in demand seems to have made little impact, and his discussion of entrepreneurial expectations to have been largely ignored. Whereas Marshall's entrepreneur studies technical and market information, and assimilates this in the process of choosing factor combinations and outputs, a form of activity regarded as entirely superfluous in the perfectly competitive model, Richardson's entrepreneur is apparently incapable of doing this and requires a cartel to do it for him.

The Representative Firm and costs

The Representative Firm finds no place in Richardson's discussion, even though this was Marshall's central device for studying the response of an industry to a change in demand conditions. But even Marshall's *partial* equilibrium reasons for expecting cost curves to rise after a certain point disappear – managerial diseconomies are dismissed without evidence (Richardson 1960: 211–14). For Richardson, cost curves are expected to rise only because of general equilibrium considerations in the form of rising factor prices for the industry as a whole (*ibid.*: 16–21). At this point one suspects an incipient confusion between partial and general equilibrium in the argument; and this suspicion is reinforced by the failure to consider how large an *industry* has to be in relation to the *economy* before this rise in factor prices – and the consequent increase in costs – can be expected. In fact, as Lionel Robbins (1934) pointed out, the problem makes little sense as formulated; factor prices cannot be considered in isolation from demand changes. If firms attempt to expand output without an increase in demand they will have to bid factors of production away from more highly valued uses, and thus costs will rise; if, however, firms expand output after a shift in demand has freed resources in another industry, there is no reason for factor prices to rise.

The attempt to remedy the defects in perfect competition by introducing Marshallian elements was always doomed to failure. While Richardson had correctly diagnosed the fundamental incoherence of perfect competition as a theory of actual competition, a system which exhibits fundamental incoherence cannot be patched up by the introduction of ad hoc expedients; and the attempt to marry Marshallian competition with a fundamentally different research programme was bound to fail – as Coddington's critique implies.

But, having got this far, Richardson went on to use the failed marriage between Marshallian and perfect competition in two ways, the discussions of cartels and of planning, which were, in my judgement, unfortunate.

THE DEFENCE OF CARTELISATION

The 1956 Restrictive Trade Practices Act seems to have acted as an unacknowledged background to Richardson's book. Certainly this is the suspicion raised by a reading of some points in it. It is also apparent that Richardson believed that the 1956 Act was predicated on the basis of perfect competition (Richardson 1960: 70–1; 1965: especially 434–6, 440; 1967: 369). At all events, the stages in the argument outlined so far led in *Information and Investment* to a favourable attitude towards cartels (Richardson 1960: 67, 76–9, 95–6). The non-sequitur involved should be clear. It is that, because perfect competition cannot work, real competition needs cartels. While he was prepared to concede that there might be some sub-optimality involved in cartelised industries, he believed that the abolition of cartels – as envisaged by the 1956 Act – could make things worse by increasing uncertainty.

Richardson saw cartels as institutions embodying those 'frictions' which made competition more stable than his attempts to apply the perfectly competitive model to the real world would suggest it would otherwise be. He recognised that, in the real world, investment and expansion might take place as established firms increased output to maintain their market share (*ibid.*: 55), and that if this was the pattern followed the result would be predictable. He also recognised that capital market imperfections and managerial limitations could constrain expansion and be stabilising (*ibid.*: 58–60). But he clearly believed that the existence of these stabilising forces was accidental and that it was better to stabilise matters through a cartel. Firstly, he did not believe that firms in cartels engaged in joint profit maximisation (since, if they did, marginal revenue would be positive and elasticity of demand greater than one, yet Richardson indicated that elasticity of demand facing cartels was low, e.g. *ibid.*: 13; 1965: 444). Secondly, he believed that the conduct of firms in cartels was compatible with efficient allocation (Richardson 1960: ch. VII, especially 130–2). Not only did he believe that it was possible for a cartel to improve selection of efficient firms – through the avoidance of price cutting – but he also believed that cartels would not achieve supernormal profits.

He buttressed his faith in this argument – though without reference to any actual cartels – with discussion of what he conceived to be the inadequacies of the market in achieving both the selection of efficient firms and the competitive constraint of profits to a normal level. There was, he believed, a significant role for chance in the availability of both internal and external finance to firms, and thus in firm selection, this element of chance being in turn related to chance variations in the supply of adequate information. He also – though the reasoning here is not entirely clear – seems to have doubted that the market would, unaided, constrain profits to a normal level; again the implication is that market selection was affected by risk associated with inadequate information. In all this Richardson does not discuss the question of whether such imperfections were quantitatively sufficient to justify cartels.

Consistently with the perfectly competitive model, Richardson ignored the open economy aspects of the problem. If the possibility of imports is allowed for, then shortages – particularly of produced inputs – can be made good by imports which in turn signal the extent of the shortfall in the market to all the existing participants. It is perhaps an interesting reflection on the nature of progress in economics that a *nineteenth-century* economist, J. R. McCulloch, not only anticipated Richardson's thesis about over-entry but pointed out that, in an open economy, the availability of imports would prevent such over-entry (McCulloch 1826).

Richardson felt able to argue that cartels would be beneficial in preventing what he later called 'short-run competition' (Richardson 1965, 1966, 1967; see also 1960: 130–40; for criticism, see O'Brien and Swann 1968: 234) and also that co-operation between firms might lead to operations at minimum efficient scale (Richardson 1960: 91–4). There was also the possibility of vertical integration or joint subsidiaries as a way round uncertainty affecting business decisions (*ibid.*: 83–4). He even suggested that cartels could somehow or other co-ordinate new products (*ibid.*: 115) – even though cartels more often than not, in practice, interpreted 'co-ordination' as suppression which removed even the vestiges of competition through product variation. They also impeded technical progress; but an appreciation of this aspect of competition is absent not only from *Information and Investment* but also from later work by Richardson (1965, 1966, 1967).

Apart from outright cartels, Richardson also later came to defend information agreements (Richardson 1967) even though, as pioneered in the United States by A. J. Eddy, they had a long (collusive) history (Scherer 1980: 224–5, 521–3; Neale and Goyder 1980: 43–50) and, as it turned out, were also cartels in all but name in this country (O'Brien and Swann 1966, 1968; Swann and O'Brien 1967). Richardson's belief in the need for industrial co-ordination through cartels led him to adopt a position distinctly favourable to such ill-fated 1960s developments as indicative planning and the National Economic Development Office (Richardson 1960: 36–7, 99, 115), but to explore that issue here would take us too far away from the main path.

THE PLANNED ECONOMY

Richardson made clear in *Information and Investment* that he did not subscribe to totalitarianism (Richardson 1960: 217–20). Yet throughout the book there are comments which suggest a naive attitude towards central planning – and above all to its knowledge problems (e.g. *ibid.*: 45, 70). Richardson's basic argument against perfectly competitive general equilibrium theory actually supports directly Hayek's criticism of the use of such general equilibrium by people like Lange to 'justify' planning – Hayek pointed out that these people had shown only that *any* (statically) efficient economy must meet the Lausanne conditions for such static efficiency, without showing *how*, under planning, this could be done (Hayek 1949: 92–106, 148–80). Yet Richardson, while pointing out the fundamental problems of knowledge as applied to perfect competition, appears to assume that in that context where the knowledge problem is completely *insoluble* – central planning – it does not even *exist*. Thus, according to Richardson, 'It is perfectly possible to conceive of conditions under which the adjustment of capacity, whether to an increase or a reduction in demand, would be best accompanied by central planning, whether by the government or by the industry itself' (Richardson 1960: 70).

One might interpret this to be a reference to activities of the kind pursued in the 1960s by Britain's National Economic Development Office, were it not for Chapter 10 of *Information and Investment*, which appears to be a late insertion into the book. In this the naiveté about planning becomes very marked; and costs are held to be higher in a decentralised economy than in a planned one because of the greater degree of uncertainty (Richardson 1960: 198). Falling into the trap into which micro textbooks still sometimes fall,[3]

Richardson had earlier in the book asserted that 'in principle' Pareto optimality could be brought about by central planning (*ibid.*: 45). Of course it could not, both because a knowledge of preferences is required and because there are no proper factor markets in a planned economy. Mises (1932) had, long before *Information and Investment*, shown that, without competitive markets, there was no way of registering the preferences of consumers in the form of factor prices, although this was necessary to ensure the allocation of factors between the satisfaction of different wants in a way which reflected such preferences. The knowledge problem was insoluble. Similar problems occur at various points, especially towards the end of the book. In particular we find the curious argument that a redistribution of gains and losses would increase certainty (Richardson 1960: 207–8) – which would only be true if the redistributing authority were provided, by magic, with the information to undertake this.

CONSIDERATIONS FROM THE WIDER LITERATURE

As indicated already, *Information and Investment* proceeded from a critique of a hypothetical axiomatic construct – perfect competition – to the consideration of actual competition and of potential problems which could arise in the course of its operation. It is, however, rather surprising that much earlier literature with a direct bearing on these problems does not seem to have impinged on Richardson's formulation of them. Given the subject matter of Richardson's book, some of the omissions seem rather remarkable. Particularly noteworthy, given Richardson's stress on the possibility of over-investment in the absence of 'frictions', is the omission of any reference to over-investment theories of the trade cycle, associated with writers like Aftalion, Spiethoff and even Robertson (Haberler 1937: ch. 3; Presley 1978, 1981). The lack of discussion of alternative approaches to competition – some of which one might have expected Richardson to find sympathetic – is also striking. P. W. S. Andrews receives only one mention, and not in this context. Yet Andrews insisted that the characteristic of 'perfect competition' was the absence of competition. The roles of belief and plans in the operation of the price system figure in the work of Mises and Hayek; Mises is not referred to at all, and Hayek only once (Richardson 1960: 6). The Austrians, as well as Smith and Marshall, stressed that markets generate knowledge; yet Smith is mentioned only once (and as an historical figure), though Richardson has, in later work, repaired this gap (Richardson 1975). In the context of discussions of the firm it is even more remarkable, since an issue of co-ordination is involved, that the name of Ronald Coase does not appear in the book.[4]

The most prominent omission is that of any reference to empirical material. The apparent innocence of the practical operation of information agreements has already been alluded to; but this is symptomatic of a much wider problem. Scherer, after an excellent summary of Richardson's thesis, has pointed out that collusive agreements are as apt to *destabilise* investment as to stabilise it – *and there is empirical evidence on this*. Market sharing and cartels can actually produce investment races – again *there is empirical evidence*. Oligopolistic price fixing can lead to competition in capacity. Scherer himself provides further econometric evidence that investment *instability* is *positively* related to concentration (Scherer 1980: 370–4). A subsequent investigation found that neither the level nor the variability of investment was adversely affected by the ending of cartels (O'Brien *et al.* 1979).

Richardson's book suggests testable propositions, but the author seems to have been inhibited at the time of writing by what I have called elsewhere 'Ivory Tower empiricism' (O'Brien 1984: 252), peculiarly Oxbridge in form. Indeed Walter Eltis has recently documented the Oxbridge resistance to the suspiciously newfangled econometrics as late as the mid-1960s (Eltis 1993: xi). Observations such as that 'one may wonder' if adjustment to a common joint price 'might not involve a degree of instability' (Richardson 1960: 134) cannot substitute for empirical research.

CONCLUSION

There seems to be little doubt that Richardson's work has been seriously neglected. There have been fruitful later manifestations of his influence, notably in the work of Brian Loasby (1991), but the very fundamental difficulty which he identified in the axiomatic 'perfectly competitive' model has been largely ignored. Even Coddington's incisive critique of some extravagant claims made on behalf of general equilibrium failed to make the point which was at the centre of Richardson's concern. Part of the reason for the neglect of the message must lie in the belief that, by specifying a full set of contingent markets, general equilibrium theorists had somehow solved knowledge problems – as distinct from assuming them away. Part of the problem may also lie in Richardson having become sidetracked into an endorsement of cartelisation. Yet the economics profession as a whole has lost a good deal by this neglect. *Information and Investment* contains an outstanding discussion of demand in terms of attributes (Richardson 1960: 102–4).[5] It contains an analysis of uncertainty which is highly suggestive, even though the discussion tails off and the various coefficients formulated are unused (*ibid.*: ch. VIII). It introduces the important idea of dislocation effects for both producers and consumers; and it contains an outstanding chapter on risk (*ibid.*: ch. IX) – with a critique of Friedman and Savage – which could have been the basis for much further work. Finally, it contains a most interesting suggestion of the way in which information affects the yield of an investment because of the need for an *adaptable* programme (*ibid.*:

188–90). A certain outcome is preferred to an uncertain one with the same expected value. All of these issues deserved further exploration and – since Richardson's original background was in maths and physics – there is no reason why that exploration should not have been pursued. Even so, the fundamental perception of *Information and Investment* remains one of the greatest importance.

NOTES

1. I am extremely grateful to Professor John Creedy, Dr Julia Stapleton, Professor Peter Johnson and Mr Richard Morley for detailed and helpful comments on earlier versions of this paper.
2. John Creedy has pointed out to me that while *tâtonnement* and recontracting are highly artificial mechanisms for dealing with the problem of information, modern readers wonder why such attention is paid to these artificial constructs – without appreciating the issue with which they were trying to cope. Marshall also employed a special case so that disequilibrium trading did not affect the final price, and while that too was a very special case he was extremely upset by criticism from Edgeworth (Marshall 1920, vol. II: 791–8).
3. A poignant example of this kind of thing may be found in a widely distributed textbook by Chacholiades: 'In a centrally planned economy, a planning bureau could intentionally allocate resources at some point on the contract curve' (Cacholiades 1986: 462).
4. The only reference to Coase in the work of Richardson appears as a footnote appended right at the end of Richardson's 1972 article.
5. Lancaster's classic 1960 article appeared only in the same year that *Information and Investment* was *published*, having passed through the process of publishing, so Richardson's contribution deserves independent recognition. (John Creedy, however, has pointed out to me that the characteristics model was *first* produced by Alan Brown.)

REFERENCES

Andrews, P. W. S. (1949) *Manufacturing Business*, London: Macmillan.
—— (1964) *On Competition in Economic Theory*, London: Macmillan.
Arrow, K. and Hahn, F. (1971) *General Competitive Analysis*, Edinburgh: Oliver & Boyd.
Chacholiades, M. (1986) *Microeconomics*, London: Collier Macmillan.
Chamberlin, E. H. (1933) *Monopolistic Competition*; 2nd edition 1936, Cambridge, Mass.: Harvard University Press.
Coase, R. (1937) 'The nature of the firm', *Economica*, NS 4: 386–405.
Coddington, A. (1975) 'The rationale of general equilibrium theory', *Economic Inquiry* 13: 539–58.
Edgeworth, F.Y. (1889) 'The Mathematical Theory of Political Economy,' *Nature*, 40: 434–436.
Eltis, W. (1993) *Classical Economics, Public Expenditure and Growth*, Aldershot: Elgar.
Haberler, G. (1937) *Prosperity and Depression*, Geneva: League of Nations.
Hayek, F. A. (1942–4) 'Scientism and the study of society', *Economica* 9: 267–91; 10: 34–63; 11: 27–39.

—— (1949) *Individualism and Economic Order*, London: Routledge.
Kirzner, I. M. (1973) *Competition and Entrepreneurship*, Chicago: University of Chicago Press.
Lancaster, K. (1960) 'A new approach to consumer theory', *Journal of Political Economy* 68: 132–57.
—— (1972) 'Review of K. Arrow and F. Hahn *General Competitive Analysis* (1971)', *Journal of Economic Literature* 10: 1202–4.
Leontief, W. (1937) 'Implicit theorising: a methodological criticism of the neo-Cambridge school', *Quarterly Journal of Economics* 51: 337–51.
Lerner, A. P. (1933–4) 'The concept of monopoly and the measurement of monopoly power', *Review of Economic Studies* 1: 157–75.
Loasby, B. (1991) *Equilibrium and Evolution*, Manchester: Manchester University Press.
[McCulloch, J. R.] (1826) 'Commercial revulsions', *Edinburgh Review* 44 (June): 70–93.
Marshall, A. (1920) *Principles of Economics*, 8th edn; repr. ed. C. W. Guillebaud, London: Macmillan for the Royal Economic Society, 1961.
Mises, L. (1932) *Gemeinwirtschaft*, trans. as *Socialism* by J. Kahane, repr. Indianapolis: Liberty Classics, 1979.
Neale, A. D. and Goyder, D. G. (1980) *The Antitrust Laws of the United States of America*, 3rd edn, Cambridge: Cambridge University Press.
O'Brien, D. P. (1983) 'Research programmes in competitive structure', repr. in *Methodology, Money and the Firm*, vol. I, pp. 277–99, Aldershot: Elgar, 1994.
—— (1984) 'The evolution of the theory of the firm', repr. in *Methodology, Money and the Firm*, vol. I, pp. 247–76, Aldershot: Elgar, 1994.
O'Brien, D. P. and Swann, D. (1966) 'Information agreements – a problem in search of a policy', *Manchester School* 24: 285–306.
—— (1968) *Information Agreements, Competition and Efficiency*, London: Macmillan.
O'Brien, D. P., Howe, W. S., Wright, D.M. and O'Brien, R.J. (1979) *Competition Policy, Profitability and Growth*, London: Macmillan.
Opie, R. (1931) 'Marshall's time analysis', *Economic Journal* 41: 199–215.
Pigou, A. C. (1928) 'An analysis of supply', *Economic Journal* 38: 238–57.
Presley, J. R. (1978) *Robertsonian Economics*, London: Macmillan.
—— (1981) 'D. H. Robertson, 1890–1963', in D. P. O'Brien and J. R. Presley *Pioneers of Modern Economics in Britain*, London: Macmillan.
Richardson, G. B. (1959) 'Equilibrium, expectations and information', *Economic Journal* 69: 223–37.
—— (1960) *Information and Investment: A Study in the Working of the Competitive Economy*, Oxford: Oxford University Press.
—— (1965) 'The theory of restrictive trade practices', *Oxford Economic Papers* 17: 432–49.
—— (1966) 'The pricing of heavy electrical equipment: competition or agreement', *Bulletin of the Oxford University Institute of Economics and Statistics* 28: 73–92.
—— (1967) 'Price notification schemes', *Oxford Economic Papers* 19: 359–69.
—— (1972) 'The organisation of industry', *Economic Journal* 82: 883–96.
—— (1975) 'Adam Smith on competition and increasing returns', in A. S. Skinner and T. Wilson (eds) *Essays on Adam Smith*, Oxford: Clarendon.

Robbins, L. (1934) 'Remarks upon certain aspects of the theory of costs', *Economic Journal* 44: 1–18.
Robinson, J. V. (1933) *The Economics of Imperfect Competition*, London: Macmillan.
Scherer, F. M. (1980) *Industrial Market Structure and Economic Performance*, 2nd edn, Chicago: Rand McNally.
Shackle, G. L. S. (1967) *The Years of High Theory*, Cambridge: Cambridge University Press.
Stigler, G. J. (1941) *Production and Distribution Theories*, New York: Macmillan.
Swann, D. and O'Brien, D. P. (1967) 'Information agreements: a further contribution', *Manchester School* 25: 285–8.
Swann, D., O'Brien, D. P., Maunder, W. P. and Howe, W. S. (1974) *Competition in British Industry*, London: Allen & Unwin.
Triffin, R. (1941) *Monopolistic Competition and General Equilibrium Theory*, Cambridge, Mass.: Harvard University Press.

7

INFORMATION AND CO-ORDINATION IN AN EFFECTIVE COMPETITIVE PROCESS

Downie's evolutionary model as a means of resolving Richardson's problem with competition in the context of post-Marshallian economics

John Nightingale[1]

INTRODUCTION

The task of the present chapter is to show that the problems of market co-ordination posed by Richardson are at least partially met by an evolutionary approach which recognises proprietary information, the passing of historical time and non-homogeneous expectations. This was demonstrated as early as Jack Downie's work *The Competitive Process*, also emanating from Oxford in the 1950s. Downie shared with Richardson not only a scepticism of Cambridge microeconomics, but also many of the solutions to the problems inherent in that orthodoxy. My argument will be that Richardson saw fundamental problems in the emerging neoclassical orthodoxy, while Downie presented a potential solution by replacing it with an alternative. While Richardson posed a problem and Downie at least implicitly suggested a solution all those years ago, the profession has chosen to examine either the problem or potential solutions only relatively recently.[2]

Richardson was attempting a potentially fatal attack on the orthodox theory of markets by destroying its logical foundations. Like Philip Andrews (1964), Richardson was intent on demonstrating that the theory at the centre of our discipline was logically flawed and incapable of supporting the application made of that theory by academics and policy-makers. But, unlike Andrews, Richardson was not an evangelist for some grand alternative scheme. Richardson's work examined in detail the logical gaps in orthodox theory (Richardson 1960: 1–2), but he did not in *Information and Investment* suggest major theoretical innovation. His suggestions remained at the level of the implications of his analysis for the efficacy of atomistic competition for resource allocation.

Richardson argues that a perfectly competitive equilibrium cannot be approached because there is no means by which the information required for decision-makers can be provided; as a consequence, he argues, institutional forms observed in the world around us are attempts at solving the information problem so identified. These forms are generally identified by orthodox theory as 'market imperfections', but are required if the market is to work at all.

Jack Downie was a contemporary of Richardson at Oxford, though their paths barely crossed. Downie became a civil servant, one of the earliest cohorts of professional economists in the Economic Section, under Robert Hall.[3] He wrote *The Competitive Process* (1958) while on leave at the Oxford Institute of Statistics. That was the only academic phase of his career. *The Competitive Process* was an investigation of the question of reform of monopoly and restrictive practices law, an exploration of the significance of the 'rules of the game', as he called them, for the efficacy of competition. His concern was with economic progress, the rate of productivity change in the macro-economy. He sought insight from market processes, which he thought were the basis of economic progress, processes deeply affected by the 'rules of the game'. Thus his starting point was the theory of the firm, that is, the theory of markets comprising firms contesting those markets. He reviewed current theory, the orthodox Robinson–Chamberlin–Machlup synthesis. Imperfect and monopolistic competition provided the background which his own theory abandoned.[4]

It is my contention that Downie saw what were in effect the same problems as Richardson, and in his theory of market process showed how they are actually dealt with. His vision of an effective competitive process is very close to that of Richardson, despite very important differences. 'Time is of the essence' to the solution, the timely emergence of data, the timely emergence of the specific opportunities to which Richardson refers repeatedly. Both writers dealt with the issue of information and investment.

DOWNIE'S POPULATION ECOLOGY OF THE INDUSTRY

Downie rejects static equilibrium as a central concept, embracing instead a dynamic theory in which investment maintains growth. This is similar to Harrod's macroeconomic theory of growth. Equilibrium is defined as the situation where demand and supply growth are equal (with some special exceptions where diversification is examined). He also rejects, at least implicitly, the rational action model, using instead theory based on satisficing, target achievement and behaviour.[5]

Downie develops his theory in Chapters V–X. He begins with a concise argument for an historical theory:

> An industry has a continuous history, in the sense that it persists through time ... what we seek is an understanding of the mechanism through which the present has grown out of the past or the future will grow out of the present.... By asking such questions we are implying that historical continuity means more than mere succession; that there is causality also.
>
> (Downie 1958: 59)

His theory can be quickly summarised:[6] an industry consists of firms of differing efficiency, and thus differing profits. The industry operates at full capacity, with average price set much as Andrews's normal cost theory suggested.[7] Competition ensures that the industry's production capacity tracks demand growth via a negative feedback loop: the rate of investment required to maintain this rate of growth is regulated by profits and those in turn by prices, given the technical efficiency of firms. He defines equilibrium as production capacity growth equal to demand growth. He assumes firms reinvest a common proportion of profits, or live on depreciation charges if they are unprofitable. Those firms making above average profit will increase their share of industry capacity, those making less than average profit will lose market share, the loss-makers shrinking absolutely. Industry average efficiency will converge on industry best practice efficiency. This theory he calls the Transfer Mechanism (TM). Were this the only force acting on industry structure and performance the result would be monopoly, as suggested by Steindl (1952).[8] But Downie saw that (even relatively) declining firms would not let such a position become entrenched without some response to attempt to arrest the decline. The incentive to innovate or imitate is the loss of market share; the ability to do so is profits. Thus innovation/imitation is attempted by firms that are somewhat less than leaders but better than those at the other extreme. This elaboration, indeed reversal (Nightingale, forthcoming),[9] of Schumpeter's Creative Destruction idea he calls the Innovation Mechanism (IM). Not all attempted innovations succeed, but generally enough do so that the competitive process continues for a very long time in any industry. He does not deal with inter-industry competition for expenditures except in an interesting discussion of diversification (Downie 1958: ch. VIII). The dispersion of efficiency is essential to drive the TM. The TM by itself will be 'self-destructive and the end result would be the disappearance of anything which could plausibly be described as a market economy' (*ibid.*: 60). The seemingly Schumpeterian IM is the resolution of this problem.

Downie's replacement of the orthodox equilibrium concept with his alternative means that the co-ordination problem is rather different from that of Richardson. He had no need to concern himself any longer with the possibility of attaining static, zero economic profit, equilibrium. Our central question with Downie's theory is about the competitive process by which his own equilibrium is attained. The answer seems almost too simple:[10] imagine a mature industry, i.e. one in which its products have fully occupied their market niche, no further potential buyer discovery is available. Demand is growing at about the rate of growth of the gross domestic product (GDP), plus or minus income effects of income elasticity of demand differing from unity. The most profitable firms are investing at a rate which adds to their capacity at a greater rate than the demand growth rate; the least profitable, or loss-making, firms are not investing or are retiring capacity. If the average rate of capacity growth exceeds demand growth, a combination of falling achieved prices, unplanned unused capacity growth and growth of inventory will reduce profits and increase losses across the board, but, in particular, reduce the profits of the less than most efficient firms. Their ability and willingness to invest is thus reduced, and will continue to fall at least until their profits stop falling. Conversely, were demand growth outstripping growth of capacity achieved prices would be pressing upward, capacity utilisation would be greater than planned and inventory below planned levels, and profits would be increased, stimulating increases in the rate of capacity utilisation. Only on the knife edge of demand and capacity growth being equal will there be no general pressure to change the rate of capacity growth. This describes a stable equilibrium growth rate for an industry within a macroeconomic system which the industry does not appreciably affect.

While this description of a stable growth path appears plausible and capable of being modelled given exogenous macroeconomic growth, it does pass over quickly the problems of which firms will do how much investing and how firms learn what 'their share' of the expansion is. Downie's rather mechanical assumption is the common proportion of profits reinvested. But this is merely a simplification for the sake of exposition in Chapter VI.

Richardson's solution to the problem of co-ordination of decisions was to abandon atomistic competition as a realistic option within which a stable economic environment could emerge. I would suggest that Downie addressed the same problem constructively in his characterisation of the effects on industry behaviour over historical time of the diversity of firms' ability to make profits, command investment funds both internally and externally, and increase their capacity to produce. The historical nature of the competitive process is the key to understanding how it is that a seemingly atomistic industry could achieve some semblance of normality.[11]

In a historical context, lack of information about other firms' plans is not critical if those firms' abilities are clear in their recent past behaviour and economic performance, as reported in public company reports, financial market intelligence and industry journalism. Moreover, to the extent that industries are organised informally in Marshall's industrial districts, be they geographical or communities based on other shared attributes, the information available to inform an investment decision will be deep and rich. This information resource constitutes part of the economies external to the firm but internal to the industry which Marshall was first to notice. The seemingly atomistic industry is not atomistic in reality, but a network of interrelated communities of firms. Far from the neoclassical preoccupation with prices, including share prices, as the conveyors of information, these other forms of information present a comprehensive picture of the ability of particular firms to invest. Add this to the ordering of firms by ability to invest, as indicated by their past performance, and I would argue that the co-ordination problem of the competitive market is sufficiently well resolved to allow the observer to expect that fluctuation around the (Downian) equilibrium growth path will not be too great after all.

Downie's two mechanisms, the TM and the IM, together model the observation that efficiency is dispersed and that there is a tendency towards increased concentration. Both mechanisms work in a context of complex information matrices: prices, inventories and order books; trade journalism and gossip; the public domain information about technique and organisational methods; and the occurrence of investment and other commitment events in the industry at particular points in time. The frictionless world of perfect competition is far removed from this world. In Downie's world the competitive institutions seek out the required information and utilise it in a timely manner which allows reasonable co-ordination but does not prevent overshooting or chaotic cycles. This is what we observe in mature market economies. The TM is a negative feedback system and generally a force for stability.

However, the IM allows the possibility of positive feedback. Innovation can lead to a firm or a group of innovators enhancing their positions not merely from the immediate gains from the innovation but also from the new trajectory of efficiency gains opened by the innovation. While much innovation will be a mere reordering of the relative efficiencies of firms, the consequences of innovative change may be more dramatic than a mere change of ordering. Downie does not explore this possibility. But examples such as Henry Ford's moving production line and Sony's use of the transistor constitute dramatic illustrations of the information problem of finding a competitively co-ordinated equilibrium. Until the feedback system has generated the process of change, which cannot be anticipated, even a Downian equilibrium is not to be defined. This is Schumpeter's Creative Destruction.

Downie's argument is a brief but cogent anticipation of the main thrust of that of Richardson, that (Robinsonian) imperfections in the market are necessary to the establishment and maintenance of any form of stability, in his case a growth equilibrium.[12] To show this I first look at the (retarded) operation of the TM in a decline, or where there are firms at or below the margin of zero profitability. In a decline there will inevitably be a fringe of unprofitable but viable firms not covering their real depreciation costs (Downie 1958: 112–13). The efficient, expanding, firms will be interested in buying out these marginal firms as an alternative to investing their funds in new capacity, or in diversifying out of the declining industry. Downie argues strongly that it is the choices of the efficient which determine the path of the industry (*ibid.*: 112–13). The efficient may allow the departing firms to decay, the payoff being a rather higher profit rate but less investment in that industry; the alternative is for them to take over the inefficient and control both the ageing capital and the remaining customers still attached. Those choices, he argues, depend on the information characteristics of the marketplace in question, specifically how price information is created and disseminated to buyers and to rivals.

He distinguishes situations where prices are posted from those where prices are negotiated. In the former case customers are usually less technically well informed, being final consumers or other mass-market individual buyers. In the latter case they are usually well informed on the technical features of the products, the sellers' offering of factors creating goodwill and prices on offer from rival sellers – more so than any seller, he suggests (Downie 1958: 114). In this latter case the efficient seller can directly target its marketing at detaching custom from vulnerable rivals, using the various techniques of improved offering, price, product qualities and ancillary services. The TM can thus be seen to crush the marginal firm specifically.

The case of posted prices retards the TM, as the targeting of vulnerable firms is not so simple. Their customers are not a clearly defined group whose special needs can be addressed. Indeed, he argues that the more the market conforms to the neoclassical ideal, the more slowly market forces will work to eliminate excess capacity and restore balance between demand and capacity (Downie 1958: 117). His pointed remark that 'it is difficult to see how without [the imperfections of competition represented by such phenomena as goodwill] manufacturing industry could avoid some of the extreme instability which chronically afflicts the market for primary commodities, in spite of professional speculators' (*ibid.*: 116) drives home the point that markets which deviate from the neoclassical ideal are actually more competitive in outcomes than those which seem perfect, for reasons of information flows in those various markets. He arrives at precisely Richardson's conclusion that imperfections are necessary for equilibrium, albeit with a growth equilibrium. The posted-price industry in which the efficient cannot target marginal customers is therefore subject to periods of stasis, during which the efficient build up reserves or perhaps invest elsewhere. But when investment in the home industry occurs, it is done with maximum disruption to the inefficient, by means of price war and other alarmingly effective marketing tools (*ibid.*: 117). Here again we see the Richardson phenomenon but with Downie's solution, that information needed for investment decisions is generated over time. In a 'perfect' or frictionless (timeless) market, information about profit opportunities emerges too fast and results in lumpy and disruptive actions. But where actions and reactions take time, decisions can be appropriately based on information that will not immediately be made irrelevant. Downie is optimistic about the social function of the process, with the more efficient able to make the investment and displace the less efficient. But it is also clear that many other 'imperfections' could upset this functionality. The 'deep-pocket' effect of a parent company diversifying is mentioned (*ibid.*: 108), but many other effects, for example the propensity to invest, may differ, with less efficient firms reinvesting more in the 'home' industry, while the more efficient firms are willing to bear the risks of diversification. The question is an important one for the variety of welfare which Downie is exploring. If the normal market process is very likely to throw up the functional results Downie firmly expects (*ibid.*: ch. X, *passim*) and Metcalfe's model (1989) predicts on the basis of his simplifying but rather ad hoc assumption of equal propensity to reinvest, then a set of rules of the game to help that process will be relatively simple.

I hope it is clear from my analysis of Downie's theory that the information problem is central to his picture of evolving market structures and performance. Like Richardson, whose focus was more directly on the conditions under which decisions could sensibly be made, Downie found that the conditions under which markets would work most effectively in improving the level and variety of real incomes were not those like the structural characteristics of perfect competition but, rather, those like very 'imperfect' competition, where personal rather than impersonal relations were important, where much more than prices conveyed the required information, and where the passage of time and the temporal sequences of decisions are clearly visible to all decision-makers.[13]

RICHARDSON'S COMPETITIVE PROCESS

Most attention is usually focused on Richardson's critique of the information assumptions of orthodox theory. Less attention is given to his theory of competition, one at least as coherent as that of Downie, though less explicit in its development of the selection metaphor as the mode of unifying the theory. This theory throws much light on the role Richardson believes information must play in a functioning market. He uses many elements almost identical to those of Downie's theory. However, there are crucial differences which mark each off from the other.

Market co-ordination of investment

Richardson's (1960) chapters III to VI outline the various features of the modern competitive economy which make the competitive industry less than 'perfectly competitive' yet thereby more capable of sustaining competition as it is experienced. These so-called imperfections act to ration and implicitly sequence over time the investment decisions of potential investors, thus allowing them to make those decisions with some degree of certainty, enough certainty to allow the decisions to be made, at least. His focus in these chapters is on the features themselves, not on the characteristics of those enjoying advantage or suffering disadvantage from them. The necessary conditions for the conduct of business in a decentralised market system are thus set out.

Richardson's debt to Marshall is explicit. He takes as his starting point Marshall's own equilibrium concept:

> Our aim in identifying the equilibrium of a group, as in the case of an individual, is again to relate given objective conditions to the pattern of activities which members of the group will come to adopt in response to them. It would be possible to define equilibrium in such a way that the group as a whole could be said to be in equilibrium even although its component members were not.
> (Richardson 1960: 5; see also 14ff)

However, I would argue that Richardson, in maintaining the veil of implicit rather than explicit timeliness of decisions, missed a chance to resolve the co-ordination problem in a competitive process, a chance which Downie had taken in his historical time evolutionary model.

The difficulty into which Cambridge fell in the 1920s – what we now call 'the Richardson problem' – could have been avoided by a careful interpretation of Marshall's industry supply curve in the long run. Marshall was not imagining that all entrepreneurs would see and act immediately and simultaneously in the manner implied by the Pigovian interpretation of Marshall. The representative firm simply stands for some kind of average. Firms, in particular, would act as their individual circumstances and knowledge indicated.[14] The time-sequencing solution to Richardson's problem is thus implied by Marshall's theory of long-run supply. Information leading to expectation of profit is held not by all, but by the privileged few, and that information diffuses slowly as the decisions taken by the few make their impact on the market, and is modified by those impacts. The Marshallian long-run supply curve is finally revealed in the *ex post* equilibrium, not in the expectations initially held in the market. Chapter I of *Information and Investment* is devoted to this demonstration, thus fixing his critique firmly in the Marshallian mould as even more explicitly developed by Andrews

(1964). Richardson's demonstration of the contradiction inherent in an *ex ante* interpretation of the Marshallian long-run supply curve is remarkably neglected. Can this be attributed to the havoc its recognition would wreak on orthodox theory?[15]

Co-ordination of investments, competitive and complementary

The motto of Richardson's treatment is (paraphrasing) 'a profit opportunity for all is a profit opportunity for none' (Richardson 1960: 50 or 57 for the correct version). In order that opportunities be effective, there must be a means of ordering the potential opportunity-takers. Downie's Transfer Mechanism embodies a stylised version of an ordering mechanism: the ability to finance investment varies between firms, the amount of capacity expansion is regulated by the profits available to finance investment, the effect of increasing capacity on price, rate of growth of sales and inventory, the temporal matrix in which this process takes place. It is this latter which is of most critical importance, and it marks an important difference between Downie's picture of market competition as historical and Richardson's accurate caricature of orthodox theory in which opportunities emerge as parameter shifts outside of history.

In Richardson's discussion of the resolution of the problem, he brings forward all of those factors which mark the difference between the neoclassical world and the world in which we live. The whole of his Chapters III and IV are devoted to these differences, in an exhaustive discussion of (logical) time, capabilities, market connections and availability of funds, both internal and external. However, he remains within the broad confines of the analysis of the typical firm, with no explicit role played by the differences between firms in rationing opportunities.

All the means of providing information to potential investors adduced by Richardson are regarded as imperfections by conventional theory. He sees them as necessary to efficient markets, and 'at worst a very necessary evil' (Richardson 1960: 69). However, unlike Downie, who was motivated by the idea that different restrictive practices policies may have differential effects on economic progress, Richardson restricts his comments on monopoly policy to a few paragraphs which do not address the nature of different restrictions (*ibid.*: 70–1). His later discussion of restrictive practices has policy implications, but these he does not explicitly address.

Richardson's discussion of complementary investments is redolent of the literature on vertical integration. Indeed, he begins these chapters by pointing out that the boundaries of the individual firm 'are, in any case, to some extent arbitrary' (Richardson 1960: 73), anticipating much of this literature, as well as his 1972 article. He looks not only at information but also at assurances that would enable the entrepreneur to invest. Credible assurance has received rather less attention from industrial economics than credible threats, but the two are symmetrical, as are competing and complementary investment. Richardson's discussion of mutual assurance raises questions about 'rules of the game' explicitly. His view is that collusion by complementary investors is virtually always positive in effect. The difficulty is in balancing uncertainty and flexibility to an appropriate degree of integration. A set of integrated investments may all be an unfortunate error. But a brilliant success may be avoided by one of a set of required decision-makers having cold feet.

Competition, selection and market discipline

Chapter VII of *Information and Investment* deals in the central issues of *The Competitive Process* (Downie 1958). The analysis is startlingly close to Downie's, indeed it makes more explicit the mechanics which lie behind Downie's Transfer Mechanism, with an analysis of the foundations of that mechanism in terms of the internal and external financing of investments. But unlike Downie, Richardson explicitly uses a general equilibrium framework and uses the theoretical categories of orthodox welfare economics. Downie by contrast, sweeps aside these categories as empirically insignificant (Downie 1958: 22–4) and replaces them with the broad and simple criterion of productivity change.[16] Richardson's choice means that he has to deal with the question of optimal allocation as well as with selection of productively progressive firms. The questions he is thus forced to ask include: what are the institutions of the market which will provide the information required and yet allow optimal allocations to emerge?

The four requirements of market institutions that he sees are (1) information consistent with market operation, (2) appropriate response to uncertainty, (3) selection of the fit and productive relative to the unfit and less productive, and (4) prevention of deliberate restriction and protection of entrepreneurial rents, or 'market discipline' (Richardson 1960: 119). His earlier chapters have dealt at length with the first of these. The extensive and relatively neglected third part of *Information and Investment* deals with the second. The latter two have a close affinity with Downie's model. They are also closely interrelated. If market discipline is strong, so will be selection pressures. In the long run, short-run sequencing of decisions and actions allows information to emerge which will see any shelter from market discipline removed. The qualifications to this general statement take up the remainder of the chapter.

Both Automatic and Planned Selection can broadly be identified with the Transfer Mechanism:

> The volume of resources under the command of particular entrepreneurs may vary automatically. . . . To the extent that it is

varied directly by the profits and losses incurred in economic activity, I shall say that Automatic Selection is in operation. Selection will be termed Planned when the resources available to an entrepreneur are altered by the deliberate decision of an authority with a superior position in an organisational hierarchy, or the owners of wealth who entrust the entrepreneur with funds. In a competitive economy... firms grow both from undistributed profits and from external finance.

(Richardson 1960: 20–1)[17]

Constraints on the extent of the market are dealt with in ways that have resonances with Andrews, both deriving from Marshall's concept of the 'particular market'. And both use goodwill and reputation to extend this concept. Richardson's comments on these 'natural restraints' on competition mirror those of Andrews, whom he quotes at this point (Richardson 1960: 127). Market discipline and selection can only be said to be thwarted in a quixotic manner by superior marketing and ability to satisfy demand. This, nonetheless, is the line taken by orthodoxy in the tradition of Robinson's theory of imperfect competition.

Deliberate constraints on the market may have the same consequences as natural ones, but have no justification in the lack of alternative means of supply. Agreements which corner a market for a particular producer remove the incentive to efficiency resulting from rivalry. Neither allocative nor productive efficiency is promoted; however, the certainty inherent in such a position may allow ambition for long-run profit to be given rein in investment in R&D and capital equipment which might otherwise be too speculative for the firm. There would seem to be a potential trade-off as seen by Schumpeter, whom Richardson does not quote at this point (Richardson 1960: 128–30). Anti-competitive agreements between firms may also have some benefits, stabilising sales revenues in the face of normally fluctuating demand, stabilising market share, and so reducing uncertainty and financial risk. More directly in Richardson's sights, the adjustment of supply to demand may be facilitated by agreements which put the cost of mistakes on the firm which makes the mistake. So in markets in which goodwill is important, the new investment in capacity is clearly an addition to the supply of the particular firm's output to its own market. The informational requirements are those contained within the firm. He tries another rather subtle, and rather Andrewsian, argument about multi-product firms' costing procedures and the implications for pricing in open markets. If cost allocations are arbitrary and subject to alternative accounting treatments, then implicit or tacit collusion will not as easily lead to common outcomes. Explicit agreement, at least on accounting conventions in an industry, will be needed to expedite such tacit collusion. He notes that this is the case in a number of industries in the United States (*ibid.*: 134n.). The remainder of the chapter is devoted to discussion of yet more restrictive arrangements, such as price agreements, which have as a benefit the creation of certainty amongst investors, but at the considerable cost of poor market discipline and lack of selection force (*ibid.*: 136–7). In the light of recent experience and of recent fashions for viewing that experience (enthusiasm for microeconomic reform of economic institutions), it would seem that the gains from selection pressure are judged to outweigh by far the costs in market uncertainty and investor mistakes.

It seems clear to me that the two analyses of the industrial economy that are the subject of this chapter have a great deal of common ground. Both see the working of markets as dependent on the information available to decision-makers. Both see the effective operation of markets as requiring what neoclassical theory would describe as imperfections. The implications each draws are radically different, Richardson proposing that some form of central planning or cartels would often be required to allow co-ordination of investment, while Downie merely requires 'grit in the system' (Downie 1956: 575) to allow time to order the decisions in the context of ranking of abilities by a financial constraint. I would assert that Downie's solution provides a constructive way of understanding market co-ordination as it is seen in the modern economy, while Richardson's remains problematical.

AN ALTERNATIVE WELFARE ECONOMICS

Downie's purpose was to examine the effects of regulation of the competitive process on economic welfare. The welfare criterion which Downie advances is the growth of real incomes. Given his model, what judgements can be made about the organisation of the competitive process? Do the 'rules of the game' promote or deter innovation and its diffusion; is market share volatility increased or reduced; is concentration cemented or de-concentration encouraged (Downie 1958: 121)? My interest here is in the information characteristics of Downie's welfare-promoting suggestions, and their relation to Richardson's views, examined earlier.

He classes agreements as artefacts of depression, unstable or entrenched. The first are attempts to deal with excess capacity. If such agreements keep price above the depression floor, they will often still be below the equilibrium price in normal times. So such an agreement may dampen cycles in investment over the trade cycle, as well as reducing the financial losses suffered by both eventual failures and survivors. As the TM and the IM are both out of action in any case, the agreement makes no difference to progress (Downie 1958: 124). Downie's judgement on this is essentially based on information implications for investment. The unfettered price mechanism offers inappropriate information in the context of fluctuating fortunes of the trade cycle. If business people are subject to the excesses of optimism and pessimism which we appear to observe, such a dampening effect due to the agreement will actually improve the information about future prospects. And if the industry is truly declining, the agreement will merely slow down and perhaps reduce the social costs of the transition of the industry to its reducing state. Whether Downie is correct now, or was then, is tangential to the present argument that his judgement was taken on the basis of the information content of the agreement for the functionality of the market process.

The second type of agreement, the unstable one, is an attempt at creating stability in markets which are inherently unstable, those he identifies as 'posted-price' markets (Downie 1958: 125). He sees some unstable price agreements as attempts at restoring price levels not too far from equilibrium after the elimination of the non-viable firms whose capacity had been in excess of requirements. But the essence of functionality for economic welfare is that such agreements ought to be unstable. Were such an agreement to become entrenched it would stifle the TM. It would prevent market participants from enjoying the fruits of their efficiency in freezing market shares by preventing efficient firms from increasing market share. His argument that there are some positive functions is sometimes not very attractive to present conventional wisdom, as the problem of price wars does not seem to be that of stopping them after exit, but of distinguishing between exit due to inefficiency and exit due to financial weakness independent of real productive efficiency. The information content of such unstable agreements would seem to be small, in that the agreements are defined as unstable and known to be unstable. No one trusts the agreement to persist, thus no one takes any notice of the information it purports to purvey.

Durable agreements are to be found, on Downie's argument, in concentrated industries where the large and efficient firms agree to suspend competition in order to maintain a tail of less efficient firms who can bear the brunt of trade fluctuations while maintaining prices. The large and efficient have ample outlets for their investible funds in other industries into which they are diversifying. The agreement is thus strengthening the effects of the 'imperialistic' tendency to invest in alternative industries (Downie 1958: 127). These agreements are thus a signal that investment in the home industry is to be discouraged. The equilibrium growth rate is reduced by the elevation of price and the cementing of market shares that comes from the agreement, again reinforcing the effects of imperialism. He therefore condemns such agreements as constraining both the TM and the IM (*ibid.*: 128–9).[18]

He concludes his argument about private regulation of market behaviour with a discussion of the assumptions about information implied by trade associations' argument in favour of their various entrenched restrictive agreements (Downie 1958: 129–32). He sees the associations as fundamentally at odds with the market system, in that they are arguing that customers cannot know good value, that only the suppliers have this knowledge. Prices have to be maintained in order to allow the proper level of quality to be supplied, as price-cutting results in poor quality which is purchased unknowingly by stupid customers. In the case of innovation and research he points out that while it may be the case that what we now call pre-competitive research should be carried out co-operatively, the British trade association argument that innovation should be managed co-operatively is the recipe for British stagnation (*ibid.*: 132). Without the spur of market share and price competition the IM languishes. The wastes of competitive innovation are small in relation to the gains from rapid diffusion. Again his judgement about entrenched agreements is that they reduce the effectiveness of the competitive processes that he has identified, processes which are essentially means of conveying information from buyers to producers, and to the right producers, those which are relatively efficient.

These suggestions for competition policy are by no means incompatible with orthodox prescriptions. But they do not envisage the institution of a market that has clear optimality properties. Instead, they remove impediments to change that will usually enhance economic growth and productivity growth. The implications of evolutionary theory with no direct optimality properties are not that no improvements to economic performance can be imagined or analysed, but that policy measures are possible which will enhance measurable performance.

CONCLUSION

Richardson's analysis of the equilibrium properties of the market concluded that orthodox theory had no means of explaining the emergence of equilibrium. Richardson directed his attention to the information conditions for market process, a direction shared by the Austrian tradition, as Foss (1998) has pointed out at length. Downie chose a path not too far removed in examining the operation of workably competitive markets. These included explicitly oligopolistic markets, as had Clark and, of course, Marshall, Andrews and the Austrians. Both saw that 'grit in the system' is a requirement for decision processes and incentive, that the imperfections of orthodox market theory are often absolutely necessary to allow markets to function at all.

They share many of the concerns expressed by the more thoughtful of modern orthodox 'rational action' theorists, as exemplified by Stiglitz (1994). The problems addressed by Stiglitz seem to be substantially the same as those addressed by Richardson thirty years earlier, also from the viewpoint of the analysis of information problems. The solutions to those problems seem to be no further advanced. Stiglitz specifically rejects evolutionary solutions which threaten the rational action framework, leading to a casuistic or even an empty welfare economics.

It is my argument that Downie and those evolutionary economists who have developed those same ideas more recently have constructively begun to deal with the problems of information and co-ordination which detain rational action theories at roughly the stage at which Richardson encountered them some forty years ago.

NOTES

1 I have benefited from the comments and suggestions of Harry Bloch, Peter Earl, Peter Forsyth, Nicolai Foss, Don Lamberton, Stan Metcalfe, Richard Nelson, Denis O'Brien and John Pullen. George Richardson has steered me away from some of my more extreme interpretations of his work, while encouraging my efforts to define the respective contributions of himself and Downie.
2 As readers of this volume will usually be familiar with Richardson's work, I will spend a relatively large proportion of my paper explaining Downie's contribution.
3 For a short outline of his career, see Nightingale (1993, in press).
4 It seems clear from *The Competitive Process* that Downie accepted uncritically the conventional conflation of Chamberlin's work with that of Robinson. This is a position Chamberlin himself had always strenuously rejected (Chamberlin 1961).
5 This is clear in his discussion of orthodox equilibrium (Downie 1958: 28–9) and the section 'Motives and means for growth' (*ibid.*: 63–7).
6 A more detailed exposition can be seen in Nightingale (1993, in press).
7 Downie does not acknowledge Andrews, but the similarity is clear (see Nightingale, in press).
8 Steindl saw economies of scale as the force leading to monopoly, whereas Downie needs only to assume that investment is monotonically and positively related to profit.
9 While Schumpeter saw innovation as a bolt from the blue, suddenly striking down old industries, Downie saw innovation as a response to the stimulus of threat.
10 A more formal approach to this can be found in Metcalfe (1994).
11 This is the burden of O'Brien (1995), who argues that the temporal context of real markets is the critical difference that sets the most radical implications of Richardson's theory (cartelisation or central planning) at odds with much of experience.
12 Zero growth is merely a particular growth rate, perhaps the consequence of zero macroeconomic growth, or some coincidence of growth factors.
13 Richardson comments critically on Alchian's attempt at a biological analogy to a competitive market (Alchian 1950). Does his comment carry over to theory of the kind which Downie develops? Richardson's concern (Richardson 1960: 140n) is partly with the random process which Alchian uses as an extreme, a process which eliminates conscious or rational choice, partly with the biological element in Alchian's argument. His critique has something in common with the well-known Penrose article (1952) attacking Alchian, in that his focus is on the inappropriate biological processes which Alchian adduces, namely random natural selection as an analogue for conscious decision-making.
14 Marshall's explicit use of the assumption that firms differ in their circumstances and knowledge is again to the fore. His explanation of equilibrium (Marshall 1920: 345) – including the following: 'those who were just on the margin of doubt as to whether to go on producing' – is quoted by Richardson (Richardson 1960: 23).

15 Richardson comments on this very matter (Richardson 1960: 138n.). He would have been familiar with the views of Hicks (his tutor as an undergraduate), as expressed in *Value and Capital*, about the choice between general equilibrium theory and abandonment of perfect competition (Hicks 1946: 83–5).
16 Richardson maintains his position on this question, arguing strongly against Downie's position in response to an earlier draft of this paper:

> You simply cannot 'sweep aside' the theoretical categories of orthodox welfare economics as 'empirically insignificant' and replace them with 'the broad and simple criterion of productivity change'. An increase in production can be identified unambiguously if all outputs increase, inputs remaining unchanged. Generally, however, the output of some goods will have increased and that of others decreased. In order to decide whether total output has risen or fallen, we need to attach 'weights' to each output, and do so typically by using their prices. In other words, productivity change, for an economy as a whole, is far from being a broad and simple criterion; it is measured by index numbers, and the prices that are used as weights can only mean something interesting if they are proportional to marginal utilities, only, in other words, if something like a Pareto configuration obtains.
>
> (Richardson 1995)

17 Richardson distinguishes internal funds, as an Automatic Selection factor, from external funding as Planned Selection. I find this distinction a little strange, in that decisions to invest funds taken by the firm's own Board (an authority in a superior position in an organisational hierarchy?) is planning to about the same extent as decisions to permit the raising of capital.
18 Denis O'Brien tells of G. C. Allen, one of his teachers and a member of the Monopolies and Mergers Commission, explaining that the Commission in the early 1950s had no intention of seeking to impose or be limited by a 'Paretian ideal'. The idea, as exemplified by the Collective Discrimination report, was to free the industrial structure so that a selection process could transfer resources from less to more productive uses, to operate not only on firms but also on products and the product/service mix. This set of goals is clearly very much in line with Downie's analysis.

REFERENCES

Alchian, A. (1950) 'Uncertainty, evolution and economic theory', *Journal of Political Economy* 58: 211–21.

Andrews, P. W. S. (1949) *Manufacturing Business*, London: Macmillan.

—— (1964) *On Competition in Economic Theory*, London: Macmillan.

Caves, R. and Porter, M. E. (1977) 'From entry barriers to mobility barriers', *Quarterly Journal of Economics* 91: 240–61.

Chamberlin, E. H. (1961) 'The origin and early development of monopolistic competition theory', *Quarterly Journal of Economics* 75(4): 515–43.

Clark, J. M. (1940) 'Toward a concept of workable competition', *American Economic Review* 45 (June): 241–56.

Cyert, R. M. and March, J. G. (1963) *Behavioural Theory of the Firm*, Englewood Cliffs, N.J.: Prentice Hall.

Devine, P. J., Lee, N., Jones, R. M. and Tyson, W. J. (1973) *An Introduction to Industrial Economics*, London: Allen & Unwin; 4th edn 1985.
Downie, J. (1956) 'How should we control monopoly? II', *Economic Journal* 66: 573–7.
—— (1958) *The Competitive Process*, London: Duckworth.
Foss, N. (1994) 'The economic thought of an Austrian Marshallian: George Barclay Richardson', *Journal of Economic Studies* 22: 23–44.
—— (1998) 'Austrian and post-Marshallian economics: change and organisation in the context of George Richardson's work', in N. J. Foss and B. J. Loasby *Economic Organization, Capabilities and Co-ordination*, London: Routledge.
Hicks, J. R. (1946) *Value and Capital*, Oxford: Oxford University Press.
Loasby, B. (1991) *Equilibrium and Evolution*, Manchester: Manchester University Press.
Marshall, A. (1920) *Principles of Economics: An Introductory Volume*, London: Macmillan.
Metcalfe, J. S. (1984) 'Technological innovation and the competitive process', *Greek Economic Review* (November): 287–316.
—— (1989) 'Evolution and economic change', in A. Silberston (ed.) *Technology and Economic Progress*, London: Macmillan.
—— (1994) 'Competition, Fisher's principle and increasing returns in the selection process', *Journal of Evolutionary Economics* 4: 327–46.
Nelson, R. R. and Winter, S. (1982) *An Evolutionary Theory of Economic Change*, Cambridge, Mass.: Belknap Press of the Harvard University Press.
Nightingale, J. (1993) 'Solving Marshall's problem with the biological analogy', *History of Economics Review* 20: 75–94; reproduced in G. Hodgson (ed.) (1995) *Economics and Biology*, Cheltenham: Edward Elgar.
—— (in press) 'Jack Downie's *Competitive Process*: the first articulated population ecology model in economics', *History of Political Economy*; currently available as *School of Economics Working Paper No. 9*, Griffith University, May 1996.
O'Brien, D. (1995) 'Information and investment in a wider context', *Working Paper No. 145*, Durham: Durham University Economics Department.
Penrose, E. T. (1952) 'Biological analogies in the theory of the firm', *American Economic Review* 42: 814–15.
Richardson, G. B. (1960) *Information and Investment: A Study in the Working of the Competitive Economy*, Oxford: Oxford University Press; 2nd edn 1990.
—— (1972) 'The organisation of industry', *Economic Journal* 82: 883–96.
—— (1995) personal communication.
Salter, W. E. G. (1969) *Productivity and Technical Change*, Cambridge: Cambridge University Press.
Steindl, J. (1942) 'Capitalist enterprise and risk', *Oxford Economic Papers* 7: 21–35.
—— (1945) *Small and Big Business*, Oxford: Blackwell.
—— (1952) *Maturity and Stagnation in American Capitalism*, Oxford: Blackwell; 2nd edn 1976.
Stiglitz, J. E. (1994) *Whither Socialism*, Cambridge, Mass.: MIT Press.
Wilson, T. (1984) 'The microeconomic basis of microeconomic policy', *Inflation, Unemployment and the Market*, Oxford: Oxford University Press.
Young, W. and Lee, F. S. (1994) *Oxford Economics and Oxford Economists, 1920–1990*, Oxford: Oxford University Press.

8

AUSTRIAN AND POST-MARSHALLIAN ECONOMICS

The bridging work of George Richardson

Nicolai J. Foss

INTRODUCTION[1]

At first glance, there seems to be little similarity between Austrian and post-Marshallian economics. On the one side, we have one of the three distinct marginalist traditions, originating in Austria in 1871, and recently flourishing in the United States (Vaughn 1994). In its modern incarnation, the Austrian school has laid particular emphasis on economic methodology and research into the entrepreneurial role in the market process. On the other side, we confront representatives of the genuine Marshallian tradition, who have mainly written on industrial organisation and firm behaviour.

In contrast, Austrians have written relatively little on these subjects, and do not seem to have been particularly comfortable with Marshallian doctrines. For example, to Austrians Marshall's halfway house between Ricardian cost theory and subjective value theory is a hopeless muddle that neglects the utility dimension of costs; his understanding of economics as being occupied with material well-being smacks of an objectivism that is foreign to Austrian subjectivism; and Marshall's claim that 'Economics contains no long chains of deductive reasoning' (Marshall 1925: 781) will certainly not appeal to Austrians brought up on Mises's apriorist methodology. On the whole, there seem to be numerous and deep differences between the Marshallian and the Austrian traditions.

However, in a broader perspective, the differences between Marshall and at least some of the Austrians, particularly Carl Menger, may be smaller than their differences from the kind of neoclassical economics that came to dominate during the 1930s. In fact, as Brian Loasby (1993b) tells in his 'Counterfactual history of twentieth century economics', the leaders of the anti-Walrasian opposition were Menger and Marshall, who shared the central concern of (some of) the classical economists: the growth and organisation of productive knowledge. By implication, Mengerians and Marshallians may share similar concerns.

In the present chapter I link up with this more conciliatory reading of the Marshallian/Austrian relationship. I begin by providing a brief and admittedly somewhat superficial *tour d'horizon* over the relevant issues, arguing that the ideas of Marshall's true heirs – from D. H. MacGregor, over Philip Andrews, Edith Penrose, Jack Downie and George Richardson to Brian Loasby – are, in a number of dimensions, closely related to Austrian doctrines (see 'Marshall, the post-Marshallians and Austrian economics', pp. 140–4). Both traditions are ultimately deeply concerned with change, including unanticipated change, and how to adapt effectively to such change.

In particular, this emphasis on change is accompanied by an understanding of institutions and organisations as means to adapt to change. For example, the Austrians had, at least since the socialist calculation debate of the 1930s, a clear grasp of the incentive properties of alternative institutions, but their later emphasis on the growth and co-ordination of knowledge does not in all (or even most) dimensions reduce to static incentive considerations.

Relatedly, the post-Marshallian understanding of the firm as a repository of productive knowledge is quite different from the modern contractual view of firms as incentive systems (Holmstrom and Milgrom 1994). Both the Austrian and the post-Marshallian perspectives on economic organisation are therefore distinct from the contemporary Coasian strand of organisational economics.

More focus on the Austrian/post-Marshallian connection is provided by an attempt to uncover those themes that are particularly germane to Austrian economics in the work of George Richardson (see 'George Richardson: Marshallian answers to Austrian problems', pp. 144–52). While Richardson's contributions have not gone completely unnoticed among Austrian economists,[2] I am not aware of any comprehensive analysis of the similarities. But they are there; and the more obvious similarities have to do with Richardson's concern with the co-ordination problem, his welfare economics, his process view of the market, his subjectivism, and his Marshallian view of markets and their various 'imperfections' as information structures.

Because of this, Richardson's work is particularly likely to serve as a *bridge* for a future dialogue between Austrians and post-Marshallians. Specifically, I argue that points of contact may well lie in the emerging 'capabilities perspective' on the firm, which in many respects reflects the issues that have traditionally been central to Austrians and post-Marshallians (see 'Austrian and post-Marshallian economics: the theory of the firm', pp. 152–6).

MARSHALL, THE POST-MARSHALLIANS AND AUSTRIAN ECONOMICS

That it may be worthwhile to examine the Austrian/post-Marshallian connection is indicated by, for example, Peter Earl's reference to a group of 'English economists who have been concerned ... with the theory of the firm in its market context ... [and] share a ... subjectivist, disequilibrium view' (Earl 1983: 91). Now, Austrians traditionally have not been much concerned with 'the theory of the firm in its market context', but they too share 'a subjectivist, disequilibrium view' that goes back – in its essentials – to Menger (Streissler 1972).[3] In the Austrian scheme of things, we look to economic theory 'to help us understand how the decisions of individual participants in the market interact to generate the market forces which compel *changes* in prices, in outputs, and in the methods of production, and the allocation of resources' (Kirzner 1973: 6).

Post-Marshallians are likely to agree with this causal–genetic approach to economic explanation. For example, George Richardson argued that 'a proper understanding and evaluation of the competitive economy [is] to be obtained by studying the actual process of adaptation and not by taking the illusory short cut ... of equilibrium' (Richardson 1960: 107). Where post-Marshallians and Austrians may differ, however, is rather in the attention paid to some of the constituent mechanisms of the market process, particularly firm behaviour. Furthermore, rather than tending to see the market process as predominantly a matter of successful entrepreneurial discovery (as in Kirzner 1973), post-Marshallians tend to invest their view of the process with more distinctly evolutionary elements, explicitly emphasising processes of differential firm growth.[4] This evolutionary, disequilibrium view arguably dates back to Marshall (Loasby 1990). So Marshall is where we should start in order to understand the post-Marshallians.

Marshall and the new theory of value

One sometimes becomes tempted to say that the important thing about Marshall is that he did *not* invent 'intermediate microeconomics'; that particular type of 'Marshallian' doctrine was developed primarily by Pigou, Viner and Robinson. Instead, Marshall – at least in his later years – saw the development of the mechanical theory of equilibrium as merely a stepping stone to the development of a more comprehensive and satisfactory theory of economic change, inspired by the work of Charles Darwin and particularly Herbert Spencer. That story is fairly well known, as is the fact that the biologically inspired theory largely remained ill developed (Thomas 1991).

From the beginning of the 1920s, Marshall's programme seemed to be progressively accumulating empirical and theoretical anomalies. The Pigou–Clapham 'boxes' debate was the first serious manifestation of this.

Crucially, in 1926 Piero Sraffa changed the terms of the 'boxes' debate from a debate about the empirical significance of Marshallian categories to a debate about the theoretical consistency of the Marshallian edifice. The focus changed from empirical to theoretical anomalies. Sraffa's message was that theorists either had to adopt monopoly theory as the standard market theory or had to work with general equilibrium analysis. Sraffa himself clearly preferred the first option, and Joan Robinson followed him in this. As we know well today, however, in a somewhat longer perspective, the profession turned towards the second option.

The new value theory represented a true *break* with Marshall's theoretical edifice – rather than a continuation, refinement and elaboration of it. It is noteworthy that the new theoretical style that became dominant during the 1930s also had the effect of squeezing out the Mengerian tradition.[5] On the whole, the new value theory implied a successful suppression of processual approaches to economics. From a subjectivist or process perspective, this implied a substantial Kuhnian 'loss of content' (O'Brien 1984): on an overall level, all of that in Marshall's and also – albeit more indirectly – Menger's work which can be said to have had an 'evolutionary', developmental, institutional or historical character was effectively eliminated by the new value theory.

That a clean break was involved is perhaps clearest with regard to the theory of the firm. Here, Marshall's analysis of organisation, his 'trees in the forest' metaphor, etc., all of which were designed to emphasise the essential heterogeneity of firms, were discarded in favour of the uniform equilibrium firm, which logically made evolutionary reasoning impossible and suppressed any co-ordination problems between firms.

The post-Marshallian and Austrian rearguard actions

Not everybody accepted the changes brought about by the new value theory. In hindsight, the two groups who put forward the most sophisticated and sustained critique of the new microeconomics were the post-Marshallians, primarily Philip Andrews, Jack Downie, Edith Penrose and George Richardson, and the Austrians, particularly Hayek, Lachmann and, somewhat later, Kirzner. Where Hayek's strictures (Hayek 1948) broadly centred on the suppression in the new value theory of the dispersal of knowledge and the unfortunate consequences of this for understanding the competitive process in its entirety, the post-Marshallians had a somewhat more narrow orientation, and chose the firm in its market setting as their prime object of analysis.

Assuredly, both groups strongly criticised the conceptualisation of competition in the new value theory, and promoted a process approach in its stead. It is telling in this respect to compare, for example, Hayek's 'The meaning of competition' (1946) with Andrews's (1964) or Richardson's

(1960) reflections on the same subject. Like the Austrians, the post-Marshallians all rejected the perfect competition framework for practically all analytical purposes. This was a matter of its flagrant descriptive unrealism (Andrews), its suppression of any scope for evolutionary (Downie) or developmental (Penrose) reasoning, and its logical inconsistencies and suppression of any co-ordination problems (Richardson).

Hand in hand with the rejection of the perfect competition framework went also a rejection of the 'marginalist' theory of the firm (Andrews 1949, 1964; Downie 1958: ch. 2; Penrose 1959; Lee and Earl 1993); in fact, one sometimes gets the impression – particularly from Andrews's work – that perfect competition is rejected *because* it implies a distorted view of the firm. On the positive side, the post-Marshallians reacted by turning their attention either to detailing the behaviour of oligopolistic firms (Penrose, Andrews) or to elaborating the evolutionary intentions in Marshall's work (Downie). The one attempt to keep an eye on both the firm and the industry level is represented by Richardson's overall work. Here we find both an emphasis on the skill and capability endowments of individual firms (Richardson 1972), and an emphasis on industry-level selection forces (Richardson 1960: ch. 7).[6]

Subjectivism and economic change

Apart from their shared interest in the firm, the post-Marshallians were also united in an overall subjectivist perspective: like the Austrians, they (most obviously Penrose (1959: 41) and Richardson) are subjectivists in the sense that they see subjectively held, dispersed and changing knowledge, as well as the expectations produced on the basis of this knowledge, as absolutely crucial for understanding economic events. As Penrose was at pains to emphasise (*ibid.*: ch. 2), interpretive frameworks differ over firms, and it is to a large extent such differences that are determinative of market dynamics. For example, the experience of the management team determines its interpretative framework and therefore the 'productive opportunity set' it can conceive of. It is the market that sorts among such interpretive frameworks; indeed, according to Downie (1958: 13), who did most out of this, the market acts as a Hayekian discovery procedure (Hayek 1968).

In other words, both traditions conceptualise the economic problem as one 'not only of allocative logic but of search and discovery' (Richardson 1971: 244; compare Hayek 1946, 1968), so that 'concentrating on growth and change rather than equilibrium' (Downie 1958: 7) is warranted. This change-oriented perspective is, in both traditions, accompanied by a perspective on institutions and organisations as devices for adapting to change. Such a perspective was clearly championed by Marshall when he argued that 'organisation' was intimately related to 'forecasting the future ... and [the] willingness to make provisions for it' (Marshall 1925:

139). It was later echoed in Hayek's claim that 'economic problems arise always and only in consequence of change' (Hayek 1945: 82), and that this warranted attention to organisations and (primarily) institutions.

Theory and empirical reality

Where the post-Marshallians may perhaps diverge from the Austrians has to do with their strong empirical orientation. This led them to emphasise that conceptualisations of reality should be allowed significantly to influence theorising, rather than the perception of economic reality being wholly determined by the theoretical armoury at hand (as argued most directly by Lucas 1980). Therefore, case studies were seen as an important way of furthering research (Penrose 1960; Lee and Earl 1993).

This strongly empirical orientation, as well as the accompanying methodological perspective on the interaction between theory and empirical reality, may seem to clash head on with the apriorist tendency that has traditionally characterised (plagued?) Austrian economics. But need it be so? No other than Mises (1949: 59–64) emphasised that the categories of pure economics could only be fully utilised in applied research when combined with insight in the meaning structures through which real-world actors orient themselves. This is the more interpretivistic – dating back to the Austrians' debt to the German hermeneutics of the nineteenth century – side of Austrian economics, perhaps best represented by the work of Ludwig Lachmann (1986). And this type of Austrian economics may not at all be in conflict with the 'anthropological' (O'Brien 1985: 38) research strategy favoured by some of the post-Marshallians (notably Andrews). In fact, a modern Austrian, Don Lavoie (1990), has even been close to endorsing Lester's attack on marginalism as against Machlup's defence, and has advocated precisely a more anthropological/interpretive approach to the study of firms.

Summing up

The similarities between Austrians and post-Marshallians are in many respects more numerous than their similarities to formalist mainstream economics. They share the fundamental emphasis on subjectivism, dispersed knowledge, disequilibrium and the need for causal–genetic explanation; they emphasise the need to adapt to (unforeseen) economic change, and view institutions and organisations in this light. Both are 'economics of time and ignorance' (O'Driscoll and Rizzo 1985), and their relative lack of awareness of each other arguably cannot be explained by inconsistent *Weltanschauungen*. Where they differ lies primarily in their *focusing* on the basic disequilibrium, subjectivist stance in different ways.

Notably, the post-Marshallians and the Austrians differ in terms of attention paid to *the firm*. Whereas firm behaviour and organisation are probably the single most important problem area of post-Marshallian economics, they are almost entirely neglected in Austrian economics. Before I discuss this problem, I further examine the relation between post-Marshallian and Austrian economics, focusing on Richardson's work. His work is, for several reasons, particularly interesting in the present context. For example, he stands out among the post-Marshallians as being explicitly influenced by Austrian economics. Possibly for this reason, the frequency of shared themes is remarkably high. As a result, Richardson's work is particularly likely to serve a bridging role between the two traditions.

GEORGE RICHARDSON: MARSHALLIAN ANSWERS TO AUSTRIAN PROBLEMS

Marshall and Hayek

For more than twenty years, from the early 1950s well into the 1970s, George Richardson produced a string of extremely original contributions to the post-Marshallian tradition, many of which were strongly mixed with Austrian spices. Thus, he is the first economist to forge explicit links between the two traditions. Although Marshall is arguably the major influence, Hayek's influence on Richardson almost rivals Marshall's. In particular, Hayek's famous 1937 essay 'Economics and knowledge' left a strong imprint on Richardson's thinking (Richardson 1953: 136n.; 1960: 6; 1993a, 1993b).[7] However, it is notable that those aspects of Marshall's work that seem to have inspired Richardson the most are also those that are most broadly compatible with Austrian thinking. For example, the Marshallian influence is clearly present in Richardson's methodological discussions, for example in his scepticism towards analogies from physics (Richardson 1953: 153; 1960: 41n.), a view that any Austrian would clearly endorse (e.g. Hayek 1943).

Equally Marshallian is the warning against excessive reification of economic concepts, something which may 'distort our vision of the plain facts of economic life' (Richardson 1971: 244). As Richardson further explains, the history of economics demonstrates how awareness of 'of important aspects of reality may be inhibited ... by the particular conceptual framework we employ' (Richardson 1960: 138). Austrians would be likely to agree with this. It has been a constant theme in Austrian economics that, most notably, the perfect competition framework is likely seriously to distort our comprehension of economic reality (for example Hayek 1946). In this connection, Austrians would wish to point to the so-called 'socialist calculation debate' as a particularly illuminating example: the fact that the market socialists of the 1930s based their theorising on the perfect competition model and were thought to have won the debate meant that attention to many relevant issues (identified by the Austrians) became suppressed for decades (Lavoie 1985; Foss 1994a: ch. 4). Although incentives and dispersed knowledge were formally treated in mechanism design models, the roles of tacit knowledge, process and discovery were neglected. From a subjectivist perspective, these models therefore cannot satisfactorily confront the real alternatives: the tacit and process aspects of the real-world economic problem are suppressed.

Richardson's perspective on economic organisation is quite similar to this: he rejects ascribing exorbitant amounts of knowledge to agents,[8] and emphasises that the problem of economic organisation must begin from the Marshallian premise that in the real world 'Organization aids knowledge' (Marshall 1925: 138). But before we can understand why organisation aids knowledge, we must understand why (dispersed) knowledge raises a problem at all. In clarifying this, Richardson seems to have been strongly influenced by Hayek's (1937) carefully elaborated distinction between the pure logic of choice, which we utilise for understanding individual decisions, and the societal problem of co-ordination, which is a matter of making all the different pieces of knowledge mesh (for example Richardson 1959: 224–5). According to Hayek (1937), economic theory had not successfully established a correspondence between these two different allocation problems, basically because of its suppression of the issue of how economic agents get access to knowledge that will allow them to implement equilibrium plans.

This is indeed a – perhaps *the* – crucial theme in Richardson's writings, too. In fact, at least one of his articles (Richardson 1959) is essentially a restatement of the problems Hayek had identified in more Marshallian terms, and therefore explicitly formulated in the context of a *production* economy. However, Richardson basically supplies Marshallian answers to the Austrian problem of co-ordination; in a way, he suggests Marshallian 'statements about how knowledge is acquired and communicated' (Hayek 1937: 33). Let us take a brief look at how Richardson conceives of the problem and the answers he provides.

Information and investment

Consistent with the research strategy he had been taught by his one-time thesis adviser, John Hicks, namely to go back to the older influential writers rather than to modern writers, Richardson opens *Information and Investment* with a critique of Walras. It is appropriate that Richardson's main work should begin with such a critique, for, as he later recalled, 'It was indeed while reading Walras that I came to realise the confusion at the core of the General Equilibrium Theory' (Richardson 1993a). Predictably, Walras is criticised for his specific way of suppressing the co-ordination problem with the fictitious *auctionarius*. This leads into a more general critique of how economists have traditionally described 'The tendency to equilibrium' (the title of the first chapter). Today such a discussion would probably have taken place under the title 'the stability problem' (Fisher 1983), that is to say, the problem of how economic agents can hope to implement consistent plans when they are initially ignorant about with whom, on what terms, when, where, etc. they can trade.

It is important to emphasise this *informational* interpretation of the stability problem, since in its older (and non-informational) version it implies an analogy to mechanics that was, and remains, wholly alien to Richardson's outlook (Richardson 1993b). The reason that the problem has to be cast in informational terms is essentially that 'no direct connection can exist between objective conditions and purposive activity; the immediate relationship is between *beliefs* about relevant conditions and *planned* activities which it may or may not prove possible to implement' (Richardson 1959: 224).

This subjectivist statement clearly echoes to Hayek's earlier insight that 'The equilibrium relationships cannot be deduced merely from the objective facts, since the analysis of what people will do can start only from what is known to them' (Hayek 1937: 44).

Although he is not without predecessors (e.g. Morgenstern 1935; Hayek 1937), Richardson presents what is probably the most acute critique of economists' excessive preoccupation with equilibrium positions to the neglect of how these positions are actually attained, before Frank Hahn, Franklin Fisher and others voiced some the same concerns ten years later.[9] According to Richardson, the problems with the usual adjustment stories are that they are unrealistic, mechanical, ad hoc, and violate the principle of methodological individualism (Richardson 1960: 24). All this implies that, in a methodological sense, no satisfactory *explanation* of equilibrium has been provided, only a description of the explanandum, with a fundamentally ad hoc explanans tagged on.

However, it is more serious than that; for Richardson is strongly questioning the very possibility of demonstrating any tendency towards equilibrium within the Walrasian model. One can, for the sake of hypothesis, assume that somehow – for example, by pure luck – agents were able to home in on a co-ordinated state. If in this situation a disequilibrium should develop, it will not be possible to return to the equilibrium. More generally, 'the familiar "general equilibrium of production and exchange" cannot properly be regarded as a configuration towards which a hypothetical perfectly competitive economy would gravitate' (Richardson 1959: 19).[10] So, as Joan Robinson is reported to have said, 'In order to get into equilibrium, one has to be in equilibrium'. Let us see why.

Suppose that producers are hit by some increase in demand that affects them all and is expected to persist. What will be their responses; how much plant should they order? The problem is that the information on other firms' investment decisions that would be necessary for calculating optimal investments is not available to anyone, given the assumptions of the model. It is not incorporated in any given Debreu-type states of nature. Firms may guess, of course, but those guesses must involve the guesses of other firms, which would seem to lead into an infinite regress. The endogenous uncertainty created implies that there is no equilibrium in the sequence of guesses, which implies that there is no single exit solution for any agent in the system. This is how we end up with the proposition that 'A general profit opportunity, which is both known to everyone, and equally capable of being exploited by everyone, is, in an important sense, a profit opportunity for no one in particular' (Richardson 1960: 57).

This counter-finality indicates the existence of an internal theoretical anomaly in the form of an internal contradiction deep at the heart of neoclassical economics, or at least general equilibrium economics. It is not merely that neoclassical economics does not contain any causal mechanisms that help us understand how order comes about, as Hayek (1937) argued; the problem is that the whole operation is condemned from the beginning: an institutionless Walrasian production economy simply cannot function.[11]

Rationality and ad-hocery

In his critique of the Walrasian model, Richardson has two distinguished Austrian precursors. Like Hayek (1937), Richardson is criticising the assumption that there is a direct connection between the allocation problem of the perfectly rational representative agent and market-level allocation; in the absence of specification of the institutions under which agents interact, and therefore the information they may gain access to, there is no such connection. And, like Morgenstern (1935), Richardson points out the problems of endogenous uncertainty that perfect rationality may imply. Mainstream economists are not quite ignorant of problems of endogenous uncertainty per se, although to the extent that they are discussed, it is mostly in the context of certain oligopolistic market structures. As Richardson demonstrated, however, the problem applies to all market structures. In terms of its overall scope, Richardson's critique of received theory has a superficial similarity to Sraffa's theory of three decades earlier, in identifying an internal theoretical anomaly in price theory and in its concentration on the supply curve. However, his is by far the more fundamental.

Richardson is not only questioning the use of equilibrium theory in the absence of a sound stability theoretic foundation (Richardson 1960: ch. 1); he is also pointing out that neoclassical economics has *its* amount of ad hoc theorising. Fundamentally, this has to do with the kind of indeterminacy that Richardson highlighted in the Walrasian model, an indeterminacy that is most obvious in the case of dynamic adjustment processes and which is eliminated by routinely adding various ad hoc devices to the formal theory. A catalogue of these devices would begin, of course, with Walras's auctioneer, continue with Milton Friedman's (1953) appeal to strong selection forces on the supply side of the market in order to justify maximisation and equilibrium, and proceed to the ad hoc auctions that are routinely postulated in some of the modern neoclassical literature on innovation (see Reinganum 1989) and on capacity expansion problems in oligopolies when entry is allowed (Ghemawat 1986).

These devices allow the analyst to sidestep precisely the adjustment problems that Richardson highlighted. However, they are essentially theoretically unrelated to the formal theory. For example, the evolutionary market processes that Friedman (1953) appeals to do not incorporate maximisation and equilibrium. But these processes are the basis on which the validity of these two concepts are *really* argued. Thus, a quite natural question to ask is: Why not take them seriously?, that is, theoretically approach them (cf. Nelson and Winter 1982). By the same token, if our faith in the relative efficiency of the market system lies not only in ascribing rationality to agents, but also in the institutions and constraints the system incorporates, why not theoretically approach them, too? This would seem necessary, particularly when we consider the Richardsonian recognition that there cannot be exchange in isolation from market institutions.

Institutions

Much of modern economics has recently taken an 'institutional turn', as witnessed by work on, for example, transaction cost economics, property rights theory, agency theory, etc. However, also economists who are not directly affiliated with the neo-institutionalist movement have argued for more attention being paid to the institutional dimension – and often for reasons that are closely akin to the problems that Richardson was taken up with. For example, in the context of an examination of convergence to rational expectations equilibrium, Roman Frydman (1982) concluded that the possibility of demonstrating such convergence under decentralisation is remote, very much in the same spirit that Richardson concluded that perfect competition could not be regarded as a configuration that a competitive system would approach. Furthermore, Frydman suggested that

> in addition to information contained in market prices, social norms (in particular business practice) imposing some restrictions and coherence on the individual decisions and information generated by institutions external to the market may play important roles in understanding decentralized market processes.
>
> (Frydman 1982: 664)

It is very much from a similar perspective that Richardson approaches 'imperfections' and 'business practices'. For example, capital market imperfections limit access to investment funds and thereby keep in check expansion plans; and price agreements, cartel arrangement, etc. play similar roles. They exist because they allow complementary investments to be co-ordinated and hinder excessive competitive investment in the face of, for example, unforeseen changes in demand. Thus, institutions are approached in terms of their ability to accommodate economic change, much as Mises (1981) and Hayek (1945) approached the market system.

As early as 1937, Hayek also noticed that the perfectly competitive ideal made it impossible to address the existence of a number of institutions. Focusing on the dissemination of knowledge, he noted that the dominance of the perfect competition model would 'go far to account for the fact that pure analysis seems to have so extraordinarily little to say about institutions, such as the press, the purpose of which is to communicate knowledge' (Hayek 1937: 55). Hayek found that economic theory was unable to come up with a convincing answer to how plan co-ordination came about in a decentralised economy, and it can be argued that it was basically this circumstance that led Hayek to leave economics and seek a solution to the co-ordination problem in the traditional classical–liberal emphasis on evolved institutions.

Thus, both Hayek and Richardson concentrate on 'institutions' in a broad sense as the phenomena that dampen the co-ordination problem and ease adaptation to changed and perhaps unforeseen circumstances. However, Richardson seeks a solution that is internal to economic theory, while Hayek does not. Where Hayek (1973) focuses on society-wide and mostly tacit rules of behaviour, Richardson focuses solely on industry-specific 'imperfections', some of which are quite explicit (such as collusion). Therefore, Richardson may be seen as supplying Austrian economics with a much needed analysis of specific market institutions, since he addresses these institutions as solutions to essentially Austrian-type co-ordination problems. Among the Austrians, such institutions captured the interest only of Lachmann (1956, 1986).

The importance of 'imperfection' for the effective working of industry is perhaps most obvious in the case of the co-ordination of investment projects that are complementary to each other. Here, Richardson is again linking up with a favourite Austrian theme, namely the intertemporal complementarity of capital goods (Hayek 1941; Lachmann 1956). The basic theme of Austrian capital theory – that production is staged and that capital goods stand in a relation of intertemporal complementarity to each other – was attacked by Frank Knight in the 1930s as a non-issue, and survived only in development economics and in a distorted form in input–output analysis. Co-ordination problems in the intertemporal chain of production were of course the main concern of the Austrian business cycle theory of the 1930s

(Hayek 1931): co-ordination problems that could be avoided through appropriately chosen monetary policies.

In a sense, the efficient co-ordination of complementary investments is also a main message and a policy concern in Richardson's analysis; thus, here too he is reviving and elaborating an older Austrian theme. Where Richardson differs from the early Hayek is of course in denying that the price mechanism generally will do the job of co-ordinating complementary investments unassisted. This is argued in much the same way as it is argued that the pure price mechanism cannot yield an optimal amount of competitive investment (Richardson 1960: 76–7). Again, 'imperfections' such as reputation, trust and contractual agreements perform the tasks of easing knowledge flows over stages of production and contributing commitments.

Planning and investments

There is a direct, though neglected, link from Richardson's early work (1953, 1956, 1959, 1960) on co-ordination problems to his acclaimed work on inter-firm relations (1972). The link is provided by Richardson's 1969 consultancy report for the British Electrical and Allied Manufacturers' Association (BEAMA), *The Future of the Heavy Electrical Plant Industry*, and his 1971 article on 'Planning versus competititon'.

The report was written in the context of the aftermath of a co-ordination failure for complementary investments associated with projections of economic growth in the Labour Government's 1965 National Plan (Richardson 1969: 8), a co-ordination failure that Austrians may invoke in support of their views on public intervention. Specifically, there had been wide and unpredictable fluctuations taking place in the electricity authorities' demand for heavy plant; in fact, a massive over-ordering of generating equipment, which was the price of consistency with the Plan. This lack of co-ordination of complementary investments was only part of the problem; for there was also a problem of co-ordination of competitive investments that arose because of the particular organisation of the power station equipment industry. The industry in fact confronted the destructive situation that relates to the co-ordination of competitive investments under competition so dramatically portrayed by Richardson in *Information and Investment*. As a result, it was virtually impossible for firms in the industry to operate on a profitable basis under competitive tendering.

Given that Richardson's 1969 report was very much written in the context of indicative planning gone wrong, it is perhaps not surprising that he should turn his attention towards comparative systems issues. In addition to putting forward a number of fresh arguments on the particular issue under consideration, 'Planning versus competition' (1971) is also noteworthy for its anticipation of some of the central points in the much better known 1972 article on 'The organisation of industry'. It is here that

Richardson for the first time systematically inquires into alternative forms of economic organisation – markets, inter-firm arrangements, firms – in a private property market economy.

The organisation of industry

Thus, we finally emerge at Richardson's 1972 masterpiece. Industry, says Richardson, may be thought of as composed of numerous 'activities' (R&D, manufacturing, sales and service, etc.), which have to be carried out by firms with the requisite 'capabilities'. Activities which require the same or closely related capabilities are 'similar'. Similar activities are seldom complementary, since complementary activities typically occupy different stages of production. Firms find it expedient to concentrate on similar activities, since incorporating 'dissimilar' activities bring diseconomies of scope and/or increased information costs. This forms a basis for a theory of 'co-operation', that is, of inter-firm relations, such as long-term contracts, joint ventures, licensing agreements, etc.: firms enter into co-operative relations when they need access to upstream or downstream complementary but dissimilar activities. Activities that are 'closely complementary' will typically be under common ownership.

In this view of industry, the existence of numerous bonds, ties, commitments, etc. between firms, developed because activities may be dissimilar but complementary, *stabilises* the system and secures its effective working. Richardson's work during the 1960s primarily focused on *horizontal* inter-firm relations and agreements (Richardson 1965, 1967), such as price notification schemes, and therefore primarily addressed the issue of the co-ordination of *competitive* investments. His 1972 article, partially preceded by the 1969 BEAMA consultancy report and the 1971 article, extended the focus to vertical arrangements, addressing *complementary* investments.

Clearly, the argument to a large extent turns on the tacit knowledge underlying capabilities; it is because this knowledge can be transferred and acquired only at great cost that firms avoid integrating dissimilar activities (cf. Demsetz 1988). And partly because of such tacitness, the individual firm will not normally have superior or even precise knowledge about the whole of the production process into which its products enter. It is likely that nobody will in fact possess all of this knowledge. However, to paraphrase Hayek (1945) with a bow to Richardson, 'the marvel' is precisely that competition *and co-operation* ensure that effective use is made of capabilities that are not possessed by any single firm. Firms are not completely self-contained; as Richardson (1972: 885) points out, effective co-operation will normally require some knowledge of 'neighbouring' capabilities (those possessed by other firms) in order for 'their limited individual fields of vision sufficiently [to] overlap so that the relevant information is communicated' (Hayek 1945: 86).

Richardson also links up with the Austrian understanding of the market in a somewhat different way. In Richardson's perspective, much of 'the organisation of industry' is a matter of discovering which capabilities are best for you (as a producer), where and when. Now, Hayek saw 'The function of competition' as primarily a matter of teaching us *'who* will serve us well; which grocer or travel agency, which department store or hotel, which doctor or solicitor, we can expect to provide the most satisfactory solution for whatever particular personal problem we may have to face' (Hayek 1946: 97; italics in original). Thus, one of the benefits of the market system, including its modes of competition and co-operation, is that it makes *capabilities* visible to the participants.

Summing up

While Richardson *focuses* his basic insights in economic organisation in ways that are often (due to the Marshallian heritage) different from Austrian economics, the fact that these insights are in themselves quite close to basic Austrian themes remains. For example, like Marshall (Loasby 1990), Richardson is concerned with the organisation and growth of knowledge. But so is Hayek; indeed, perhaps his primary argument for market organisation is precisely that it is (compared to central planning) a superior means of discovering and testing new knowledge, and he quite explicitly draws on the growth of knowledge literature in developing this argument (Hayek 1968).

Moreover, much of Richardson's work may be seen as complementary to an Austrian process view of the market. In this perspective, he supplies that analysis of market institutions which is so sorely missing in most Austrian accounts of the market process. In, for example, Israel Kirzner's account of the entrepreneurial market process (Kirzner 1973), the entrepreneur is portrayed as acting in an institutional vacuum; this is one reason why it is so hard meaningfully to evaluate Kirzner's claim that the market process is inherently equilibrating. Moreover, like other post-Marshallians but unlike the Austrians, Richardson theorises the firm. In the following section, I further explore the complementarity between Richardson's capabilities view and Austrian economics, focusing on the firm. I offer this as an example of a common hunting ground for the Austrian and post-Marshallian traditions.

AUSTRIAN AND POST-MARSHALLIAN ECONOMICS: THE THEORY OF THE FIRM

Austrian economics and the theory of the firm

It has often been observed that Austrian economics does not feature a theory of the firm (O'Driscoll and Rizzo 1985; Loasby 1989, 1992; Langlois

1992b; Foss 1994b; Minkler 1993). This is a paradoxical feature, since what may arguably be 'the most obvious deficiency in Austrian economics' (Loasby 1989: 166) lies in the market process itself. Austrians have next to nothing to say about pricing, buyer–seller relations, vertical integration and other aspects of economic organisation; in other words, one of the most important constituent mechanisms of the market process, namely firm behaviour, is simply not theorised in Austrian economics. In contrast, firm behaviour has captured the lion's share of interest among post-Marshallians. This is perhaps not surprising, given that Marshall was the first economist (at least among the neoclassicals) to give much attention to the firm.

Elsewhere I have observed that it is really something of a doctrinal puzzle that the Austrians never came forward with a theory of the firm (Foss 1994b). This is the case because they had so many of the necessary elements of modern theories of the firm, such as a basic understanding of the principal–agent relationship (Mises 1981), dispersed knowledge (Hayek 1945), 'routines' (broadly conceived) (Hayek 1973), knowledge costs (Hayek 1937), asset specificity and complementarity (Hayek 1931), and an emphasis on unexpected change (Hayek 1945). The reason for this apparent lack may well be that the Austrians were busy defending themselves against the attacks of Keynes, Sraffa, Knight and the market socialists. Another, more trivial, reason may simply be that they, like most other contemporary economists, were not interested in the firm and therefore never thought of approaching firms in terms of the above theoretical insights.

Malmgren (1961): Richardsonian arguments and the firm

Whatever that may be, it is still possible to distil Austrian insights of relevance to the theory of the firm. For example, in a splendid essay, Richard Langlois (1992b) argues that the Austrian (Hayekian) understanding of social institutions as spontaneously emerging and generalised rules of behaviour may be able to further the capabilities view of the firm associated with post-Marshallians such as Penrose and Richardson and evolutionary economists Nelson and Winter (1982). However, Langlois is not the first to forge links between Austrian economics and the post-Marshallian understanding of the firm. In an article published long ago, Harold Malmgren (1961) not only significantly furthered the Coasian (1937) view of the firm, but also managed to integrate Coase's insights with post-Marshallian and Austrian insights.[12]

According to Malmgren, firms are 'put together' for a number of reasons that have little to do with the modern standard view of firm organisation, that is, as efficient institutional responses to potential misalignment of incentives (Holmstrom and Milgrom 1994). Rather than transforming non-cooperative behaviour in potential prisoner's dilemma games to co-operative behaviour, the role of firms is to provide an institutional setting that solves co-ordination-type games (cf. Foss 1993; Langlois and Robertson 1993). Thus, the 'precedents' and 'customs' of firms provide co-ordinating Schelling points, help to stabilise the expectations of input-owners, and therefore reduce transaction costs. Moreover, firms harmonise expectations in situations in which the 'output and profitability of various production units are closely interdependent'; under such circumstances, 'the firm is formed to undertake decisions concerning all or some of the production units simultaneously, so as to maximize the joint profit and total output' (Malmgren 1961: 412). Notice that all this is essentially an *application* of Richardson's (1960) industry-specific reasoning to the level of the firm: the firm is seen as an instance of particularly tight co-ordination between closely complementary assets and investments.

Arguably, the Richardson–Malmgren co-ordination view of the firm and vertical integration is in some dimension closer to Coase's (1937) original story than modern purportedly Coasian theories (such as Williamson 1985; Holmstrom and Milgrom 1994) are. Coase (1937) says nothing about misaligned incentives and he emphasises the superior adaptability – the superior co-ordinating capabilities – of the firm for some (by him unspecified) activities. These activities may typically involve closely complementary activities, and particularly *changes* in closely complementary activities are needed. Here Richardson points out that

> An entrepreneur may believe that only by gaining some degree of control over the firm responsible for some complementary investment will he be fully assured of it being undertaken; vertical integration may be carried out with this end in view.
> (Richardson 1960: 83–4)

As Morris Silver (1984) argued in a neglected contribution more then a decade ago, the economic reason why integration may be necessary under such circumstances is because of the presence of prohibitive communication costs; the relevant knowledge is wholly 'impacted' in the entrepreneur's 'vision' or in the capabilities of the firm.[13] As Malmgren put it, 'the firm predicts the costs of production of its commodities better than the market could' (Malmgren 1961: 405), and therefore may have difficulties entering into satisfactory market contracts with outside suppliers (see also Penrose 1959: 148). In other words, economic organisation largely reflects the economics of conservation of expenditures on knowledge transmission (Demsetz 1988).

This view should appeal to Austrians and post-Marshallians alike; it should appeal to post-Marshallians because it is perfectly consistent with an overall capabilities view of the firm; it should appeal to Austrians because it takes seriously the subjectivist positions that 'different men know different things' (Hayek), that 'different men have different thoughts' (Lachmann), and that communicating knowledge and thoughts is not costless. It should appeal to both groups because it explicitly places economic organisation in a dynamic context.

Economic organisation and flexibility

The idea, promoted by Coase, Malmgren and Richardson, that organisations and institutions may derive their efficiency rationales from their ability to react to economic change – that is, from 'the need for adaptability' (Richardson 1960: ch. 8) – is one that should be sympathetic to Austrians. For example, Menger's (1871) liquidity theory of *money* entails a notion of money as a flexibility-providing asset. And clearly Mises (1981) and Hayek (1945) saw the main virtue of the *market* as its superior ability to react flexibly to unexpected change (Foss 1994a). Ludwig Lachmann extended the perspective to the *entrepreneur*: 'We are living in a world of unexpected change; hence, [asset] combinations ... will ever be changing, will be dissolved and reformed. In this activity, we find the real function of the entrepreneur' (Lachmann 1956: 131). Although the Austrians never explicitly applied the idea of institutions as embodying responses to change to the firm, we may tentatively extend their perspective by suggesting that 'the real function of the firm' may lie in rapidly deploying assets in the way Lachmann saw the entrepreneurial role.

Starting a firm is one way of capturing rents on specific human capital; one that may be particularly attractive to people with entrepreneurial abilities, since it will, for a variety of reasons, be hard to trade entrepreneurial services in the market (information impactedness, moral hazard problems, etc.). Thus, in an Austrian perspective, firms may be seen as means to realise entrepreneurial visions that would not be realised in their absence. In his attempt to carry out his entrepreneurial plan, the entrepreneur will not bring all the capabilities that are complementary to his own entrepreneurial capabilities under his own direction; the services of capabilities that are not *closely* complementary can normally be acquired without problems in the market. But 'in a world of unexpected change' there will sometimes arise a need for new asset combinations and new inputs. Unexpected change feeds plan revisions, and such revisions may have implications for the boundaries of the firm. The reason? The change of the asset mix that is necessary for realising the revised plan may require new inputs from new activities and capabilities, some of which may now be closely complementary to the firm/the entrepreneur. As Richardson (1972) tells us, closely complementary (similar) activities and their underlying capabilities should be governed inside the firm. Furthermore, as Coase (1937) and Malmgren (1961) suggest, firm organisation may have cost advantages relative to the market in rapidly redeploying assets (of the sort described by Silver 1984; Langlois 1992a; Langlois and Robertson 1993; Foss 1993).

Thus, if markets, in the Austrian tradition, may be seen to incorporate capabilities of flexible adaptation to unforeseen change (Mises 1981; Hayek 1945), firms may be seen in much the same light (Richardson 1960: ch. 8; Malmgren 1961).[14] This perspective on both firms and markets as flexibility-providing institutions is one that dispels simplistic ideas of the one as inherently superior to the other in terms of flexibility; an idea that has marred much of the debate on 'Fordism v. flexible specialisation'. Clearly, firms may sometimes be more flexible than markets; Alfred Chandler's work in business history is testimony to that. On the other hand, decentralised networks of firms may be more flexible in terms of rapidly testing a number of, for example, technological designs; however, as William Lazonick (1991) argues, there are several historical examples (particularly British examples) of decentralised networks of firms being unable to adopt new (systemic) innovations, thus being in some sense inflexible. In other words, what may count more than the kind of economic organisation is the *kind* of capabilities that are involved.

CONCLUSION

I have argued that Austrians and post-Marshallians share some important characteristics that set them apart from the mainstream in modern economics. Considerations of space have allowed me only to scratch the surface; more specific similarities and dissimilarities have not been discussed, merely the important overall shared characteristics. These characteristics have to do with a subjectivist perspective on knowledge, an emphasis on disequilibrium and a concern with institutional change. Another way to phrase the issue is that the Austrians and the post-Marshallians are united in a concern with those aspects of the classical (particularly Smithian) edifice that, although they survived the marginalist revolution (primarily in Marshall and Menger's work), became suppressed with the advent of the formalist revolution in the 1930s: change, evolution, institutions and a concern with the role of knowledge in economic life. The features are particularly visible in the work of George Richardson; as a result, his work is particularly likely to serve as a bridge between the two traditions.

In terms of today's economics, the natural allies of post-Marshallians and Austrians are neo-institutionalists and evolutionary economists. But they may also benefit from dialogue. That dialogue seems to be slowly beginning. For quite some years, Brian Loasby has done much to get it started (Loasby 1989, 1992, 1993a, 1993b), and the recent work of Richard Langlois (1992a, 1992b), Alanson P. Minkler (1993) and Roger Koppl (1992) may in many respects be seen as attempts to combine Austrian and post-Marshallian insights. As I have indicated, the liaison may begin with the theory of the firm, since modern work on the capabilities view of the firm already incorporates notions that are very close to both Austrian and post-Marshallian ideas.

NOTES

1 A number of comments from Richard Arena, Peter Earl, Brian Loasby, Jaques Ravix and George Richardson on earlier versions of this paper are gratefully acknowledged. Some of the sections in this paper draw on my earlier work on Richardson (Foss 1994c, 1995).
2 See Kirzner (1962: 380n; 1973: 93n.), O'Driscoll and Rizzo (1985: 90, 223) and Lachmann (1986: 8, 11, 57n.). Littlechild mentions Richardson along with Loasby and Shackle, and observes that 'Nevertheless, these British writers have not worked consciously in the Austrian tradition, and in some respects they have gone further than the Austrians in emphasizing the unpredictability of economic events and the limited role of general equilibrium' (Littlechild 1977: 16).
3 It should be noted that the post-Marshallian–Austrian economics connection strongly depends on which *kind* of Austrian economics one focuses on. Here I primarily associate Austrian economics with Hayek (1937, 1945, 1946, 1973), Lachmann (1956, 1971, 1986), Kirzner (1973, 1986), and O'Driscoll and Rizzo (1985), rather than with the more Misesian branches of Austrian economics. Also pertinent is the interpretation of Marshall's work that is adopted. My understanding follows Loasby (1990) and O'Brien (1990) (rather than Shove, Frisch or Levine).
4 Thus, Downie (1958) talked about the 'transfer mechanism', and Richardson about (1960: 119) about 'Efficient Selection'. In contrast, Austrian interest in variety–retention–selection processes mostly relates to institutional evolution (see Hayek 1973), that is to say, to changes in the rules within which market processes take place.
5 For example, one of the most decisive events behind the elimination of the Austrian school was the debate with market socialists who had thoroughly adopted the new style. Arguably, it was as a result of this debate that the Austrians began to understand their distinctiveness (Lavoie 1985; Foss 1994a; Vaughn 1994).
6 This is despite a quite strong critique of Alchian (1950), which closely parallels Penrose's (1952) in criticising Alchian's playing down the role of intention and rationality. Evolutionary arguments are, however, not inconsistent with some measure of intention and rationality. It adds to the irony when it is recognised that Alchian explicitly saw his analysis as a continuation of *Marshall's* evolutionary thought (Alchian 1950: 19n.).
7 Though not Hayek's other writings. When *Information and Investment* was published, Richardson sent a copy to Hayek, expressing appreciation of his article, but got no reply. Political aspects may have played a role, since Richardson's somewhat more activistic emphasis on the need for government action in a market economy may not have been wholly congenial to Hayek's more radical outlook (Richardson 1993a). It should also be noted that there are no references in Richardson's work to other Austrians than Hayek, except for a brief and approving reference to Menger's liquidity theory of money (Menger 1871: ch. 8), which is correctly seen as anticipating Keynes's monetary theory (Richardson 1960: 157n.).

8 Richardson's first published article (Richardson 1953) is a very Hayekian piece on welfare economics, written in the days when enthusiasm about social welfare functions was strongest. Almost paraphrasing Hayek's famous 1945 article on 'The use of knowledge in society', Richardson argues that the economic problem of society in 'our theoretical system would most closely represent . . . that facing a single mind to which all the relevant knowledge regarding means and ends were known with certainty and as a whole; that which confronts us is entirely different . . . [T]he actual economic problem . . . is . . . to ensure that the fullest use will be made of the . . . knowledge which is dispersed among many minds' (Richardson 1953: 136).

9 Strictly speaking, Arrow (1959) had voiced *some* – but by no means all – of the same concerns before. Of course, it was Arrow's contribution that became widely quoted, and not Richardson's much richer discussion.

10 However, Richardson's version of perfect competition may differ somewhat from modern conceptions: his is a non-perfectly contestable (since investments are partially irreversible; Richardson 1960: 50), non-rational expectations set-up. Furthermore, absence of forward markets is implicitly assumed, so that expectations based on local knowledge must be substituted. Well, as Richardson shows, such expectations in fact *cannot* substitute for forward markets under atomism.

11 Clearly, simple exchange economies would not experience the sort of co-ordination failures that Richardson describes.

12 Malmgren acknowledges the help of Andrews and refers to Penrose (1959), Richardson (1960), Hayek (1937) and Lachmann (1956).

13 See Langlois (1992a), Langlois and Robertson (1993) and Foss (1993) for analyses in the spirit of Silver.

14 As Brian Loasby (1993a) argues, the market is an institutional structure that largely exists by virtue of its flexible ability to supply *options for future contracts*, whereas the firm is an institutional structure that exists because of its provision of *contracts for future options*. Thus, they are both devices for creating and preserving the possibilities of future trade when the future is uncertain to the extent that present commitments cannot be justified; they derive their value to economic agents from these characteristics.

REFERENCES

Alchian, A. A. (1950) 'Uncertainty, evolution, and economic theory', in Alchian (1977) *Economic Forces at Work*, Indianapolis: Liberty Press.

Andrews, P. W. S. (1949) *Manufacturing Business*, London: Macmillan.

—— (1964) *On Competition in Economic Theory*, London: Macmillan.

Arrow, K. J. (1959) 'Toward a theory of price adjustment', in M. Abramovitz (ed.) *The Allocation of Economic Resources: Essays in Honor of Bernard Francis Haley*, Stanford, Calif.: Stanford University Press.

Caldwell, B. and Böhm, S. (eds) (1992) *Austrian Economics: Tensions and New Directions*, Boston, Mass.: Kluwer.

Coase, R. H. (1937) 'The nature of the firm', in J. B. Barney and W. G. Ouchi (eds) (1988) *Organizational Economics*, San Francisco: Jossey-Bass.

Demsetz, H. (1988) 'The theory of the firm revisited', *Journal of Law, Economics, and Organization* 4: 141–62.

Downie, J. (1958) *The Competitive Process* London: Duckworth.

Earl, P. E. (1983) 'A behavioral theory of economists' behavior', in A. S. Eichner (ed.) *Why Economics Is Not Yet a Science*, London: Macmillan.
—— (1993) 'Whatever happened to Andrews' industrial economics', in F. S. Lee and P. E. Earl *The Economics of Competitive Enterprise: Selected Essays of P. W. S. Andrews*, Aldershot: Edward Elgar.
Fisher, F. M. (1983) *Disequilibrium Foundations of Equilibrium Economics*, Cambridge: Cambridge University Press.
Foss, N. J. (1993) 'The theory of the firm: contractual and competence perspectives', *Journal of Evolutionary Economics* 3 : 127–44.
—— (1994a) *The Austrian School and Modern Economics: Essays in Reassessment*, Copenhagen: Copenhagen Business School Press.
—— (1994b) 'The theory of the firm: the Austrians as precursors and critics of contemporary theory', *Review of Austrian Economics* 7: 31–65.
—— (1994c) 'Cooperation is competition: George Richardson on coordination and interfirm relations', *British Review of Economic Issues* 16: 25–49.
—— (1995) 'The economic doctrines of an Austrian Marshallian: George Barclay Richardson', *Journal of Economic Studies* 22: 23–44.
Friedman, M. (1953) 'The methodology of positive economics', *Essays on Positive Economics*, Chicago: University of Chicago Press.
Frydman, R. (1982) 'Towards an understanding of market processes: individual expectations, learning and convergence to rational expectations equilibrium', *American Economic Review* 72: 652–68.
Ghemawat, P. (1986) 'Investment in lumpy capacity', *Journal of Economic Behavior and Organization* 8: 265–77.
Hayek, F. A. von (1931) *Prices and Production*, London: Routledge.
—— (1937) 'Economics and knowledge', *Individualism and Economic Order*, Chicago: University of Chicago Press.
—— (1941) *The Pure Theory of Capital*, Chicago: University of Chicago Press.
—— (1943) 'The facts of the social sciences', *Individualism and Economic Order*, Chicago: University of Chicago Press.
—— (1945) 'The use of knowledge in society', *Individualism and Economic Order*, Chicago: University of Chicago Press.
—— (1946) 'The meaning of competition', *Individualism and Economic Order*, Chicago: University of Chicago Press.
—— (1948) *Individualism and Economic Order*, Chicago: University of Chicago Press.
—— (1968) 'Competition as a discovery procedure', in Hayek (1978) *New Studies in Philosophy, Politics, Economics, and the History of Ideas*, London: Routledge.
—— (1973) *Law, Legislation, and Liberty, Vol.1: Rules and Order*, Chicago: University of Chicago Press.
Holmstrom, B. and Milgrom, P. (1994) 'The firm as an incentive system', *American Economic Review* 84: 972–91.
Kirzner, I. M. (1962) 'Rational action and economic theory', *Journal of Political Economy* 70: 380–5.
—— (1973) *Competition and Entrepreneurship*, Chicago: University of Chicago Press.
—— (ed.) (1986) *Subjectivism, Intelligibility, and Economic Understanding: Essays in Honor of Ludwig M. Lachmann*, London: Macmillan.

Koppl, R. (1992) 'Invisible-hand explanations and neoclassical economics: towards a post-marginalist economics', *Journal of Institutional and Theoretical Economics* 148: 292–313.
Lachmann, L. M. (1956) *Capital and Its Structure*, 1978 edn, Kansas City: Sheed Andrews & McNeel.
—— (1971) *The Legacy of Max Weber*, London: Heinemann.
—— (1986) *The Market as an Economic Process*, Oxford: Basil Blackwell.
Langlois, R. N. (1992a) 'Transaction cost economics in real time', *Industrial and Corporate Change* 1: 99–127.
—— (1992b) 'Orders and organizations: toward an Austrian theory of social institutions', in B. Caldwell and S. Böhm (eds) *Austrian Economics: Tensions and New Directions*, Boston, Mass.: Kluwer.
Langlois, R. N. and Robertson, P. (1993) 'Business organization as a coordination problem: towards a dynamic theory of the boundaries of the firm', *Business and Economic History* 22: 31–41.
Lavoie, D. (1985) *Rivalry and Central Planning*, Cambridge: Cambridge University Press.
—— (1990) 'Hermeneutics, subjectivity, and the Lester/Machlup debate: toward a more anthropological approach to empirical economics', in D. Lavoie (ed.) *Hermeneutics and Economics*, Boston, Mass.: Kluwer.
Lazonick, W. (1991) *Business Organization and the Myth of the Market Economy*, Cambridge: Cambridge University Press.
Lee, F. S. and Earl, P. E. (1993) *The Economics of Competitive Enterprise: Selected Essays of P. W. S. Andrews*, Aldershot: Edward Elgar.
Littlechild, S. (1977) *The Fallacy of the Mixed Economy*, London: Institute of Economic Affairs.
Loasby, B. J. (1976) *Choice, Complexity, and Ignorance*, Cambridge: Cambridge University Press.
—— (1989) *The Minds and Methods of Economists*, Cambridge: Cambridge University Press.
—— (1990) 'Firms, markets, and the principle of continuity', in J. K. Whitaker (ed.) *Centenary Essays on Alfred Marshall*, Cambridge: Cambridge University Press.
—— (1992) 'Market co-ordination', in B. J. Caldwell and S. Böhm (eds) *Austrian Economics: Tensions and New Directions*, Boston, Mass.: Kluwer.
—— (1993a) *Understanding Markets*, Working Paper, Stirling: University of Stirling.
—— (1993b) 'Change and evolution: a counterfactual history of twentieth century economics', *Papers on Economics and Evolution 9304*, edited by the European Study Group for Evolutionary Economics.
Lucas, R. E. (1980) 'Methods and problems in business cycle theory': reprinted in *Studies in Business Cycle Theory*, Cambridge: MIT Press, 1981.
Malmgren, H. B. (1961) 'Information, expectations and the theory of the firm', *Quarterly Journal of Economics* 75: 399–421.
Marshall, A. (1925) *Principles of Economics*, London: Macmillan.
Menger, C. (1871) *Principles of Economics*, New York: New York University Press.
Minkler, A. P. (1993) 'The problem with dispersed knowledge: firms in theory and practice', *Kyklos* 46: 569–87.

Mises, L. von (1949) *Human Action*, London: William Hodge.
—— (1981) *Socialism*, Indianapolis: Liberty Press.
Morgenstern, O. (1935) 'Perfect foresight and economic equilibrium', in A. Schotter (ed.) (1976) *Selected Writings of Oskar Morgenstern*, New York: New York University Press.
Nelson, R. R. and Winter, S. G. (1982) *An Evolutionary Theory of Economic Change*, Harvard: Belknap Press.
O'Brien, D. P. (1984) 'The evolution of the theory of the firm', in F. H. Stephen (ed.) *Firms, Organization, and Labour*, London: Macmillan.
—— (1985) 'Research programmes in competitive structure', *Journal of Economic Studies* 10: 29–51.
—— (1990) 'Marshall's industrial analysis', *Scottish Journal of Political Economy* 37: 61–84.
O'Driscoll, G. P. and Rizzo, M. (1985) *The Economics of Time and Ignorance*, Oxford: Basil Blackwell.
Penrose, E. T. (1952) 'Biological analogies in the theory of the firm', *American Economic Review* 42: 804–19.
—— (1959) *The Theory of the Growth of the Firm*, Oxford: Oxford University Press.
—— (1960) 'The growth of the firm – a case study: the Hercules Powder Company', *Business History Review* 34: 1–23.
Prahalad, C. K. and Hamel, G. (1990) 'The core competence of the corporation', *Harvard Business Review* 66: 79–91.
Reinganum, J. F. (1989) 'The timing of innovation: research, development, and diffusion', in R. Schmalensee and R. D. Willig (eds) *Handbook of Industrial Organization*, Amsterdam: North Holland.
Richardson, G. B. (1953) 'Imperfect knowledge and economic efficiency', *Oxford Economic Papers* 5: 136–56.
—— (1956) 'Demand and supply reconsidered', *Oxford Economic Papers* 8: 113–26.
—— (1959) 'Equilibrium, expectations and information', *The Economic Journal* 69: 223–37.
—— (1960) *Information and Investment: A Study in the Working of the Competitive Economy*, Oxford: Oxford University Press; 2nd edn 1990.
—— (1965) 'The theory of restrictive trade practices', *Oxford Economic Papers* 17: 432–49.
—— (1967) 'Price notification schemes', *Oxford Economic Papers* 19: 359–69.
—— (1969) *The Future of the Heavy Electrical Plant Industry*, London: British Electrical and Allied Manufacturers' Association Ltd.
—— (1971) 'Planning versus competition', Annex to *Information and Investment*, Oxford: Oxford University Press.
—— (1972) 'The organisation of industry', *Economic Journal* 82: 883–96.
—— (1975) 'Adam Smith on competition and increasing returns', in A. S. Skinner and T. Wilson (eds) *Essays on Adam Smith*, Oxford: Clarendon Press.
—— (1993a) personal communication, 14 May.
—— (1993b) personal communication, 19 October.
Silver, M. (1984) *Enterprise and the Scope of the Firm*, Aldershot: Martin Robertson.
Sraffa, P. (1926) 'The laws of return under competitive conditions', in G. J. Stigler and K. E. Boulding (eds) (1952) *Readings in Price Theory*, Homewood, Ill.: Irwin.

Streissler, E. (1972) 'To what extent was the Austrian school marginalist?', *History of Political Economy* 6: 426–41.
Thomas, B. (1991) 'Alfred Marshall on economic biology', *Review of Political Economy* 3: 1–14.
Vaughn, K. I. (1994) *Austrian Economics in America: The Migration of a Tradition*, Cambridge: Cambridge University Press.
Williamson, O. E. (1985) *The Economic Institutions of Capitalism*, New York: Free Press.

9
THE CONCEPT OF CAPABILITIES

Brian J. Loasby

INTRODUCTION

> It is convenient to think of industry as carrying out an indefinitely large number of *activities*, activities related to the discovery and estimation of future wants, to research, development, and design, to the execution and co-ordination of processes of physical transformation, the marketing of goods, and so on. And we have to recognise that these activities have to be carried out by organisations with appropriate *capabilities*, or, in other words, with appropriate knowledge, experience, and skills.
>
> (Richardson 1972: 888)

In these two sentences George Richardson set out the agenda for what has come to be called the capabilities theory of the firm. It is a theory which seeks to explain what any particular firm does by what its decision-makers believe that they know, what they believe they have learnt, and what they believe they can now do; that seeks to explain the evolution of a firm's activities by the evolution of its knowledge and skills, which is the result in part of deliberate efforts to guide that evolution, and in part of the unintended consequences of its actions; and that pays particular attention to the firm's internal arrangements and patterns of behaviour and also to its connections with other firms – but does not attempt to explain these features entirely by their implications for transaction costs. That is a broad agenda; and in this chapter I propose to explore the concept of capabilities. The concept is not well defined, and my primary purpose is to improve the definition.

The first requirement is to make a clear distinction between capabilities and production functions, in which the relationship between input combinations and outputs is isomorphic to the relationship between combinations of consumption goods and the satisfaction that they provide. Production and consumption functions are designed to show how the combinations chosen, of inputs and consumption goods, respectively, reflect relative prices; they ignore the activities, and the skills, which are necessary in order to transform inputs into outputs, or to use consumption goods effectively. The use of the word 'capabilities' by an economist signifies that the universe of discourse is not the universe of rational choice and equilibrium allocations which is the natural habitat of consumption and production functions, but one in which skill, and therefore the quality of performance, is important and problematic. We should therefore begin by investigating the universe of discourse in which the concept of capabilities can flourish.

THE DIVISION OF LABOUR AND THE ORGANISATION OF KNOWLEDGE

The relevant economic context for the concept of capabilities, as Richardson (1975) himself has pointed out, is the increase of wealth through the division of labour, which is the fundamental principle of Adam Smith's (1976) economic theory. (For an extended treatment, see Loasby 1996.) It is especially relevant to note that the central importance of the division of labour in Smith's scheme derives not from its power to make the best use of differences in natural aptitudes, which had long been recognised, but from its power to create increased, and also novel, specialist competences (Smith 1976: 28–30). Smith's basic theme was not allocative efficiency but economic development through increased productivity. Allocative efficiency was important, but secondary; as Richardson (1975: 353) has observed, any economist who thinks of increasing return as a threat to optimal allocation is not developing Smith's theory but denying it. Capabilities belong in a theory of change, and are themselves subject to change. Unlike production functions, they are endogenous, for their development is endogenous; and they are idiosyncratic, for this development is influenced by its context, and the way in which this context is interpreted.

Hayek (1937: 49) criticised economic theories of equilibrium for neglecting the problems caused by the division of knowledge – a neglect which provided the theme of Richardson's *Information and Investment* (1960); but Hayek did not recognise that the principal cause of the division of knowledge is the division of labour, for knowledge grows by division. Marshall extended Smith's analysis by identifying knowledge as 'our most powerful engine of production' (Marshall 1920: 138), and by drawing attention to the forms of industrial organisation which aid knowledge. Specialisation allows each person to learn more about a particular group of activities, and then to create new knowledge about them; and it is a simple inference from Smith's (1976: 20–1) account of the different sources of invention that each kind of specialist knowledge develops in ways which are likely to be in some degree peculiar to that specialism. The growth of knowledge proceeds through the differentiation and dispersion of knowledge, and the co-ordination of economic activity should respect the diversity of knowledge-generating systems. There is no calculable destination for this process of increasing productive knowledge, either for those engaged in that process or for those who seek to analyse it. Thus the capabilities theory of the firm can be comfortably accommodated within Smith's theory of economic development. It is much more difficult to assimilate it to orthodox kinds of equilibrium theory, including endogenous growth theory, for the set of future possibilities can never be specified — though, as Shackle frequently reminded us, it may be imagined. That a different concept of equilibrium may nevertheless be helpful in understanding change, and even the emergence of novelty, I have argued elsewhere (Loasby 1991).

In this chapter I would like to examine capabilities from the perspective of knowledge, and I will begin by identifying four kinds of knowledge, which may be arranged in a simple 2 × 2 matrix. One dimension is introduced into Richardson's (1972: 895) own examination of the organisation of industry, through his reference to Gilbert Ryle's (1949: 28) distinction between 'knowing that' and 'knowing how'. 'Knowing that' is knowledge of facts and relationships, the primary subject matter of formal education and the news; it may be subdivided into 'knowing what' and 'knowing why' (Lundvall and Johnson 1994). 'Knowing how', by contrast, is the ability to perform the appropriate actions to achieve a desired result. It includes skill both in performance and in recognising when and where this skill should be applied. A production function, as used in economic theories, is 'knowledge that' specific quantities of output may be produced from certain combinations of inputs; it makes no reference to 'knowledge how' they may be produced. The other dimension is provided by the distinction between direct and indirect knowledge. In relation to 'knowing that', the usual reference is to Dr Johnson's observation: 'Knowledge is of two kinds. We know a subject ourselves, or we know where we can find information about it' (Dr Johnson; quoted by Rosenberg 1994: 12), while Nelson and Winter (1982: 86) emphasise the distinction between knowing how to do something and knowing how to get something done. Capabilities are know-how, both direct and indirect; they represent the kind of knowledge which plays little or no formal part in mainstream economics, but which is crucial to the performance of a firm, an industry and an economy.

Ryle's analysis is particularly, though unintentionally, appropriate because he was criticising the traditional focus on the mind as the arena for intellectual operations and as the location for 'knowledge that', separate from and superior to the practical management of the machinery of the body. He claimed that 'In ordinary life . . . we are much more concerned with people's competences than with their cognitive repertoires, with the operations than the truths that they learn' (Ryle 1949: 28), and observed that it is generally not the case that effective operations depend on the understanding of truth, nor that the understanding of truth leads directly to effective operations. 'Knowing how' is not a consequence of 'knowing that', but deserves separate attention.

What is true of ordinary life is also true of economic activity, but not of orthodox theorising about economic activity. The exaltation of rational choice is the exaltation of intellectual operations (even though most economists are extremely uncomfortable when the agents in their models are actually free to choose). These intellectual operations clearly depend on 'knowledge that', and readily encompass the analysis of information, when that is treated as manipulable and authentic data. Economists are prepared to make heroic, even incredible, assumptions about such knowledge, and may be encouraged to do so by the Nobel Prize Committee; few of them seem to be aware that they are also making heroic, even incredible, assumptions about agents' ability to perform successfully the operations of production and exchange that they are supposed to have rationally chosen. Indeed the formulation of standard models assumes that the only obstacles to successful performance arise from inadequate incentives: knowing how is never a problem. For example, Arrow and Hahn's definition of the production possibility set as 'a description of the state of the firm's knowledge about the possibilities of transforming commodities' (Arrow and Hahn 1971: 53) thoroughly confuses the knowledge *that* it is possible, for example, to convert crude oil into a wide range of plastics with the knowledge of *how* precisely this is to be accomplished. This is precisely the sort of model of the mind that Ryle was criticising. Far from providing, as Becker (1976) has claimed, the only proper basis for theory in the social sciences, it confines economists to a single, though not negligible, aspect of complex social phenomena. It is a notable handicap to our understanding of the organisation of industry.

George Richardson, along with Edith Penrose (1959), Nelson and Winter (1982), and Rosenberg (1982, 1994), among others, has argued that we need to understand the performance of firms and of individuals, and that we shall not do so by confining our attention to 'knowledge that' (though such knowledge is certainly relevant, as we shall see later). Knowing how to achieve a desired result may be quite independent of any understanding of the reasons why the procedure appears to work; all of us make use of procedures that we do not understand. Yet, as Ryle points out, such activity often displays intelligence: 'It is of the essence of merely habitual practices that one performance is a replica of its predecessors. It is of the essence of intelligent practices that one performance is modified by its predecessors. The agent is still learning' (Ryle 1949: 42). Like all learning, this is a process of trial and error, and intelligence is required if people are to make appropriate trials and to interpret the results sensibly – in particular, to decide which parts of the procedure to think about *next*.

> We learn *how* by practice, schooled indeed by criticism and example, but often quite unaided by any lessons in the theory.... Even when efficient practice is the deliberate application of considered prescriptions, the intelligence involved in putting the prescriptions into practice is not identical to that involved in intellectually grasping the prescriptions.
>
> (Ryle 1949: 41, 49)

Indeed those proficient in developing and expounding the theoretical structure of a discipline often seem to be remarkably ineffective in its practical application.

DIRECT 'KNOWLEDGE HOW'

Let us explore for a few paragraphs the psychological basis of individual 'knowledge how'. Hayek declared that 'hypotheses or assumptions that people do learn from experience, and about how they acquire knowledge... constitute the empirical content of our propositions about what happens in the real world' (Hayek 1937: 45). Recognition of the importance of 'knowledge how' reinforces the argument for an approach to learning which does not rely on an extension of rational choice theorising. The modern interest in the evolution of neural networks and classifier models looks more attractive; and it is fitting that an approach of this kind was advocated in Hayek's *Sensory Order* (1952), an evolutionary theory of psychology which contains four references to Ryle's *Concept of Mind*. The problem that stimulated Hayek's interest was the disparity between the account of the external world which has been developed by the physical sciences and our sensory perceptions of that world:

> events which to our senses may appear to be of the same kind may have to be treated as different in the physical order, while events which physically may be of the same or at least a similar kind may appear as altogether different to our senses.
>
> (Hayek 1952: 4)

Hayek's proposed solution to this problem is that each individual's sensory order is a network of relationships in the brain which develops as a means of classifying particular stimuli or clusters of stimuli and connects each category to a suitable action or sequence of actions. The criterion of this process, which predates consciousness, is effective performance, or 'knowing how', whereas the later construction of a physical order is 'knowledge that', which is not designed for direct application. Science and technology are oriented differently; that is why their relationship is rarely straightforward, as Rosenberg (1982, 1994) has reminded us.

We may prefer to say, with Kelly, that experience 'is made up of the successive construing of events. It is not constituted merely by the events themselves' (Kelly 1963: 73), although, as Kelly observes, the particular kinds of events and the sequence in which they occur will typically have some effect on the construction systems which an individual develops. In Kelly's account there are many possible construction systems, and in Hayek's there are many possible networks of relationships; but in both accounts the establishment of one particular pattern of interpretation or response inhibits the development of many alternatives (as happens when an infant learns to speak a particular language). Learning is a path-dependent process, in which the acquisition of certain kinds of 'knowledge how' facilitates the acquisition of further knowledge of the same kind, and impedes the acquisition of knowledge of incompatible kinds; and this principle applies both to the performance of productive operations and, as we shall see, to the procedures by which we seek to develop new 'knowledge that'. That is why the division of labour leads to different kinds of 'knowledge how', and why even within a specialism people will acquire skills that differ somewhat in context and scope, as well as quality, thus generating the variety which Marshall expected within each of the forms of organisation that aid knowledge.

A sketch of a similar kind of psychological theory, in which 'knowledge how' was acquired through the formation and reinforcement of connections, was worked out by Marshall, in a paper probably written for a discussion group in Cambridge in the 1860s, and recently published for the first time. Marshall (1994) imagines a robot, in which one set of wheels receives impressions from its environment and another set controls its actions. These wheels are linked by a multitude of bands, most of them inoperative, but others fitting tightly enough to transmit motion, though sometimes imperfectly. The linkages between impressions and those actions which appear to generate new and satisfactory impressions become tighter and the machine's responses stronger and more certain; and cross-linkages develop which allow the machine to respond to specific clusters of stimuli with specific sets of complementary actions. But what is of particular interest in Marshall's model is that his machine has a higher level of control, which functions only when the lower level can establish no satisfactory connections, or where cross-linkages generate conflicting motions. The wheels at this higher level represent, not impressions and actions, but ideas of impression and action, and the bands thus form connections between possible actions and envisaged consequences. The addition of consciousness to the unconscious process of network formation at the operating level allows actions to be tested in the imagination before they are put into practice. It thus introduces to the evolutionary process both the deliberate generation of alternatives and selection among these alternatives in anticipation of outcomes; and Marshall drew attention in his *Principles* to the importance of 'deliberate choice and forethought' (Marshall 1920: 5) in improving the rate of economic progress.

If this higher level of connections allows the machine to take better actions, and especially if the capacity to think ahead allows it to avoid serious error, it confers important advantages; but these advantages have to be paid for. Not only is there a whole new set of machinery; this set is more elaborate and consumes much more energy (Woo 1992). Thus it is important that as much as possible should be left at the operating level, or returned to that level after the higher authority has rearranged the pattern of connections. Marshall thus extends the principle of the division of labour to intellectual operations within the human brain, and later developed this application in his analysis of the organisation of industry (Raffaelli 1995). The problems of living are made much easier, and perhaps they are only made soluble, by our ability to be instrumentally knowledgeable while substantively ignorant – even when we do not know how to set about reducing that ignorance.

The natural history of Marshall's 'machine' respects the evolutionary priority of skills for survival, which require an effective, and often immediate, response to complex, and often ambiguous, stimuli. In the early stages of human development, natural selection therefore favours rapid information retrieval and pattern recognition over the linear sequences of information processing that we associate with logical thought. The architecture of the human brain and its propensity to form patterns and to evoke connections between apparently unrelated phenomena has not produced an ideal instrument for rational thought. It is therefore important not to place too much reliance on the concept of rational action. 'Knowing how' comes before 'knowing that', and, as in Marshall's model, is not superseded by it. We might recall Whitehead's warning that 'operations of thought are like cavalry charges in battle – they are strictly limited in number, they require fresh horses, and must only be made at decisive moments' (Whitehead 1948: 42).

It is not appropriate in this chapter to pay systematic attention to 'knowledge that'. But it is relevant to note that its production and its effective use depend on particular kinds of knowledge how; archaeological knowledge, for example, rests on the skills with which archaeologists conduct a dig, and on their ability to interpret their discoveries by making connection to a pattern of relationships, or occasionally by the invention of novel patterns. Ziman (1978) has argued that the reliability of scientific knowledge depends primarily on the processes by which it is generated and tested, and on the appropriateness of these processes to the subject matter; there may be fundamental principles which are common to all branches of science, but these branches do not share a common body of know-how, and it would not be helpful if they did. Moreover, the content, as well as the reliability, of knowledge depends on the procedures that are followed.

The knowledge that is presented in economics textbooks is conditioned by the ways in which economists have sought to develop it, and economics students learn by practice how to deal with problems in ways which are approved within the profession, thereby avoiding issues, and potential 'knowledge that', which are not amenable to their 'knowledge how'. That can be seen most clearly by observing what is left out of standard economics, for example in the explanation of firms solely in terms of market failure and incentive problems and the lack of interest in inter-firm differences in productivity, which are often substantial and persistent, and also, as Hahn and Solow (1995: 2) have noted, by the exclusion of involuntary unemployment from the knowledge that can be produced within new classical macroeconomics. What we know is not without influence on what we can do; but it is itself strongly influenced by how we know (Loasby 1998). We should also note that the centrality of rational choice in modern economics has not perceptibly improved the ability of trained economists to make rational choices, either as managers or as policy-makers. This is not solely because the ability to make good decisions is not closely related to an understanding of the logical principles of choice; it is primarily because economists use choice theory as an instrument for developing propositions about the economy. Their skills are not in making choices, but in using particular concepts of choice in creating knowledge – or perhaps, remembering Popper's warning that all scientific knowledge is conjectural, we should say in creating knowledge claims.

INDIRECT 'KNOWLEDGE HOW'

Knowing how to do things ourselves is not enough. Anyone who is not self-sufficient needs to know how to get many things done; indeed, if we consider the standard co-ordination problem in economics from the point of view of the individual, as Adam Smith (1976: 26–7) did, it appears precisely to be the problem of how to get many things done on which that individual depends for comfort or even survival, but which, because of the differentiation of skills as a consequence of the division of labour, must be entrusted to others. The standard answer to this problem is, in rigorous models, to enter into an appropriate set of contracts or, in a more casual exposition, to buy and sell in appropriate markets. Coase suggested in 1937 that this was not always the best answer, for what is essentially Hayek's reason – that a good deal of knowledge is required in order to use markets, especially unorganised markets, effectively; and this, though neither Coase nor Hayek make the point explicitly, is primarily knowledge how.

A better way of getting some things done, Coase argued, was to enter into a continuing relationship with people who will agree to do them as required. This avoids the need for precise forecasts, but, as Coase explicitly recognised, it requires a general agreement on the kinds of things which are to be done and, as he did not explicitly recognise, on who is competent to do them. Since Coase's problem was to explain why all activity was not co-ordinated in markets, it is not surprising that his focus is on the costs of transacting for activities, rather than the activities themselves; but this focus was unfortunate, as Coase (1991: 65) has admitted, because the attempt to explain the scope of firms exclusively by the desire to reduce transaction costs has added very little to our understanding of what firms actually do. (See Chapters 4 and 10.) But to Coase's suggestion that collecting a particular group of activities within a firm may be transactionally efficient we may add Smith's proposition that such an arrangement may lead to these activities being better performed, either by deliberate design or as an unintended consequence of this form of organisation. It certainly seems reasonable to assert that in considering a firm, as in considering an individual, we need to pay attention to both direct and indirect know-how. We should also recognise that many activities within firms depend on know-how which goes well beyond knowledge of facts or reasons, and that reliance on such know-how is an important cause both of outstanding success and of spectacular failure.

All four kinds of knowledge are acquired by trial and error, which may be carefully designed, especially for the acquisition of scientific knowledge, fairly casual, or often controlled by the unconscious processes of our brain. Not one of the four kinds can ever be more than provisional, or, in Popper's terms, conjectural. The next time that we try to use any piece of knowledge it may be falsified. Our theorem may fail, a previously reliable source of information may lead us astray, a well-proven routine may fail to produce the expected result, a colleague or regular supplier may be unable to deliver what we expect. As we shall see, there are ways of protecting ourselves against the consequences of falsification, but these in turn are fallible.

COMPETITIVE ADVANTAGE

If we are not satisfied with the notion of the firm as a production function, when production functions are treated as public goods, or with the notion of the firm as a governance structure, when production functions and (with some ambiguity) governance structures are both treated as public goods, then it is natural to look for sources of difference between firms. This we shall do. For anyone who has been thoroughly trained in the use of equilibrium concepts, it may also seem natural to look for sources of permanent difference. This, however, we shall not do. Not only are permanent differences unnecessary to an analysis of processes, but an insistence on permanent differences excludes some kinds of analysis and prevents us from explaining many historical episodes. Persistence is both theoretically and empirically important; permanence is not. The maintenance of a particular level and kind of productive capability will not suffice to maintain a firm's position; continuing advantage depends on the continuing development of capabilities. It does, however, seem reasonable to pay particular attention to those assets which are not readily traded and therefore tend to provide an organisation with distinguishing characteristics, and distinctive paths of development. In the emerging terminology in this field, such embedded characteristics are usually called capabilities rather than resources.

At a first approximation, this distinction between capabilities and resources appears to match the distinction between 'knowing how' and 'knowing that'. If the latter is indeed, as Popper has called it, 'knowledge without a knowing subject' (Popper 1972: 109), which can be stored and communicated, then there is apparently no reason why a person or a firm which at a particular time happens to have exclusive possession of such knowledge should be able to gain more by using it than by selling it. Any rents from first ownership should be capitalised, as with the discovery of a new source of any valuable input. By contrast, know-how, if embodied in practices which are difficult to explain and hard to transfer except in the persons of those who have learnt them, provides an advantage which loses much of its value on sale, especially if these practices form an interdependent – and therefore almost certainly idiosyncratic – cluster.

The focus of economists' attention on 'knowledge that', encouraged by such expedients as the representation of technology by information sets, has fostered a belief that the knowledge required for effective performance will become increasingly codified, and sometimes, in the long-established tradition of considering knowledge as a public good, that such codification should be promoted by government action. Others have argued that Polanyi's (1968) emphasis on the tacit element in know-how will continue to be valid. It is tempting to seek a resolution of this debate by assimilating the distinction between 'knowing that' and 'knowing how' to a distinction between codified and tacit knowledge; but that is too simple. Know-how can often be partially codified, even without an understanding of the reasons why the procedures work; there are plenty of manuals, even on the rules for producing winning strategies. But codification of know-how is never complete. Close attention to recipes does not ensure excellent results, and even detailed manuals often make crucial, if unconscious, assumptions about the user's skills. It is notorious that standard operating procedures, followed to the letter, produce unsatisfactory levels of performance; and although patents are supposed to be granted in exchange for full disclosure, a good deal of know-how is often needed in order to operate a patent. In the chemical industry, where licensing of patents is common, one of the important functions of R&D departments is the development of skills in adapting technologies which have been developed elsewhere (Cohen and Levinthal 1989) – for as my former colleague Professor Bradbury, who had much experience in these processes, insisted, innovations are always adapted and never merely adopted. Know-how is never identical on both sides of the transfer of technology. Even when improved methods which have been learnt by doing are transferable, the transfer does not include the skills by which further improvements may be achieved.

However, the codification of objective knowledge is never complete either, as is demonstrated in classrooms and lecture halls every day. The significance of any item of objective knowledge depends on the context, which is supplied by the selections and simplifications of each individual. In particular, both the development and the use of objective knowledge rely on procedural skills which often seem to require personal tuition and a great deal of time, whether or not these skills are securely anchored in theory. Transfers of scientific or technological knowledge are rarely simple or speedy; and the codification which the transferer finds convenient may not be appropriate to the recipient. So in seeking to identify those capabilities which may provide a firm with more than an evanescent advantage, one should beware both of including those procedures which are more readily codifiable and of excluding apparently objective knowledge which requires idiosyncratic skills if it is to be used effectively.

The capabilities of individuals do not provide sufficient reason for a firm, which is, from this perspective, one way of organising the capabilities of a collection of people. The justification for a firm derives from the interdependence of direct capabilities, both in the advantages of mutual learning among those with similar skills and in the close complementarities between skills which are different but compatible; a given set of activities will facilitate the carrying out of activities which rely on similar kinds of knowing how, but hinder the performance of others in which ways of knowing how are radically different. A successful organisation is a set of people who know how to get things done – indeed, as Winter (1991: 185) has pointed out, who know how to get things done within an organisation that none of them would know how to get done as an individual. The division of labour is a division of knowledge, and knowledge grows because it is divided; consequently the knowledge of each person becomes a smaller fraction of the whole; even if much of it is codified, there is no time to learn the many different codes. The knowledge is distributed within the system and can only be assembled by the particular combination of indirect knowledge how which has been accumulated within that system. Know-how is combined with 'know whom' – and indeed with knowing who knows whom; and this is precisely what we get when we add Smith's founding principle to Coase's firm.

But, as Hayek (1948: 97) emphasised, knowing who will provide what we want is important in markets also; and though Hayek's examples were all consumer goods and services, knowledge of that kind is necessary for the successful running of a business. As Marshall saw more clearly than any other economist, the relationships created within a firm must be complemented by the creation of relationships with suppliers, customers and providers of the various services which a firm may need. Just as each of us relies on the capabilities of many other people to whom we have no formal or kinship connection, so a firm relies on the capabilities of many people, and many organisations, which are formally quite independent; and a firm may achieve distinctive advantages through the ways in which it combines these external capabilities with its own.

Where capabilities can be combined in a modular structure – where there are no externalities – it is sufficient (but also necessary) to know how these capabilities may be acquired. Often they are acquired by the purchase of commodities in which they are packaged, as consumers acquire the capability of reproducing music, washing clothes or taking high-quality photographs. This kind of exchange comes closest to the familiar economic model of a market, although we need to know how to use a market effectively. Very few of us would risk attempting to acquire any significant capability from a source which did not possess a distinctive identity. Thus every supplier needs to develop a reputation; often this reputation will not allow that supplier to charge more than competitors, but it may allow a larger volume of sales, or a smaller selling effort, because it provides knowledge to customers and reduces their costs of deciding what to do. Building a market requires skills, just as does building an organisation, and these skills may be specific to particular kinds of markets or particular kinds of organisation.

However, as Richardson reminded us in 1972, the combination of capabilities often requires some interactive shaping, especially if a firm is seeking to develop a substantial innovation. Sometimes this may be most effectively accomplished within a single firm, and indeed some firms develop distinctive capabilities in the handling of such processes. But the kinds of knowledge which need to be combined may be so dissimilar that they create major difficulties of management within a single structure; the assumptions and procedures which generate exemplary results in one activity may be disastrous in another – as some firms have discovered in their attempts to diversify. If these dissimilar capabilities are each closely linked to a cluster of other capabilities which are used to support a distinctive range of activities, then it may be impossible to extract the desired capability from its cluster without seriously impairing its effectiveness, and impossible to contain the diversity of activities which is supported by all those clusters within a coherent business. Many mergers and acquisitions have been designed to exploit complementarities, which often appear to be readily identifiable from outside, only to founder on the dissimilarities which may not be appreciated until people come face to face with incompatible know-how.

Then the best, if sometimes difficult, option may be to create some kind of inter-organisational arrangement to manage the intersection of these dissimilar capabilities, perhaps in the form of a joint venture, perhaps by creating joint teams at the working level, as, for example, staff from logistics companies work on their customers' premises. Skill in this kind of management may itself provide a distinctive capability, which may be especially valuable in a rapidly changing high-technology industry. What is important is not the minimisation of transaction costs but the maximisation of net benefits; and sometimes an acceptance of higher transaction costs may be the only means of securing much greater increases in benefits (Zajac and Olsen 1993). Similar arguments may also apply within firms: a highly efficient governance structure may prevent people within an organisation from making good use of the capabilities which they possess. We should not assume that senior managers, who design and operate this governance structure, always know what these capabilities are. Know-how is differentiated and dispersed, and not easily translated into the language of information and control systems.

Every firm relies on capabilities which it does not control, and some of those capabilities may be destroyed by the attempt to control them. If a firm buys up a supplier, not only may the imposition of governance structures which are appropriate to that firm's core business impede the supplier's ability to learn, but also by denying that supplier access to other customers it may cut off some crucial opportunities to learn. Every industry, similarly, relies on capabilities which are distributed among the firms within that industry and among other firms that have trading links with them. These capabilities form a structure of complementarities; but it is also, in part, a structure of substitutes. Substantial diversity usually requires separate organisations; but substantial diversity may be a major capability for the industry as a whole, widening the range of activities which can be undertaken and increasing the possibilities of improving some relevant kinds of knowledge. Although diversity implies rivalry among firms with different capabilities, it may also be a source of strength even to firms whose apparent capabilities seem to be deficient; for it may give such firms a means of learning from their more successful local rivals before their markets are taken over by international competition.

The more important the tacit component in skills, the greater the advantage in being able to learn from other firms which are geographically and psychologically close. This is a major part of the old argument for industrial districts, recently revived in the form of national clusters of firms within particular industries (e.g. Porter 1990). Another part is provided by Hayek's later emphasis on the co-ordinative function of social rules, for we should not forget that firms and industries are social as well as economic systems, each embodying its particular network of direct and indirect know-how. Diversity is necessarily a system property: it may allow an industry, or an economy, to do what no firm knows how to do. But we should recognise that an industry or economy may be able to do this only as long as no one tries to control the system, because the knowledge required for control cannot be extracted from that system.

Unless we restrict ourselves to explaining the past, our interest in capabilities, whether direct or indirect, and whether embedded within individuals, firms, industrial districts or economies, is in their future uses and their future development, and neither are fit subjects for rational expectations. In Menger's (1871) terms, capabilities provide a reserve when the list of future contingencies cannot be closed: they are a structure of complementary skills oriented towards a particular range of possible futures. (We should have learnt from Austrian economists to think of capital in terms of both its structure and its orientation.) But if the set of future contingencies can rarely be precisely defined, neither can the capabilities of an individual or a firm. As Ryle (1949: 33) pointed out, skills are not acts, and should not be identified with any particular performance, or even set of performances, which they have made possible. 'Knowing *how* is a disposition, but not a single-track disposition like a reflex or a habit. Its exercises are observances of rules or canons or the applications of criteria' (*ibid.*: 46). Moreover, capabilities may be, and clusters of capabilities always are, clusters of dispositions, which may be realised in many ways; and, through the exercise of intelligence, they may be developed in ways which are not foreseeable.

The limitations on their development cannot be foreseen either, for, as Nelson and Winter remind us, 'performance takes place in a context set by the values of a large number of variables; the effectiveness of the performance depends on those variables being in appropriate ranges' (Nelson and Winter 1982: 84); and we cannot possibly know what all the ranges – or indeed all the relevant variables – are. Nelson and Winter's emphasis on the ambiguity of scope inherent in any skill should be matched by an emphasis on the variability of its quality. 'We never speak of a person having partial knowledge of a fact or truth. . . . On the other hand, it is proper and normal to speak of a person knowing in part how to do something' (Ryle 1949: 57–8). Thus many firms may know how to make cars, market new products or manage a supply chain, but not all firms know how to do so equally well; and what level of performance is 'good enough' is never definitively established.

Nevertheless, the scope and level of capabilities sought, and also the rate of improvement, must depend on a view of future possibilities, for no one can afford to prepare for every prospect that can be imagined, let alone those that cannot. So capabilities involve a double conjecture, about the kinds of future that it is reasonable to prepare for and about the appropriateness of particular capabilities to those kinds of future. Both judgements must be right if a firm is to be able to undertake the activities which match the requirements of the situation. Despite a long record of imperfect success, it is apparently still very common for firms to misjudge their capacity to manage successfully businesses that they propose to take over (Norburn and Schoenberg 1994: 32). On the other hand, firms, like individuals, may have pleasant surprises. Even intelligent procedures do not preclude unintended consequences, welcome or unwelcome.

Even after allowing for uncertainty, if we wish to explain a firm's activities we need to go beyond capabilities. A conspectus of capabilities resembles a production set in one important respect: it specifies (with some ambiguity and a significant potential for error) a range of possibilities; we need something else to explain what is chosen. For that it is helpful to turn to Penrose's (1959) analytical distinction between a firm's capabilities and its 'productive opportunity', which combines those capabilities with a perception of the ways in which they might be used. Since Penrose is interested in explaining the growth of those firms which succeed in growing, she considers only those productive opportunities that are genuine, although she explicitly recognises that even successful firms may fail to identify opportunities which they are capable of exploiting. A productive opportunity may well depend on a conjunction between 'knowing how' and 'knowing that': a combination of factual knowledge (which, of course, may be incomplete or even false) about a new need or a new scientific discovery, for example, and skills which seem to be applicable to the exploitation of that need or discovery. Here is another important role for 'knowledge that', and also for skills which enable people to discover and interpret such knowledge. Even though the knowledge may be public, the connection may not be; and the ability to make such connections may provide a distinctive capability. The particular kind of alertness which distinguishes each of Kirzner's (1973) entrepreneurs is such a capability. Sony is a good example, most spectacularly in its perception of the productive opportunity in portable radios that was offered by Bell Labs' development of the transistor. But because both kinds of knowledge are fallible, so too may be the conjectured connections, as has been illustrated more than once by Clive Sinclair; and Sony was apparently so impressed by the doubtful complementarities between its television business and Hollywood film-making that it underrated the rather obvious contrasts in 'knowledge how'.

Without explicitly making the distinction, Marshall (1920: 297–8) clearly indicates the need for businessmen to know both how and that: how to apply the principle of substitution to achieve better performance and what opportunities for new commodities are becoming available. Indeed, a principal function of the external organisation which Marshall thought so important is to provide information about customers, actual and potential, and about materials and machinery. Successful firms know many things directly (or, rather, through the individuals within the business) and they know how to find out many other things indirectly, though small organisations sometimes know much better than large ones how to combine such 'knowledge that' with the capabilities that could make good use of it. Indeed, much of the drive towards 'empowerment' of relatively junior members of large organisations is motivated by the desire to find better ways of making such combinations.

CAPABILITIES IN DECISION-MAKING

The division of labour in decision-making, whether through empowerment or on any other principle, helps people to learn how to make particular kinds of decisions in particular contexts. There may be universal principles of optimisation, which is a branch of 'knowledge that', but there can be no universal procedure for applying them; 'knowing how' is a practical skill, developed in a limited range of contexts and of uncertain, and often negative, value outside that range. Nelson and Winter (1982) highlighted the range of procedures for making decisions within a single firm by distinguishing between operating, investment and search routines, and cited Schumpeter in support of their argument that decisions have to be made not only in choosing a technology but also in the process of operating the technology that is chosen. Schumpeter observed that:

> the necessity of taking decisions occurs in any work. No cobbler's apprentice can repair a shoe without making some resolutions and without deciding independently some questions, however small. The 'what' and 'how' are taught him; but this does not relieve him of the necessity of a certain independence.
>
> (Schumpeter 1934: 20)

After noting tasks which entail greater discretion, Schumpeter continues:

> Now the director or independent owner of a business has certainly most to decide and most resolutions to make. But the how and the why are also taught him.... He acts, not on the basis of the prevailing condition of things, but much more according to certain symptoms of which he has learned to take heed.
>
> (Schumpeter 1934: 21)

At each level, people know how to take the relevant kind of decision (though, as noted earlier, the level of skill may be high or low). Nelson and Winter were particularly anxious to elide the standard distinction between technologies as data and the choices of what technology to use, by drawing attention both to the technologies of choice and to the scope for choices within technologies, which generate improvements in the manner of Smith and Marshall.

I would like to reinforce this elision by emphasising the importance in all situations where action is required of what Simon (1959) has called 'decision premises', which provide partial closure by specifying assumptions about the possibilities and the criteria by which to choose between them. One can hardly overestimate the importance of decision premises in determining the effectiveness of each particular kind of know-how. For the cobbler's apprentice, the closure is almost, though not quite, complete; for the director it is a good deal less, though the how and the why are closely specified. All capabilities depend on the pre-selection of phenomena and of the methods by which to handle them. Marshall's 'machine' relies on evolving systems of linkages both to perform operations and to organise ideas; we make choices by making connections. Effective interaction between phenomena and methods produces capability; ineffective interaction produces intractable problems. That is true both of business and of academic disciplines (consider the products which British companies have abandoned to foreigners and the problems which economists avoid handling). Moreover, interactions which are effective for one purpose are likely to be ineffective for others, and so attempts to tackle unfamiliar classes of problems by proven methods often produce disappointing results. Far from being surprising, that is a natural corollary of the advantages of specialisation; the opportunity cost of capabilities in one kind of activity is incapabilities in many other kinds.

It is an important function of both formal and informal organisation to guide members towards pre-selected premises which are believed to be relevant to the purposes of the organisation and which will facilitate co-ordination among the membership. Simon (1992: 6) has suggested that people may be encouraged to join an organisation because they can then accept the organisational definition of problems as their own: they therefore know, without deliberation, what they should be thinking about, and can begin to develop their knowledge of how to handle a particular category of problems in ways which are compatible with the capabilities of other members of that organisation. He has even claimed that it is 'more important, in some circumstances, to have *agreement* on the facts than to be certain that what is agreed on is really fact' (Simon, 1982, vol. 2: 339), because shared decision premises facilitate the co-ordination of activities. Academic disciplines likewise develop categories for phenomena, methods of structuring problems and analytical techniques; and academic education is largely designed to induce students, by precept and example, to accept these, in the dual belief that these decision premises will provide sufficient closure to focus attention and sufficient commonality to make communication easy. By operating within the shared routines of 'normal science', well-educated members of a discipline learn not only how to improve their own objective knowledge but also how to gain access to the objective knowledge and know-how of others. Much the same is true of a highly capable business.

THE EVOLUTION OF CAPABILITIES

Schumpeter (1943) claimed that capitalism could never be static. His emphasis was on the process of creative destruction, and what is destroyed is an existing network of direct and indirect capabilities; the resultant co-ordination failure, not surprisingly, produces a recession, because people no longer know how to decide what to do. Nelson and Winter (1982), however, although invoking Schumpeter, describe a process which is much closer to Marshall's theory of continuous improvement through the enhancement of capabilities. They even appear to replicate the distinction in Marshall's 'machine' between the modification of operational know-how and the generation and trial of new ideas. Their discussion of the role of routines in preserving an organisational truce may be regarded as an important complement to the argument in this chapter that an effective process of trial and error within a community, whether this be an academic discipline or a business, requires a set of broadly compatible decision premises – what might be called an interpretative framework, a paradigm, a research programme or, in Ryle's terminology, similar ways of knowing how. Such compatibility is especially important if improvements in different activities need to be co-ordinated. Organisations create stability at this level in order to encourage orderly change. Hayek (1979: 167) has argued that all progress is based on tradition, and it appears that even self-proclaimed revolutionaries are unable to discard significant elements of past systems, whether these systems be scientific, political or commercial. But because of transaction and cognition costs, even minor changes are not simply reversible, and so path-dependency is endemic. Incremental change is often cumulative, and may in due course produce the appearance of a paradigm shift. It generates barriers to entry for outsiders, and barriers to exit for those who have efficiently internalised the kinds of know-how which enable them both to perform certain activities efficiently and to get appropriate activities performed by others.

One consequence is that the development of an organisation's capabilities may take it in directions which were not anticipated. Thus strategy itself may need to be malleable, as Henry Mintzberg (1994) has argued for many years. Another is that options are continually being closed as capabilities evolve; and however unattractive those options may appear when they are relinquished, it is impossible to be certain that they will never become attractive again. Selection processes must operate within contemporary perspectives: they may reflect views of the future, but they cannot reflect the future itself. Thus capabilities may be lost which we may later wish were available. Reproducing an extinct capability is not quite as difficult as reproducing an extinct species, but it is likely to be costly; and reproducing a network of direct and indirect capabilities, which may depend on extinct social rules, may be a formidable challenge. Thus there may be value in diversity; but if there is to be substantial diversity it must almost certainly be found within a system, not within a single organisation. Compatibility of know-how imposes constraints, as it is meant to do; for capabilities are improved by exploiting such constraints. We are back to Smith's theory of development through the division of labour; but of course we have never left it. Our investigation of the concept of capabilities needs to be matched with an investigation of selection processes; but that is a topic for other papers.

REFERENCES

Arrow, K. J. and Hahn, F. H. (1971) *General Competitive Analysis*, San Francisco: Holden-Day.

Becker, G. (1976) *The Economic Approach to Human Behavior*, Chicago: University of Chicago Press.

Coase, R. H. (1937) 'The nature of the firm', *Economica*, NS, 4: 386–405; reprinted in R. H. Coase (1988) *The Firm, the Market, and the Law*, Chicago: University of Chicago Press.

—— (1991) 'The nature of the firm: influence', in O. E. Williamson and S. G. Winter (eds) *The Nature of the Firm: Origins, Evolution and Development*, New York and Oxford: Oxford University Press.

Cohen, W. M. and Levinthal, D. A. (1989) 'Innovation and learning: the two faces of R&D', *Economic Journal* 99: 569–96.

Hahn, F. H. and Solow, R. M. (1995) *A Critical Survey of Modern Macroeconomic Theory*, Cambridge, Mass., and London: MIT Press.

Hayek, F. A. (1937) 'Economics and knowledge', *Economica*, NS, 4: 33–54.

—— (1948) 'The meaning of competition', *Individualism and Economic Order*, Chicago: University of Chicago Press.

—— (1952) *The Sensory Order*, Chicago: University of Chicago Press.

—— (1979) *Law, Legislation and Liberty*, vol. 3, London: Routledge and Kegan Paul.

Hounshell, D. A. and Smith, J. K. (1988) *Science and Corporate Strategy*, Cambridge: Cambridge University Press.

Kelly, G. A. (1963) *A Theory of Personality*, New York: W. W. Norton.

Kirzner, I. M. (1973) *Competition and Entrepreneurship*, Chicago: University of Chicago Press.

Loasby, B. J. (1991) *Equilibrium and Evolution*, Manchester: Manchester University Press.

Loasby, B. J. (1996) 'The division of labour', *History of Economic Ideas*, 4:299–323.

—— (1997) 'How do we know', in S. Boehm (ed.) *Economics as the Art of Thought: Essays in Memory of G. L. S. Shackle*, London: Routledge.

Lundvall, B. A. and Johnson, B. (1994) 'The learning economy', *Journal of Industry Studies* 1: 23–42.

Marshall, A. (1920) *Principles of Economics*, 8th edn, London: Macmillan.

—— (1994) 'Ye machine', *Research in the History of Economic Thought and Methodology* Archival Supplement: 116–32.

Menger, C. (1871 [1950]), *Principles of Economics*, translated by J. Dingwall and B. F. Hoselitz, Glencoe, Ill.: Free Press.

Mintzberg, H. (1994) *The Rise and Fall of Strategic Planning*, New York and London: Prentice-Hall.

Nelson, R. R. and Winter, S. G. (1982) *An Evolutionary Theory of Economic Change*, Cambridge, Mass.: Harvard University Press.

Norburn, D. and Schoenberg, R. (1994) 'European cross-border acquisition: how was it for you?', *Long Range Planning* 27(4): 25–34.
Penrose, E. T. (1959) *The Theory of the Growth of the Firm*, Oxford: Basil Blackwell; 2nd edn 1995, Oxford: Oxford University Press.
Polanyi, M. (1968) *Personal Knowledge*, London: Routledge & Kegan Paul.
Popper, K. R. (1972) *Objective Knowledge: An Evolutionary Approach*, Oxford: Clarendon Press.
Porter, M. E. (1990) *The Competitive Advantage of Nations*, London: Macmillan.
Raffaelli, T. (1995) 'The principles of organisation: a forgotten chapter of Marshallian economics', paper presented to the European Conference on the History of Economics, Rotterdam, 10–11 February.
Richardson, G. B. (1960) *Information and Investment: A Study in the Working of the Competitive Economy*, Oxford: Oxford University Press.
—— (1972) 'The organisation of industry', *Economic Journal* 82: 883–96.
—— (1975) 'Adam Smith on competition and increasing returns', in A. S. Skinner and T. Wilson (eds) *Essays on Adam Smith*, Oxford: Oxford University Press.
—— (1990) *Information and Investment: A Study in the Working of the Competitive Economy*, 2nd edn, Oxford: Oxford University Press.
Rosenberg, N. (1982) *Inside the Black Box: Technology and Economics*, Cambridge: Cambridge University Press.
—— (1994) *Exploring the Black Box: Technology, Economics, and History*, Cambridge: Cambridge University Press.
Ryle, G. (1949) *The Concept of Mind*, London: Hutchinson.
Schumpeter, J. A. (1934) *The Theory of Economic Development*, Cambridge, Mass.: Harvard University Press.
—— (1943) *Capitalism, Socialism and Democracy*, London: Allen & Unwin.
Simon, H.A. (1959) 'Theories of Decision-Making in economics and behavioural sciences,' *American Economic Review*, 49: 253–283.
—— (1982) *Models of Bounded Rationality*, 2 vols, Cambridge, Mass.: MIT Press.
—— (1992) *Economics, Bounded Rationality and the Cognitive Revolution*, Aldershot: Edward Elgar.
Smith, A. (1976) *An Inquiry into the Nature and Causes of the Wealth of Nations*, ed. R. H. Campbell, A. S. Skinner and W. B. Todd, 2 vols, Oxford: Oxford University Press.
—— (1980) 'The principles which lead and direct philosophical enquiries: illustrated by the history of astronomy', in W. P. D. Wightman (ed.) *Essays on Philosophical Subjects*, Oxford: Oxford University Press.
Whitehead, A. N. (1948) *An Introduction to Mathematics*, Oxford: Oxford University Press (1st edn 1911).
Winter, S. G. (1991) 'On Coase, competence, and the corporation', in O. E. Williamson and S. G. Winter (eds) *The Nature of the Firm: Origins, Evolution, and Development*, Oxford: Oxford University Press.
Woo, H. K. (1992) *Cognition, Value and Price*, Ann Arbor, Mich.: University of Michigan Press.
Zajac, E. J. and Olsen, C. P. (1993) 'From transaction cost to transactional value analysis: implications for the study of interorganizational strategies', *Journal of Management Studies* 30: 131–45.
Ziman, J. M. (1978) *Reliable Knowledge*, Cambridge: Cambridge University Press.

10

CAPABILITIES AND THE THEORY OF THE FIRM

Richard N. Langlois

INTRODUCTION

It is a long-established habit of economists (and other intellectuals) to unearth precursors who can help support their claims to legitimacy. Keynes offered Malthus and the mercantilists; Jevons dredged up Dionysius Lardner and Fleeming Jenkins. Such precursors are always easy to find. As Alfred North Whitehead is supposed to have written, 'everything new has been said before by someone who didn't discover it'. The implication is that discovery is a matter not of saying something for the first time but of saying it at the right time, that is, of offering a new idea precisely when the relevant intellectual community is prepared, for whatever reasons, to accept it.[1] But the very idea of 'precursors' already implies an exercise in Whig history. We can understand those who came before us only to the extent that what they had to say fits the frame of our ideas today; and to the extent that their ideas do not fit the frame, our precursors are but imperfect, albeit perhaps influential, prefigurations of what we now know to be true.[2]

This chapter seeks to locate the ideas of G. B. Richardson within the present-day discussion of the theory of the boundaries of the firm. In doing so, however, it seeks to avoid making of Richardson a precursor. Although it is quite true – and quite significant – that Richardson anticipated ideas that form the core of today's dominant explanation of the firm's boundaries (Teece 1990), it is also true that his ideas have not by any means been completely absorbed or appreciated, at least not within the main current of thought on this topic since Coase. Like most 'precursors' properly read, Richardson is as much a critic as he is an ally.

The ways in which Richardson differs from the modern-day mainstream in transaction-cost economics go beyond the obvious, that is, the latter's comparative neglect of networks, inter-firm arrangements and strategic relationships – topics recently seized by a growing, if peripheral, literature that is certainly well represented at this colloquium. At a more fundamental level, Richardson differs from the mainstream of transaction-cost economics in that, like Coase and Knight before him, Richardson sees the problem of (long-term) market contracting as a matter of difficult co-ordination rather than as a problem of 'opportunism' in the face of contractual hazards, and in that Richardson effectively links together transaction costs and production costs, categories sharply partitioned by traditional price theory (which largely ignored the former) and by transaction-cost economics (which largely ignores the latter). The result of these differences is that, as Loasby (1991) has observed, Richardson stands on its head a principal presumption of transaction-cost economics, namely that contractual relationships among firms must be fraught with hazards and thus that integration must be widely desirable.

PRODUCTION COSTS I:
PIGOVIAN PRICE THEORY

The appropriate place to begin a discussion of Richardson's ideas, of course, is with Marshall. That is a task, however, that one can safely leave to others at this colloquium. Moreover, my objective is to locate Richardson in the context not of Marshall's ideas but of the main current of ideas. And, as Loasby (1976), Moss (1984) and others have argued, what we think of as mainstream 'Marshallian' theory today is in many ways more Pigovian than it is Marshallian. Rather than thinking in population terms as Marshall did, and constructing a 'representative firm' that reflects the characteristics of the population of firms as a whole (rather than the characteristics of any particular firm), the neoclassical theory of the firm since Pigou begins with identical idealised firms and then builds *up* to the industry by simple addition. It is this later methodological standpoint, not any logical problem with Marshall's own conception, that led to the famous controversy over increasing returns early in the twentieth century.[3]

The 'theory of the firm' in modern-day price theory builds on the Pigovian foundation. It begins with firms as production functions, each one identical and each one transforming homogeneous inputs into homogeneous outputs according to given technical 'blueprints' known to all. One effect of these assumptions has been to reduce the margins on which firms operate to two only: price and quantity. This in turn has led to the notion of 'perfect' competition, in which a technically desirable set of assumptions replaces the common-sense notion of competition (Hayek 1948; McNulty 1968).

Now, price theory – whether appreciative[4] Marshallian or heavy-metal Pigovian – was never intended to be a theory of the firm as an organisation or an institution. As Marshall understood, the firm in price theory is a theoretical link in the explanation of changes in price and quantity (supplied, demanded or traded) in response to changes in exogenous factors (Langlois and Koppl 1991). It was never intended to explain industrial structure, let alone to serve as a guide to industrial policy. More to the point, using this sort of price theory to explain the boundaries of the firm is just plain illogical, since the firm's boundaries in price theory are a matter of assumption.

The spectre of illogic has not stopped a good many people from trying, however. Since Pigovian price theory rules out by assumption any qualitative elements, it must interpret all of industrial activity in terms of price and quantity. And, since these are purely quantitative variables, the only issue is whether they are of the right magnitude, that is, whether price and quantity are socially optimal (which is good) or not socially optimal (which is bad). Qualitative elements like distinctive knowledge, ongoing relationships or exchanges of information do not appear on the radar screen of price theory – or, rather, when they do appear, they are often interpreted as unfriendly bogeys. In what Williamson (1985) calls the inhospitality tradition, the least hint of a non-impersonal relationship among firms is viewed with suspicion, since the only possible purpose of non-arm's-length arrangements (when seen through the price theory lens) is collusion to raise prices above the social optimum and to lower quantity below it.[5]

The attempt to appraise institutions – including the kinds of inter-firm arrangements Richardson discussed – with an institution-free theory is an enterprise that has extended even to questions of the firm's boundaries. There exists a large literature attempting to explain vertical arrangements of various sorts, including vertical integration itself, using only the tools of price theory. One long-standing bit of inhospitality lore held, for example, that a firm could 'leverage' its monopoly position at one stage in the chain of production into another stage by tying the sale of its product to the purchase of an input. This is, of course, a fuzzy-headed idea, one that the Chicago school eventually cut to ribbons.[6] Posner (1979) has argued that the genius of the Chicago school in this respect lay in its rigorous and unflinching application of price theory.[7] And what price theory shows is that, in a world of pure neoclassical production costs alone, 'market power' does not explain inter-firm contractual relationships (apart, perhaps, from simple collusion to raise prices) or the boundaries of the firm. This is, of course, quite to be expected, as it is a corollary of the proposition that, in a world of pure neoclassical production costs alone, *nothing* explains the boundaries of the firm.

TRANSACTION COSTS

Many economists, probably going as far back as Cantillon and Smith, have understood that the costs the firm faces are rather different in character from the fully known and purely technological costs of the production function. In this century, however, that recognition crystallised in a form that strongly challenged the price-theoretic formulation – while, in an odd way, simultaneously reinforcing it.

In 1937 Ronald Coase enquired into the nature of the firm and observed that, in the world of price theory, firms have no reason to exist. According to the textbook, the decentralised price system is the ideal structure for carrying out economic co-ordination. Why, then, do we observe some transactions to be removed from the price system to the interior of organisations called firms? The answer, Coase reasoned, must be that there is a 'cost to using the price system' (Coase 1937: 390). Thus was born the idea of transaction costs:[8] costs that stand separate from and in addition to ordinary production costs. It is transaction costs that explain, as it were, the institutional overlay of production. Production costs determine technical (substitution) choices, but transaction costs determine which stages of the productive process are assigned to the institution of the price system and which to the institution of the firm. The two kinds of costs are logically distinct; they are orthogonal to one another.

One salutary effect of the invention of the idea of transaction costs is that it made clear the extent to which the price theory approach tends to sneak institutional judgements in the back door. This is true even of the basic idea of supra-competitive pricing applied to antitrust policy. As I enjoy pointing out to my students, the very idea of monopoly pricing, which seems so obviously a pure artefact of price theory, is actually just a transaction-cost problem. The deadweight-loss triangle monopoly pricing creates is in fact an unexploited source of gains from trade, since, with an appropriate split of the rents, consumers could bribe the monopolist to produce at the social optimum in a way that is strictly Pareto-improving. The reason that these gains are not exploited is that, in some institutional settings, it is costly for the consumers to organise and bargain with the monopolist: so costly, indeed, that these transaction costs – in the sense of Coase (1960) if not Coase (1937)[9] – outweigh the costs of the deadweight loss. And, as Demsetz (1969) has pointed out in a related context, to pronounce an inefficiency and call for government intervention in such a case is in fact to propose replacing one institutional structure with another without having taken the trouble to examine the full costs of either.

Coase's approach in 'The nature of the firm', which Richardson mentions only in a footnote in 'The organisation of industry', is in some ways different from and in some ways similar to Richardson's own. One clear difference is that Coase formulated a sharp break between firm and market, thus ignoring the various inter-firm arrangements Richardson highlighted.[10] This was a significant methodological choice in that it directed attention for some years away from inter-firm complexities. But there is, in the end, nothing about the idea of transaction costs that implies such a sharp dichotomy.

What is more interesting are the similarities between Coase and Richardson. Both are arguably concerned with the issue of qualitative co-ordination. Although it is not well recognised, the need for qualitative co-ordination of activities – indeed, co-ordination of activities over time – lies at the heart of Coase's conception of organisation within the firm. 'It may be desired to make a long-term contract for the supply of some article or service', Coase writes, continuing:

> Now, owing to the difficulty of forecasting, the longer the period of the contract is for the supply of the commodity or service, the less possible, and indeed, the less desirable it is for the person purchasing to specify what the other contracting party is expected to do. It may well be a matter of indifference to the person supplying the service or commodity which of several courses of action is taken, but not to the purchaser of that commodity or service. But the purchaser will not know which of these several courses he will want the supplier to take. Therefore, the service which is being provided is expressed in general terms, the exact details being left until a later date.... The details of what the supplier is expected to do is not stated in the contract but is decided later by the purchaser. When the direction of resources (within the limits of the contract) becomes dependent on the buyer in this way, that relationship which I term a 'firm' may be obtained.
> (Coase 1937: 391–2)

This is clearly close to Richardson's concerns, in *Information and Investment*, with the co-ordination of complementary investments. In Chapter IV Richardson also considers the problems of executing fully specified long-term contracts:

> The longer the future period which is envisaged, the more flexible will the entrepreneur's investment programme become; both the quantities, and frequently also the kinds of outputs and inputs will become a matter of subsequent decision according to the circumstances which come to prevail. Contracts which extend into this more distant period, therefore, are likely to diminish the entrepreneur's ability to modify his plans in order to meet unexpected developments, without at the same time producing a very substantial reduction in uncertainty. The point will be reached where the greater predictability yielded by contracts does not justify the loss of flexibility which they involve. Attempts to secure a more perfect co-ordination of complementary activities by means of binding agreements between firms, will, therefore, encounter a barrier, the existence of which is the consequence of the inherent imperfectibility of both technical and market information. Because of this, the efficiency of any economy, viewed as a system of communication, can

never be made perfect; there is a resemblance in this respect to electrical networks, the efficiency of which for communication is limited by the irreducible element of random molecular motion known technically as 'noise'.

(Richardson 1960: 81)

For Richardson as for Coase, such 'noise' – perhaps a better physical image for transaction costs than the more usual one of friction – may lead to alternative institutional forms that include 'agglomeration' (Richardson 1960: 84). And, for both writers, the relevant 'costs of the price system' are costs of co-ordination over time.

MODERN TRANSACTION-COST THEORY

Since Coase, the economics of transaction costs as applied to organisation has burgeoned into a major subfield of the discipline. Largely in a quest to make Coase's ideas more 'operational', this literature has arguably both narrowed his explanation for the firm and moved its focus away from issues of co-ordination, especially qualitative co-ordination. Oliver Williamson, the standard-bearer of the field since the 1970s, cannot be accused of having a narrow conception of transaction-cost economics. But it was Williamson (1975) who introduced the idea of *opportunism* and made it coequal with *bounded rationality* as a pillar of the transaction-cost approach. The latter, which is Herbert Simon's famous term, leads naturally to the Richardsonian concern with co-ordination. Because economic agents have cognitive limits,[11] in an uncertain world they cannot fully anticipate all future contingencies, which may make long-term contracting difficult. Relatedly, they may be afflicted with *information impactedness*, which means, more or less, that information important to a transaction can get stuck and not flow to where it is needed.[12] Opportunism, however, is a behavioural (or quasi-behavioural) postulate rather than a strictly cognitive or informational one. In part, opportunism is just self-interested or rent-seeking behaviour, something tacitly assumed at some level by Coase, Richardson and most others. But Williamson embellishes the idea to become 'self-interest seeking with guile' (*ibid.*: 9). The 'guile' part surreptitiously mixes in some information impactedness again. It also arguably both narrows and amplifies the presupposition of rent-seeking behaviour, implying, if not necessarily requiring, that agents craftily seek to take advantage of others at every turn in a manner not typically constrained by wider or longer-run considerations.[13]

In Williamson's work, especially his early work, opportunism and bounded rationality proved to be versatile tools that helped create a smorgasbord of explanations for organisational forms and features. Issues of co-ordination figured prominently in these explanations. For example,

Williamson argued that internal organisation may be a superior mode of co-ordination whenever boundedly rational transactors confront uncertainty.

> If, in consideration of these [cognitive] limits, it is very costly or impossible to identify future contingencies and specify, *ex ante*, appropriate adaptations thereto, long-term contracts may be supplanted by internal organization. Recourse to the latter permits adaptations to uncertainty to be accomplished by administrative processes in a sequential fashion. Thus, rather than attempt to anticipate all possible contingencies from the outset, the future is permitted to unfold. Internal organization in this way economizes on the bounded rationality attributes of decision makers in circumstances in which prices are not 'sufficient statistics' and uncertainty is substantial.
>
> (Williamson 1975: 9)

What Williamson means here by prices not being 'sufficient statistics' – a reference to his interpretation of Hayek (1945) on the virtues of the price system – is that internal organisation may be superior in situations requiring qualitative co-ordination, that is, the transmission and use of information beyond price and quantity.

The breadth of Williamson's approach was met, however, with impatience from the larger profession, now becoming increasingly interested in moving, albeit gingerly, beyond the margins of price theory *strictu senso* into the economics of institutions. To most economists, even sympathetic ones, transaction-cost theory remained insufficiently 'operational', meaning that it was too rich to be crammed into a mathematical model. Williamson (1985) himself helped solve that problem when, along with Klein *et al.* (1978), he focused in on asset specificity as a variable first among (what had been) equals in explaining vertical integration.[14] Here was a variable that was quantifiable and whose relationship to the boundaries of the firm was clear: the greater the degree of asset specificity in a transaction, the higher the probability that the transaction would be internalised.

The logic is quite simple. Assets are highly specific when they have value within the context of a particular transaction but have relatively little value outside the transaction. This opens the door to opportunism. Once the contract is signed and the assets deployed, one of the parties may threaten to pull out of the arrangement – thereby reducing the value of the specific assets – unless a greater share of the quasi-rents of joint production find their way into the threat-maker's pockets. Fear of such 'hold-up' *ex post* will affect investment choices *ex ante*. In the absence of appropriate contractual safeguards,[15] the transacting parties may choose less specific – and therefore less specialised and less productive – technology. If, by contrast, the transacting parties were to pool their capital into a single enterprise in whose profits they jointly shared, the incentives for unproductive rent-seeking would be attenuated. And, because such unified organisations would choose the more productive specialised technology, they would win out in the competitive struggle against the contractual alternative.[16]

As Williamson suggests, this logic depends as much on bounded rationality as it does on opportunism.[17] 'Guile' serves little when information is perfect. And, in a world of certainty and unrestricted cognitive ability (if one could imagine such a place), it would be easy to write and enforce long-term contracts that pre-empt *ex ante* unproductive rent-seeking behaviour *ex post* and thus obviate internalisation. This insight, indeed, has inspired one important formal strand of the literature. The work of Oliver Hart and others (Grossman and Hart 1986; Hart 1988, 1989; Moore 1992) – called the incomplete-contracts literature or, increasingly, the 'property rights' approach[18] – distinguishes two types of rights under contract: specific rights and residual rights. The latter are generic rights to make production decisions in circumstances not spelt out in the contract. In this literature, the choice between contract and internal organisation reduces to a question of the efficient allocation of the residual rights of control when contracts are incomplete and assets highly specific. Suppose there are two parties co-operating in production, each bringing to the arrangement a bundle of assets. If none of the assets is highly specific, opportunism is impossible ceteris paribus, as either party can liquidate at no cost as soon as troublesome unforeseen contingencies arise. If, however, assets are specific, or if opportunism becomes possible for other reasons, it may be efficient to place the residual rights of control in the hands of only one of the parties by giving that party ownership of both sets of assets.[19] In general, the owner ought to be the party whose possession of the residual right minimises rent-seeking costs, which typically means the party whose contribution to the quasi-rents of co-operation is greater.

Another strand of the transaction-cost literature since Coase has reached a similar conclusion by a slightly different path. This strand has also emphasised opportunism and the hazards of contracting. In this case, however, the contractual hazards involved are not those of hold-up in the presence of highly specific assets but those arising from the costs of measuring the inputs to and monitoring the outputs of production.[20] A well-known milestone along this path was Alchian and Demsetz's (1972) analysis of monitoring team production. When individual contributions to joint production cannot be distinguished, opportunistic contributors have the incentive to shirk, that is, to supply less effort than they contracted to supply. (Such shirking, and related problems in other formulations, is an instance of *moral hazard* broadly understood.) Alchian and Demsetz propose that this problem be solved by assigning one party to be a specialist in monitoring – a boss – who possesses the rights to the residual income and is thus monitored by the market. *Voilà* the firm.

As Alchian and Woodward (1988) point out, transaction costs emanating from situations of moral hazard are ultimately related to those emanating from problems of hold-up: both arise because cognitive limits create in contracts a certain 'plasticity' that allows conduct *ex post* to deviate from what was agreed upon *ex ante*. In the hands of Barzel (1987), indeed, the moral-hazard approach tells a story quite similar to that of Hart *et al.* Imagine again two parties co-operating in production. If the output of one of the parties is hard to monitor, that party is tempted to moral hazard. If in addition the shirking party's contribution to the joint quasi-rents is large, it may be efficient to assign the residual rights to this hard-to-monitor partner, who is then effectively disciplined by the desire to maximise residual income.[21] Although it is less clearly spelt out, Barzel's story is also one of incomplete contracts. Routine tasks are generally easy to monitor. The less routine the agent's actions – the larger the uncertainty in the tasks the agent may be called upon to execute (Stinchcombe 1990: ch. 2) – the harder it will be to monitor the agent and the harder to specify in a contract what the agent is supposed to do.[22]

In the end, then, we might argue that the modern transaction-cost literature has not in fact strayed too far from the concern with co-ordination over time in Richardson (and in Coase),[23] even if the literature has buried those concerns behind secondary concepts like asset specificity and moral hazard. Especially in *Information and Investment*, we can see Richardson's connection in particular to the asset-specificity literature, with which he shares a concern for the co-ordination of complementary assets. Yet, there are differences.

Richardson clearly understands the difficulties of inflexibility and lock-in posed by assets specialised to particular uses.

> Under any technological conditions, except the most primitive, production requires the service of skills, experience, and equipment which are highly specific in character. There may, of course, be occasion when the maximum adaptability, such as is conferred by investment exclusively in money, provides the expectation of greatest gain or smallest loss. . . . Generally, however, it is only by allowing himself to be trammelled by a particular production programme that the entrepreneur can hope to make any substantial return.
> (Richardson 1960: 152)

In Chapter VIII, indeed, Richardson even offers measures of asset specificity, namely *separation loss*, which is the difference between value in sale and value in use, and the *coefficient of dispensability*, which is the ratio of value in sale to value in use.

What is interesting, however, is that, unlike modern-day transaction-cost theorists, Richardson does not see asset specificity as leading principally to problems of opportunism and inefficient rent dissipation. Rather, asset specificity creates problems of co-ordination even when, as he seems to assume in the following passage, there is no opportunism.

> It may be very difficult . . . to arrange that the terms of a long-term contract are such as to offer each of the parties a prospective return which is in proportion to the risks which they are assuming. One manufacturer might be asked, for example, to supply another with a specialized component, the manufacture of which requires heavy investment. If all went well, he would be assured of a market for his output for some years ahead, and at a price fixed by the terms of the contract; but, however profitable the sale of the final product, he could not expect more than this return. If, on the other hand, the purchaser's enterprise fared very badly, then the contract would likely be broken and the supplier would suffer loss. In order to obtain a more equitable distribution of possible gains and losses, a form of co-operation more intimate than that of a simple contract would be sought; the two companies might form a subsidiary in which they both possessed some equity interest or might decide wholly to amalgamate.
>
> (Richardson 1960: 84)

In Richardson, it is not the threat of hold-up that leads to integration (or, significantly, to other possible institutional forms, including joint venture). Rather, it is the inflexibility of highly specific assets that leads the contracting parties to choose an organisational form precisely *because* it allows them to redistribute quasi-rents *ex post*.

We can see this focus on qualitative co-ordination – so lacking in the asset-specificity literature – perhaps even more clearly in 'The organisation of industry'. Here Richardson talks of how the activities of contracting parties need to be 'co-ordinated both quantitatively and qualitatively', and he notes that the neoclassical habit of thinking in terms of a fixed list of goods is partly responsible for the neglect of qualitative co-ordination (Richardson 1972: 884). And this need for qualitative co-ordination is at least coequal with the hazards of asset specificity in the explanation of 'governance structures' – like long-term subcontracting relationships – alternative to spot contracting.[24] The stability of a subcontracting relationship, he writes, is important for two reasons:

> It is necessary, in the first place, to induce sub-contractors to assume risks inherent in a rather narrow specialization in skills and equipment; and, secondly, it permits continuing co-operation between those concerned in the development of specifications, processes and designs.
>
> (Richardson 1972: 885)

We might encapsulate the difference between Richardson and the present-day literature of asset specificity in the following way: Richardson is interested in the *co-ordination of production*, not merely in the *co-ordination of commitments*.[25] This wider orientation is perhaps more evident in 'The organisation of industry' (1972) than in *Information and Investment* (1960). The earlier work is centrally about commitments, albeit with an awareness of the larger problems of co-ordination. The later work, however, is less worried about the problem of commitments and more worried about the difficulties of qualitative co-ordination. The reason for this, I believe, is at least in part because the 1972 paper develops and emphasises an idea present only in embryonic form in the 1960 book: namely, the idea of *capabilities* and its concurrent implication that productive knowledge is widely dispersed and non-homogeneous.

PRODUCTION COSTS REDUX: CAPABILITIES

As I have suggested, one effect of the invention of the concept of transaction costs has been a partition between those costs and the costs of production, a partition rigidly upheld (in principle) by both price theory and transaction-cost economics. Williamson, for example, maintains that, although he sees organisational structures as somehow resulting from the minimising of the sum of production costs and transaction costs, his own analytical interest has lain in transaction costs alone (Williamson 1988: 361). That is, he (and most others) have sought to hold production costs constant and investigate the effects on organisational form of differences in transaction costs *tous seuls*. This is by no means a nonsensical methodological position. In the end, however, production costs and transaction costs do affect one another, and they cannot be so neatly separated.

Indeed, the very notion of asset specificity brings production costs back in centrally, albeit in a somewhat ad hoc way. In the basic asset-specificity story, the nature of the rent dissipation that integration avoids is the inefficient choice of technology. Absent joint ownership of assets, the contracting party or parties at risk would choose a less productive but more liquid technology as a defence against hold-up, thus dissipating quasi-rents in the same sense that residents of crime-ridden areas 'waste' resources on locks and security guards in order to reduce the likelihood of becoming the victims of directly unproductive rent-seeking activities. But what makes choosing more liquid assets inefficient in this case is the old Smithian production-cost trade-off. As Richardson puts it, the 'sacrifice of adaptability which any act of real investment inevitably imposes should be regarded as simply the obverse side of the gains from specialization' (Richardson 1960: 151). The division of labour is limited not merely by the extent of the market, but also by the *predictability* of the extent of the market. Organisation matters, then, because various organisational forms have quite different abilities to eliminate sources of uncertainty – and therefore to support a more elaborate division of labour.[26]

But production costs and transaction costs are also arguably intertwined in a much more subtle and fundamental way. If one relaxes the rather stern assumption that productive knowledge is always in the nature of 'blueprints', the line between production costs and transaction costs begins to blur.

As we have seen, standard Pigovian price theory partakes of the epistemology of old spy movies, in which complete knowledge of how to build and launch an ICBM could somehow be transcribed onto a microdot and hidden under a postage stamp. Michael Polanyi (1958) has taught us, however, that knowledge is not all of a form that can be articulated in words or pictures for easy transmission. Much knowledge – including, importantly, much knowledge about production – is *tacit* and can be acquired only through a time-consuming process of learning by doing. In a world of tacit knowledge, having the same blueprints as one's competitors is unlikely to translate into having the same costs of production.[27] Moreover, in a world of diffuse and variegated knowledge, the costs that can make transacting difficult – the costs that may lead to internalization or various other business institutions – may go beyond those that arise in the course of defending against opportunism. In such a world, economic activity may be afflicted with what I call dynamic transaction costs,[28] the costs that arise in real time in the process of acquiring and co-ordinating productive knowledge (Langlois 1992b; Langlois and Robertson 1995).

In order to understand this point, we need to recognise that production faces two rather different kinds of co-ordination problem, which I have already labelled problems of the co-ordination of commitments and problems of the co-ordination of production. The former arise, in effect, when flexibility inhibits specialisation. The latter – the obverse side – arise when specialisation inhibits flexibility, especially the flexibility to seize profitable opportunities.

As we have seen, the main current of the transaction-cost literature (and, in a larger sense, so-called industrial organisation in general)[29] concentrates almost exclusively on problems of the co-ordination of commitments. And, again, such problems were a dominant concern in *Information and Investment*. Solutions to such problems typically follow the lines set out by Schelling (1960) and defined, among other places, in the domain of constitutional economics (Buchanan 1990). In certain situations, interacting parties can increase their welfare (severally as well as jointly) by committing themselves in a credible way to one particular course of action. Paradoxically (from a standard economic point of view), the parties can actually make themselves better off by *reducing* the size of their choice set. In the case of specific assets, the reasons for this should be clear. By following inflexibly a predictable course of action, one can reduce uncertainty, thus allowing others to plan effectively and encouraging efficient specialisation. One way to gain predictability is to follow codes of behaviour, which, by restricting one's freedom of action, increase predictability (Heiner 1983; Langlois 1986). This is, of course, vintage Richardson, and the theme of his 'Les Relations entre firmes' (1965).

But it is also a theme in Richardson that flexibility too is valuable. The cost of specialisation is the ability to adapt to an uncertain future, which may mean, in particular, foregoing profitable market opportunities and emerging technological possibilities. Specialisation is certainly a matter of highly specific tangible assets. But, even in *Information and Investment*, Richardson is clear that transactional inertia (if we may call it that) is also a cognitive and behavioural matter. Production, as we saw, requires the service not just of plant and equipment but of 'skills and experience' that are highly specific in character (Richardson 1960: 152). 'From some points of view', indeed, 'management itself, together with the skills, experience, and traditions which it embodies, may restrict a firm's freedom of manoeuvre as much as, if not more than, the fixed equipment which it owns' (*ibid.*: 153).

Although it is not developed in the 1960 book, the idea of accumulated and inertial 'skills, experience, and traditions' prefigures the notion of *capabilities* introduced in the 1972 essay. Capabilities, Richardson says there, are 'the knowledge, experience, and skills' of the firm (Richardson 1972: 888). It is, in fact, the emphasis on capabilities that distinguishes the theme of 'The organisation of industry' from that of *Information and Investment*. Taking issue with the representation of knowledge in the production-function approach, Richardson writes:

> Of course I realise that production functions presume a certain level of managerial and material technology. The point is not that production is thus dependent on the state of the arts but that it has to be undertaken (as Mrs Penrose has so very well explained) by organisations embodying specifically appropriate experience and skill. It is this circumstance that formal production theory tends to put out of focus, and justifiably, no doubt, given the character of the optimisation problem that it is designed to handle; nevertheless, it seems to me that we cannot hope to construct an adequate theory of industrial organisation and in particular to answer our question about the division of labour between firm and market, unless the elements of organisation, knowledge, experience and skills are brought back to the foreground of our vision.
>
> (Richardson 1972: 888)

The reference to Penrose is, of course, to *The Theory of the Growth of the Firm* (1959), which appears to have crystallised for Richardson the idea of capabilities that was embryonic in *Information and Investment*.

Richardson's entire discussion of capabilities in 'The organisation of industry' is clearly indebted to Penrose. In her theory, firms consist of acquired pools of resources – including, importantly, managerial resources – that come in lumpy bundles. In order to take advantage of excess capacity in some of the lumps, the firm may expand or diversify into areas in which that capacity is useful. This, in turn, may lead the firm to acquire other complementary capabilities, which will lead to further excess capacity etc. In Richardson's terminology, production can be broken down into various stages or *activities*. Some activities are *similar*, in that they draw on the same general capabilities. Activities can also be *complementary*, in that they are connected in the chain of production and therefore need to be co-ordinated with one another. For Richardson (1972), the central problem of economic co-ordination lies in the fact that what is complementary need not be similar:

> Where activities are both similar and complementary they could be co-ordinated by direction within an individual business. Generally, however, this would not be the case and the activities to be co-ordinated, being dissimilar, would be the responsibility of different firms. Co-ordination would then have to be brought about either through co-operation, firms agreeing to match their plans *ex ante*, or through the processes of adjustment set in train by the market mechanism.
>
> (Richardson 1972: 895)

Clearly, co-ordination – the matching, 'in level or specification' (Richardson 1972: 895), of complementary activities – could still be a matter of co-ordinating commitments. In many respects, this is the view taken by David Teece (1980, 1982, 1986), one of the few major scholars to have incorporated Richardson's ideas.[30] Unlike Richardson, who has switched from discussing the co-ordination of complementary *investments* to discussing the co-ordination of complementary *activities*, Teece talks about complementary *assets* that might be *cospecialised* to one another. As with Richardson's closely complementary activities, cospecialised assets may be difficult to co-ordinate. But, unlike Richardson, Teece is inclined, with the broader asset-specificity literature that has influenced him, to believe that cospecialised assets may be a cause of integration more than of co-operation, especially to the extent that integration allows an innovator to appropriate the gains from innovation in regimes in which intellectual property rights are ineffective.[31]

Thus, we might say that, for Teece, problems of co-ordination arise because markets (narrowly understood) exhibit *too little* 'friction'. Governance structures alternative to the market arise to prevent slippery innovative knowledge from escaping the grasp of its creators, just as, in the main current of the transaction-cost literature,[32] alternative governance structures emerge to protect transactors from the 'plasticity' of contract. An admixture of Penrose, however, suggests the opposite possibility. Co-ordination problems may arise because markets – or, indeed, any structure of business institutions, including large vertically integrated firms – exhibit *too much* 'friction'. If Penrose and Richardson are right, the knowledge, skills and traditions embodied in existing governance structures (be they firms, markets or in between) may be too inflexible, especially in the face of major 'Schumpeterian' change, to seize market and technological opportunities. In such circumstances, other governance structures that can muster the necessary capabilities may arise and prosper.

Morris Silver (1984) has suggested, for example, that much vertical integration arises not when firms venture into areas of similar capabilities but when firms are dragged, kicking and screaming, as it were, into complementary but dissimilar activities because only in that way can they bring about a profitable reconfiguration of production or distribution.[33] For example, consider the once-famous calculator-maker Bowmar. After losing a defence contract, Bowmar was looking for some way of selling its light-emitting diodes (LEDs). The company tried to interest makers of larger calculators in using the LEDs, to no avail. So Bowmar designed its own hand calculator, and the rest is history (Schnaars 1994).[34] On the other side of the ledger, we might tell a similar story about IBM's motives for turning to the market rather than to its in-house capabilities in producing the original PC (Langlois 1992a). Paul Robertson and I (Langlois and Robertson 1995) have tried to think in some depth about the implications of these sorts of co-ordination problem.

I do not want to be read as implying that Richardson was in any way inconsistent in shifting his emphasis between 1960 and 1972. Both kinds of co-ordination problem are important, and both can involve the qualitative aspects of co-ordination. We need to investigate both kinds of co-ordination problems, which may mean, for the profession as a whole, a major shift of emphasis away from problems of co-ordinating commitments toward problems of co-ordinating production. If we work hard, Richardson may yet be a precursor – of a theory we have still to develop fully.

NOTES

1 In that respect, innovation in matters intellectual operates in a manner similar to – and partakes of many of the same communications difficulties as – innovation in industry (on which see Robertson in this volume).

2 A good example of this is neoclassical scholarship on Frank Knight. (See Langlois and Cosgel 1993.)

3 This is a point on which Richardson agrees: 'the apparent necessity of finding some reason why long-run marginal costs should ultimately rise is created not by the phenomena themselves, but by the nature of the theoretical schema through which we have chosen to study them' (Richardson 1960: 213).

4 On the distinction between formal and appreciative theory, see Nelson and Winter (1982: 46).
5 'Economic relationships are never perfectly competitive if they involve any personal relationships between economic units' (Stigler 1946: 24).
6 A firm cannot raise the price of a tied complement above competitive levels without thereby raising above the rent-maximising level the effective price of the monopolised good to which the complement is tied. When the two tied goods are substitutes in production at the same horizontal level, it is possible to conjure up situations in which tying might in theory reduce welfare (Scherer and Ross 1990: 566). But those would not be vertical arrangements.
7 There is, however, another interpretation. Rather than applying price theory more rigorously, the Chicago school was arguably *broadening* price theory to include a wider range of phenomena. For example, the classic Chicago explanation for tying arrangements (Director and Levi 1956) is that they solve what is in effect a transaction-cost problem: tying allows a manufacturer to 'meter' the output of a monopolised product in order to engage in price discrimination. The welfare implications of price discrimination are ambiguous, and such behaviour is probably typically welfare-enhancing. More to the present point, however, price discrimination (or, rather, the lack thereof) is a transaction-cost problem that tying helps mitigate.
8 Even though Coase did not actually use the term in the 1937 article.
9 It is in fact an interesting question whether the 'costs of using the price system' in Coase's 1937 article are transaction costs in the same sense as the bargaining and other costs given the name transaction costs in Coase's 1960 article. Although I will try below to shed some light on the 'transaction costs' in the 1937 article, answering the comparative question is beyond the scope of this chapter.
10 In his fifty-year retrospective on 'The nature of the firm', Coase (1988) cites this black-and-white dichotomy as perhaps his chief regret.
11 And it is, of course, cognition, not rationality, that is limited. That Simon labelled the problem a limitation of 'rationality' says much about his own conception of rationality (Langlois 1990).
12 'Information impactedness is a derivative condition in the organizational failures framework. It is mainly attributable to the pairing of uncertainty with opportunism. It exists in circumstances in which one of the parties to an exchange is much better informed than is the other regarding underlying conditions germane to the trade, and the second party cannot achieve information parity except at great cost – because he cannot rely on the first party to disclose the information in a fully candid manner' (Williamson 1975: 14).
13 The assumption of opportunism has come under most violent attack by sociologists, who have usually offered to substitute their own excesses in the direction of communitarian postulates. A sensible middle ground is Granovetter (1985), who argues that, although self-interested, behaviour is 'imbedded' in a network of relationships that go well beyond the boundaries of an individual transaction and that constrain in many cases the impulse to opportunism. I should add in Williamson's defence that he does mention trust and even atmosphere as important organisational variables (Williamson 1993). As I will argue below, however, the postulate of opportunism, coupled with a comparative neglect of production-cost differences, has led transaction-cost economics to overemphasise the costliness of the price system (broadly understood).
14 'The main factor to which transaction-cost economics appeals to explain vertical integration is asset specificity' (Williamson 1986: 189).

15 For example, a hostage. (See Williamson 1985: chs 7 and 8.)
16 This way of putting it gives an explicitly evolutionary spin to the functionalist argument more typical in transaction-cost economics.
17 Indeed, as I have long maintained, it is the bounded rationality part rather than the opportunism part that is the important factor in explaining internalisation (Langlois 1984). Even if the parties were perfectly content always to split rents fairly and amicably, they would still be unable to write fully specified contacts in a world of what I call structural – that is, qualitative – uncertainty. Although the lack of opportunism would attenuate the need for internalisation as a safeguard against intentional rent-seeking behaviour, joint ownership may still have advantages in respect of flexibility and as a way of reconciling divergent visions of the uncertain future.
18 We might more properly call this literature the 'new' property-rights approach to distinguish it from the older literature of property rights emerging directly from Coase (1960) and associated with such names as Alchian, Demsetz, Furubotn and Pejovich. On this older literature, see De Alessi (1983).
19 Hart and his colleagues hold that the possession of the residual rights of control necessitates ownership of the firm's capital assets, whether tangible or intangible. This allows them to do something few in the literature have been able to do: to *define* the boundaries of the firm crisply and consistently. For them, a firm is defined by the bundle of assets under common ownership. (This stands in contrast to the 'nexus of contracts' view, which sees the firm as a far more fuzzy notion.) While I find Hart's approach appealing, I wonder, with Louis Putterman (1988), whether it is not in fact possible to possess the right to direct the production programme (that is, the residual rights of control) without also possessing the firm's capital.
20 Williamson (1985: 24) distinguishes his *governance* approach to transaction-cost economics from the *measurement* approach. I would also lump agency theory in with the measurement-cost approach, since that literature is also driven by monitoring costs (which are a form of measurement costs, namely, the costs of measuring performance *ex post*, as distinct from the *ex ante* measurement costs of searching or sorting inputs).
21 Also like Hart, Barzel (1987) believes possession of the residual rights should involve ownership of capital, in this case because capital ownership serves as a bond to guarantee the fixed-income claims of the other parties.
22 Barzel's (1987) own example is of co-operation between a manufacturer and a 'business expert'. Because the business expert is the harder to monitor, says Barzel, he ought to become the entrepreneur and possess the residual claim. But this is because the business expert is the one whose tasks involve greater uncertainty and are more difficult to specify in a contract. That the expert can disguise shirking as bad luck (as Barzel puts it) is a manifestation of contractual incompleteness, not its cause.
23 And let's not forget Frank Knight, on which see Langlois and Cosgel (1993).
24 It is perhaps significant that Coase also rejects the centrality of asset specificity in explaining the firm. He notes that, in formulating the thesis of 'The nature of the firm', he considered – but then rejected – asset specificity as an explanation (Coase 1988).
25 I am indebted to Sergey Rumyantsev for this terminology.
26 For example, the co-operating parties may choose a trading relationship 'which is stable enough to make demand expectations more reliable and therefore to facilitate production planning' (Richardson 1972: 884). Consider also Alfred Chandler's (1977) notion that large American firms in the nineteenth century

often sought vertical integration as a way of assuring predictable inputs in the service of 'economies of speed'.
27 Indeed, having the same *equipment* may not guarantee the same production costs, as suggested by Polanyi's own example of the Hungarians unable to make function a light-bulb machine identical to one operating flawlessly in Austria.
28 Loosely, and perhaps somewhat cryptically, dynamic transaction costs are the costs of not having the capabilities you need when you need them (Langlois 1992b).
29 Problems of the co-ordination of commitments are tailor-made for game-theoretic modelling, an approach that arguably dominates the high-brow regions of the field of industrial organisation today. See, for example, the textbook by Tirole (1988).
30 It is interesting that, in developing a theory of firm diversification not unlike that of Richardson (1972), Teece refers only once to Richardson (in Teece 1982), and that reference is to *Information and Investment*. When I showed Teece a draft of what became Langlois (1988), his principal response, as I remember it, was that I had reminded him of the importance of Richardson (1972).
31 Richardson (1972: 894n.) seems much more sanguine about the workability of markets for licences.
32 Indeed, the formal economics of organisation has lately begun to take cognisance of the idea of capabilities. But, rather than adopting the stance towards productive knowledge taken by Penrose and Richardson, it seeks to explain the tendency of firms to concentrate on specific activities in terms of problems of co-ordinating commitments. In Milgrom and Roberts (1992), for example, a commitment to a narrow strategy allows managers engaged in a co-ordination game to avoid dominated equilibria. And Rotemberg and Saloner (1994) use the incomplete-contracts framework to argue that a firm may choose a narrow strategy (and thus ignore profitable opportunities) because strategic breadth leads to implementation problems *ex post* that distort *ex ante* incentives. Rotemberg and Saloner note that 'increasing returns to specialization' (Rotemberg and Saloner 1994: 1131) – which comes closer to the Penrose–Richardson idea – may also be a reason for narrow strategies, but they do not investigate that possibility.
33 Richardson recognises this motive for integration when he writes that '[a]n entrepreneur may believe that only by gaining some degree of control over the firm responsible for some complementary investment will he be fully assured of it being undertaken; vertical integration may be carried out with this end in view' (Richardson 1960: 83).
34 As, soon, was Bowmar, which went belly-up a few years later, the victim of larger firms wielding Teecean complementary assets. I am indebted to Paul Robertson for this example and the Schnaars reference.

REFERENCES

Alchian, A. and Demsetz, H. (1972) 'Production, information costs, and economic organization', *American Economic Review* 62(5): 772–95.

Alchian, A. and Woodward, S. (1988) 'The firm is dead; long live the firm: a review of Oliver E. Williamson's *The Economic Institutions of Capitalism*', *Journal of Economic Literature* 26(1) (March): 65–79.

Barzel, Y. (1987) 'The entrepreneur's reward for self-policing', *Economic Inquiry* 25: 103–16.

Buchanan, J. M. (1990) 'The domain of constitutional economics', *Constitutional Political Economy* 1(1): 1–18.

Chandler, A. D., Jr (1977) *The Visible Hand: the Managerial Revolution in American Business*, Cambridge: Belknap Press of Harvard University Press.

Coase, R. H. (1937) 'The nature of the firm', *Economica*, NS, 4 (November): 386–405.

—— (1960) 'The problem of social cost', *Journal of Law and Economics* 3: 1–44.

—— (1988) 'The nature of the firm: origin, meaning, influence', *Journal of Law, Economics, and Organization* 4(1) (spring): 3–47.

De Alessi, L. (1983) 'Property rights, transaction costs, and X-efficiency', *American Economic Review* 73 (March): 64–81.

Demsetz, H. (1969) 'Information and efficiency: another viewpoint', *Journal of Law and Economics* 12: 1–22.

Director, A. and Levi, E. (1956) 'Law and the future: trade regulation', *Northwestern University Law Review* 512: 81.

Granovetter, M. (1985) 'Economic action and social structure: the problem of embeddedness', *American Journal of Sociology* 91(3) (November): 481–510.

Grossman, S. and Hart, O. (1986) 'The costs and benefits of ownership: a theory of vertical integration', *Journal of Political Economy* 94: 691–719.

Hart, O. D. (1988) 'Incomplete contracts and the theory of the firm', *Journal of Law, Economics, and Organization* 4(1) (spring): 119–40.

—— (1989) 'An economist's perspective on the theory of the firm', *Columbia Law Review* 89(7): 1757–74.

Hayek, F. A. (1945) 'The use of knowledge in society', *American Economic Review* 35(4): 519–30.

—— (1948) 'The meaning of competition', *Individualism and Economic Order*, Chicago: University of Chicago Press.

Heiner, R. A. (1983) 'The origin of predictable behavior', *American Economic Review* 73: 560–95.

Klein, B., Crawford, R. G. and Alchian, A. (1978) 'Vertical integration, appropriable rents, and the competitive contracting process', *Journal of Law and Economics* 21(2): 297–326.

Langlois, R. N. (1984) 'Internal organization in a dynamic context: some theoretical considerations', in M. Jussawalla and H. Ebenfield (eds) *Communication and Information Economics: New Perspectives*, Amsterdam: North Holland.

—— (1986) 'Coherence and flexibility: social institutions in a world of radical uncertainty', in I. Kirzner (ed.) *Subjectivism, Intelligibility, and Economic Understanding: Essays in Honor of the Eightieth Birthday of Ludwig Lachmann*, New York: New York University Press.

—— (1988) 'Economic change and the boundaries of the firm', *Journal of Institutional and Theoretical Economics* 144(4): 635–57.

—— (1990) 'Bounded rationality and behavioralism: a clarification and critique', *Journal of Institutional and Theoretical Economics* 146(4): 691–5.

—— (1992a) 'External economies and economic progress: the case of the microcomputer industry', *Business History Review* 66(1) (spring): 1–52.

—— (1992b) 'Transaction-cost economics in real time', *Industrial and Corporate Change* 1(1): 99–127.

Langlois, R. N. and Cosgel, M. M. (1993) 'Frank Knight on risk, uncertainty, and the firm: a new interpretation', *Economic Inquiry* 31 (July): 456–65.

Langlois, R. N. and Koppl, R. G. (1991) 'Fritz Machlup and marginalism: a reevaluation', *Methodus* 3(2) (December): 86–102.

Langlois, R. N. and Robertson, P. L. (1995) *Firms, Markets, and Economic Change: a Dynamic Theory of Business Institutions*, London: Routledge.

Loasby, B. J. (1976) *Choice, Complexity, and Ignorance*, Cambridge: Cambridge University Press.

—— (1991) *Equilibrium and Evolution: an Exploration of Connecting Principles in Economics*, Manchester: Manchester University Press.

McNulty, P. J. (1968) 'Economic Theory and the Meaning of Competition', *Quarterly Journal of Economics* 82: 639–56.

Milgrom, P. and Roberts, J. D. (1992) *Economics, Organization, and Management*, New York: Prentice Hall.

Moore, J. (1992) 'The firm as a collection of assets', *European Economic Review* 36: 493–507.

Moss, S. (1984) 'The history of the theory of the firm from Marshall to Robinson and Chamberlin: the source of positivism in economics', *Economica* 51: 307–18.

Nelson, R. R. and Winter, S. G. (1982) *An Evolutionary Theory of Economic Change*, Cambridge: Harvard University Press.

Penrose, E. T. (1959) *The Theory of the Growth of the Firm*, Oxford: Basil Blackwell.

Polanyi, M. (1958) *Personal Knowledge*, Chicago: University of Chicago Press.

Posner, R. A. (1979) 'The Chicago school of antitrust analysis', *University of Pennsylvania Law Review* 127: 925.

Putterman, L. (1988) 'The firm as association versus the firm as commodity: efficiency, rights, and ownership', *Economics and Philosophy* 4(2) (October): 243–66.

Richardson, G. B. (1960) *Information and Investment: A Study in the Working of the Competitive Economy*, Oxford: Oxford University Press; 2nd edn 1990.

—— (1965) 'Les Relations entre firmes', *Economie appliquée* 18(3): 407–30.

—— (1972) 'The organisation of industry', *Economic Journal* 82: 883–96.

Rotemberg, J. J. and Saloner, G. (1994) 'Benefits of narrow business strategies', *American Economic Review* 84(5) (December): 1330–49.

Schelling, T. C. (1960) *The Strategy of Conflict*, Cambridge: Harvard University Press.

Scherer, F. M. and Ross, D. (1990) *Industrial Market Structure and Economic Performance*, 3rd edn, Boston, Mass.: Houghton Mifflin.

Schnaars, S. P. (1994) *Managing Imitation Strategies: How Later Entrants Seize Markets from Pioneers*, New York: Free Press.

Silver, M. (1984) *Enterprise and the Scope of the Firm*, Aldershot: Martin Robertson.

Stigler, G. J. (1946) *The Theory of Price*, 1st edn, New York: Macmillan.

Stinchcombe, A. L. (1990) *Information and Organizations*, Berkeley, Calif.: University of California Press.

Teece, D. J. (1980) 'Economies of scope and the scope of the enterprise', *Journal of Economic Behavior and Organization* 1(3): 223–47.

—— (1982) 'Towards an economic theory of the multiproduct firm', *Journal of Economic Behavior and Organization* 3(1): 39–63.

—— (1986) 'Profiting from technological innovation: implications for integration, collaboration, licensing, and public policy', *Research Policy* 15: 285–305.

—— (1990) 'Foreword' to 2nd edn of G. B. Richardson *Information and Investment*, Oxford: Oxford University Press.
Tirole, J. (1988) *The Theory of Industrial Organization*, Cambridge: MIT Press.
Williamson, O. E. (1975) *Markets and Hierarchies: Analysis and Antitrust Implications*, New York: Free Press.
—— (1985) *The Economic Institutions of Capitalism*, New York: Free Press.
—— (1986) 'The economics of governance: framework and implications', in R. N. Langlois (ed.) *Economics as a Process: Essays in the New Institutional Economics*, New York: Cambridge University Press.
—— (1988) 'Technology and transaction cost economics: a reply', *Journal of Economic Behavior and Organization* 10: 355–63.
—— (1993) 'Calculativeness, trust, and economic organisation,' *Journal of Law and Economics*, 36: 221–270.

11
INFORMATION COSTS AND THE ORGANISATIONAL STRUCTURE OF THE MULTINATIONAL ENTERPRISE

Mark Casson

INTRODUCTION

This Chapter uses the economic theory of information costs to analyse the determinants of the organisational structure of the multinational enterprise (MNE). It offers a rigorous alternative to theories of organisational structure derived from sociology and political science. The theory explains the derivation of rules and procedures, the structuring of information flow and other aspects of organisation as a rational response to information costs. It represents a practical implementation of the research agenda set out in Richardson (1960). It shows, in particular, that bounded rationality need not be invoked to explain the internal mechanisms of the firm. The phenomena imputed to bounded rationality can be explained quite simply as a rational response to information costs. Furthermore, specific assumptions about the magnitude of information costs generate important predictions about the way in which organisational structure will adapt to changes in the environment.

While its primary focus is on the *quantity* of information used by the firm, the theory can be extended to cover the *quality* of information too. For example, managerial employees may understate potential revenues or overstate potential costs in order to create a budgetary surplus that they can appropriate for themselves. Controlling misinformation incurs transaction costs in the firm's internal markets, and these internal transaction costs cause the boundaries of the firm to contract. An efficient organisational structure will optimise both the quantity and quality aspects of information. It will minimise the sum of information costs and transaction costs to determine simultaneously both the organisational structure and the boundaries of the firm.

Information costs have important implications for the debate over whether hierarchies are becoming flatter and, indeed, are being supplanted by 'networking' (Kanter 1989). The theory provides a rigorous argument linking the globalisation of markets to the flatness of hierarchy. At the same time, it suggests an important refinement – that it is not so much the number of levels in the hierarchy that is important as the amount of informal consultation that goes on. Intensifying global competition means that competitive threats can originate from a much greater diversity of places. More information therefore needs to be synthesised before decisions are taken, and the sources from which this information must be obtained are more difficult to identify in advance. Abolition of social differences between superiors and subordinates promotes effective synthesis of information, so 'flatness' in this sense is desirable. But simply reducing the height of the hierarchy will, beyond a certain point, actually impair the synthesis of information. Taking time to consult – as in Japanese firms – may be better than speeding up decision-making by reducing the number of people involved. The next section (pp. 206–9) sets out the general principles governing the modelling of the firm using information costs. The section on 'Meta-rationality' (pp. 209–11) shows how the concept of information reconciles bounded rationality and complete rationality, by determining the firm's optimal exposure to the risk of mistakes in managerial decisions. The subsequent section ('Decisiveness, consultation and the internal balance of power', pp. 211–213) considers the consequences of combining two distinct types of information in order to make a decision. The first is marketing information on the intensity of demand and the second is production information on the level of costs. It is shown that the relative influence of marketing executives and production executives on the firm's output plans depends upon the relative volatility of fluctuations in demand and cost and the relative impact of these fluctuations on profit. This is a special case of the general proposition that the internal distribution of power within an efficient organisation is governed by the relative volatility of different aspects of the firm's environment.

Then there is a section (pp. 213–16) which introduces the quality aspect of information and considers its implications for the organisation of the firm. It applies the analysis to the special case of dual sourcing, showing how rival plants can be played off against each other to elicit truthful information from their managers.

The final section (pp. 216–20) applies these insights to the MNE as a whole. It is shown that the height of trade barriers has an important influence on the organisational structure of the MNE. When barriers are high, only limited consultation is required when setting the output for each plant. But when barriers are lowered as a consequence of tariff reductions or transport economies, greater consultation is required and output decisions for each plant need to be made at a global rather than at a local level. Even so, it may be efficient to constrain the level of consultation so that total output requirements are determined from marketing information before cost information is invoked to allocate output between different plants. Theory indicates the exact conditions under which simplifications of this kind are worthwhile and the conditions under which they are not. It therefore offers detailed predictions about how the organisational structure of the firm varies according to the relative volatility and the relative impact of fluctuations in demand and cost at different locations.

GENERAL PRINCIPLES

The general principles underlying the theory of information costs may be set out as follows (Casson 1994):

1 Organisations use information to co-ordinate activities. Co-ordination is a continuing process because activities are regularly disturbed in an unpredictable way.
2 Co-ordination is effected through a sequence of decisions. Each period a set of related decisions is taken in response to information which has become available since the last decision was made. Such new information relates, for example, to current changes in the firm's environment, such as changing demand and cost conditions.
3 Information is logically constructed by partitioning the set of all possible states of the environment into subsets and then asserting that reality belongs to one of these subsets, and so, by implication, not to the others. The simplest partition is a binary one – for example, into 'good' and 'bad' conditions. When analysing MNE co-ordination problems, local conditions for demand and for costs may be partitioned in this way to create a simple model.
4 Just as information is constructed by partitioning the set of all possible states of the environment, so decisions are constructed by partitioning the set of all possible strategies. A decision asserts that the strategy must belong to one subset and not to the others. An organisation is characterised by a rule which associates a unique strategic choice with each partition of the environment that is recognised.
5 Uncertainty is captured by assigning subjective probabilities to the different subsets. Uncertainty is great when all the subsets carry roughly equal probabilities, and it is small when one subset carries a probability close to unity.
6 An organisation has stakeholders who determine its objective. In a Western-style MNE the stakeholders are the equity shareholders. If they are risk-neutral their objective is the maximisation of expected profit. The ordinary members of the MNE organisation are its employees. The managerial employees collect information, communicate it to one another and take decisions on the shareholders' behalf.
7 Information is costly to collect, to communicate and to use in decisions. Profit is maximised net of information costs. An efficient organisation

minimises the information cost of achieving a given degree of co-ordination (as measured by expected gross profit). An optimal organisation trades off information cost against the degree of co-ordination (expected gross profit) to maximise expected net profit.

8 In some cases the amount of information that is collected each period will be determined in advance. But in other cases the amount of information that is collected can be determined in response to what the initial information that is collected turns out to be. The organisation can employ a rule which specifies which item(s) of information should be collected first and what subsequent items should be collected in the light of what has been discovered. Thus the organisation consists of a rule for gathering information as well as a rule for acting on it. It is the use of sequential information-gathering rules that gives organisations their distinctive 'procedural' quality.

9 Sources of information within an organisation tend to be dispersed (Radner 1992). This dispersion reflects a division of labour in the collection of information. This division of labour in information gathering often emerges as a spin-off from a division of labour in other activities. Information is often acquired as a by-product of other activities. Thus if one person is assigned to making a product and another person to selling it, then the former has a natural advantage in observing cost conditions and the latter a natural advantage in observing the state of demand.

10 Information from different sources may have to be synthesised before a decision can be made. This incurs costs of interpersonal communication. The greater the interpersonal flow of information, the higher the communication costs become. One of the people who collects information may be appointed to receive information from others. Alternatively, a specialist synthesiser may be appointed to receive information from everyone.

11 The concept of the specialist synthesiser extends the division of labour from the collection of information to the processing of it. An individual collector may lack the skill to understand what other people are telling him, whereas a specialist synthesiser can be chosen for his ability to understand different types of information from different sources. The use of a specialist synthesiser increases the amount of information that has to be communicated (since when a collector acts as synthesiser he has no need to communicate with himself) but may still reduce the overall cost because the information that is communicated is more readily understood.

12 The reason why certain types of information are difficult to understand lies in their tacit nature (Polanyi 1964). Explaining the nature of the partition that the observer has made, and identifying the subset in which reality lies, is often more tricky than it appears when the idea has

to be expressed in formal terms. The more tacit the information, the higher the costs of interpersonal communication will be.

13 Decisions are easier to communicate than tacit information because they are more explicit. It is easier to give an order than to brief someone else on the situation. Thus communication costs are normally minimised by giving the synthesiser the authority to make a decision. It is cheaper to localise authority at the point of synthesis than to require the synthesiser to communicate his synthesis to other people. The advantage of identifying certain people as synthesisers and vesting authority in them explains why organisations tend to evolve a hierarchical structure in which subordinates gather information and their superiors act upon it.

14 To each possible pair of rules, as identified above, there corresponds an optimal division of labour in implementation, which minimises overall information cost. Different rules effect different degrees of co-ordination. Those that collect the most information generally offer the best co-ordination but incur the highest information costs. The optimal pair of rules, and hence the optimal organisational structure, trades off the degree of co-ordination and the information cost in the appropriate way.

This is illustrated in Figure 11.1. Each possible pair of rules affords a particular combination of degree of co-ordination (as measured horizontally by expected gross profit) and expected information cost (measured vertically). For any given degree of co-ordination there is a rule – which we suppose to be unique – which minimises the expected information cost. This is the efficient rule for that degree of co-ordination, as defined above. The information cost function LC_0EC_1 identifies the minimum information cost for each degree of co-ordination. It is shown for convenience as a continuously increasing function, although under the conditions assumed below it will in fact comprise a series of straight-line segments instead. The rule which collects all available information in order to make the best possible decision corresponds to the point C_1, while the rule which collects no information corresponds to the point L (where, as shown here, a loss is made). The information cost required for the firm to break even (in terms of gross profit) is OC.

With perfect co-ordination at C_1 the expected gross profit is OG_1 and the net profit, measured from the vertical intercept of the 45° line C_1N_1 is ON_1. But a higher net profit is achieved at E with imperfect co-ordination. The information cost falls to OC^e, but gross profit falls only to OG^e, giving a net profit ON^e. The point E corresponds, in fact, to a maximum of net profit. The 45° line N^eQ is tangent to the information cost function at E, indicating that net profit cannot be further increased.

INFORMATION COSTS AND ORGANISATIONAL STRUCTURE

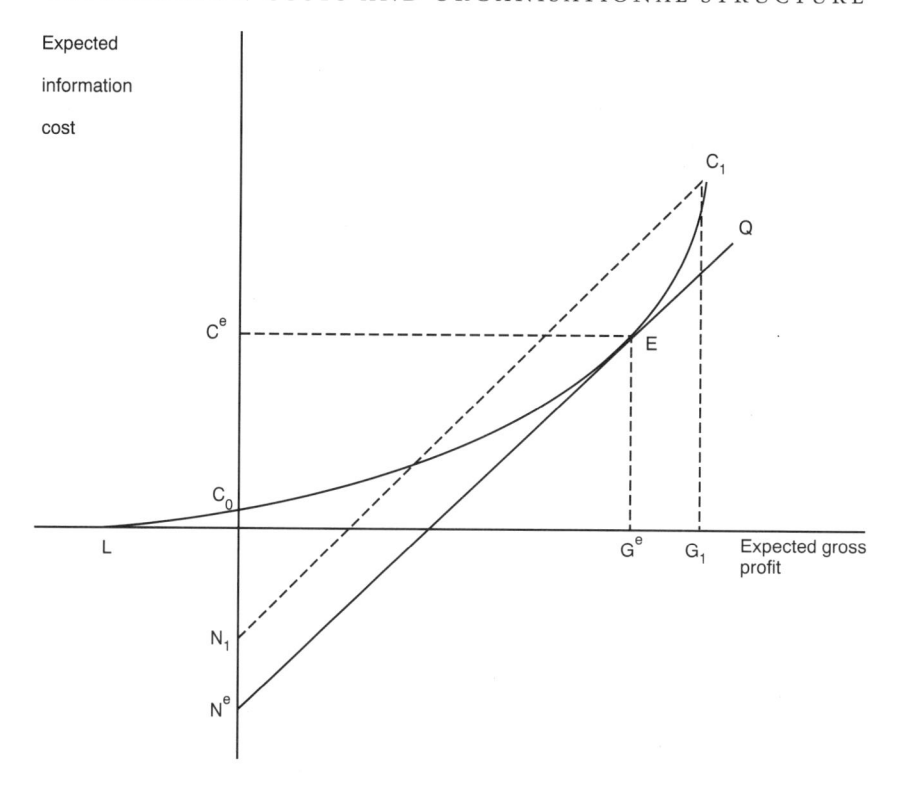

Figure 11.1 Maximisation of expected profit net of information cost

META-RATIONALITY: MINIMISING THE RISK OF MISTAKES

The significance of information costs can be appreciated from a simple example. Suppose a firm faces a market of unit size in which a price of 10 units prevails. The cost of a unit output is 7 units if production conditions are good and 12 units if they are bad. The subjective probability that conditions are bad is p ($0 \leq p \leq 1$). If management maximises expected profit, will it pay to incur the cost c of investigating production conditions before the output decision is made?

The firm maximises expected profit net of information cost using two instruments: the output decision and the observation decision. Given that the observation is perfectly accurate, the output decision is obvious once the observation has been made; namely to produce if conditions are good and not to produce if conditions are bad. Without observation, however, the output decision depends on the probability p.

The problem can be solved in a simple diagrammatic way, by noting that there are two kinds of error that can be made (Marschak and Radner 1972). The first is to assume that conditions are bad when in fact they are good. If conditions are assumed to be bad, then no output will be produced because a loss of two units is anticipated. If conditions are in fact good, then the output should be produced because a profit of 3 units can be made. Thus the first error is to produce no output when conditions are good and to lose 3 units of profit as a result. The second error is the converse of this, namely to produce the output when conditions are bad and sustain a loss of 2 units as a result. The probability that producing no output results in an error is $1 - p$, namely the probability that good conditions occur, while the probability that producing output results in an error is p, the probability that bad conditions occur. Thus as p increases the expected value of the first error declines and the second increases.

This is illustrated in Figure 11.2, which plots the expected cost vertically and the probability p horizontally. The expected cost of the no production strategy is illustrated by the downward sloping schedule AA', with its intercept of 3 units on the left-hand vertical axis. The expected cost of the production strategy is illustrated by the upward-sloping schedule BB', which has an intercept of 2 units on the right-hand axis. They intersect at E, which determines the critical probability $p^* = 0.6$ at which the firm ceases producing output. The expected cost of an error attains a maximum at this point. This critical probability reflects the relative magnitude of the two types of error – in fact it is the ratio of the first error (3 units) to the sum of the two errors (5 units).

Observation eliminates both types of error, but at a cost. If the cost of observation is less than the expected cost of error at p^*, then management will observe production conditions for a range of probabilities around this critical value. Thus if the cost of observation is one unit, as indicated by the horizontal line CC' in the figure, then observation is efficient within the range $p_1 = 0.5$ and $p_2 = 0.67$, determined by the points of intersection F and G. But when the probability is outside this range, and so closer to either 0 or 1 – so that management feels subjectively more certain about the situation – then no observation will be made.

This demonstrates that with confident beliefs it is rational for management to risk making a mistake in order to save the observation cost. The model therefore suggests that it is misleading to ascribe mistaken management decisions to 'bounded rationality' when in fact management is being meta-rational in optimising its exposure to the risk of making a mistake. Specifically, the model shows that management exposes itself to the risk of error when observation costs are high, when subjective certainty prevails, and when the costs of error are low.

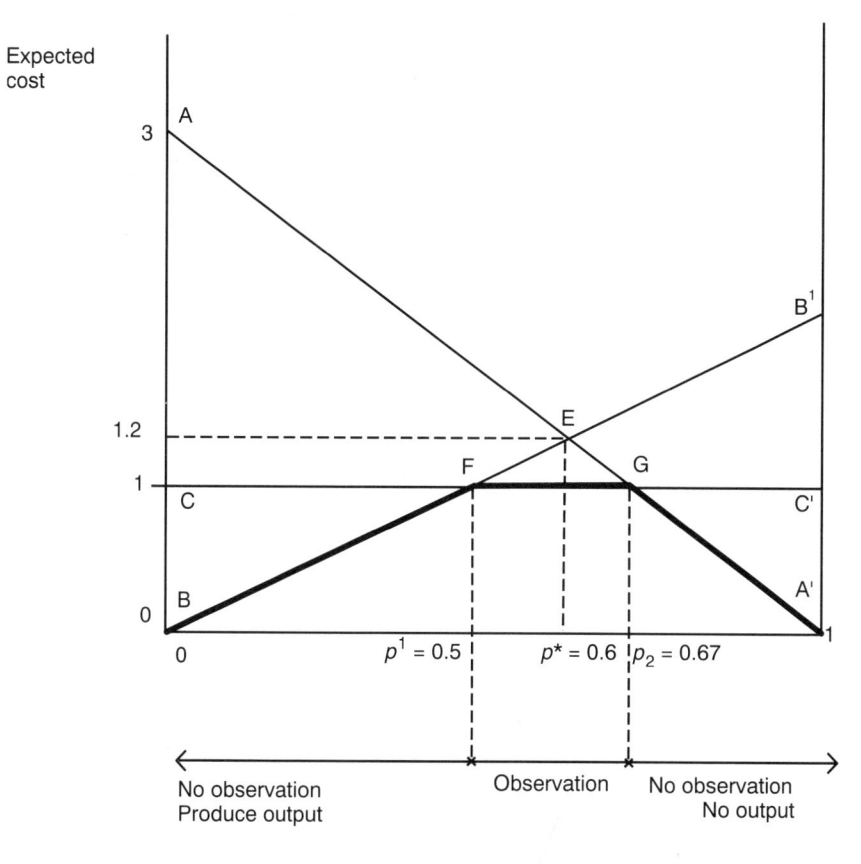

INFORMATION COSTS AND ORGANISATIONAL STRUCTURE

Figure 11.2 Optimising the collection of costly information

DECISIVENESS, CONSULTATION AND THE INTERNAL BALANCE OF POWER

Access to information is an important source of power within the firm. The stronger the implications of a given item of information, the more power accrues to those who possess it. To see this, suppose that in the previous example the price was uncertain too. Imagine, to begin with, that buoyant demand sustains a price of 14 units whereas depressed demand affords only the price of 10 units assumed above. Then if it is known that demand is buoyant, it is obvious that the output should be produced whatever the cost conditions turn out to be. It is only if demand is depressed that the cost conditions need to be considered. It may be said that in this case the state of demand is *conditionally decisive* for output, in the sense that if appropriate conditions prevail, output can be determined with reference only to the state of demand. If one person knows the state of demand and another person knows the cost conditions, then conditional decisiveness allows the first person to determine output without consulting the second person when appropriate conditions prevail. Moreover it is logical to allow the first person to decide whether to consult the second person, given that the former, and not the latter, has the relevant information at his or her disposal.

It is possible to envisage a more extreme situation, in which the state of demand is *absolutely decisive* for output. Suppose, for example, that the price under depressed demand falls to 6 units, while the price under buoyant conditions remains at 14 units. It is now obvious that if demand is depressed no output should be produced whatever the cost conditions turn out to be. Thus the person who possesses the marketing information can determine output without consulting the person who knows the cost conditions at all. This is because the variation in the price of 8 units is so much larger than the variation in the costs of 4 units. More specifically, it is because the range of price variation between 6 and 14 encompasses the range of cost variation between 7 and 12.

Absolute decisiveness of this kind provides a justification for the marketing-led firm in which output decisions are governed by the state of demand, as reported by the sales director, and not by cost conditions as reported by the production director. Indeed no one really wants to know what the cost conditions are so far as the determination of output is concerned.

It may be questioned how far decisiveness of this kind naturally occurs in business situations. It is important to note, however, that even when decisiveness does not naturally occur, the effect of information costs is to encourage management to impose decisiveness by simplifying the way that decisions are made. Suppose, for example, that depressed demand generates a price of 8 units while buoyant demand continues to generate a price of 14 units. This makes both buoyant demand and low costs conditionally decisive for positive output. It is only where either demand is depressed or costs are high that the other item of information is required in order to make the correct output decision.

Without information costs, there is nothing to choose between allowing the sales manager who knows demand to decide whether to consult the production manager who knows the costs or the other way round. But with information costs it may turn out that one of these items is never worth collecting.

Thus if the owners of the firm feel more confident about the cost conditions than about the marketing conditions, then they may decide that cost information should be ignored altogether. If the owners are pessimistic about cost conditions, then they will instruct the sales manager to produce output only if demand is buoyant. In this case demand information is treated as if it were absolutely decisive even though it is not. If, on the other hand, the owners are optimistic about cost conditions, then they will require output to be produced whatever the demand conditions turn out to be. In this case power is taken away from both the production manager and the sales manager. They are both told that the output will be produced whatever the conditions.

On the other hand, if the owners are more confident about marketing conditions than about cost conditions they may decide to ignore marketing information instead. This seems less likely in practice, though. In modern industrial societies fashion changes tend to generate regular fluctuations in demand, so that marketing information is normally crucial, and marketing executives acquire considerable power as a result.

THE QUALITY OF INFORMATION

So far it has been assumed that the information that managers supply to one another is perfectly accurate. There are two main reasons why this may not, in fact, be the case. The first is a question of competence. It is often difficult to observe the true state of demand or the true cost conditions directly. What is observed is a symptom of the underlying reality. A favourable symptom usually indicates good conditions, but this is not invariably so. Different managers may use different symptoms, and those that use the best symptoms will obtain, on average, the best results. The owners of the firm can address the issue of competence by careful recruitment and training of the managers they employ.

Matters are rather different with the second source of information error – dishonesty. Where the interests of owners and managers conflict, managers who know the decision rules used by the people to whom they report can calculate the decision implications of alternative reports, in order to make dishonest reports which serve their own selfish interests (Milgrom and Roberts 1992). In the example above, for example, the production manager might always report 'bad conditions' in order to obtain a surplus budget under good conditions, which can be spent on 'perks' for himself.

Five main strategies are available to the owners for dealing with this problem:

1 *Ignore information that is not reliable* – do not bother to collect what you will not believe. This approach is characteristic of the autocratic firm. It is a feasible approach when there is only a small amount of relevant information to be collected, for then the owners can collect all of the relevant information themselves. Perhaps for this reason, the autocratic approach seems to be most common in small firms.
2 *Conceal the decision rules* from those who collect the information. This is difficult to do, because most managers can make plausible guesses as to the use of the information that they communicate to others. The rules

are most likely to be opaque in large organisations. In some cases the rules can be made difficult to discern by deliberately introducing a random element into decisions – as exemplified by the 'maverick' management style which often accompanies autocracy.

3 *Offer performance-related pay* based on *ex post* corroboration of information. Although information is often difficult to check before the decision is made (but see 4 below), the true state of the environment often becomes obvious once the outcome of a decision is known. By monitoring outcomes the owners can reward managers who provide correct reports with bonuses paid in arrears. This requires the managers to believe that the assessment of performance will be fair and accurate, and that promised bonuses will actually be paid. It also requires that the truth is known without too much delay. So far as the owners are concerned, it is also important that the collection of information on outcomes is not too costly. It is easiest to implement performance-related pay when the performance information would in any case be needed for other purposes. The recent introduction of sophisticated management accounting practices exploiting modern information technology has reduced the costs of collecting performance-related information and of using this information for general strategic purposes. Such information is of particular strategic value in diversified consumer-oriented firms, and many firms of this kind have indeed adopted performance-related pay.

4 *Replicate the reporting of information* by having different managers report independently on the same aspect of the environment. This is potentially very costly, and is warranted only when mistakes must be avoided at all costs. It is thus quite common in hospitals, public passenger transportation and other areas where safety considerations are paramount. It is usually associated with a large formal bureaucracy. It is predicated, moreover, on the view that the majority report is correct and that the minority is therefore deviant. By branding the minority view as dishonest and punishing the person who offers it, it clearly discourages entrepreneurial behaviour by people who have good reason to dissent from the majority view.

5 *Require information to be communicated indirectly in the form of prices.* This method works only when each manager believes that the activity on which he is reporting could be dropped in favour of some other activity which would be substituted for it. Suppose, for example, that the market described in section 4 could be sourced from two plants in two different locations. Each plant has a manager who knows the conditions at his own plant but not the conditions in the other one. Each manager is told that there is a fixed budget for producing output which is independent of the local cost conditions. He is simply asked each period whether he is willing to supply output or not. The discrepancy between

the budgeted sum and the actual cost accrues to the manager as either profit or loss.

By setting an appropriate budget the owners can induce each production manager to disclose production conditions honestly in the following way. If production conditions are bad it pays the manager to decline to supply because a loss is certain to be made. This is because the budget is less than the costs incurred under unfavourable conditions. On the other hand, if production conditions are good it pays the manager to agree to supply because a profit will be made. Thus the decision whether to supply indirectly embodies the report of the production conditions.

There is a complication, however. If conditions at both locations are bad, then no output will be forthcoming at all. Yet if market conditions are good the owners may wish to elicit some output, and to do this they must increase the budget – i.e. raise the supply price. Thus each manager knows that if he declines to supply at the initial terms, then the terms may subsequently improve because the other manager has declined as well. The question is then whether the other manager will decline only when his own production conditions are genuinely bad or whether he will decline strategically. If each believes the other will decline strategically it encourages them to decline themselves, since the price is then certain to rise if demand conditions are good, and so each manager's expectations of the other's behaviour are self-fulfilling. Conversely, if each believes that the other will not decline strategically it encourages them not to decline, because the price is unlikely to rise if they do, and so again the expectations tend to be self-fulfilling.

It is clearly in the interests of the owners to create an expectation by each manager that the other manager will always offer to supply when his local conditions are good, because this promotes a competitive outlook amongst them. By setting an appropriate level for the initial budget the owners can then ensure that each manager finds it in his or her interests to agree to supply whenever conditions are favourable. Thus, even with these strategic complications, the owners can elicit supply responses which are truthful indirect reports of the local production conditions by selecting a suitable budgeting strategy.

This last approach to assuring the quality of information is of particular importance for the boundaries of the firm. It effectively creates an arm's length contractual arrangement between the managers and the owners of the firm; the managers become independent subcontractors and the budget becomes the price at which the deal between the two parties is struck. It effectively 'dis-integrates' the firm into three independent firms – the original firm, together with two independent subcontractors.

The rationale is that it encourages the honest reporting of production conditions. Replication of reporting and performance-related pay also encourage honesty, but they work within the firm and tend, if anything, to make it more bureaucratic and less entrepreneurial than it would otherwise be. The great advantage of the subcontracting approach is that it incentivises honesty without the cost of cross-checking or retrospectively examining the report that is made. Its great disadvantage is that it hinges crucially on the existence of substitution possibilities and the absence of any collusion between the managers of the rival activities. It also tends to expose the managers to financial risks connected with aspects of the environment that they cannot monitor and control, and which the shareholders of the subcontracting firm are better placed to bear. It is the balance between these advantages and disadvantages that determines whether the firm will disintegrate or not.

This analysis of the quality of information reveals the interdependence between organisational structure and the boundaries of the firm. When substitution possibilities are limited, quality assurance for information impacts mainly upon the internal structure of the organisation and leaves its boundaries unchanged, whereas when substitution possibilities are significant, quality assurance tends to redraw the firm's boundaries instead. Internal organisational structure and the external boundaries of the firm are thus two different aspects of a single, much wider phenomenon – the optimal organisation of economic activity as a whole.

APPLICATIONS TO THE MULTINATIONAL ENTERPRISE

The MNE is of course more complex than the ordinary firm and it is therefore advisable to be more formal in the way that it is analysed. Figure 11.3 illustrates a simple set of multinational operations.

By making a simple assumption about cost conditions it is possible to decompose the analysis further. It is assumed that each upstream plant operates under constant marginal cost (whatever local cost conditions prevail). This means that the output the plant supplies for any one of the two downstream plants can be determined independently of the output it supplies to the other. Thus, with one important qualification (noted below) the system shown in Figure 11.3 decomposes into two subsystems. The first is concerned with alternative methods of sourcing the home market – i.e. domestic production v. off-shore production – and the second with alternative methods of sourcing the foreign market – the classic issue of exporting v. foreign production.

Both of these subsystems have a similar structure. There are two produc-

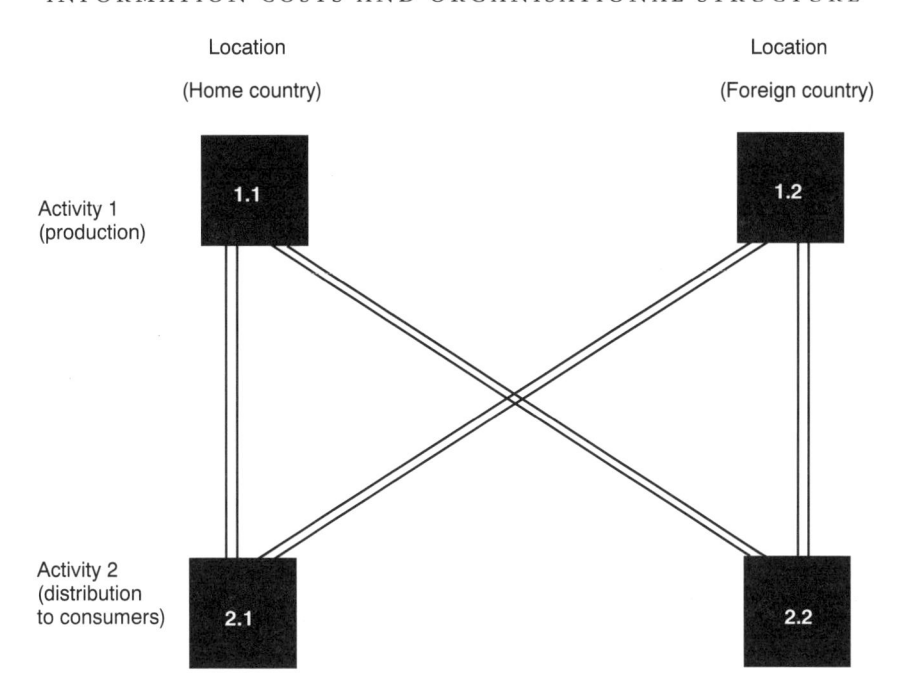

INFORMATION COSTS AND ORGANISATIONAL STRUCTURE

	Location (Home country)	Location (Foreign country)
Activity 1 (production)	1.1	1.2
Activity 2 (distribution to consumers)	2.1	2.2

Key: A square box denotes a plant
Double lines indicate a tangible intermediate product flow
Arrow indicates direction of flow
The convention is that, unless otherwise shown, the outputs for each box are perfect substitutes for each other and the inputs to each box are also perfect substitutes for each other

Principal sourcing options
　　Exporting: (1.1) to (2.1) and (2.2)
　　Foreign direct investment in production:
　　　　Import-substitution: (1.1) to (2.1); (1.2) to (2.2)
　　　　Off-shore production: (1.2) to (2.1) and (2.2)

　　　　Internationally rationalised production:
　　　　　　Either exporting from home (1.1) to (2.1) and (2.2)
　　　　　　or exporting from aboard (1.2) to (2.1) and (2.2)
　　　　　　depending on relative production costs

Figure 11.3　　　　Basic model of intermediate product flow in a multinational enterprise

tion facilities from which a given demand can be sourced. Each source is a substitute for the other. One source is, however, advantaged compared to the other because it is a local one. The advantage lies principally in avoiding tariffs and international transport costs. For simplicity, tariffs and domestic transport costs will be ignored and it will be assumed that international transport costs are the same in each direction.

Suppose, furthermore, that the cost implications of good and bad conditions are the same in each country. Good conditions give a marginal cost of 7 units and bad conditions a marginal cost of 12 units, as before. In a situation of this kind international comparative advantage switches back and forth between the countries according to which country has good conditions at the same time as the other has bad ones.

Consider, to begin with, the issues relating to the quantity of information. If transport costs exceed 5 units it is obvious that foreign sourcing is never worthwhile. So far as production is concerned, the multinational resembles two autarkic firms, one in each country. At the opposite extreme, if transport costs are zero, then the local source and the foreign source are on an equal footing. If conditions are the same in each location, then the optimal source is indeterminate.

The most interesting and relevant case is the intermediate one in which transport costs are positive but less than 5 units. Here the local source is favoured when either conditions are the same or the local conditions are good, and the foreign source is favoured when local conditions are bad and the foreign conditions are good.

The fact that the two sources are substitutes might suggest that information will normally be required on both, but this is not in fact the case. Consider, for example, the sourcing of home-country demand. If foreign conditions are thought to be almost certainly bad, then they may not be deemed worth investigating. Off-shore processing is not regularly evaluated because an initial subjective assessment has suggested that the occasional benefits do not outweigh the regular observation costs incurred.

However, if local conditions are thought to be almost certainly bad it is more likely that they will be investigated. This is because local sourcing is used whenever local conditions happen to be good, whereas foreign sourcing is used only when foreign conditions happen to be good and local conditions are bad at the same time. Transport costs therefore create a bias in favour of collecting local information which is quite independent of the fact that local information may be cheaper to collect anyway.

There is also the issue of whether production conditions at either location need to be observed independently of what the local state of the market turns out to be. If the local market is buoyant, then more output needs to be produced (under the circumstances assumed earlier), and so the savings available from making the right sourcing decision are increased. Whether production information should still be collected when it is known that demand is depressed and that additional output is not warranted depends a great deal on how much output is actually required by the depressed market. If a depressed market requires no output at all, then clearly the sourcing decision is irrelevant. A depressed market is decisive not only for output but also for the observation of production conditions. If, on the other hand, a depressed market still affords a substantial level of demand, then the cost savings from the correct sourcing decision may still be quite considerable. In this case it may be decided to observe production conditions independently of the state of demand.

When the two markets are considered together the presence of information costs creates an important externality. For the information on the foreign source for one market is the information on the local source for the other market. Thus the fact that each source can be used for either market strengthens the case for observing both. Because the firm is sourcing two markets rather than one it is advantageous to observe conditions in each market's 'foreign' location. Thus a firm sourcing two markets will generally be better informed about production conditions than would a pair of firms each sourcing just one. This reveals the sharing of information on cost conditions as an important economy of the MNE. It also explains why MNEs may be more adept at switching the sourcing of markets than are single-country firms. It is more advantageous for a multi-market firm to learn about foreign production conditions than it is for the single-market firm.

The information advantage to the multi-market firm will be greatest when production conditions in the two locations are uncorrelated, since then nothing can be inferred about foreign conditions from the local ones. If the conditions are believed to be negatively correlated, then sourcing decisions can be based on local information alone. Bad local conditions imply good foreign conditions and so dictate foreign sourcing, making local conditions decisive for the sourcing strategy. Thus the single-market firm can decide almost as well as the multi-market firm.

The advantage to the multi-market firm is also small when conditions are positively correlated, but for a quite different reason. If conditions are positively correlated, then, quite simply, local sourcing is always likely to be the best strategy. Indeed, with positive correlation there may even be little point in finding out what local conditions are, particularly if local demand is decisive for the level of output.

In some cases even the multi-market firm may not bother to collect information on production conditions, particularly if observation costs are high. Information is most likely to be collected in the absence of positive correlation and where conditions are relatively uncertain – in other words, where conditions at each location are equally likely to be good or bad. Low transport costs and large cost differentials also favour the observation of production conditions by the multi-market firm.

Turning to the quality of information issue, it is evident that the method of assuring truthful reporting of cost conditions through subcontracting is potentially relevant in the MNE case. Indeed, the lower transport costs and tariffs are, the closer the substitution possibilities between the plants, and hence the greater the potential for 'playing off' the managers of independent plants against each other.

This suggests an organisational structure in which the MNE synthesises marketing information from the downstream plants and uses it to set prices for delivery to each downstream plant which are quoted to the upstream plants. The managers of these independent plants indicate whether they are willing to supply or not. If a market is buoyant but neither producer is willing to supply it, then the price is raised. Each producer is encouraged to believe that the other will behave in a competitive manner, so that neither is tempted to withhold supplies when conditions are good in the hope of a higher price.

Combining the discussions of the quantity and quality of information indicates reasons why greater competition in global markets may be leading to flatter, more dis-integrated firms. Few large firms are any longer dominant suppliers of protected national markets. A single local source of marketing information is no longer decisive for the output decisions of any given plant. There are many sources of volatility to which each plant must respond, and information on these sources must be synthesised before any decision is made. If managerial honesty can be guaranteed by cultural norms, then synthesis is most readily achieved by passing the information up to higher levels of a hierarchy where specialist synthesisers receive reports from a wide range of subordinates. The primary role of these synthesisers is not to control their subordinates, however, but to listen to what they have to say. The hierarchy must therefore be a consultative one, in which the social differences between superior and subordinate are relatively low. The hierarchy therefore needs to be 'flat' in social terms, but not necessarily in the number of levels involved.

While it is possible to reduce the number of levels by replacing specialised synthesis with group-centred interaction, in which everyone shares information directly with everyone else, it is not immediately obvious that this is the best strategy, despite its apparent success in some 'Japanese-style' companies (Aoki 1990). The group approach is most likely to work under conditions of very radical change, where it is not possible to design in advance a hierarchical system because it is difficult to know the underlying pattern of environmental volatility. When the underlying pattern of volatility *is* known, it pays to impose a hierarchical structure of some kind because this economises on information costs.

As national markets become less protected, each firm becomes free to search around the globe for the lowest-cost sources of supply. This means that different national subsidiaries of the MNE become competitive suppliers for one another's markets. If cultural norms of integrity are weak, then competition provides the MNE with a mechanism for eliminating budgetary slack by turning national production facilities into independent subcontractors, competing with each other to supply national sales and distribution affiliates in different parts of the world. The boundaries of the MNE are redrawn to concentrate on the sales and distribution function, with production being subcontracted wherever possible. Sales strategies in different parts of the world need to be co-ordinated in a highly consultative manner, particularly where the same standardised product is used to meet the needs of several different national markets. In this new economic order there is no scope for the traditional national subsidiary which integrates local production and local sales. A global sales organisation backed up by international subcontracting is the logic response to modern conditions, because with weak cultural norms it optimises both the quantity and the quality of management information.

REFERENCES

Aoki, M. (1990) 'Towards an economic model of the Japanese firm', *Journal of Economic Literature* 28: 1–27.

Casson, M. (1994) 'Why are firms hierarchical?', *Journal of the Economics of Business* 1(1): 47–76.

Kanter, R. M. (1989) *When Giants Learn to Dance: Mastering the Challenge of Strategy, Management and Careers in the 1990s*, London: Simon & Schuster.

Marschak, J. and Radner, R. (1972) *Economic Theory of Teams*, New Haven, Conn.: Yale University Press.

Milgrom, P. R. and Roberts, J. (1992) *Economics of Organization and Management*, Englewood Cliffs, N.J.: Prentice Hall.

Polanyi, M. (1964) *Science, Faith and Society*, Chicago: University of Chicago Press.

Radner, R. (1992) 'Hierarchy: the economics of managing', *Journal of Economic Literature* 30: 1382–415.

Richardson, G.B. (1960) *Information and Investment*, Oxford: Oxford University Press.

12

CLUSTERS OF COLLABORATION

The firm, joint ventures, alliances and clubs

Neil M. Kay

INTRODUCTION

This paper looks at co-operative activity involving firms at three different levels; co-operative activity at the business level (such as joint venture), co-operative activity at firm level (alliances or partnerships between firms) and co-operative activity involving groups of firms (networks or clubs). Following Richardson, our interest is in trying to understand aspects of 'the complex and inter-locking clusters, groups and alliances which represent co-operation fully and formally developed' (Richardson 1972: 887). It is argued here that the key to developing such understanding lies in recognising the interaction and interplay between different levels of analysis in this context. A number of elements in the paper may be seen as following from, or consistent with, Richardson's 1972 paper, including his 'triple distinction' (*ibid.*: 896) between firm, co-operative and market modes of resource co-ordination; the role of complementary activities in collaboration; the role of *future* decisions in stimulating co-operative arrangements; and the picture of the firm as a bundle of capabilities represented by appropriate knowledge, experience and skills.

In the first section below, joint venture is compared to alternative modes of organisation, and it is argued that joint venture typically appears to be clearly inferior (costly and inefficient) compared to simpler single-firm options. We then place joint venture and its alternatives into the context of corporate diversification and analyse how and when joint venture may appear as an efficient mode of organisation. The next section develops the analysis to argue that the behaviour of networks or groups at industry level cannot be understood by analysing one level in isolation, but must be seen as a phenomenon encompassing and integrating business, corporate and group levels of analysis. The chapter finishes with a short concluding section.

THE EVOLUTION OF COLLABORATIVE ACTIVITY

Complementary activities or assets have been analysed as providing basic foundations for collaborative activity (Richardson 1972; Teece 1986). A variety of skills and resources running through the value chain will be required to bring any complex venture to fruition, and not all of them may be possessed to the required degree or quality by a single firm. However, there are a variety of ways in which the different resources can be brought together. As Richardson points out, 'Co-ordination (of complementary activities) can be effected in three ways; by *direction*, by co-operation, or through market transactions' (Richardson 1972: 890). Market transactions involving the trading of assets are the obvious and traditional means through which resource deficiencies can be compensated. Direction can be readily provided by intra-firm co-ordination, and merger is one mechanism through which the possibility of such co-ordination can be effected. Thus, co-operative or collaborative activity between firms is only one way in which complementary assets may be combined to produce efficiency-oriented economic activity. this is illustrated in Figure 12.1, which shows a possible venture opportunity (the middle business unit) which could be set up with the help of resources provided by two other single business firms (the end business units). One firm could provide marketing resources (such as shared assets in marketing, distribution, advertising and/or reputation), while the other could provide technological resources (such as shared assets in plant, equipment, work force and/or R&D).

As Richardson's distinction between direction, co-operation and market modes of co-ordination makes clear, the new venture could combine complementary assets in a variety of ways. If an asset can be directed it can also be contracted; in principle, contracts can be written through which two or more firms can co-ordinate any gain derivable from shared resources that could be obtained through direction. Licensing, leasing, rental, consultancy,

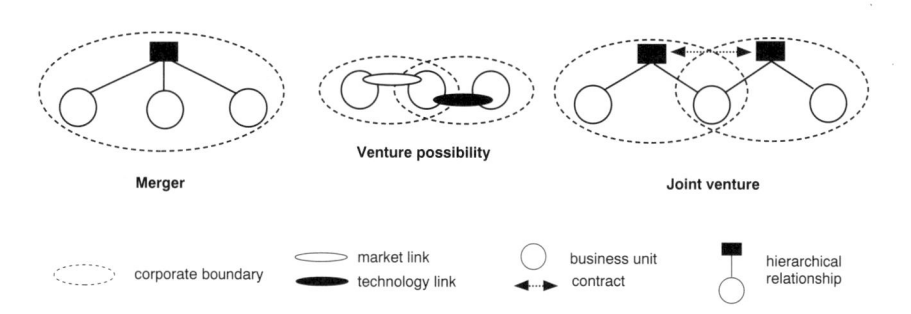

Figure 12.1   Joint venture strategy and structure

commission and tie-in are examples of contractual modes that can help firms jointly exploit potential gains from asset trading or sharing.[1]

Any purely market solution would involve a maze of contracts between the two donor firms and the new business venture. However, both merger and joint venture would involve the installation of hierarchy to provide decision-making capabilities, and these possibilities are illustrated in Figure 12.1. The merger option is assumed here to create a multidivisional or M-form corporation (Williamson 1975) around the three business units, with each unit or division reporting to a single HQ. However, a joint venture typically adds three other elements compared to the merger solution: (1) the joint venture contract which exists as a statement of the obligations and rights of the respective parties; (2) a dual system of hierarchical control, with the respective 'parents' having a continuing authority relation with the joint venture 'child'; and (3) overlapping property rights (and firm boundaries) with respect to the assets associated with the new venture opportunity. Therefore joint venture includes both market or contract and direction or hierarchical elements. In analysing the different circumstances in which the respective modes of organisation identified by Richardson might be adopted, it may be useful to split the question into two parts. First, what circumstances are likely to favour the adoption of hierarchical solutions (such as merger or joint venture) over purely market or contractual solutions? Second, what circumstances are likely to favour the adoption of a joint venture solution over the merger alternative? We shall consider both questions in turn.

As far as the first question is concerned, markets and contractual modes of organisation tend to perform effectively in allocating resources in circumstances in which goods and services are standardised, their characteristics are well specified, and there are many competing buyers and sellers (Williamson 1975). In such circumstances, the market may offer the standard gains associated with specialisation, flexibility, competitive pressure and choice. There is likely to be little point in a firm owning and producing all the assets relevant to its ventures if the market can offer a range of competing suppliers on a sufficient scale to exploit economies of scale in production. Market solutions also tend to be widely observed in cases of well-established and stable technologies in which standard or off-the-shelf solutions such as licensing, rental, leasing and franchising may be adopted.

By way of contrast, contractual solutions tend to encounter problems or break down completely in situations involving ambiguity, uncertainty and novelty. These conditions tend to hold where firms are contemplating innovative ventures, as in the case of technological innovation and market entry. If contracts cannot be well specified, then potential problems of opportunism (self-interest seeking with guile) appear (Williamson 1985). The costs of co-ordinating contracts characterised by incomplete or vague elements may be intolerable for either or both of the potential parties to the transaction, and internalised or hierarchical alternatives may be preferred at this point. Hierarchy incorporates decision-making capacity to allow for the making of future decisions relevant to a particular ventures; contracts embody past or present decisions; 'where buyer and seller accept no obligation with respect to their *future* conduct however loose and implicit the obligation might be, then co-operation does not take place and we can refer to a pure market transaction' (Richardson 1972: 886; italics mine). For example, old or established technologies may be traded between firms in the form of licences, while the R&D stage itself is typically carried out in-house within corporate boundaries. This is consistent with the findings of Davidson and McFetridge (1985), who studied 1,200 intra-firm and market technology transactions by US firms in the period 1945–78. Their study indicated that the probability of internal intra-firm hierarchical transfer was greater for R&D-intensive companies, and for newer technologies and technologies with few previous transfers.

Hierarchy may therefore make provision for future decisions to be made with respect to venture possibilities, and this can be an important attribute in venture opportunities characterised by innovative elements. However, this raises the issue of our second question above; we have two modes of hierarchical organisation in Figure 12.1: merger leading to single firm operation, and joint venture. What circumstances should lead to joint venture being preferred to single-firm or merger alternatives?

The obvious way to approach this question is to compare the characteristics of the respective modes in terms of their potential efficiency implications. We have already noted that joint venture tends to have three distinctive characteristics compared to single-firm operation; the contract itself, dual hierarchical control and overlapping firm boundaries. Each feature is likely to have efficiency implications.

The joint venture *contract* itself is unlikely to be a free good, but will involve managerial and legal resources to set up, administer and police. The *dual control system* itself is more complex and cumbersome than the simple unified hierarchy associated with the single-firm option; even if the respective parents are paragons of virtue, such dual control is likely to lead to confusion and conflict to the extent that the parents have different objectives and expectations. Add the possibility of opportunistic intent, and the potential difficulties associated with dual control are magnified. Also, *overlapping firm boundaries* can provide unique opportunities for one firm to observe the other, and possibly assist access to trade secrets, proprietary knowledge and other intangible assets that would normally be protected by the cloak of secrecy provided by corporate walls (Richardson 1972). The fear of this potential leakage of sources of competitive advantage to outside firms may provide a disincentive to firms considering joint venture.

Therefore, the characteristics of joint venture illustrated in Figure 12.1 all appear to represent potential barriers to joint-venture formation compared to the single-firm solution obtainable through merger. Joint venture typically has the more complex and potentially costly administrative structure, it necessitates a supporting contractual apparatus absent in single-firm operation, and it may pose the threat of leakage of intellectual property and other intangible assets. Contractual, hierarchical and property rights issues all suggest that joint venture is likely to be regarded by firms as an inferior mode of organisation to the single-firm alternative. This conclusion is consistent with the point frequently made in the managerial literature that joint venture is typically treated as a device of last resort by management (Kay 1992). This leaves us with a problem: if joint venture is an unambiguously inferior mode of organisation compared to single-firm operation, how can its existence ever be justified on efficiency grounds? Unless we are prepared to argue that firms adopting this mode are making expensive mistakes, the analysis so far must be incomplete. In the next section we explore circumstances in which joint venture might evolve as an efficient mode for combining and organising venture opportunities.

THE EVOLUTION OF COLLABORATION IN THE DIVERSIFIED FIRM

In practice it is not difficult to find examples of joint-venture activity being adopted even where it is perceived to be less efficient than the single-firm option. The obvious examples are cases in which third world governments make joint venture with a local firm a condition for market access. It does not matter if joint venture is the most expensive mode of organising activities; if it is the only mode permitted, then firms may have to take it in a Hobson's choice situation. However, these circumstances do not appear to apply so obviously to many of the joint ventures formed between developed-country firms in recent years. Joint ventures between US, Japanese and European partners tend not to be characterised by the forced partnerships so frequently observed in Third World cases. It still leaves the puzzle of why such an apparently inferior mode of organisation should have become so prevalent in recent years.

The problem with much conventional analysis of the merits and demerits of alternative forms of organisation is that they tend to restrict consideration to the business units directly involved in the venture opportunity. For example, Figure 12.1 identifies the business units directly involved in the joint venture, their relationship with each other and the child joint venture. This is consistent with the common representation of the relationships involved in joint-venture activity. However, these business units may themselves be part of a larger diversified firm in the respective cases, and while the other businesses associated with the respective firms may not be directly involved in the venture opportunity, their existence may still have important

||||||| potential link

◯ new venture opportunity

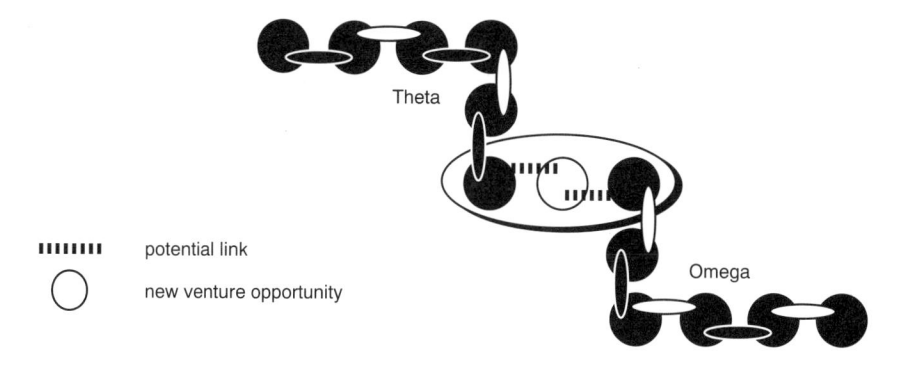

Figure 12.2   New venture opportunity for large diversified firms

implications for how the new venture may be organised. Figure 12.2 extends the analysis of Figure 12.1 to include this possibility.

The new venture opportunity of Figure 12.1 is represented on the central oval mat in Figure 12.2. The links that might be established between it and the two donor businesses are illustrated by dotted lines. However, each donor business is itself only a division within a highly diversified firms. There are two such firms, Theta and Omega. In both cases the two firms have pursued related linked diversification (Rumelt 1986), with a series of different market and technological links exploited by the corporate strategy.

If we focus only on the region represented by the central oval mat, we shall effectively replicate the analysis of Figure 12.1. At this level, the level of business strategy, joint venture is still likely to appear as unambiguously inferior to single-firm operation which could obtain through the merger of the two firms. Analysed at this level, there is still no obvious way to make sense of joint-venture activity. However, expanding the perspective to include the respective firms in their entirety makes it clear that the single-firm option is not likely to be restricted to the donor businesses directly involved with the new venture. As Figure 12.3 makes clear, merger of Theta and Omega to fully internalise the new business opportunity would create an extremely large firm. Such a solution could be tantamount to taking a sledgehammer to crack a nut (Kay *et al.* 1987), points also made separately by Hennart (1988) and Buckley and Casson (1987). The expanded firm has a scale of operation an order of magnitude many times greater than that of the new venture opportunity, and any gains directly associated with the new venture may be swamped by the wider implications of the expanded firm. The full-scale merger of Theta and Omega to co-ordinate the new venture possibility may generate diseconomies as a consequence of putting together a hybrid collection of disparate and dissimilar activities. Much of the recent concern in the managerial literature with 'focus' and 'sticking to the knitting' is evidence of managerial concern with the adverse efficiency consequences of overexpansion and extreme corporate diversity. Further, both Theta and Omega may have businesses which, if combined, could attract antitrust attention and even sanctions. Consequently, the full-scale merger of Theta and Omega to exploit the new business opportunities may have significant efficiency and antitrust implications that go far beyond the efficiency implications of the merger option at the level of the new business opportunity itself. On the other hand, the efficiency implications of the joint-venture option will tend to be more highly localised around the region of the joint venture itself and its participating businesses in Figure 12.3. Otherwise, Theta and Omega retain their independence and their scale of operation is only marginally expanded to the extent of their participation in the joint venture. Therefore, while joint venture may be more costly than single-firm operation over the domain of the venture itself, single-firm options such as merger may bring with them significant additional complications. This indicates how it may be possible to reconcile the apparent general inferiority of joint venture as a mode of organisation at the level of the *venture*, with its adoption as a preferred mode of organisation in certain cases by highly diversified firms. Once the perspective is extended to the level of the participating firms, joint venture may be clearly seen to offer efficiency advantages for large diversified firms pursuing new ventures opportunities. As Hennart comments:

> besides the obvious case when governments restrict mergers and acquisitions, joint venture will be preferred when the assets that yield the desired services are a small and inseparable part of the total assets held by both potential partners or when a merger or a total acquisition would significantly increase management costs.
>
> (Hennart 1991: 99)

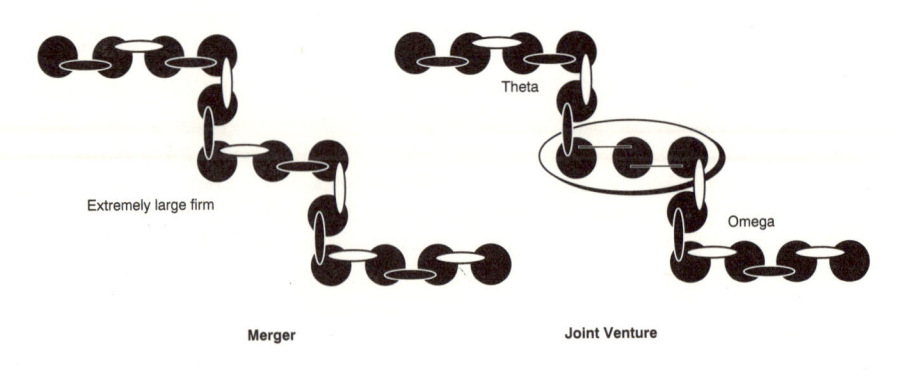

Figure 12.3   Merger and joint venture options for diversified firms

Selective disinvestment by one or other of the parties may be an alternative to full-scale merger in certain cases. For example, Theta or Omega could sell the relevant donor business to the other firm. In Figure 12.3, if Theta sold the potential donor business to Omega, it would allow the domain of the venture to be fully internalised within Omega's corporate boundaries, with resulting expansion of Omega's boundaries and shrinkage of Theta's. This combines the advantages of full-scale internalisation with relatively modest adjustment in terms of the scale of the respective firms. However, such a solution may be impractical in the case of many large diversified firms such as Omega or Theta. Selling the respective donor business to the other firm would cut across an existing technological link between the donor and another division in the case of Theta, and a marketing link between the donor and another division in the case of Omega. Of course, the respective link might still be exploited by forming a co-operative agreement between the traded business and its previous owner. However, such co-ordination is what selective disinvestment was intended to avoid the need for, and so this rather negates the purpose of the whole exercise.[2] Kay *et al.* (1987) and Hennart (1988) point out that it may be difficult to decompose or disengage the various businesses in a firm pursuing related diversification because of 'tangled assets' (Hennart 1988), and so selective disinvestment may not be available as a means of redesigning the boundaries of the firm to maintain a single unified hierarchy.

This leads to a simple conclusion. Corporate diversification may be the crucial trigger that stimulates joint-venture activity. Corporate strategy (diversification) can influence business strategy (joint venture). Such a perspective also helps us to make sense of a variety of related phenomena. It helps to explain why the proliferation of collaborative activity is a relatively recent phenomenon; it can be seen as essentially a post-diversification mode of organisation, the extensive diversification of the modern corporation being itself mostly a post-war phenomenon. We would also expect to find a positive link between size of firm and the level of joint-venture activity, and this tends to be confirmed by empirical analysis (Boyle 1968; Berg and Friedman 1978). Much post-war corporate diversification was merger-driven,[3] which suggests that merger and joint venture may be complements as well as substitutes; it was earlier merger activity which created the precondition of diversification that led to subsequent joint-venture activity.

The essential point is that collaborative activity such as joint venture has to be analysed by looking at different levels of analysis simultaneously, that holding at the level of the venture and that holding at the level of the firm. We hope to show in the next section that more complex co-operative phenomena such as alliances and clubs or networks may also have to be analysed by recognising the influence of different levels of analysis.

THE EVOLUTION OF STRATEGIC BUSINESS ALLIANCES

Up until now we have been concerned with the development of one particular type of co-operative activity, the joint venture. This has meant looking at individual collaborative agreements in the context of business strategy. In this section we shift up a level in that we consider the possibility that co-operation may take place at the level of the firm and not just individual businesses. This is the domain of strategic business alliances, also described in the literature as coalitions or partnerships between firms.

Porter and Fuller define coalitions as 'formal, long-term alliances between firms that link aspects of their businesses but fall short of merger' (1986: 315). Porter and Fuller point out that strategic business alliances may encompass joint ventures, licensing arrangements, supply agreements and marketing agreements amongst other arrangements. Porter and Fuller also suggest that coalitions or alliances only be properly analysed in the context of a firm's overall global strategy (which may involve multiple alliances; *ibid.*: 316), and the opportunity cost of alternative strategies must always be compared to that of alliance formation if it is to be justified as the preferred option (*ibid.*: 327).

Alliances link businesses of the firm by providing for future decision to be made by the firms in areas of specified mutual interest. As a solution that tends to go beyond contract and involve hierarchy as a mode of resource allocation, we would expect to find alliances at firm level to operate in similar areas to those associated with joint ventures at business level; that is, domains involving new markets and new technologies, and associated with incomplete and poorly specified problems. The surveys of this area in Porter and Fuller (1986) and Dunning (1993) suggest that issues such as these tend to be major factors encouraging alliance formation. Daimler Benz and Mitsubishi provide a good example of an alliance in practice, with the partners collaborating in a variety of link-ups at business level, Daimler Benz generally providing access to mechanical technology and European markets for Mitsubishi, and Mitsubishi providing access to electronic technology and Japanese markets for Daimler Benz (*The Financial Times*, 7 March 1990, and 31 December 1993).

However, it appears that the propensity to form alliances is not evenly distributed throughout industry, but tends to be particularly associated with certain sectors. One sector which appears to be especially characterised by alliance formation is biotechnology. This is illustrated by Delapierre and Mytelka (1994), who use the MERIT-CATI data base to analyse the emerging networks in the biotech-based pharmaceutical industry (Figure 12.4). They identify both intensity and clustering (nodes) of technology co-operation agreements, with major nodes in Figure 12.4 illustrated by the oval mats.

CLUSTERS OF COLLABORATION

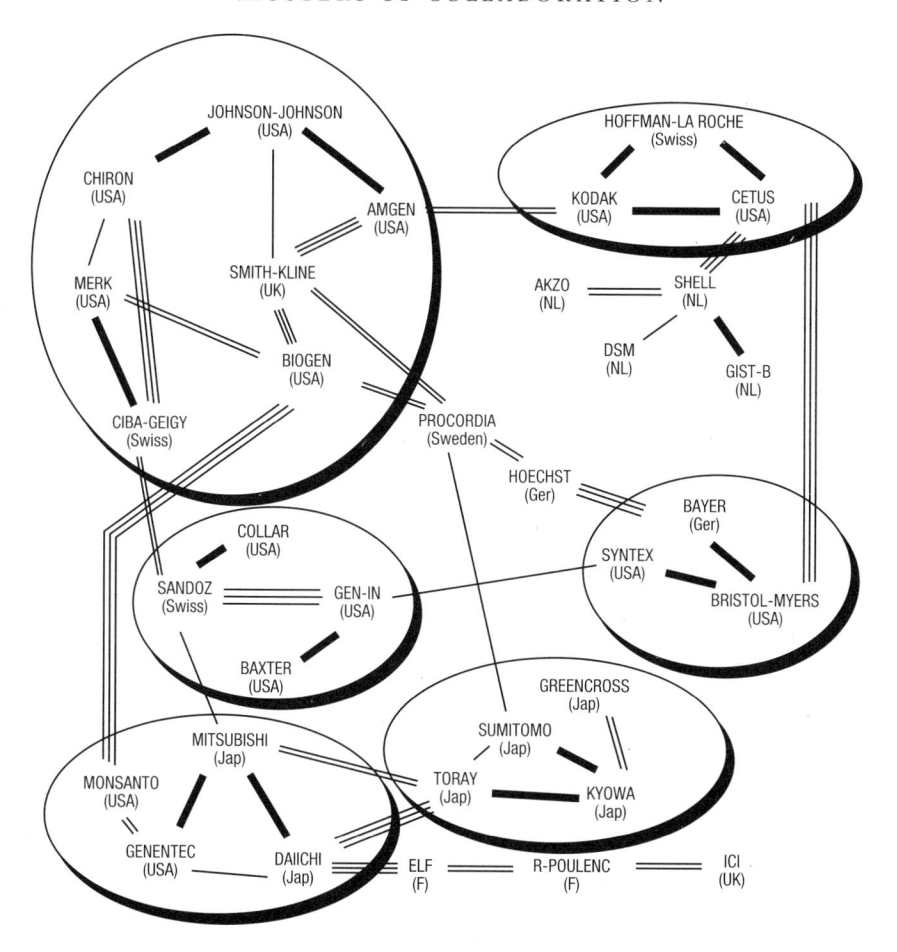

Figure 12.4   Main nodes of the networked knowledge-based oligopoly in the biotech-based pharmaceutical industry

Source: Delapierre and Mytelka (1994)

Note: Based on technology co-operation agreements established between 1985 and 1989; number of links indicated by thin lines, with four or more links indicated by heavy black lines

The first point to note is that, to the extent these technology co-operation agreements involve new or evolving technology, wholly owned or co-operative hierarchical solutions will be preferred to standard contractual solutions such as licensing. The contingent issue of which option (wholly owned or co-operative) should generally prevail in such circumstances can be made more tractable by noting that supplanting all collaboration with merger in this case would result in a single firm called the biotech based pharmaceutical industry – all firms here are eventually linked to each other through the network. Even if merger turns out consistently to be the simplest and most effective way of co-ordinating resources at the level of individual *businesses* in the biotechnology industry, there would clearly come a point where further merger proposals to exploit individual business-level opportunities would threaten to create outsized firms, trigger antitrust alarm bells or both. The question is not whether this would happen in such an industry, but when.

In this respect, it is useful to regard Figure 12.2 and Figure 12.4 as complementary. Figure 12.2 focuses on the complexity of linkages *within* firms for two hypothetical firms, while Figure 12.4 illustrates the complexity of linkages *between* firms for a real-world industry. If Delapierre and Mytelka's analysis in Figure 12.4 was to be expanded to include the complexity of linkages between divisions and businesses for each of the firms in Figure 12.4, it would be transformed into a dense thicket of intra-firm and inter-firm linkages. It is difficult and indeed probably unhelpful to illustrate the full complexity of intra- and inter-firm linkages for a single industry such as biotechnology. It is easier to analyse such an industry by looking at the complexity of intra-firm linkages (Figure 12.2) and inter-firm linkages (Figure 12.4) separately. The important point as far as reading a map such as that provided by Delapierre and Mytelka in Figure 12.4 is concerned is to remember that parties such as Kodak, ICI and Mitsubishi are themselves highly diversified systems with complex systems of internal linkages. Reducing them to single points is analytically convenient in Figure 12.4; however, it is crucial to remember that this illustrates only one dimension as far as linkages is concerned, and that the resource linkages exploited between businesses within such firms may be considerably more important and extensive than the resource linkages exploited across firm boundaries through such mechanisms as technical co-operation agreements.

Thus, previous diversification on the part of firms may represent the crucial trigger that stimulates collaborative activity between firms. Hoffman-La Roche and Kodak may discount merging with each other as a means of pooling their expertise in order to exploit some common venture opportunities, just as Daimler Benz and Mitsubishi appear to have done in setting up their particular series of collaborative arrangements. However, Delapierre and Mytelka's mapping of co-operative arrangements raises other questions. First, why are collaborative arrangements frequently arranged in clusters between pairs of corporations? Second, why do there appear to be nodes or networks of multiple firms linked together through a rich network of agreements? Third, if diversification is generally a prerequisite for the evolution of collaborative activity as we have suggested, how can we explain the extensive participation of many relatively small and specialised firms in collaborative activity? Delapierre and Mytelka (1994: 13) point out that each of the major nodes or clusters in Figure 12.4 contains one or more small biotech firms, such as Genentec and Chiron, and that this is similar to the pattern of clusters in information technology, each of which contains a semiconductor manufacturer.

To begin to explore such questions, we shall start with an example of collaborative ventures along the lines discussed in Figure 12.3, and then consider the issues that may be of importance to relevant participants as new opportunities emerge. Figure 12.5 shows three firms; the firm in the middle has been considering a new business opportunity, and, while it has the relevant technical expertise, it needs complementary marketing expertise to develop the venture. Both the other firms in Figure 12.5 possess the relevant expertise, and indeed they provide equally attractive matches in this respect as far as our original firm is concerned. As in the case of the joint venture in Figure 12.3, the venture is judged to be small scale relative to the scale of the respective firms, and so merger with either match is rejected as a potential solution. Consequently, collaboration is adopted as the preferred option in this case. Our original firm is indifferent between collaborating with either match; however, the firm on the left responds first to overtures, and a collaborative agreement jointly to exploit the new venture is set up between these two firms. Considerations such as these may lead to the appearance of collaborative activity in the first place as in Figure 12.4.

Figure 12.5 indicates that collaboration can be exclusive as well as inclusive. The corollary of the choice of the firm on the left as collaborator is the rejection of the firm on the top right in the same capacity. While this may represent a loss of opportunity for the latter firm in the context of the present venture, it may well have further consequences. Suppose that our middle firm is now considering more business opportunities and either of the other two firms could provide the requisite complementary resources, just as in the first case. While the middle firm may still be indifferent

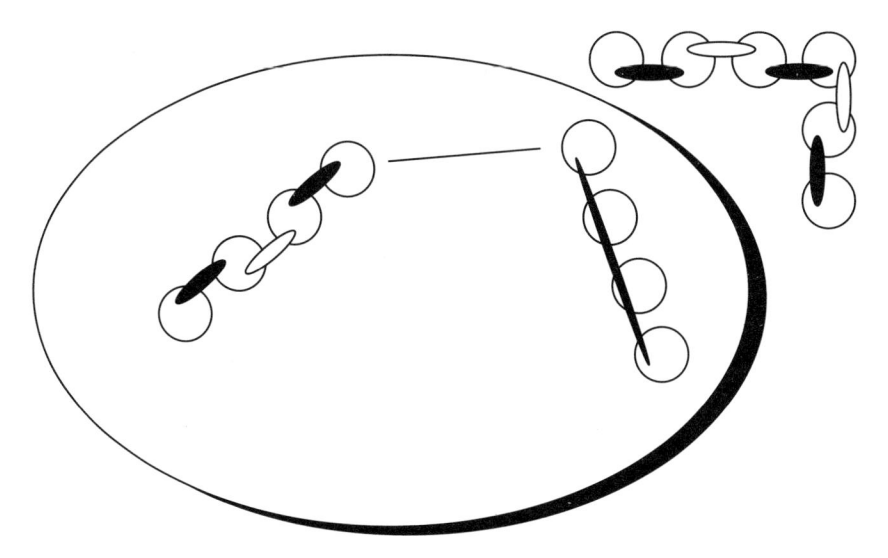

Figure 12.5   Collaboration

between either of the other two firms as potential collaborators considered in terms of potential resource matches, other considerations may now come into play. The location of its existing collaboration with the firm on the left may influence its decision as to which firm to choose for future collaborative agreements. The firm may be concerned about the possibility of opportunistic behaviour on the part of its collaborator, and the fact that its existing collaborative agreement with the firm on the left may be seen as providing a potential hostage helping to encourage good behaviour on the part of that firm. Indeed, the argument is symmetric, in that the other firm may perceive the co-ordination costs of collaboration to have been lessened through alliance formation as it can also use the existing collaborative agreement to encourage good behaviour on the part of its partner. This may lead to the consolidation of a formal or informal alliance between the two firms, as shown in Figure 12.6.

In Figure 12.6, the two diversified firms exploit multiple collaborations between business units. Formally or informally, these two firms have developed an alliance. In such cases, there can be clear and strong efficiency advantages for an alliance over alternative arrangements that take no note of the identity of business-level collaborators. Alliances can help provide an umbrella to encourage and sustain a variety of collaborative arrangements operating at business-unit level between alliance partners, just as can twinning agreements between pairs of cities or universities. Twinning agreements at the level of the overall systems can foster and sustain lower-level projects carried out between individuals, groups and departments located in the

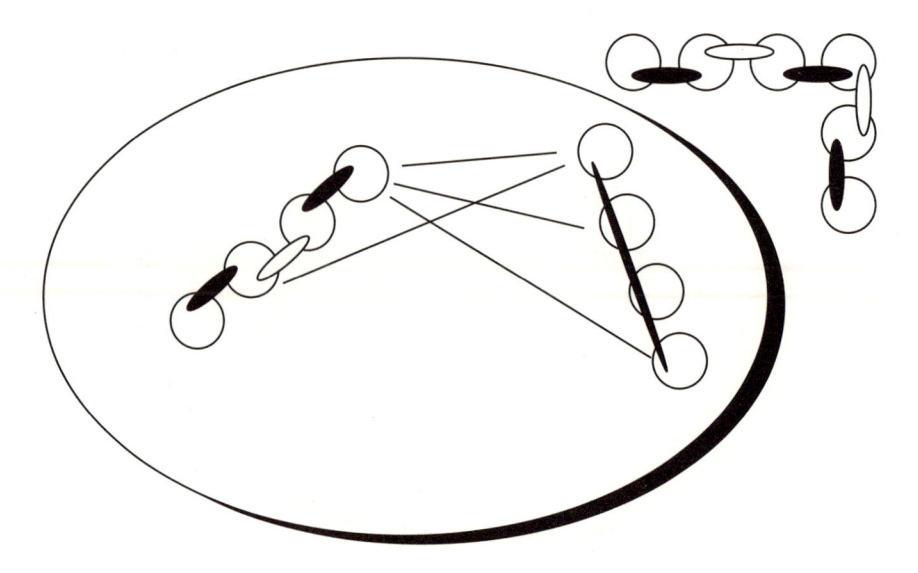

Figure 12.6   Alliance

respective partners. An efficiency rationale for alliances would start by noting that they may reduce co-ordination costs and guard against potential opportunism. Cheating on a distant, isolated collaborator is one thing; projects being conducted or planned by others within your system which can be endangered by knock-on reputation or retaliatory effects are likely to represent a hostage ensuring good behaviour. What is also worth noting about such arguments is that they raise the possibility that the formation and maintenance of alliances may be characterised by path-dependency, in that 'important influences upon the eventual outcome can be exerted by temporally remote events, including happenings dominated by chance elements rather than systematic forces' (David 1985: 332). Firms brought into contact and subsequent alliance through earlier collaboration may find it worthwhile to maintain the partnership after the original collaboration has been wound up. Once patterns of collaboration have been established, they are likely to influence where and between which parties future collaborative agreements are established.

In short, corporate and business strategy levels interact and influence each other. The growth of diversification (corporate strategy) stimulates collaboration (business strategy). But diversified firms that are pursuing multiple collaborative opportunities (business strategy) may seek to concentrate clusters of linkages with a limited number of partners (corporate strategy) where possible because of the reduced co-ordination costs that alliance may afford.[4] Both corporate and business strategy levels contribute to this resolution; in such cases the phenomenon of alliance cannot be understood without explicitly recognising the potential influence and interplay of both levels of analysis.

Up to this point we have focused on a rationale for business-level collaboration and firm-level alliances, in both cases involving co-operating pairs. There remains the further interesting possibility that co-operation may take place at even higher levels, involving groups or nodes of firms. However, there is a simple question that turns out on closer examination to be extremely complicated in such cases; what are the boundaries of a specific alliance? In some cases this question is straightforward even for cases involving multiple firms. Airbus Industrie, with its multiple partners, and the IBM–Motorola–Apple alliance to develop the RISC microprocessor are good examples of alliances created around shared projects. However, in networks the answer is frequently less obvious.

While these issues obviously require further investigation, there is one striking pattern which is embedded in Delapierre and Mytelka's (1994) analysis and is worth noting. Almost all the firms have more than one partner, though none has more than four. However, just as collaborative arrangements tend to cluster between selected *partners*, so alliances themselves appear to exhibit a strong tendency to cluster. This can be expressed in a single statement; for any given alliance, there is a strong probability that both partners share a further *partner* as well as specific technology cooperation agreements.

Thus, Figure 12.4 illustrates seven triads in which participating firms share partners – that is, Hoffman-La Roche–Kodak–Cetus, Merk–Chiron–Ciba-Geigy, two triads involving Smith Kline and three triads involving Japanese firms plus Genentec. The reasons for the triads are not immediately obvious. It could be that complementarities or technological convergence drew the partners together; but, whatever the particular reasons, it may be worthwhile considering possible efficiency implications of clustering partners within a club or network. Some such implications can be pursued using Figure 12.7, which adds a new firm to the analysis of Figure 12.6. Our new firm is a three-business firm based around a common marketing expertise and is shown on the mat in Figure 12.7.

Suppose that our new firm has already set up an alliance with the firm on the left, and this is embodied in three collaborative agreements between the two firms. It has two other potential venture opportunities, and in this case it could have chosen the third firm on the mat or the firm outside the mat. Suppose also, as in the previous cases, that the firm outside the mat would have provided as satisfactory a resource match as could be provided by the firm on the mat. Why should our new firm prefer the other firm on the mat over the firm outside, either as collaborator or as alliance partner?

A possible stimulus in this respect is provided by the new firm's existing alliance with the firm on the left. If our new firm was to be adversely affected through opportunistic behaviour inflicted in other collaborative

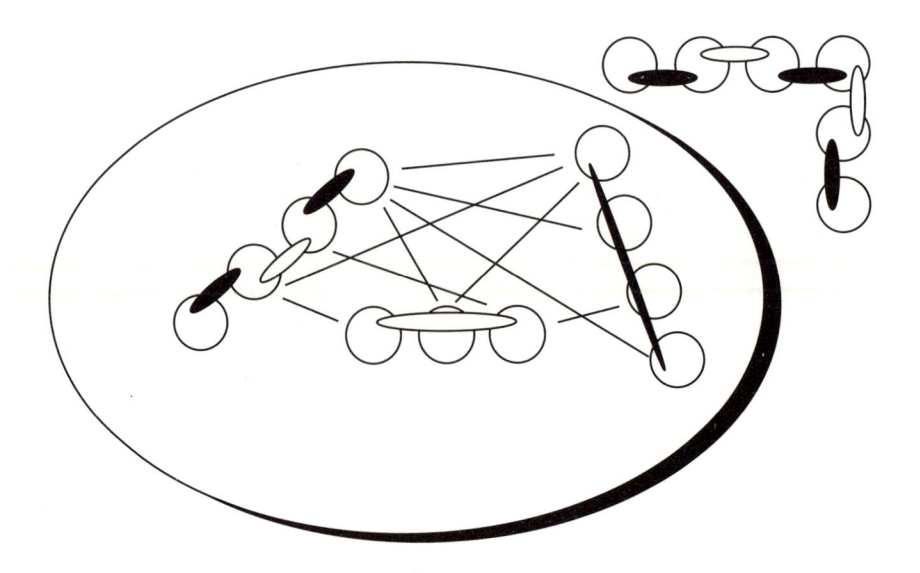

Figure 12.7   Club or network

agreements or alliances, the firm's original partner is likely to be concerned if such damage could impair the new firm's ability to function effectively in its original partnership. A partner's overall health (and ultimately survival) is likely to be of direct relevance in any alliance, and threats to a firm may be regarded as an indirect threat to its partners. Consequently, our new firm may be more relaxed concerning the possibility of collaborating with the other firm on the mat, given that its existing partner also has an alliance with the other firm on the mat and could presumably use the constituent collaborative agreements to coerce it into good behaviour if necessary. In short, hurt me and you might also indirectly hurt your other partner, who might retaliate. However, the potential reduction in co-ordination costs that the new firm might enjoy through being hooked into such a network or club is not limited to its transactions with the third firm, or indeed limited to the new firm itself. Each of the three firms on the mat in Figure 12.7 might enjoy increased security and associated reduction in co-ordination costs in each of its alliances through being a member of this club.

Group sticks or carrots encouraging or enforcing responsible individual behaviour could also operate at the level of broadly defined networks or nodes of the type identified by Delapierre and Mytelka (1994). It reinforces the point made earlier that the apparently simple question 'What are the boundaries of the alliance?' is not so simple. It may even be the case that there may be clubs within clubs, with tightly integrated triads embedded in more loosely coupled networks or modes in some cases. If political alliances can tolerate the possibility of 'variable geometry' or 'multi-speed' coalitions, as in the case of European integration, then similar possibilities may be entertained for industrial alliances.

The efficiency implications of clubs and networks are not straightforward, but one point that can be made here is that they must involve different levels of analysis, just as did the relationships between business-level collaboration and corporate-level alliances or partnering. If networks or clubs of closely associated firms exist, then a firm's choice of partners is likely to be influenced by the club(s) it belongs to, or would like to belong to. Similarly, what partners a firm has, or would like to have, is likely to influence the club(s) it joins. The levels interact, with choice of specific partners influencing and limiting choice of clubs, and choice of clubs influencing and limiting choice of partners. Thus, clustering in our example takes place here at three levels: clusters of collaborative agreements *around* individual firms (diversification driven), clustering of collaborative agreements *between* firms (alliance motives) and clustering *of* co-operating firms (club behaviour). Each level of behaviour interacts with the one above or below, and if any level of behaviour was studied in isolation, it would obscure or overlook major influences on the pattern of co-operative behaviour.

This type of approach can also help us analyse the participation of small specialised firms in collaborative agreements. We have argued that decisions such as those on technical co-operation tend to favour hierarchical solutions, while small size and specialisation favour merger solutions over collaborative alternatives. At first glance the involvement of small specialised firms in these clusters appears inconsistent with such arguments.

In fact, diversification can still be seen to exert a powerful influence over collaborative activity in such cases, though one step removed – here it is sufficient that some of the small specialised firm's multiple *partners* are large and diversified for collaborative solutions to be stimulated. For example, merging Genentec and Chiron with *all* of their direct partners in the respective cases would force marriages of Monsanto and Mitsubishi, and Ciba-Geigy with Johnson-Johnson, respectively. This leads us into the barriers to merging diversified systems discussed earlier and illustrated in Figures 12.2 and 12.3. However, if a small specialised biotech firm was to merge with only *one* of its existing partners, this would only fully internalise one set of agreements while leaving the rest still to be exploited through co-operation agreements. Against the limited gains that such partial internalisation offers must be set the potential impediments to existing and future collaboration in cases where loss of independence, and assimilation within a potential or actual competitor, is seen to matter. This is illustrated in Figure 12.8, where a small specialised firm is added to the mat of Figure 12.7. This firm only has three collaborative agreements, but if the merger option was to be adopted in each case, it would indirectly lead to the combination of all four firms on the mat into a single large firm. Thus, the small single-business-unit firm illustrated in the four-firm cluster in Figure 12.8 remains independent and does not merge with any or all of its partners. Diversification still plays an important role in inhibiting further merger activity, though in this case it is the diversification of the small firm's multiple collaborators that is particularly relevant.

It is useful to contrast this with circumstances in which clustering of collaborative agreements would tend to favour the *merger* alternative. If a small specialised firm has multiple actual or potential knowledge-based links with other small specialised firms, then multi-firm merger to create a multi-business firm is the obvious solution. Alternatively, if a small specialised firm has multiple actual or potential knowledge-based links with *one* partner, then merger with its partner is still the obvious solution, whether or not the partner is large and diversified. It is the special case of multiple partners, some of whom turn out to be large and diversified, that creates the special circumstances in which partnership arrangements are favoured over merger in systems characterised by a dense thicket of knowledge-based agreements in which a small specialised firm is involved.

Figure 12.9 puts the club or network of Figure 12.8 in a broader context by recognising that firms may have to go beyond the boundaries of particular clubs to pursue collaborative opportunities in certain cases. In Figure 12.9 two of the firms in our club have had to search outside for collaborators

CLUSTERS OF COLLABORATION

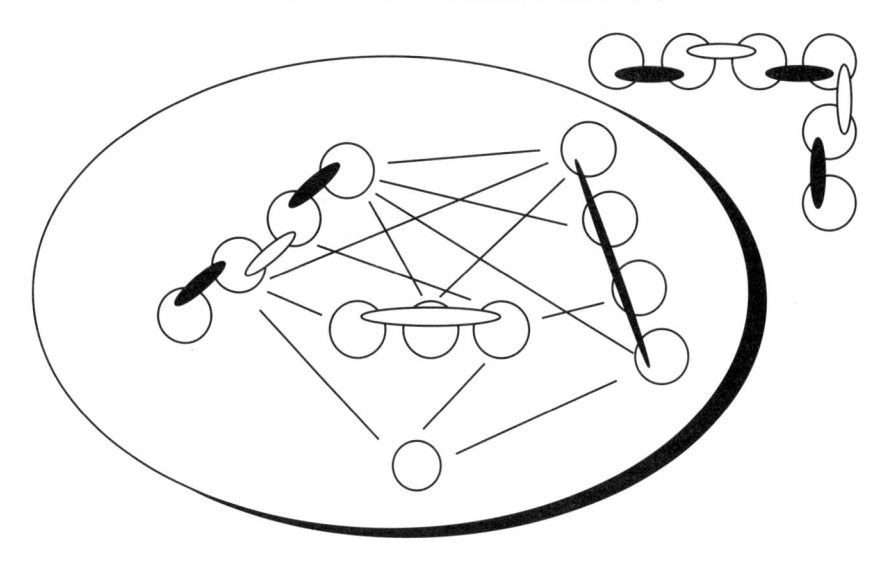

Figure 12.8   Small-firm involvement in collaboration

to provide complementary resources for new ventures. In this example we have restricted consideration to the new collaborators themselves. However, these new firms may well be members of other clubs or networks, and these clubs may be weakly linked in similar fashion to other clubs and networks, as in the interrelated nodes illustrated in Figure 12.4. Figure 12.9 now displays all the major elements contained or implied in Delapierre and Mytelka's analysis in Figure 12.4; notably, clustering of links in the form of highly diversified firms, clustering of links within alliances, clustering of firms within clubs and involvement of small firms in collaborative activity. The perspective here sees corporate diversification as the critical trigger leading to the formation of first collaborative activity, and subsequently alliances and clubs. In this perspective there is no conflict between the relative costliness of collaborative activity, such as joint venture at business-unit level, and its proliferation in recent years. Indeed, if joint venture was *not* a generally inferior and inefficient mode of organisation compared to single-firm alternatives when analysed solely at individual-business level we would have expected to have seen its appearance in the earlier stages of industrial development when smaller, more specialised firms predominated. For large diversified firms, collaborative activity such as joint venture may be locally inefficient (at the level of the participating business units) but globally efficient (at the level of entire firms). This is the essential starting point for analysing the evolution of the different levels of co-operative activity that we have explored here.

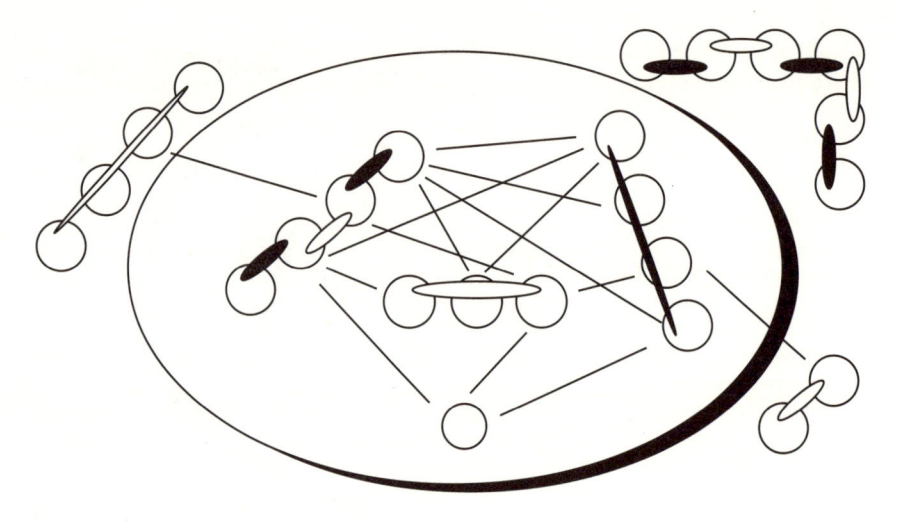

Figure 12.9   Club and extra-club linkages

CONCLUSIONS

The perspective outlined here helps integrate multiple levels of co-operative activity in the firm; it was argued that business-, firm- and group-level co-operative activity may all be distinctive phenomena, with each level influencing the formation and maintenance of co-operation at other levels. Corporate diversification was seen as playing a crucial role in stimulating the development of co-operative activity at business level in the first place, and merger was analysed as a potential complement as well as a substitute for collaborative activity such as joint venture. The paper helps to reconcile the costliness of business-level co-operative activity such as joint venture with the proliferation of such agreements in recent years.

Co-operative activity in many sectors typically involves clustering behaviour in at least four levels: clustering of linkages within firms (diversification), clustering of co-operative agreements around firms (joint venture and other collaborative activity), clustering of agreements between selected partners (alliances) and clustering of partners themselves (networks or clubs). Analysis of, say, alliances necessarily implies co-operative behaviour at business, corporate and group or network levels. The levels typically will interact, and analysis has to recognise both the multiple levels of co-operation and their potential interaction if it is not to present an incomplete and partial analysis of the alliance phenomenon.

Finally, as Richardson points out, 'Firms form partners for the dance, when the music stops, they can change them' (Richardson 1972: 896). But does clustering introduce elements of stability that bond partners together when the music stops, or does fickleness and opportunism override the advantages of stable alliances and club membership? It is questions such as these that can be raised by the analysis of collaboration as a multi-level clustered phenomenon.

NOTES

1 Kay (1982) looks at this issue in more detail.
2 Similar arguments for and against selective disinvestment hold in the case of firms wishing to disinvest in businesses which might otherwise invite antitrust attention if combined with a related business of the other firm.
3 For example, Scherer and Ross (1990: 92) show that the diversification of US corporations during the period 1950–75 was largely due to merger and not internal growth.
4 This, of course, may mean that partnership considerations may override business strategy considerations. The most attractive collaborator seen from the level of individual opportunities and businesses may not be the chosen collaborator once partnership considerations are taken into account.

REFERENCES

Arthur, W. B. (1989) 'Competing technologies, increasing returns and lock-in by historical events', *Economic Journal* 99: 116–31.

Berg, S. V. and Friedman, P. (1978) 'Joint ventures in American industry: an overview', *Mergers and Acquisitions* (summer): 28–41.

Boyle, S. E. (1968) 'An estimate of the number and size distribution of domestic joint subsidiaries', *Antitrust Law and Economic Review* (spring): 81–92.

Buckley, P. and Casson, M. (1987) 'A theory of cooperation in international business', in F. Contractor and P Lorange (eds) *Cooperative Strategies in International Business*, Lexington, Mass.: Lexington Books.

David, P. A. (1985) 'Clio and the economics of QWERTY', *American Economic Review, Papers and Proceedings* 75: 332–7.

Davidson, W. H. and McFetridge, D. G. (1985) 'Key characteristics in the choice of international technology transfer mode', *Journal of International Business Studies* 16: 5–21.

Delapierre, M. and Mytelka, L. K. (1994) 'Blurring boundaries: new inter-firm relationships and the emergence of network, knowledge-based oligopolies', EMOT Workshop on 'The Changing Boundaries of the Firm', Como, Villa Olmo, 21–23 October.

Dunning, J. H. (1993) *Multinational Enterprises and the Global Economy*, Washington, D.C.: Addison-Wesley.

Hennart, J.-F. (1988) 'A transaction costs theory of equity joint ventures', *Strategic Management Journal* 9: 361–74.

—— (1991) 'The transaction cost theory of the multinational enterprise', in C. N. Pitelis and R. Sugden (eds) *The Nature of the Transnational Firm*, London: Routledge.

Kay, N. M. (1982) *The Evolving Firm: Strategy and Structure in Industrial Organisation*, London: Macmillan.

—— (1992) 'Collaborative strategies of firms: theory and evidence', in A. Del Monte (ed.) *Recent Developments in the Theory of Industrial Organisation*, London: Macmillan.

Kay, N. M., Robé, J.-P. and Zagnoli, P. (1987) 'An approach to the analysis of joint venture', Florence: European University Institute, working paper.

Mintzberg, H. (1979) *The Structuring of Organizations: A Synthesis of the Research*, Englewood Cliffs, N.J.: Prentice Hall.

Porter, M. and Fuller, M. B. (1986) 'Coalitions and global strategy', in M. Porter (ed.) *Competition in Global Industries*, Boston, Mass.: Harvard Business School.

Richardson, G. B. (1972) 'The organisation of industry', *Economic Journal* 82: 883–96.

Rumelt, R. P. (1986) *Strategy Structure and Economic Performance*, rev. edn, Boston, Mass.: Harvard Business School.

Scherer, F. M. and Ross, D. (1990) *Industrial Market Structure and Economic Performance*, 3rd edn, Boston, Mass.: Houghton-Mifflin.

Teece, D. (1986) 'Profiting from technological innovation', *Research Policy* 15: 286–305.

Williamson, O. E. (1975) *Markets and Hierarchies: Analysis and Antitrust Implications*, New York: Free Press.

—— (1985) *The Economic Institutions of Capitalism*, New York: Free Press.

13

LIMITS TO A FIRM'S RATE OF GROWTH

The Richardsonian view and its contemporary empirical significance

Gavin C. Reid

INTRODUCTION

In a special issue of *Oxford Economic Papers* in 1964 two notable papers, by Leyland (1964) and Richardson (1964), on the growth of the firm were published. They were the product of an enquiry into 'Business Policy in an Expanding Economy' which had been undertaken by the Oxford Economic Research Group under the chairmanship of George Richardson. Richardson's own contribution 'The limits to a firm's rate of growth' is an elegant piece. It is an example of 'grounded theory'.[1] Thus his starting point was the empirical evidence from the enquiry which illuminated perceived constraints upon a firm's growth rate. Based on evidence from interviews with sixteen businessmen over three years, he identified four principal constraints: (1) labour or physical inputs; (2) finance; (3) lack of suitable investment opportunities; and (4) lack of sufficient managerial capacity. His evaluation of the potential significance of each of these constraints was not theoretical (i.e. not based merely on a priori reasoning) but, rather, empirical. He simply asked: 'What did the respondents report?' His unqualified conclusion was: 'A very striking number of our guests expressed the view without hesitation that the availability of suitable management had been, and was, the operative check on their expansion' (Richardson 1964: 10). He went on to elucidate the meaning of a managerial limit to expansion of the firm.

It is this which is the focus of the paper. I address the problem of managerial limits to growth by first making reference to Richardson's 'grounded theory'. I then turn to a modern body of data, gathered by similar grounded methods to those used by the Oxford Economic Research Group in its enquiry. Relating Richardson's own work to subsequent advances in the analysis and testing of a theory of managerial limits to growth, I present new estimates of the growth/profitability trade-off. These emphasise the roles of both organisational and financial structures in limiting a firm's growth.

RICHARDSON'S VIEW ON RESTRAINTS TO GROWTH

Richardson's (1964) starting point was to ask why a shortage of good managers did not simply lead to their prices being bid up. Why did not interviewees report a rising price of talent, rather than reporting, as they did, a scarcity of talent? He identified obvious and perhaps minor reasons: conventionality in determining salaries (especially in the underpayment of senior personnel) and 'lock-in' features of contracts, like non-transferable pension rights. More important, however, was the problem of what we would today call *adverse selection*: 'To hire outsiders is to invest in assets of uncertain yield; the rate of new recruitment, at least to the higher levels, may therefore be limited by considerations of risk' (*ibid.*: 11). In drawing attention to the problem of information asymmetry in recruiting new management, Richardson referred in a modern way to 'insiders', whom directors are able to size up more easily than 'outsiders', because their performance capabilities are better known than those of new managerial recruits. A further problem was that 'new-comers are at an inevitable disadvantage [compared] to established personnel in terms of the experience of the firm's products, markets and internal organisation' (*ibid.*: 11). There was a learning curve to be ascended, or what Arrow called 'learning by doing', to be experienced by new recruits to management as 'their services can be developed fully only after experience of the particular circumstances of their job' (Arrow 1962: 11). The argument advanced by Edith Penrose in *The Theory of the Growth of the Firm* (1959) was noted as being supported by direct evidence from one of the respondents, who had observed that 'the real curb is the lack of managerial ability in the sense that it takes a long time to train people into the ways of the firm and its wide range of activities' (Penrose 1959: 11). As a consequence, Richardson concludes that 'there is a functional relationship between the "organizational efficiency" of a firm and its rate of growth, and that the former will decline, after a point, as the latter rises' (Richardson 1964: 11). That is, there is ultimately a growth/efficiency trade-off. In the modern literature of industrial organisation, this is often called the Penrose Effect.[2]

Richardson noted that firms with greater adaptability would be less subject to this trade-off than those with inferior adaptability.[3] In a growth context, whilst longer-term planning requires greater flexibility, the attempt to reduce uncertainty by a more close co-ordination, using futures contracts, of complementary activities militates against achieving this flexibility. As

Langlois (1995) indicates, the cognitive limits of managers may make long-term contracting difficult in an uncertain world. The current capabilities of managers in a firm may set limits on flexibility, in much the same way as do fixed plant and equipment. However, such costs are more properly regarded as fixed, rather than sunk, so no issue of asset specificity, in the sense of Williamson (1975), arises. That other plank of the Williamson construction – opportunism – is largely concerned with the strategic issue of 'guile', rather than with the more central issue of cognitive limits of managers and the implied growth–profitability trade-off emphasised by Richardson. Moral hazard, as a potential further source of incompleteness or inefficiency in the co-ordination of future contractual commitments, pales into insignificance compared to difficulties of co-ordinating complementary production activities. Thus, as Langlois emphasises, a move towards a Richardsonian, rather than a Williamsonian, approach requires 'a major shift of emphasis away from problems of coordinating commitments toward problems of coordinating production' (Chapter 10).

In seeking superior co-ordination of production within the firm, consideration must be given not only to the magnitude of its contemplated growth, but also to its proposed direction. Expansion into new markets is likely to raise more acute problems of the co-ordination of production than expansion within existing markets. Thus one is confronted with the paradox, recognised by Richardson, that 'the most creative and enterprising' directors are the 'most likely to stress the managerial and organizational restraint on expansion' (Richardson 1964: 12).

By reference to the *Principles* (1890/1961) of Alfred Marshall,[4] Richardson reminds us that his own argument is not simply that managerial diseconomies of scale cause long-run unit cost curves to be U-shaped. For such curves, the relevant levels of unit cost are 'those attainable by a firm already endowed with an organizational structure appropriate to the corresponding scales of output' (Richardson 1964: 13). But, in the case Richardson is exploring, these levels of unit costs are irrelevant, for 'the firm lacks the appropriate organization and cannot hope to build it up during the planning period' (*ibid.*: 13). He rejects the possibility of constructing a modified long-run unit-cost curve which takes account of the inverse relationship between organisational efficiency and the growth rate because the particular position and shape of such a curve 'would depend upon the size and the elasticity of the managerial resources at the firm's disposal' (*ibid.*: 14): in short, it would be indeterminate. He argues against narrowly conceiving the managerial function as keeping down the costs of production, because 'part of their job is to decide upon the precise character of the product, or products, to be made, and to find, or create, a market for them' (*ibid.*: 14). Thus Richardson concludes that 'managerial difficulties, associated with an unduly high rate of growth, will show up, not just in costs, but in all of the determinants of profitability' (*ibid.*: 14). The import of all this is that the efficiency/growth trade-off also implies a profitability/growth trade-off: 'If an increasing rate of growth causes, after a point, decreasing organizational efficiency, then this should show up in profits' (*ibid.*: 14). A major purpose of this paper is to address this question of whether such a trade-off exists. In doing so, I make appeal in the next section to a contemporary body of data, gathered by fieldwork methods. I use it first in a descriptive way, and then turn in the subsequent section ('Limits to small-firm growth', pp. 252–6) to an econometric investigation of the hypothesised growth/profitability trade-off.

CONTEMPORARY EVIDENCE ON LIMITS TO A FIRM'S GROWTH

In this section I shall introduce new fieldwork evidence on small firms which can be used to cast light, in a contemporary fashion, on Richardson's 'limits to growth' argument. Three types of firms will be identified, and their organisational features will be explored. Descriptive data on growth and profitability will then be related to these organisational forms of firms.

We have seen that Richardson had case study evidence to the effect that 'for most of the firms dealt with, managerial capacity . . . was the strongest restraint on their rate of growth' (Richardson 1964: 10). As a consequence, he argued that limitations to managerial capacity caused organisational inefficiencies to arise as energetic and creative directors tried to push forward a firm's growth rate. This suggests that investigation of the organisational forms which firms assume is worthwhile. Their relative efficiencies can then be related to their performance. In this way one gets a transactionally based account of how an efficiency/growth trade-off might arise, in turn leading to the Penrose Effect of a profitability/growth trade-off. The aim is to build upon the Richardson insights in a way that has now become possible since the development of the markets, hierarchies and bureaucracies literature.[5] This done, I move on to statistical analysis of the implications of this organisational approach.

In his own work, Richardson did not attempt to go from direct observation based on case studies to statistical inference based on market data. A profitability/growth trade-off is implied by the analytical argument he constructed (or 'grounded') on case study evidence, but this is not something he explored empirically. In fact this trade-off relationship has since been widely explored, by authors like Cubbin and Leech (1986), and Dobson and Gerrard (1989). It has also been the focus of my own recent work (as in Reid 1993, 1995), where all the businesses analysed were small.

However, most of this new empirical work has been preoccupied with testing models of industrial economics. Notably, so-called 'managerial theories of the firm' have been tested against neoclassical alternatives, without much attention being given explicitly to the organisational form of the firm. The greater concern has been with agency problems arising from the so-called 'divorce of ownership and control'. My approach is naturally different from the managerial theory of the firm literature, because none of the small business enterprises (SBEs) analysed had outside equity participation. Even so, a choice of organisational form had to be made by owner-managers. Even with an SBE of, say, twenty people, choices arise as to how authority is delegated in terms of span of control and levels of hierarchy. Whilst lacking the organisational complexity of the larger corporations that one conventionally associates with managerial theories, small firms raise important organisational issues. My purpose in this section is to put these distinctive organisational issues of the SBE at centre stage. In the next section, I then make appeal to, and report upon, new econometric work on the growth/profitability trade-off relationship.

Richardson's own evidence was based on interviews with sixteen senior managers of firms which had experienced a good growth performance. Over a three-year period they came to Oxford University to participate in interviews which, according to Richardson and Leyland, 'dealt primarily with the methods of formal planning, with the motive for growth and with the limits to growth' (Richardson and Leyland 1964: 1). A summary of these responses has been provided by Leyland (1964). My own evidence is similarly 'grounded', and was also gathered over a three-year period. However, the sample was considerably larger (seventy-three rather than sixteen respondents) and also provided more detailed and systematic information.

I have reported on this evidence at several points in the recent past[6] so I shall be relatively brief here. In 1985 I engaged in fieldwork with Lowell Jacobsen that created a data base composed of the responses from seventy-three detailed structured interviews. These were conducted with a random sample of Scottish owner-managers of SBEs. These SBEs had an average employment size of nine (counting full-timers as one and part-timers as a half) and an average age of 3½ years (from financial inception). In 1988 I returned to the field again with other co-workers, and traced all surviving firms to obtain a further forty-seven follow-up structured interviews. In addition, in 1985 a sub-sample of seventeen owner-managers were taken through a semi-structured interview on small-business strategy. The 1985 structured interviews looked at general features (e.g. employment, products), pricing, costs, sales and competition, and finance. The 1985 semi-structured interviews looked at competitive forces, competitive strategy and defensive strategy. The follow-up interviews in 1988 looked at general features, competitiveness, innovation, skills and financial structure. The largest body of evidence was gathered in the 1985 structured interview, and it is primarily this evidence that I appeal to, although all the evidence available has been influential in the way I formulate and test hypotheses.

Before looking at explicitly model-based evidence, it is useful to look at two revealing cross-tabulations of the data. The first of these is contained in Table 13.1, which relates size of SBE (measured by sales and employment) to business type. Within the sample, there were three business types: sole proprietorship (30 per cent), partnership (21 per cent) and private company (49 per cent). These categories are exhaustive and mutually exclusive. The three business types may be ranked, in increasing order of size, as follows: sole proprietorship, partnership and private company. This is true by sales and by employment, both absolutely and by maximum size in each category. Thus, measuring sales at 1985 prices, sole proprietorships had average sales of about £60,000; and the corresponding figures for partnerships and private companies were £105,000 and £190,000, respectively.[7] The categories of firms I have identified tend also to be the forms assumed, typically in sequence, as the SBE grows over a period of years. Thus a sole proprietorship, perhaps initially started from home, might become a partnership some months after it has been seriously launched, and then be transformed into a private company after some years, as it enjoys further success. It is possible that an SBE starts as a partnership and then is transformed into a private company, or that the partnership form is skipped, with the SBE going directly from a sole proprietorship to a private company; but generally speaking the ordering is progressive, in terms of business development.

An important feature of Richardson's work, with the emphasis on the organisational disabilities which accompany new management recruitment, is that it anticipates the later transactions-cost-based analysis of the likes of Williamson (1975, 1985). In deference to Richardson's insight, in this paper written in his honour, I should like to make some observations about organisational form which are essentially transactions-cost-based, and which I think

Table 13.1   Size and business type

Business Type/Size	Sales Mean (Std. Dev.)	(Max, Min)	Employment Mean (Std. Dev.)	(Max, Min)
Sole Proprietorship (n=22)	2.1818 (1.4019)	(5,1)	2.6818 (2.4570)	(9,0)
Partnership (n=15)	3.1333 (1.7674)	(6,1)	5.4000 (4.8374)	(21,2)
Private Company (n=36)	4.7500 (2.7710)	(9,2)	12.833 (15.046)	(52,0)

Note: Employment = full-time employees; sales = 1 for £0–50k; 2 for >£50k–£100k; 3 for >£100k–£150k; 4 for >£150k–£200k; 5 for >£200k–£250k; 6 for >£250k–£300k; 7 for >£300k–£350k; 8 for >£350k–£400k; 9 for >£400k, all ranges measured in 1985 prices

are in sympathy with his general approach. The inspiration for this is the famed analysis of evolving organisational forms by Williamson (1975: ch. 3).

Clearly one of the consequences of growth is the tendency for it to be accompanied by the use of hierarchy to control the firm. Using the figures of Table 13.1, we see that the mean employment sizes for each of the three firm types were: 3 for a sole proprietorship; 5 for a partnership; and 13 for a private company. These average figures suggest possible organisational forms of the types indicated in Figure 13.1.

In (a) the 'peak co-ordinator' at the top is the owner-manager, or proprietor, and he or she has three subordinates. In (b), the five members of the firm are of equal status and if they each wish freely to communicate with

(a)

Sole proprietorship

(b)

Partnership

(c)

Private company

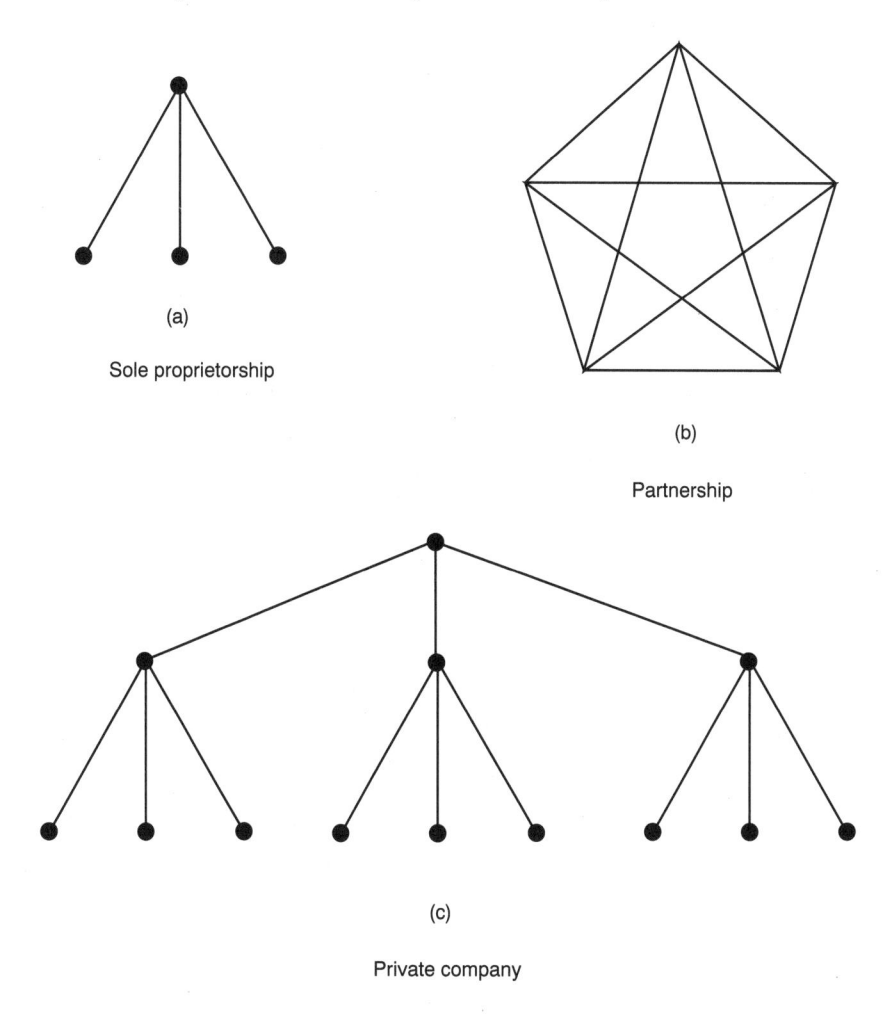

Figure 13.1   Possible organisational forms for three small-firm types

other partners, in so-called 'all-channel communication' it is necessary to have ten channels open, as indicated by the connecting lines. When the firm size is larger, this organisational form becomes inefficient. For the n-firm members case, the required number of two-way communication channels is $n(n - 1)/2$, which grows at a rate which is governed by n^2 as n becomes large.[8] For example, if thirteen firm members are involved, seventy-eight channels of communication are required. However, if hierarchy, and thus a system of superiors and subordinates, is used, the number of two-way channels is $n - 1$ in simple hierarchy; that is, it is possible to economise on channels. This is illustrated in (c), where a simple serial replication of (a) is displayed, indicating how thirteen people might be organised in a private company, with one managing director, three managers (e.g. production, marketing, accounts) and nine workers. Now it just so happens that the statistics of Table 13.1, by business type, all closely tally with the illustrations of Figure 13.1 in (a), (b) and (c). I did this to make the evidence 'come alive'. However, I think there is more than a lecturing trick behind both the data and the illustrations of it, because modifying organisational forms from (a) to (b), from (b) to (c), or even from (a) to (b) to (c) is a transition that my fieldwork suggests is typical of real SBEs over a period of around three years.[9]

Consider first the transition from (a) to (c) in Figure 13.1. If an SBE with a boss and three workers is to change to an SBE with a boss and twelve workers, the boss will have to keep twelve channels open if he is to communicate directly with all subordinates; that is, four times what he is used to dealing with. This might overstretch his supervisory capabilities, and in this sense it is a cognitive problem. It will most certainly divert him significantly from those strategic and entrepreneurial functions which first made him an active rather than passive player in the job market. His solution, to ease the transactional costs of business transformation with growth, is to appoint three managers. These might be the same three who were his first employees, but who have now learnt, in some measure, the ropes of the business and can be entrusted with some level of responsibility. They, in turn, will supervise three new employees each, and in learning how to do this will appeal to the previous experience of the boss. Amongst the tasks they confront will that of guiding new employees up the learning curve. Thus, promoted employees are learning new managerial skills, and new employees are being trained in skills relevant to the firm they have just joined. To the extent that organisational transformation occurs in a frictionless way, there are no 'costs of growth'. But, most realistically, the process of change in itself is costly, in the way which Richardson has emphasised, and in a way which I have illustrated above. To express the matter in modern terms, change is costly because it involves the creation of a new organisational technology. This will only be contemplated if the anticipated benefits outweigh the costs in the long run. In the short run the goal will be to minimise the transactional costs of change. The voluntary change from an SBE of form (a) to one of form (b) would be expected to reflect this.

It has been indicated that Richardson saw the process of growth as leading to costs. Today we might choose to call these 'convex adjustment costs', and we would expect their existence to be reflected in reduced business performance.[10] Before examining their performance implications more precisely, it is useful to refer to another cross-tabulation from this SBE data base, as displayed in Table 13.2. Here, two measures of performance, asset growth and profitability are cross-tabulated against the three forms of SBE in the sample. It is clear that the private company enjoys a higher growth rate than the partnership, which in turn enjoys a higher growth rate than the sole proprietorship. This is true both for average growth rates and for maximal growth rates within each category of SBE. Turning now to profitability, it is equally clear that the private company is less profitable on average than the other forms of SBE, and this is true also of peak profitability within each category of firm. Without looking at causality or determinants of growth and profitability, Table 13.2 at least suggests an inverse association between growth and profitability.

However, these data have to be treated with caution. They do not, for example, imply that larger SBEs grow faster than smaller SBEs. Indeed, for the sample as a whole, setting aside firm type, we know this is not the case.[11] Thus, within each firm type there is a tendency for the smaller SBEs to grow faster than the larger ones. Further, the data do not simply show that private companies are less profitable than sole proprietorships. Setting aside possible problems in comparing profitability figures across firm types, it has to be borne in mind that, on average, private companies in the sample are much

Table 13.2   Performance and business type

Performance *Business Type*	*Asset Growth* Mean (Std. Dev.)	(Max, Min)	*Profitability* Mean (Std. Dev.)	(Max, Min)
Sole Proprietorship (n=22)	22.755 (52.150)	243.20 −8.330	31.745 (49.938)	164.00 -40.00
Partnership (n=15)	56.373 (140.50)	554.20 −2.000	33.987 (42.293)	121.20 −18.000
Private Company (n=36)	78.303 (234.30)	1333.4 −4.7600	5.8472 (33.227)	62.500 −100.00

Note: Asset growth = [real assets $(t + \tau)$ − real assets (τ)] ([Age × real assets (τ)] expressed as a percentage; profitability = [net profit]. [Book value of assets] expressed as a percentage, as reported in 1988 for the year 1985.

older than the other forms of SBE. They might therefore be more advanced in their 'life-cycle', confronting the effects of declining performance first highlighted by Alfred Marshall (1890), and since confirmed in the small-firms literature.[12] Finally, I turn now to a more formal treatment of what is suggested by Table 13.2, that is, the possibility of a growth/profitability trade-off, at least partly explained by the choice of the form of the SBE.

LIMITS TO SMALL-FIRM GROWTH: THE TRADE-OFF RELATIONSHIP

In previous work (Reid 1993: ch. 11), I have explored the possibility of a growth/profitability trade-off in the context of a simultaneous equations model in which growth both causes and is caused by profitability; that is, $g = F(\pi)$ and $\pi = f(g)$, where g is the growth rate and π is profitability.[13] A 'cumulative causation' hypothesis concerning growth and profitability, with the one positively reinforcing the other, was rejected in favour of a growth/profitability 'trade-off' hypothesis. Furthermore, this latter hypothesis was supported by a model which was shown to be stable and able to generate equilibrium values which were close to the mean values for growth and profitability in the sample.[14]

A first look at the data might be made by reference to Table 13.3, which displays a profitability equation, estimated by ordinary least squares, using White's heteroscedastic-consistent covariance matrix. About 30 per cent of the variation in profitability is explained by the thirteen variables used as regressors. The F statistic is significant at the 5 per cent level. However, given the large number of regressors and the relatively small sample size, few of the coefficients are estimated with precision. With more parsimonious models this situation improves (cf. Reid 1993: ch. 11). From the standpoint of this paper, the important coefficients to note are those for the *Bsns* and *PGear* variables. The variable *Bsns* denotes 'business type' and is a categorical variable equal to unity for sole proprietorships, to 2 for partnerships and to 3 for private companies. The effect of this variable on profitability is clearly negative, confirming the initial impression of Table 13.2. If instead of this categorical variable for type of business one uses instead two dummy variables, the first for a sole proprietorship and the second for a partnership (with the private company being included in the constant term), the results obtained are the same, with positive and significant coefficients on both dummy variables. One therefore concludes with some confidence that as the SBE ascends the ladder of firm structure, it does so, in the short run, at the sacrifice of profitability.

With so many variables included, for exploratory purposes, the significance of any one variable will be difficult to establish, given limited degrees of freedom. The most obvious point to note is that the equity gearing ratio

Table 13.3 Profitability equation (dependent variable: *ProfRate*)

Variable	Coefficient	(t-ratio)
Bsns	−14.018	(−2.2316)
Mmkt	1.4716	(0.46116)
Share	1.1942	(0.60839)
CompNo	−1.2433	(−0.41711)
PCruc	18.609	(1.8300)
ProdDes	−8.1809	(−1.0036)
Adv	−9.7803	(−1.7013)
Cfp	−18.308	(−1.4001)
AddDebt	1.9991	(0.20915)
Pgear	−0.10802	(−3.4754)
DesComp	6.3928	(0.77049)
Age	0.064201	(1.0278)
Grate	−0.016316	(−0.76262)

Note: $R^2 = 0.2846$; $F = 1.805 = F(14,59)_{0.05}$; see Appendix for definition of variables

(*Pgear*) is negatively related to profitability, and this effect is highly significant (probability value < 0.0005). Thus SBEs which overstretch their indebtedness, in relation to equity invested in the firm, depress their profitability. On the one hand, such SBEs incur debt-servicing obligations which are onerous and dissipate gross profit surplus; and, on the other hand, they are relatively exposed to risk by their high gearing, and thus prone to negative profitability shocks. The existence of significant interdependence in pricing is indicated by the *PCruc* variable, which is equal to unity if the pricing of rivals is crucial to the SBE's own pricing, but 0 otherwise. This variable's coefficient is significant (probability level = 0.04) and suggests that those SBEs which experience marked price interdependence tend to experience higher profitability than those which do not. The evidence from earlier work is that such price interdependence may take the 'kinked demand curve' form.[15] It is interesting to note that cashflow problems (*Cfp*) and having had recourse to additional debt (*AddDebt*) do not appear to have significant effects on profitability (thought this specification of equation may not favour detecting such effects). These findings are also consonant with the analysis of Richardson (1964), where the consequences of funding difficulties are played down, in comparison with organisational difficulties, for fast-growing firms.

The crude specification of Table 13.3 does not enable one to identify a clear growth/profitability trade-off, though it is at least suggested by the negative coefficient on the growth rate variable (*GRate*). To better discover whether this growth/profitability trade-off, or 'Penrose Effect', is a feature of the data, one needs to have recourse to simultaneous equation modelling.

In Tables 13.4 and 13.5 I report on a simultaneous equations system for growth and profitability. It is estimated by iterative three-stage least squares (I3SLS).[16] The null hypothesis of a diagonal covariance matrix is rejected, according to the Breusch–Pagan LM test, for both the two-iteration (Table 13.4) and three-iteration (Table 13.5) estimates. This suggests that it is indeed appropriate to use a system method of estimation like 3SLS which assumes a non-diagonal covariance matrix. In each case, the system R^2 is high, and the overall fit is good, judged by the χ^2 statistic. Apart from the variables which define the form of SBE, the variables in each equation are the same in both Table 13.4 and Table 13.5. Furthermore, their effects are generally the same, which is one test of model stability.[17] The business form variable in Table 13.5 is again the familiar *Bsns* of Table 13.3, which is a categorical variable which rises as the business form becomes more complex. Business form is represented by two dummy variables in Table 13.4, *SoleProp* and *Partner*. According to the Richardson argument, one expects *Bsns* to be negative, and both *SoleProp* and *Partner* to be positive. These conditions are satisfied in both Table 13.4 and Table 13.5. Unfortunately, in order to improve the precision of estimation of the coefficients of the *ProfRate* and *GRate* variables in the growth and profitability equations, respectively, by increasing the number of iterations in the I3SLS estimates, one loses precision of estimation for the business form variables, *Bsns*, *SoleProp* and *Partner*. With the sample size one is dealing with this kind of difficulty is hard to surmount. Fortunately, other evidence on the importance of the form of the SBE has already been presented (Tables 13.2 and 13.3).

The main point brought out in Tables 13.4 and 13.5 is the growth/profitability trade-off. In both the growth equations of Table 13.4 and 13.5 the profit rate variable (*ProfRate*) is shown to have a significant negative coefficient; and in both the profitability equations of Tables 13.4 and 13.5 the growth rate variable (*GRate*) is shown to have a significant negative coefficient. Thus the growth/profitability trade-off is confirmed for this data set of SBEs, supporting Richardson's argument in favour of a 'Penrose Effect'. The interesting feature of this analysis is that here his argument has been extended to, and confirmed for, the case of quite small firms (sometimes called 'microfirms'). Of course, the reasons for this trade-off cannot be sought exclusively in the form of the SBE, though this clearly does play a role, and SBEs seem to function in some measure as Richardson saw larger firms functioning.

Turning to other variables, remember that for the single-equation estimation of Table 13.3 it was found that gearing (*PGear*) was powerfully negatively related to growth, and several reasons were adduced for this (risk

Table 13.4   Two iteration 3SLS estimates of growth and profitability equations

Growth equation (Dependent variable: GRate)		Profitability equation (Dependent variable: ProfRate)	
Variable	Coefficient (Asymptotic t)	Variable	Coefficient (Asymptotic t)
SoleProp	35.957 (0.40433)	SoleProp	6.1104 (0.37599)
Partner	73.934 (0.91643)	Partner	8.0096 (0.56165)
MMkt	23.987 (1.6244)	PCruc	9.5408 (0.95859)
Share	16.895 (1.9758)	PGear	−0.14039 (−2.6902)
PCruc	−10.783 (−0.19678)	DesComp	−1.6651 (−0.46520)
ProdDes	−59.481 (−1.9975)	GRate	−0.07304 (−1.7196)
AddDebt	−29.094 (−0.89770)	Constant	28.756 (2.0013)
PGear	−1.0857 (−3.4336)		
ProfRate	−5.6762 (−3.8121)		
Constant	255.80 (2.6059)		

Notes: System $R^2 = 0.7825$; $\chi^2 = 111.37 > \chi^2(15)_{0.05} = 25.0$; Breusch–Pagan LM test (for diagonal covariance matrix): $\chi^2 = 14.0006 > \chi^2(1)_{0.05} = 3.84$

exposure, debt servicing). This result seems to carry over strongly to the simultaneous equations settings of Tables 13.4 and 13.5 as well. It is, furthermore, extended in its scope in that higher gearing is also significantly associated with lower profitability.

When Leyland (1964: 3) wrote about the evidence from the Oxford Economic Research Group he referred to the common desire among respondents for an increased market share. This was often stated in the form of a target level of market share. He also noted that many of his fast growing firms were seeking what he called, in elegant terms, 'a vacant space in the lattice of competing products' (*ibid.*: 6) – what we would today call (less elegantly) 'a niche market'. In the growth equations of both Tables 13.4 and 13.5 the

Table 13.5 Three iteration estimates of growth and profitability equations

	Growth equation (Dependent variable: GRate)		Profitability equation (Dependent variable: ProfRate)
Variable	Coefficient (Asymptotic t)	Variable	Coefficient (Asymptotic t)
Bsns	−21.957 (−0.56751)	Bsns	−4.2867 (−0.66708)
MMkt	15.748 (1.2590)	PCruc	7.6594 (0.77497)
Share	10.373 (1.4612)	PGear	−0.15509 (−2.9820)
PCruc	2.9846 (0.05133)	DesComp	−1.0358 (−0.37603)
ProdDes	−40.553 (−1.5006)	Grate	−0.10096 (−2.7925)
AddDebt	−19.085 (−0.71419)	Constant	43.816 (2.6695)
PGear	−1.1405 (−3.5092)		
ProfRate	−6.0169 (−5.1373)		
Constant	327.08 (2.6753)		

Note: System R^2 = 0.9006

market share variable (*Share*) is positive and (marginally) significant. Growth is positively associated with an increase in market share, which, case study evidence suggests, often involves 'niche invasion' or the exploiting of new segments in highly fragmented markets.[18] Larger main markets offer the prospect of growth with scale economies, and the evidence is that the greater the market extent (*MMkt*), the greater the growth rate. Other variables play at least some role in explaining growth and profitability but their statistical effects are too unreliably estimated to place much faith in their importance.

CONCLUSION

This paper has taken as its starting point Richardson's quest for a grounded theory of limits to the growth of the firm. Under his chairmanship in the

1960s, the Oxford Economics Research Group laid the basis for such a grounded theory. What this suggested to Richardson was a theory which emphasised the impediments to growth of the firm which arose from the need, first, to recruit more managers as growth proceeded and, second, to integrate new managers into the firm's evolving structure.

This chapter on Richardson attempts to do three things: first, to provide evidence on the limits to growth which is as grounded in reality as was Richardson's; second, to relate modern organisational analysis of the firm to firm types that might be typical of the fast-growing SBE. It is shown that disabilities as the firm's form is rapidly adapted and discarded, or rapidly replicated, with increasing tiers of hierarchy, give rise to problems of limits to growth of the sort that Richardson discussed. These create a trade-off relationship between growth and profitability. Third, this chapter specifies and estimates such a trade-off relationship using simple single and simultaneous equations models. It is shown that business complexity militates against both growth and profitability, and that growth and profitability themselves lie in a trade-off relationship with one another.

In his paper Richardson wrote:

> the majority of our sample do not regard finance as setting the limit to growth. The operative check in this case is managerial resources, the burden upon which may be made especially heavy through the need to expand in new directions.
>
> (Richardson 1964: 18)

This has been confirmed by the models reported, for the trade-off effect is clear, business form seems to be important, and financial variables, like cash-flow problems and the raising of additional debt, often seem to have insignificant effects. However, one important exception seems to lie in capital structure, as represented by the gearing ratio. Higher gearing has a significant part to play in lowering profitability and growth. It may yet become apparent how Richardson's analysis of the relationship between the unit cost of funds and the expected unit return can be adapted to provide an explanation of this result.

When Richardson developed a grounded theory of the limits to a firm's growth, both fieldwork methods, as applied to the business enterprise, and industrial econometrics were in their infancy. His account of the limits to growth was also formulated before the organisational theory of the firm was well developed. However, both his theory and the empirical support for it stand up well to scrutiny from the standpoint of late twentieth-century economics. His insight in developing a theory of limits to a firm's growth was therefore clearly remarkable.

APPENDIX

Variables used in OLS and iterative 3SLS estimates of growth and profitability equation

Endogenous variables

GRate Growth rate per month of real assets (in 1985 prices) from inception to the AQ 1985

ProfRate Profit rate in 1985 as reported in 1988 re-interviews (RIQ 1988)

Exogenous variables

Employ Number of full-time employees
Bsns   = 1 for one-man business; = 2 for partnership; = 3 for private company
Sales   Sales revenue
MMkt   Main market: local community (1), region (2), Scotland (3), UK (4), international (5)
Share   Market share for main product group (%).
CompNo Number of competitors for main product group
PCruc   = 1 if pricing of rivals crucial to SBE's own pricing; = 0 otherwise
ProdDes Degree of product differentiation of main product group: identical (1), similar (2), different (3)
Adv   = 1 if SBE advertises; = 0 otherwise
Cfp   = 1 if SBE has experienced cash flow problems since inception: = 0 otherwise
PGear   Debt divided by owner-manager's injection of finance
Descomp Description of competition in market for main product group: intense (1), generally strong (2), generally weak (3), weak (4)
Age   Age in months from financial inception to AQ 1985
SoleProp = 1 for sole proprietorship; = 0 otherwise
Partner = 1 for partnership; = 0 otherwise
AddDebt = 1 if SBE had sought additional debt finance since inception; = 0 otherwise

NOTES

1 In the sense of Glaser and Strauss (1967). For the application of this method in industrial organisation, see Reid (1987: ch. 3).
2 See the detailed analysis of this by, for example, Hay and Morris (1991: ch. 10). A thorough mathematical treatment of it is provided by Slater (1980).
3 In Richardson's 1960 article what he was later to call 'capability' was anticipated by reference to 'management itself, together with the skills, experience and traditions which it embodies' (Richardson 1960: 153). Such fixed capability, allied to problems of cognition (essentially mental limits to problem

formulation and solution) result in limits to growth along the lines suggested in the main text. In Richardson's 1972 article capability was referred to, in a well-known passage, as 'the knowledge, experience and skills' (Richardson 1972: 88) of the firm. It is this that is often referred to in the work of business strategists like Kay (1963: 11). However, it is to be noted that capability was also referred to implicitly in the present context when Richardson spoke of 'appropriate commercial contracts, production experience and marketing skills' (Richardson 1964: 11).
4 The relevant quote from Marshall is that in the long period 'all investments of capital and effort in providing the material plant and the organisation of a business, and in acquiring trade knowledge and specialised ability, have time to be adjusted' (Marshall 1961: 377).
5 Notably by Williamson (1975).
6 Reid (1993) is the main work, but Reid and Jacobsen (1988) and Reid et al. (1993) are also relevant.
7 To arrive at these figures I have interpolated within the sales ranges given in the Notes according to the decimal fractions of Table 13.1 itself.
8 See Williamson (1975: 45–7).
9 See, for example, Profile K (electronic instrumentation) of Reid et al. (1993).
10 On these 'convex adjustment costs', see Hilten et al. (1993: ch. 5).
11 See, for example, Reid (1993: ch. 11).
12 Most notably by Evans (1987). This finding has been confirmed for this data base of SBEs by Reid (1993: ch. 11). For an exposition of the Marshallian life-cycle analysis and its relation to contemporary industrial economics, see Reid (1987: ch. 5).
13 Both g and π are measured as described in the notes to Table 13.2.
14 See Reid (1995).
15 See Bhaskar et al. (1991) and Reid (1993: ch. 10).
16 The *Shazam* software was used for the estimates in Tables 13.3, 13.4 and 13.5.
17 The exception to this is the *PCruc* variable in the growth equation, which has a positive sign in Table 13.5 and a negative sign in Table 13.4, though it is not significant in either equation; and indeed has very small asymptotic t-values.
18 See Reid et al. (1993: especially chs 5 and 6).

REFERENCES

Arrow, K. J. (1962) 'The economic implications of learning by doing', *Review of Economic Studies* 29: 155–73.

Bhaskar, V., Machin, S. and Reid, G. C. (1991) 'Testing a model of the kinked demand curve', *Journal of Industrial Economics* 39: 241–54.

Cubbin, J. and Leech, D. (1986) 'Growth versus profit maximization: a simultaneous equations approach to testing the Marris model', *Managerial and Decision Economics* 7: 123–31.

Dobson, S. and Gerrard, B. (1989) 'Growth and profitability in the Leeds engineering sector', *Scottish Journal of Political Economy* 36: 334–52.

Evans, D. D. (1987) 'Tests of alternative theories of firms growth', *Journal of Political Economy* 95: 657–74.

Glaser, B. G. and Strauss, A. L. (1967) *The Discovery of Grounded Theory: Strategies of Qualitative Research*, New York: Aldine.

Hay, D. A. and Morris, D. J. (1991) *Industrial Economics and Organization*, Oxford: Oxford University Press.
Hilten, O. von, Kort, P. M. and von Loon, P. J. J. M. von (1993) *Dynamic Policies of the Firm: An Optimal Control Approach*, Berlin: Springer-Verlag.
Kay, J. (1993) *Foundations of Corporate Success*, Oxford: Oxford University Press.
Langlois, R. N. (1995) 'Capabilities and the theory of the firm', paper presented to the Colloquium in Honour of G. B. Richardson, St John's College, Oxford.
Leyland, N. H. (1964) 'Growth and competition', *Oxford Economic Papers* 16: 3–8.
Marshall, A. (1890/1961) *Principles of Economics*, London: Macmillan, for the Royal Economic Society.
Penrose, E. T. (1959) *The Theory of the Growth of the Firm*, Oxford: Basil Blackwell.
Reid, G. C. (1987) *Theories of Industrial Organization*, Oxford: Basil Blackwell.
—— (1993) *Small Business Enterprise: An Economic Analysis*, London: Routledge.
—— (1995) 'Early life-cycle behaviour of micro-firms in Scotland', *Small Business Economics* 7: 89–95.
Reid, G. C. and Jacobsen, L. R. (1988) *The Small Entrepreneurial Firm*, Aberdeen: Aberdeen University Press.
Reid, G. C., Jacobsen, L. R. and Anderson, M. E. (1993) *Profiles in Small Business: A Competitive Strategy Approach*, London: Routledge.
Richardson, G. B. (1960) *Information and Investment: A Study in the Working of the Competitive Economy*, reprinted with a foreword by David J. Teece, Oxford: Oxford University Press, 1990.
—— (1964) 'The limits to a firm's rate of growth', *Oxford Economic Papers* 16: 9–23.
—— (1972) 'The organisation of industry', *Economic Journal* 82: 883–96.
Richardson, G. B. and Leyland, N. H. (1964) 'The growth of firms', *Oxford Economic Papers* 16: 1–2.
Slater, M. (1980) 'The managerial limitation to the growth of firms', *Economic Journal* 90: 520–8.
Williamson, O. E. (1975) *Markets and Hierarchies*, New York: Free Press.
—— (1985) *The Economic Institution of Capitalism*, New York: Free Press.

14

INFORMATION, SIMILAR AND COMPLEMENTARY ASSETS, AND INNOVATION POLICY

Paul L. Robertson

INTRODUCTION

In *Information and Investment: A Study in the Working of the Competitive Economy*, G. B. Richardson investigates the effects of imperfect knowledge on investment decisions to demonstrate that the equilibrium situations posited by neoclassical economists are unlikely to be achieved. In particular, Richardson shows that it is improbable that the investment decisions of individual producers will lead to socially optimal outcomes because, in the absence of knowledge as to the plans of their competitors, businesses will either over- or underinvest in capacity when they perceive an opportunity for expansion. If each producer of a good believes that it is in a position to take full advantage of a probable increase in demand, all producers will invest in new capacity, leading to excess expansion overall and lost profits for individual investment units. If, however, all producers assume that their competitors are likely to invest, then none will expand and the outcome will again be sub-optimal from the standpoint of consumers as well as producers. As a result, the degree of information provided by the market itself is insufficient to maximise welfare, and co-ordination among producers is needed to reduce uncertainty and allow rational investment decisions. This co-ordination can take a variety of forms, including collusion (the exchange of information among producers) and, at an extreme, central planning, in which a single set of decisions is made on behalf of all producers of a good.

Although Richardson does not place much emphasis on innovative situations, it is clear that his analysis applies a fortiori when there is uncertainty, not only about the investment decisions of other producers, but also about such factors as the size of the market for an untried product or the technical efficacy of the product or the production process. In an innovative situation, the limitations that poor information may place on the willingness to invest are so substantial that potentially promising outcomes may never be investigated in practice, leading (as in any case of underinvestment) to reductions in social welfare. To overcome this problem, government action may therefore be justified, either to improve the quality of information available or to enhance the distribution of existing information. As in Richardson's own analysis, these improvements and enhancements may be accomplished through 'collusion' or 'planning', including government efforts to bolster market-based outcomes as well as direct government intervention in the investment process.

In this chapter, in order to reach some tentative indications of the proper scope of government innovation policy, I explore several of the practical problems involved in generating and distributing information in innovative situations. As the field is so broad, I give special attention to three issues. In the next section I discuss the general problem of the communication of information that is already known by some people but which has not yet been spread to all users who might potentially benefit from it. The section entitled 'Information, Similarity and complementarity' (pp. 275–8) concentrates on the ways in which Richardson's concept of similar and complementary activities can be applied to determining which organisational forms are most conducive to innovation. The final issue that I investigate in some depth (see 'Innovation and industry maturity, pp. 278–82) is the problem of promoting innovation in established firms that produce 'mature' products. While my argument is based heavily on Richardson's work in *Information and Investment* and in his article on 'The organisation of industry' (1972), I have been perhaps influenced most by his argument that 'The appropriate methodological position is surely one of tolerance and eclecticism, of choosing the approach and terminology which seems to suit the subject in hand, of indiscriminate plundering of concepts from other fields whenever they seem illuminating' (Richardson 1990: 41, n. 1).

INFORMATION AND INNOVATION

Uncertainty and ignorance

Before proceeding further, I should indicate what I mean by 'innovation'. In an exchange in the *Economic Journal*, Stoneman and Diederen adhere to a strict Schumpeterian division between invention, innovation and diffusion in which innovation means 'the development of [new] ideas through to the first marketing or use of a technology' and diffusion refers to 'the spread of new technology across its potential market' (Stoneman and Diederen 1994: 918). In the same issue, however, Metcalfe argues that 'it is not helpful to treat innovation and the diffusion of innovation as separate categories, in fact they are inseparable, with feedback from diffusion being one of the critical elements shaping how a technology is developed' (Metcalfe 1994: 931). The position taken here is similar to Metcalfe's, although the reasoning differs somewhat. In addition to the feedback and subsequent reshaping of the original innovation that may result from diffusion, innovation may be undertaken repeatedly in different contexts as diffusion proceeds. The use of the turbine principle resulted in crucial innovations in both electricity generation and ship propulsion, and the widespread adoption of small electric motors was as important an innovation in Western European industry in the 1950s as it had been in the US thirty years earlier. Thus 'innovation policy' refers to government actions, or inactions, designed to promote both the spread and the application of technologies.

It is now generally conceded that the extent to which relevant knowledge is available is one of the most important factors influencing the innovation process, including the primary stage of invention. If knowledge is limited to a small group of people or firms, opportunities for change may be stifled. This is especially true if the knowledge is restricted to operators in a single industry. Hence the development of institutions to facilitate the spread of knowledge may be a vital contribution to the growth of technological capabilities in the economic system as a whole.

But, just as there are various reasons why knowledge may be lacking, there are also various tools that may be needed to tackle the problem. *Uncertainty* refers to the inherent inability of people to know exactly what will happen in the future. People lack information because the necessary data do not yet exist, and by the time the data are available they will have lost some of their relevance because the past cannot be changed. Although uncertainty may be reduced as experience accumulates and better predictions can be made, it can never be eliminated altogether. *Ignorance*, in contrast, applies in cases in which knowledge or information is already available somewhere or is potentially discoverable but some or all of the potential users have not yet acquired that knowledge. Ignorance may prevail, therefore, before an invention or an innovation has been made, as well as during the diffusion stage, but the incidence of ignorance changes. Prior to an invention or the discovery of a principle, everyone is ignorant of the answer to a particular problem. Subsequently, some people know the answer but others remain ignorant until diffusion occurs.

These distinctions have important implications because uncertainty and ignorance are best covered by different sets of policies. When there is uncertainty, policy-makers are concerned with reducing the uncertain area to the smallest extent feasible and also, perhaps, with providing some way of reducing the impact of failure on those who nevertheless make incorrect judgements. Ignorance requires a group of different approaches depending on its nature. When there is no known answer to a problem that is capable of being solved, a strategy of discovery is indicated. In this case, the appropriate policies could include a programme of pure research to discover underlying principles, or one of applied research and development to bring known principles to bear on a problem. But when potential solutions are already available, the task of policy-makers may be to find some way of bringing those solutions to the attention of people or organisations with problems (problem-holders) and, equally importantly, to bring problem-holders to the notice of current or potential solution-holders.

When taken together, uncertainty and ignorance involve both the *generation* and the *communication* of knowledge. Although both of these factors are susceptible to government policy, different instruments are appropriate. A great deal has been written on policies for the generation of innovative knowledge (e.g. Nelson 1993), but systematic analysis of the communication of such knowledge is relatively rare. Thus my concern here is primarily with the implications of the communication process for policy-makers.

A model of the communication process

The existence of knowledge provides no guarantee that it will be correctly perceived by those who can use it profitably. Would-be users must first be aware of what they need to know, and then they must find a way of cheaply and efficiently locating the necessary knowledge. To take these factors in turn, the way in which problems are perceived depends on the context in which they are encountered, as Clark (1985) has argued.[1] This has frequently been recognised as one aspect of the failure of firms in mature industries to adapt to fundamental change, as is discussed below, but it is also of importance to firms in earlier stages of development. Clark suggests that there are 'design hierarchies' that determine search patterns. For example, the early triumph of the internal combustion engine, as opposed to electric or steam power, set the context in which later developments in the automobile industry took place. Even quite early in the development of the automobile, designs for starting mechanisms, cylinder configuration and other features were viewed in terms of the prior commitment to internal combustion, petrol-fuelled engines (Clark 1985: 243).

Stinchcombe calls the information that is of central concern to a particular organisation the 'news' (Stinchcombe 1990: 3). Not all information is 'news'. Indeed, most information is of no use to an organisation, whose problems are therefore two-fold. In order to solve its problems, an organisation must first decide on what kind of 'news' is needed and then locate it, but it must also find efficient ways of filtering out information that is not 'news'. Various common means are used to accomplish this, including the adoption of heuristics based on the use of sources that have been valuable in the past, such as suppliers, customers and the trade press, and the adoption of organisational structures that are designed to concentrate on the collection and processing of the 'news' while reducing to a minimum the collection of useless information (Chandler 1962; J. D. Thompson 1967).

But the problem of ignorance does not only affect users of information. Generators of knowledge (solution-holders) may also have trouble in identifying the problems to which their new information can profitably be applied and in locating probable users, or problem-holders.[2] Neoclassical economists, including the so-called 'New Growth' and 'New Trade' theorists, often emphasise the negative effects that 'spillovers' may have on research and development efforts.[3] Grossman and Helpman, for example, have assumed, that 'profit maximizing and far-sighted entrepreneurs invest in research and development in order to capture monopoly rents from innovative products' (Grossman and Helpman 1991: 517–18). In a somewhat weaker statement, Romer argues that 'profit-maximizing agents make investments in the creation of new knowledge and they earn a return on these investments by charging a price for the resulting goods that is greater than the marginal cost of producing the goods' (Romer 1990: p. S89). But under certain circumstances it is possible to reconcile the institutions that protect the monopoly positions of entrepreneurs, such as the patent system, with other institutional arrangements that will allow for the wider economic and social benefits that may result from the spread of knowledge.

In fact, while conceding that inventive and innovative activity may be spurred on by an ability to capture monopoly rents, it is illogical to suppose that entrepreneurs will act only if they think that they can attract supermarginal prices on *all* of their transactions. In reality, solution-holders may be in a position to segment their markets and to charge different prices to different users. When an innovation has more than a single use, solution-holders could extract monopoly or near-monopoly rents in one industry (perhaps their own) and then license the innovation to producers in other industries at prices that bring them lower profits. Indeed, as long as they did not erode their monopoly positions in some markets, they would be non-rational if they did not permit the diffusion of an innovation up to the marginal cost of production, including the costs of spreading the necessary information.[4]

Thus solution-holders may well welcome the development of efficient institutions to bring their innovations to the notice of problem-holders even if they receive reduced marginal returns. To the degree that particular sources of 'news' are not encompassed by the heuristics of problem-holders, however, they are unlikely to be perceived. Moreover, even when they are noticed, outsiders may lack credibility as solution-holders simply because they are not members of the customary networks of contacts employed by problem-holders. In some cases, this may make it hard for sources of 'news' to find any listeners if they are beyond the borders of all networks. The spread of adoption of an innovation from industry to industry by a process of analogy will also be hampered if there is no overlap in the customary networks employed in different industries: if producers in industry A are unaware that they share problems with producers in industry X they are unlikely to consult the same

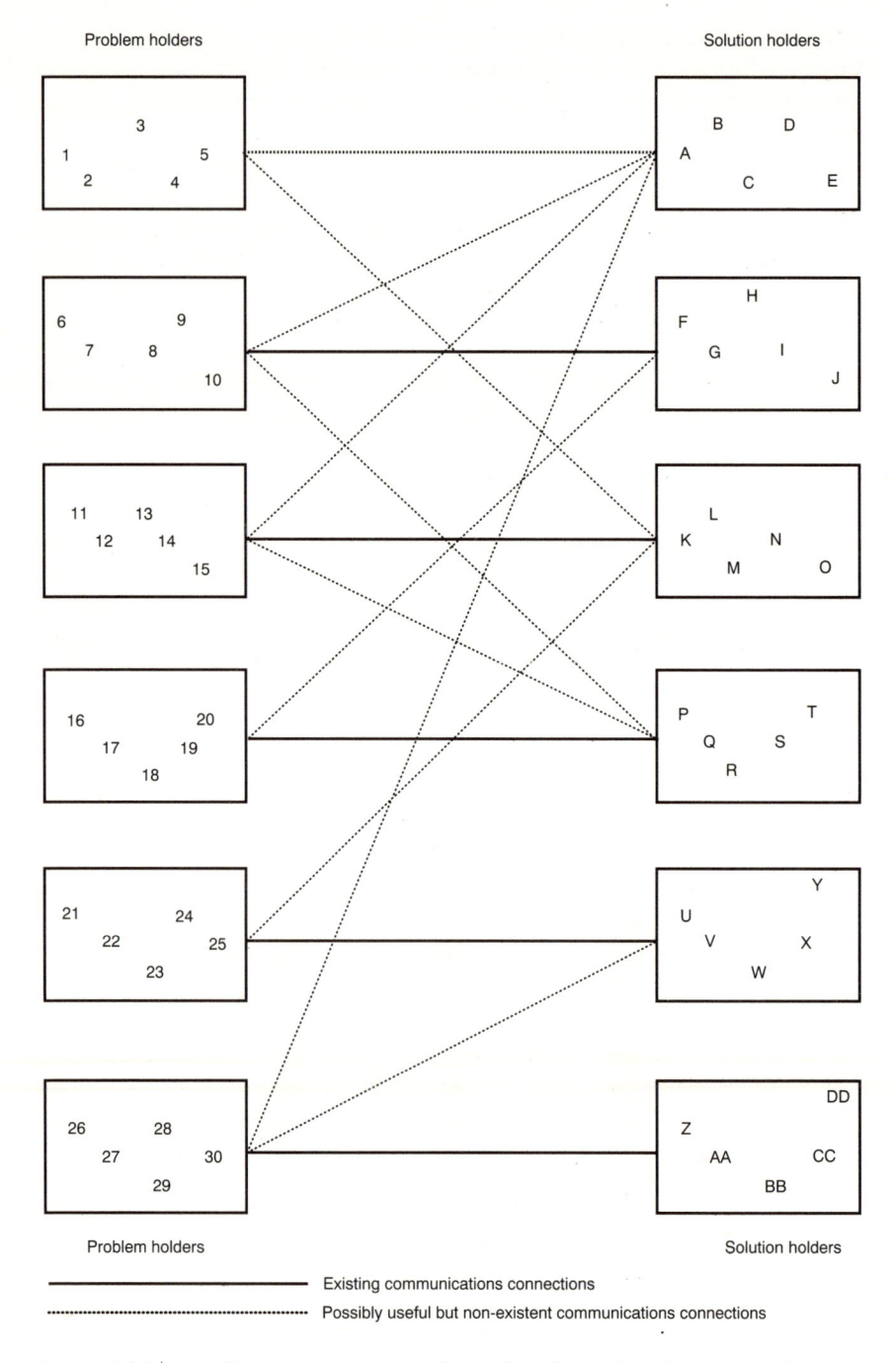

Figure 14.1   Existing and potentially useful relationships between problem holders and solution holders

sources of solutions. The upshot could be a situation like that shown in Figure 14.1, in which problem-holders have heuristic contacts with some sources of 'news'[5] (the solid lines) but lack ways of communicating with other sources from which they may possibly profit (the dashed lines).

The problem for firms – both sources and users of 'news' – is therefore to find some way of establishing the necessary communication channels, but the means of doing this will depend on why the existing channels of communication are inadequate. An elementary model of communication can help to highlight the issues. Figure 14.2[6] shows the basic stages involved in communicating information from a source (the sender) to a target (the receiver). In general, the sender initiates the communication, which can take the form of either information or a request for information. This information (or request) cannot be sent directly, however, but contains a subjective element because it must first be encoded by being translated into symbols that the sender *believes* to be an accurate representation of the information. At this point, the encoded information has become a message, which may take many forms, such as speech or a written text. The message is then sent through a communication channel or medium. For spoken words the channels could be, *inter alia*, air, radio or telephone, while a written message could be in the form of a letter, newspaper, etc. Once received, the message is then decoded, again a subjective process that involves interpretation in a way that the receiver *believes* will allow the message to be understood correctly. Finally, the process may be reversed, with the receiver sending another message as feedback to the original source.

Although codification may simplify the communication process, the

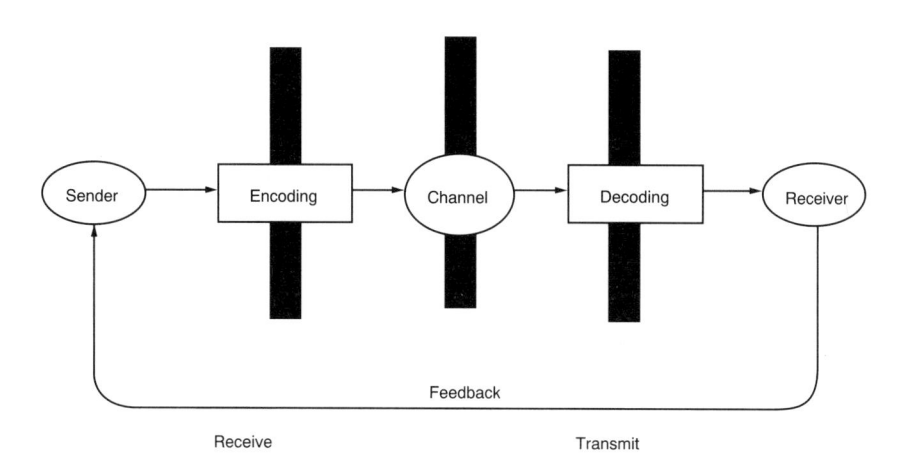

Note: Vertical shaded bars indicate noise

Figure 14.2 A model of the communication process

transmission of a message or question by no means ensures that it will be accurately received, let alone acted upon. The communication process presents pitfalls at every stage that may undermine the intentions of the sender or receiver. The most obvious problem, perhaps, is that the intended receiver may not be 'listening' or may be tuned into the wrong channel, as in Figure 14.1, but there are many other sources of 'noise'. For example, the encoding or decoding may be inaccurate. If the code is to be interpreted successfully the sender and receiver must have agreed on the meanings of the symbols used, but when a message is broadcast impersonally there is no reason to believe that an agreement would have been reached in advance. This is especially true of technical data which require specialised knowledge on the part of both parties. A source of innovative information must know how to express the innovation in terms that potential problem-holders can relate to, but since understanding is contextual, solution-holders may need to employ differently phrased messages to reach different classes of problem-holders. Thus sources may require a deep understanding of the contexts of many different potential users if a versatile innovation is to be sold widely. Similarly, questioners (problem-holders who are searching for solutions) must phrase their questions accurately in order to elicit relevant answers, and the potentially best answers from a technical perspective may be sent in languages that some problem-holders do not know.

The channel of communication may also be a source of noise. As has been shown, potential communicators often find it efficient to restrict their messages to channels that have been useful in the past. They may ignore unfamiliar locations or media and thereby miss the information that they need. Furthermore, different recipients may need different degrees of 'logical depth' in their messages (Davies 1995). Logical depth refers to the amount of knowledge that the recipient requires to be able to operationalise the material in the message. When the message relates to material that is already largely familiar to the recipient, a form of shorthand may be sufficient, but a message concerning totally unfamiliar concepts may need to provide great detail in order to achieve a high degree of logical depth. As in the case of encoding/decoding problems, the difficulty is not one of knowledge (because the necessary information already exists) but, rather, of ignorance and inadequate communication. Efforts to improve the efficiency of communication can therefore pay significant dividends by promoting the quicker solution of problems and discouraging duplicative research.

Bridging communication gaps

Entrepreneurship

Communication gaps may be tackled in the private sector through what Kirzner (1973) calls 'entrepreneurial alertness'. To Kirzner and other

Austrian economists, the role of the entrepreneur is to perceive situations in which problems and solutions already exist but have not been brought together, and then to improve efficiency by effecting a reconciliation. Such people may intentionally or accidentally become aware of situations in which potential senders and receivers of information on innovations have failed to make meaningful contact and then arrange for effective communication in return for a share of the resulting profits. Thus entrepreneurs may act as arbitrageurs by locating channels of communication, but they may also play a major role by reducing noise in the system. They may do this, for example, by acting as interpreters who present solutions in a language that problem-holders can understand, or by making problems intelligible to solution-holders by providing supplementary information that adds logical depth to messages.

Nevertheless, valuable though alertness may be, entrepreneurs may also find their work impeded by communication barriers. If they are outside established communications networks, entrepreneurs may lack credibility. Furthermore, entrepreneurs face the double task of learning about both problems and solutions in fields in which they may otherwise have no experience. And if existing firms resist their advice the only way that entrepreneurs have of exploiting their alertness may be by setting themselves up in competition, which may be expensive and risky. Although entrepreneurs are on occasion successful, especially when there is a major shift in technological paradigms, in other circumstances change may be undertaken more efficiently by individuals or organisations that are already either problem-holders or solution-holders and therefore know at least some of the language and the technical problems involved.

Standards

Communications difficulties may also be mitigated by increasing the general level of alertness in one or several industries. If noise at the encoding and decoding stages is a major drawback, then the creation of standards of language and other characteristics can ease the problem of reconciling the efforts of problem-holders and solution-holders. As time passes, each group (like members of adjacent tribes) may gain a good knowledge of the others' vocabulary and syntax, which could increase alertness on all sides and lead to higher levels of diffusion and innovation. But such a process could take considerable time, especially if the holders of problems and solutions are not adjacent but occupy distant 'social locations'. By speeding up the communication process, the conscious creation of a common language could therefore be valuable. The question is whether a government policy is needed or whether the development of a common language can be negotiated privately.

We can get an insight into this by examining the mechanisms by which standards have been developed in the past. Many items that are standardised, such as radio frequencies or the threading of screws, can be regarded metaphorically as languages because standardisation permits different users to 'speak' to each other, that is, to be compatible. In some cases, the establishment of standards has been worked out through private negotiation or left to market forces (Langlois and Robertson 1995). A number of the smaller automobile producers in the United States, for example, voluntarily agreed early in the twentieth century to standardise simple parts in order to achieve economies of scale without putting severe constraints on design (G. V. Thompson 1954). The standardisation of railway gauges in the south of England likewise occurred without government intervention when the directors of the Great Western Railway were eventually forced to agree that compatibility with adjacent lines was of more value than the technical benefits offered by Brunel's broad gauge. In fact, it is probably legitimate to generalise by saying that standardisation will almost always take place eventually whenever significant network externalities are present.

But 'eventually' may not be soon enough, in that good opportunities may be discouraged for prolonged periods or abandoned altogether if a system is fragmented. As David (1991) has shown, the diffusion of a truly systemic set of innovations, such as those associated with electrification, may take many decades. Although almost all potential users may be brought on board in the long run, there may be losses over shorter periods as problem-holders who might benefit from early access to the system fail to make contact with solution-holders. An additional, and quite opposite, problem with privately arranged standardisation is that users may be locked into a sub-optimal system if standardisation occurs too soon or is pushed through by powerful operators who stand to gain from the adoption of a technically deficient system. An example is the adoption of the 115 volt standard for most domestic and commercial electricity in the United States because early light bulb filaments wore out uneconomically quickly when higher voltages were used.

These shortcomings in what may be termed 'standardisation by consensus' would seem to provide an opening for governments to use their power to impose standards as a way of accelerating the diffusion and adoption of innovations. In practice, this sort of standardisation appears to be most common in the cases of public utilities and industries, such as communications, that have the ability to influence such public values as voting behaviour. Even in countries like the US and Australia, which have long possessed substantial privately owned broadcast networks, governments have insisted on deciding upon and allocating broadcast frequencies, in part to avoid interference which private stations that are located close to each other might cause by broadcasting on similar frequencies. More recently, governments attempted to speed up innovation by imposing standards for colour television and high-density television (HDTV) before systems became widespread in order to ensure that network externalities would be large enough to encourage large numbers of users to join the network. Finally, governments have even intervened, albeit infrequently, to change standards when advances in technical knowledge have indicated that the earlier standard was inefficient. Following the Second World War, for instance, the United States government changed the frequency band allocated to FM radio broadcasts because technical advances during the war had shed doubt on the technical efficiency of using the original band (Sterling 1968).[7]

The imposition of government standards, however, is no guarantee of uniformity or efficiency. The railway system in Australia provides an extreme example in that the gauges were all set by the various colonial governments before Federation in 1901. As one of the aims of each colony was to try to keep as much traffic as possible within its own borders,[8] the colonies deliberately chose different gauges. Even partial reconciliation took decades to achieve. Similarly, because colour television was commercialised earlier in the US than elsewhere, the standard imposed by the government turned out to be an inferior technology, in much the same way as early standardisation through private agreements has sometimes led to the adoption of systems that have later turned out to be inefficient.

In general, governments may indeed speed up innovation by adopting and enforcing standards, but this is probably most appropriate for very large systems and even then may lead to error. Private negotiation over standards seems more appropriate for the multitude of decisions affecting smaller groups who are better informed of their own needs than government agents are likely ever to be unless substantial sums of public funds are invested in educating them in the minutiae of other people's business (Hayek 1937, 1945). On an intermediate level of aggregation, either governments or private interests may work out standards. Culturally, continental European nations, with a long tradition of guild regulations, seem more favourably inclined towards imposed standards than are most English-speaking countries. It remains to be seen if, in practice, rates of innovation will accelerate or the welfare of citizens of the European Union will be increased by the imposition of 'Euro-standards' for beer, bread, condoms and other common goods for which there is often diversity in individual tastes and needs.

Accelerating diffusion and increasing absorptive capacity

Two areas in which government innovation policy has attempted to improve upon informal communication processes for several centuries are (1) the direct diffusion of innovation and (2) the generation of more conducive environments for the acceptance of innovation. One of the main features of the Mercantilist regulations enacted in most European nations in the seventeenth and eighteenth centuries was the encouragement of labour skills and innovative production processes. These policies were often coupled with others intended to reduce skills among foreign populations and prevent other nations from themselves gaining access to new techniques.

Although most of the more severe policies, such as those prohibiting the emigration of skilled workers and the export of machinery, had been repealed across Europe by the late nineteenth century, support for domestic industry has remained a policy tenet in most countries at all stages of development.

Many of the more important features of Mercantilism, including tariffs, quantitative restrictions on imports and navigation acts, are aspects of industry policy that are outside the scope of this chapter. Policies involving the direct diffusion of innovation and the creation of a conducive environment for change, however, can be viewed profitably in terms of our model of the communication process. In particular, both types of policy involve education in order to improve understanding, but on different levels of generality. Attempts to improve the diffusion of particular innovations may entail relatively specific instruction in a narrow range of skills, whereas a much broader form of education is needed to improve receptiveness to changes in the general environment.

Direct intervention by governments to promote innovation can be used as a way of economising on scarce communications skills. If there is a shortage of people in the population who are capable of sending out the right questions or of understanding and acting upon the answers, then the government may itself recruit a corps of experts to reduce noise by providing direct control over innovation policy. As in Meiji Japan or some of the German states in the nineteenth century, the government can take the lead in the collection of information and the training of skilled workers. Investment funds may also be directed into designated sectors rather than decisions being left to private investors, and, at the limit, ownership and management may even be placed in public hands.[9] Nevertheless, there are limits to how much actual direction can be imposed from above. Certain practices cannot be dictated either because they are tacit, and therefore unteachable, or because they involve the adaptation of imported techniques and need to be worked out initially by trial and error.

Hence if an innovation policy is successful, in the sense that it takes root and spreads seedlings, the need for government action should recede as skills and attitudes learnt originally in pilot projects become more generalised. Indeed, although businesses may continue to lobby for government assistance in such forms as tariffs, they will often become sceptical about the allegedly superior acumen of government functionaries. For example, a recent paper on the European computer industry complained that, despite attempts by the EC (as it then was) to foster co-operation on computer development among firms in member countries, these firms generally looked to co-operation with American or Japanese computer manufacturers for technical advances (Mytelka 1992). In practice, though, the behaviour of the firms seems rational: why should they devote their resources to communicating with other backward firms when they can enter into joint ventures or other arrangements with foreign firms that can offer some insight into the most advanced technologies?

On a more general level, perhaps the most important aspect of innovation policy that a government can undertake is in increasing the ability of a nation's people to understand and initiate innovations and to imitate and improve upon innovations that originated elsewhere. In two influential articles, Cohen and Levinthal (1989, 1990) have emphasised the importance of what they term an organisation's 'absorptive capacity'.[10] Absorptive capacity refers to the ability of an organisation to recognise and act upon information that might be competitively useful. On the corporate level, this entails developing a knowledge of technologies that lie beyond the current practices of a particular firm so that the firm can quickly take advantage of relevant new developments in other sectors. The premise is that, while firms may lose to a degree in that some of their absorptive capacity may never be needed in practice, they will gain overall because they will be better placed competitively owing to their ability to respond swiftly to change. Related to this is Stiglitz's proposition that learning in itself enhances an organisation's ability to learn (Stiglitz 1987). Thus firms that maintain a strong and active interest in new concepts should in general be able to generate and implement change more rapidly than firms that narrowly restrict their attention to their own current technologies.

On an aggregative level, absorptive capacity translates into educating the population up to a high level in both theoretical and practical subjects. If a nation's economy is to be flexible and able to respond quickly to change, then education must be provided ahead of demand and it cannot be limited to topics of current interest. This, of course, injects an element of uncertainty into curriculum design, just as research and development projects will always be uncertain to the extent that outcomes cannot be accurately predicted. Nevertheless, experience from both the past and the present supports the proposition that countries that have high levels of education and cultures that place a high intrinsic value on learning are likely to be more successful at innovation. This is illustrated by the relative success in recent decades of the Asian Tigers in comparison to Latin American countries that initially had similar levels of per capita income, and also by the growth trajectories of nations such as the United Kingdom, Germany, the United States and Switzerland after 1850.

It is arguable, for example, that one of the major reasons for the relative retardation of the British economy that began in the late Victorian and Edwardian periods is that the country lacked absorptive capacity to cope successfully with the major innovations of the era. In particular, British firms in general were in an inferior position to appropriate benefits from many branches of the developing electrical and chemical industries than were firms in countries that had already created systems of technical education because these industries required significant inputs of technically trained labour. In Germany, Switzerland and the US, governments recognised that technical education was a public good and subsidised it heavily, but in Britain the subsidies were smaller, and employers and potential students were unwilling to make up the difference through private payments (Robertson 1981). British firms depended instead on their deep stocks of skilled labour, but this confirmed their reliance on manual skills at a time when several important industries were making a transition to more highly technical job routines.[11] In the meanwhile, nations with better developed technical education facilities jumped to new technological trajectories where they were able to learn new routines rapidly and to seize market share before British firms could again become meaningful competitors. In the terms of the model of the communication process shown in Figure 14.2, by investing early in techniques for encoding and decoding technological information, the Germans, the Swiss and the Americans had reduced noise levels significantly even before important messages began to be transmitted. The British, by contrast, had to cope with noise much longer, which severely reduced their initial absorptive capacity.

Information, communication and investment

Whenever investment in innovation activities is deterred by a scarcity of information, as Richardson shows can happen, government policies may offer effective ways of improving the flows of information to individual investors, thereby increasing the overall rate of innovation. Government policy can be useful in several respects. When there is a high degree of uncertainty, governments can help to reduce the effects by providing guarantees or safety nets for innovators. These policies, which are not discussed in detail here, include ways of reducing competition for innovators or assuring markets. This can be accomplished through many common policies, such as tariff protection, direct subsidies and promises by government departments to buy only locally produced goods. As an extreme position, governments may guarantee revenues to innovative firms in the early stages of production.

Where the problem is ignorance rather than uncertainty, government policies may take different forms to improve information flows and thus make investment more attractive. In some cases, governments may encourage policies of discovery, such as promoting research and development or sending representatives to report on conditions in foreign countries. Our emphasis here, however, has been on enhancements to the communication process in which governments institute policies to spread information directly, attempt to improve information flows by providing channels of communication, or work to reduce noise through improvements in encoding and decoding.

But the fact that governments are capable of filling these roles does not mean that they are the most efficient agents. In some cases, entrepreneurial alertness may provide a superior private alternative to government action.[12] Moreover, unless governments are going to undertake detailed investment plans themselves, most policies to reduce noise do, in fact, operate by making alertness easier and thus improving the quality of private investment decisions. The maintenance of high levels of absorptive capacity in the nation as a whole, however, remains a very important responsibility for governments if the nation is to achieve the flexibility necessary to keep apace of rapid changes in technology. And, as Nelson (1993) and his co-authors have shown, government activities occupy important, even if not dominant, positions in many national systems of innovation.

It is important to remember, however, that private investment channels are highly heterogeneous and may therefore need different types of government policies to deal with their particular problems. One of the most important distinctions, to which I will turn in the next two section, is between the requirements of firms that concentrate on innovative activities and those of firms in mature industries that may be strongly affected by innovation after extended periods of quiescence.

INFORMATION, SIMILARITY AND COMPLEMENTARITY

Innovation and organisational form

The information needs of firms in 'new' industries may differ substantially from those of firms in 'mature' industries. New industries are characterised by rapid rates of product or process innovation,[13] but these decrease as dominant technologies are chosen. Because they compete in such unstable environments, firms in new industries (which, for brevity, I call innovative firms) have very substantial information needs that place strains on communication networks. Survival requires innovative firms to gain quick access to information derived elsewhere, while they frequently wish also to have exclusive access to information that they have developed in-house. In practice, it may prove difficult for such firms both to tap outside sources and to maintain confidentiality themselves because other firms are reluctant to give up information when there is no reciprocity. Furthermore, exchanges of employees, which are common among innovative firms in places such as Silicon Valley, make it hard for firms to retain proprietary access to information for very long.

Popular recommendations as to the organisational forms required to provide for the information needs of innovative firms fall into two main categories.[14] The first centres around the ideas of the economist Michael Piore and a number of sympathisers from other disciplines, including

Charles Sabel, AnnaLee Saxenian, Michael Best and Jonathan Zeitlin (Piore and Sabel 1984; Sabel 1989; Sabel and Zeitlin 1985; Saxenian 1994; Best 1990). The basic theme of their arguments is that firms are more likely to be innovative in industrial districts in which there are concentrations of small producers in close proximity who, intentionally or not, share ideas readily. As a result, firms are able to size up initiatives by their competitors very early in the game and to react equally quickly. In some cases, as in Silicon Valley, these firms may concentrate on industries in the early stages of innovation, but firms in other industrial districts, such as the Third Italy (the provinces of Emilia-Romagna and Tuscany), have reached more mature stages of development.

Real or putative network structures, like those in Silicon Valley and along Route 128, have become very popular among academics in recent years.[15] Saxenian provides a good summary of the benefits of industrial districts when they function at their best:

> Geographic proximity promotes the repeated interaction and mutual trust needed to sustain collaboration and to speed the continual recombination of technology and skill. When production is embedded in these regional social structures and institutions, firms compete by translating local knowledge and relationships into innovative products and services; and industrial specialization becomes a source of flexibility rather than of atomism and fragmentation.
> ... When technology remained relatively stable over time, vertical integration and corporate centralisation offered needed scale economies and market control. In an age of volatile technologies and markets, however, the horizontal coordination provided by interfirm networks enables firms to retain the focus and flexibility needed for continuous innovation.
> (Saxenian 1994: 161–2)

Other authors have reached the opposite conclusion based on much the same evidence. The most vocal proponent of centralisation is William Lazonick (1991). Drawing on the works of Chandler, Schumpeter, Marshall and Marx, Lazonick has concluded that markets are inefficient in providing the necessary co-ordination for successful and continuous innovation (especially systemic innovation) and that change can best be promoted by large integrated firms. Although Lazonick does not specify his vision very closely, he appears to advocate Japanese *keiretsu* organisations, or perhaps diversified and vertically integrated Chandlerian firms, as the most efficient agents of innovation.[16]

Should innovation be internalised?

These various theories, which are sometimes presented as near panaceas, appear to support different forms of industry policy. If one believes in the adaptive ability of small firms, then strict antitrust laws are required to prevent the growth of stultifying monsters. Belief in the innovative powers of vertically integrated giants and in the inadequacy of markets, however, should lead to calls for the repeal, or at least the watering-down, of antitrust legislation.

But the choice of an appropriate policy to promote innovation is in reality far more difficult because the authors that are cited have supported their views with examples from different innovative contexts. Saxenian believes that technology has entered a period of permanent revolution in which important industries will undergo continual significant changes. In essence, she is arguing that these new technologies will not offer important economies of scale and that, because product technologies will be in a state of continual flux, process technologies will never become the dominant concern, as they are in the Abernathy–Utterback model (Abernathy and Utterback 1978). Piore, Sabel, Best and Zeitlin, however, put primary emphasis on industries with limited economies of scale that have already settled most of their major technological problems and are now concerned with incremental innovation. Lazonick's argument, finally, is that large firms can best undergo continuous major change by internalising the sources of innovation, which permits them to maintain economies of scale while remaining at the forefront of their industries. Indeed, like Smith (1976), Stigler (1951) or Rosenberg (1963), Lazonick sees new industries as arising out of old ones; unlike the others, however, Lazonick maintains that the new industries should not be spun off, but should, rather, remain within large firms in which diversity feeds on itself.

Concepts developed by G. B. Richardson in 'The organisation of industry' (1972) provide tools for examining these different contentions. Richardson divides the activities undertaken in an industry into those that are *similar* to the core activities of a firm because they draw on the same capabilities as do the core activities and those that are *complementary* because, while they are needed for the final product, they draw on different capabilities. If firms are viewed as bundles of capabilities that function best when they draw on the same types of skills, then any given firm will be inclined to internalise similar activities but leave the performance of complementary activities to other firms with more appropriate capabilities. We might ask, therefore, when innovative activities are likely to be similar and when they are likely to be complementary to a firm's core activities.

Industrial districts, whether those described by Marshall (1890) or those in modern Italy, are characterised by high levels of vertical as well as horizontal disintegration. That is, firms are not only relatively small, but they are also highly specialised. This implies that there are few similar activities at any stage of the production process and (also or alternatively) that there are no important transaction costs.[17] When there are many similar activities, however, even small firms may choose to be highly vertically integrated despite limited economies of scale and low transaction costs. Furthermore, the presence of economies of scale or transaction costs encourages horizontal or vertical integration, respectively.

Given the number of complications involved, it is not surprising that the question of whether an innovation is best developed internally or externally in any particular case is more empirical than theoretical. When an innovation affects an activity that is similar to one already undertaken by a firm, then the firm might well find it advantageous to internalise the operations associated with that activity. Because they build on existing activities, such innovations are incremental. When an innovation leads to the replacement of an existing similar activity, however, the picture changes. Even though the result might be incremental in scope if the dislodged activity was of minor importance, it is less likely that the firm would have a comparative advantage in internalising the innovation. In such a situation, when the innovation involves complementary rather than similar activities, a firm might begin to outsource the new version of a component that it had previously produced itself.[18] When the innovation affects an activity that is currently complementary, the result is again indeterminate. If the innovation confirms the distinctiveness of the complementary activity, then the innovation would not lead to internalisation, but if an innovation to a component that is presently complementarily causes the production of that component to draw more heavily on capabilities similar to the core capabilities of a firm, then the outcome could be increased vertical integration.[19] As radical innovations are most commonly complementary, both their development and subsequent production are likely to be external to a firm producing the original good.

Because innovations may be either similar or complementary to the existing activities of a firm and because they may be expected to be developed either internally or externally, depending on, among other factors, the degree of radicalness of the innovation and its relationship to the current activities of the firm, no set of government policies towards firm size or diversity appears to be justified. Large and small firms as well as specialised or diversified firms can all produce important innovations if overall conditions are favourable.[20]

INNOVATION AND INDUSTRY MATURITY

It is now widely documented that firms in mature industries find it very difficult to cope successfully with major technological shifts. Although life-cycle analysis allows for incremental change to continue virtually indefinitely, more basic changes are frequently handled poorly by established firms (Henderson and Clark 1990; Iansiti 1995). Some existing firms do not even attempt to assimilate important new technologies, but the rate of success is low among those that do (Utterback 1994). As a result, changes in technological trajectories usually lead to a shake-up in industry structure, with new firms replacing many of the former leaders.

J. A. Schumpeter (1950) calls this process 'creative destruction', but he also notes that large established firms may have an advantage in generating innovations. Several more recent writers on management have likewise been rather optimistic concerning the fate of established companies. Charles Baden-Fuller and John M. Stopford (1992), for example, have written on ways of *Rejuvenating the Mature Business* and James M. Utterback (1994) contends that mature firms can survive technological transformations by *Mastering the Dynamics of Innovation*. Nevertheless, there is considerable evidence that existing firms are not always the most efficient institutions to master new technologies. As Schumpeter realised, governments are therefore faced with an unpleasant policy choice. At any given time, established firms dominate a modern industrial economy in terms of value of output. Moreover, they tend, both on average and collectively, to be larger in both the numbers of employees and the amount of funds invested than are firms dedicated to exploiting new technologies. Both the employees and investors of established firms are also voters and they have legitimate reasons for fearing innovations that will threaten their jobs and assets. Innovative firms, however, although small and unstable, have higher growth rates and promise better long-term benefits for the economy.

How, then, should governments respond to innovation? Should they oppose innovation because it is disruptive, or should they embrace it because of its promise of future prosperity? Saxenian (1994) seems to have few doubts concerning the proper course to follow. To her, large firms are dinosaurs that are to be replaced by smaller and more agile firms. She favourably portrays Silicon Valley as a land of (to my use own term) 'throwaway firms'. There, she tells us, entrepreneurs can easily start up firms to exploit new concepts. If the firms fail, as many do, the entrepreneurs suffer little stigma and can soon find high-paying jobs with their erstwhile competitors. Utterback (1994) takes the opposing position, that established firms should be saved rather than replaced. He feels that policies should be directed towards increasing the flexibility of existing companies.

Once again, the answer depends on a more detailed consideration of the nature of the innovation in question and its relationship to the capabilities of existing firms. In some cases, radical innovation does indeed upset an industry so severely that it virtually ceases to exist and is replaced by a new industry. For example, automobiles, railways and electric trams eventually displaced horse-drawn forms of transportation altogether. Although some companies may have continued to exist in other lines of business, the older technology left no important vestiges (except, perhaps, for a common reliance on the wheel).[21] The new technologies were, to use the term of Tushman and Anderson (1986), competence-destroying. Or, to adapt Richardson's (1960) term, the importance of the similar activities across technologies was not sufficiently great to allow the new technology to be grafted on to the old organisational structures. This failure to adapt was reinforced by the ways in which routines (Nelson and Winter 1982) and other aspects of organisational culture often make existing firms actively resistant to the adoption of new technologies whose use involves practices that are orthogonal to the prevailing practices of the organisation.

One of the most important aspects of the failure of established firms to adapt to innovation is that they tend to narrow down their channels of communication as they mature. The paradigm that underlies a technological trajectory can be conceived of as a set of behavioural patterns. In the words of Dosi, a technological paradigm is 'an "outlook", a set of procedures and definitions of the "relevant" problems and of the specific knowledge related to their solution' (Dosi 1982: 148). Once firms achieve sustained success with a particular paradigm they tend to reduce their absorptive capacity to encompass only activities that are related to that paradigm. As Pavitt has noted:

> Firms do not 'search' for innovations in a general 'pool' or 'stock' of knowledge, all of which is equally accessible and assimilable by them. Instead, they search in zones that are closely related to their existing skills and technologies. What firms can hope to do in technology and innovation in the future is strongly conditioned by what they have been able to do in the past.
>
> (Pavitt 1986: 174)

If the aim of policy is to allow established firms to deal successfully with innovation, then the remedies suggested above (see the subsection 'Accelerating diffusion and increasing absorptive capacity', pp. 271–4) will be helpful in increasing their absorptive capacity. But, as Dosi (1982), Nelson and Winter (1982) and others have suggested, the behavioural patterns of established firms in mature industries go well beyond tone deafness when innovations are broadcast. The routines of such firms are focused finely on doing well what they already do, and this often introduces an element of inflexibility even when the firms are aware of the challenges posed by innovations. Information alone is not sufficient to bring about successful change. The problems of established firms often appear at the implementation rather than at the planning stage because the new technologies may involve *activities*, *practices* and *capabilities* that run counter to those that the firm has long used successfully.

This raises a very real dilemma for policy-makers because it is not at all clear that governments can do anything to bring about a rapid displacement of micro-behaviour that is not conducive to change. Utterback (1994) regrets the fact that established firms tend to respond to radical innovation by perfecting their existing technologies. When they do chase perfection, as illustrated in Figure 14.3, the 'product performance' of existing technologies remains above that of newer technologies for a substantial period because the former are still being improved and bugs are still being worked out of the latter.[22] Utterback recommends that established firms immediately adopt new technologies rather than continue to tinker with existing ones so that they can go down the learning curves of the innovative technologies as rapidly as possible and thus (it is hoped) retain leadership following the transition.

Stoneman and Diederen, however, are concerned that some policies may lead to rates of diffusion that are excessive. They advocate (although they do not outline) policies that are 'aimed at fine tuning the speed of diffusion' (Stoneman and Diederen 1994: 928) As they explain:

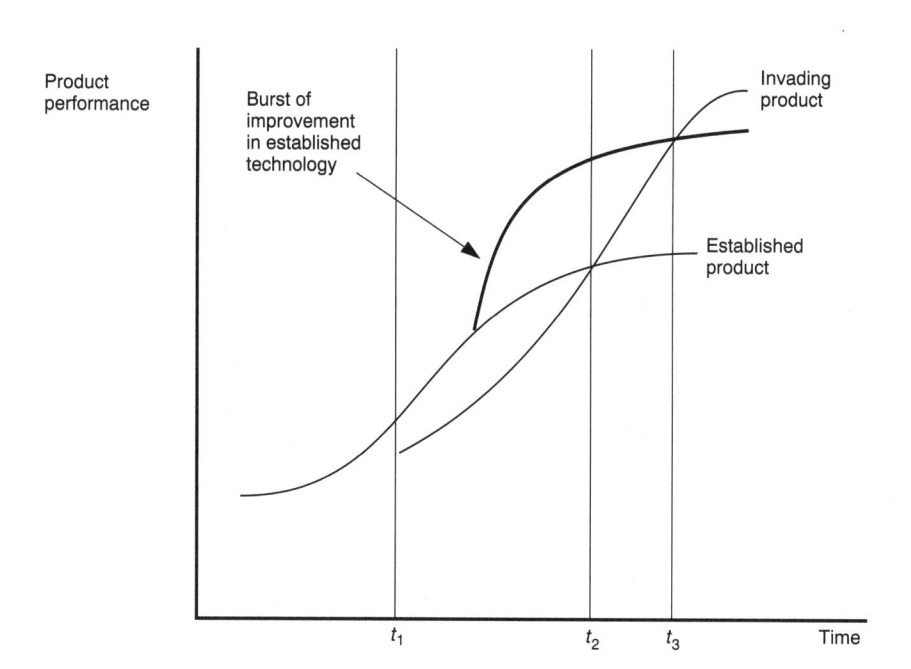

Figure 14.3 Performance of an established and an invading product: burst of improvement in established product

Source: Utterback 1994: 160

> The idea of too fast a rate of diffusion for an economy often causes some consternation amongst policy makers for whom the principle that new technology should be introduced as quickly as possible is almost a statement of faith (usually on the grounds that use of new technology will increase competitiveness). However, in the absence of significant differences between private and social costs and benefits, a rate of diffusion that is too fast could result in firms adopting a technology before it has become profitable to do so or adopting a less well developed or higher priced technology today at the expense of adopting a more developed or cheaper technology in the future.
> (Stoneman and Diederen 1994: 919)

It is difficult to conceive of the criteria that might, in practice, underpin a policy of fine-tuning the speed of diffusion. One category of fears that Stoneman and Diederen voice concerns inherent uncertainty. It is clear that firms and whole societies have become locked into inferior technologies in the past, but if policy-makers refuse to sanction the adoption of an innovation on the grounds that a better technology may someday come along, they could wait forever. Even if they do delay early adoption and then choose a superior technology, the nation may not benefit. By the time nation X acts, other important countries may be locked into an inferior technology that is incompatible. As a result, despite its 'better' decision, nation X could be shut out of potential export markets and face isolation.

A second problem arises from defining premature adoption in terms of low initial profitability. As Figure 14.3 illustrates, in its initial stages an innovation may not perform well because complementary assets, including knowledge, have not yet been developed. In time, however, these problems are overcome, giving pioneer adopters a valuable shove down their experience curves. Therefore, it may often be more reasonable to think of the low initial profits as arising out of an investment in learning rather than as a sign that the technology is not yet ready to be adopted. If subsequent adopters have to make similar investments in learning, the pioneers will have gained a competitive advantage that latecomers may find it hard to erase.[23]

CONCLUSION

This chapter discusses ways of improving the availability of relevant information to firms undertaking investment decisions, a problem highlighted in a somewhat different context by George Richardson (1960). All the evidence set out above points towards the difficulty of making policies that will improve information and lead to better investment decisions. Communications can certainly be enhanced in order to give potential investors access to better information, but action on the micro level is difficult to achieve because it presupposes that policy-makers themselves have absorbed heroic amounts of information about the needs of individual firms and industries. Policies designed to improve the absorptive capacity of society as a whole through better education are more feasible, however, and are likely to pay off well in social welfare terms.

By the same token, the use of government policy to influence firm organisation would require detailed knowledge of specific problems, since different types of innovation are likely to benefit from different types of firm and industry structure. Richardson's (1972) important distinction between similar and complementary activities has been employed to argue that innovations that depend heavily on activities similar to those fostered by the existing capabilities of a given firm might well be developed and implemented internally. When complementary capabilities are involved, innovation is often better left to outside suppliers.

Finally, firms in mature industries may or may not need help to allow them to assimilate radical innovations. Although Utterback is only one of many management writers who believes that it is desirable for innovations to be implemented by established firms rather than ceded to firms from outside an industry,[24] there is a great deal of evidence that many successful firms are highly inflexible. Contrary to Utterback's position, the situation shown in Figure 14.3 may be the best one for society. The threat of a superior competing technology pushes once complacent established firms to higher levels of productivity using the current technology while other firms that have adopted the innovative technology are still learning the routines and establishing the complementary assets needed to profit from it. In the end, the new firms with appropriate routines survive, while the older, inflexible firms die or find something else to do (Robertson and Langlois 1994). This may involve heavy social cost, but the alternative – to place barriers in the way of innovation – could be more costly in the long run.

The fact that this analysis offers no positive recommendations for government policy does not mean, however, that it lacks operational value. The same principles that underlie the policy discussion above provide guidelines appropriate for the strategy decisions of individual firms. If firms maintain high levels of absorptive capacity, concentrate on similar activities and resist the temptation to enter into activities for which their existing routines are unsuitable, they are likely to benefit.[25]

NOTES

1 Most of what Clark terms 'uncertainty' is, in fact, 'ignorance' in the terminology adopted here.
2 As Stinchcombe) points out, the sources of 'news' exist in *'distinct social locations'* (Stinchcombe 1990: 4; italics in original), and the same is true of potential recipients. What is needed is a sort of *Yellow Pages* directory combined with a

street map that allows those who are unfamiliar with the terrain to find strange locations.
3 An examination of the positive, strategic role that spillovers may play is given by Langlois and Robertson (1996).
4 To be more precise, solution-holders should be willing to accept reductions in profits in some markets up to the point at which this erosion is just matched by gains from allowing producers in other markets to use the solution.
5 If there has been a shift in technological trajectory or paradigm this may be 'old news'.
6 Similar figures may be found in many elementary management books.
7 This was a courageous decision in that it rendered obsolete all existing FM broadcasting and receiving equipment. But without being too cynical, it is possible to wonder if the same decision would have been made if the existing network had not been comparatively small.
8 For example, although Melbourne in Victoria is a more natural port than Sydney for the export of grain from the Riverina region of southern New South Wales, the New South Wales government used its control over gauges within the colony to direct traffic from the Riverina to Sydney by imposing the extra expense on shippers to Melbourne of breaking the journey and shifting goods from one set of railway wagons to another at Albury on the New South Wales–Victoria border.
9 For his views on planning versus market co-ordination, including a highly sceptical analysis of indicative planning, see Richardson (1971).
10 See also Mowery and Rosenberg (1989).
11 Richardson's distinction between similar and complementary activities (Richardson 1972) helps to explain why education is generally done in specialised institutions while the acquisition of skills is best undertaken by firms. Training in skills is a by-product of the everyday activities of firms. This is especially true, of course, of skills that are peculiar to a particular firm. Instruction in broader knowledge, on the other hand, frequently draws on routines outside the normal activities of commercial concerns and may, in fact, call on behaviour (such as questioning the person in charge) that contradicts the behaviour that a firm wants to instil in its workers. As a result, education is generally assigned to specialised institutions that are appropriate for instruction in theoretical fields but ill equipped to undertake complementary training in skills.
12 Weder and Grubel (1993) argue that certain types of private institutions, such as trade associations, industry clusters and conglomerate firm structures, may also act as agents to spread knowledge of innovations while allowing the returns to be internalised.
13 There are several life-cycle models that relate maturity to rates of change in other variables. One of the most popular, that of Abernathy and Utterback (1978), contends that the rate of product innovation is very high in new industries but slows down in mature industries. The rate of process innovation lags behind that of product innovation but it also slows down with maturity.
14 For a fuller discussion of the organisational needs of innovative firms, see Robertson and Langlois (1995).
15 See, for example, the articles in Nohria and Eccles (1992).
16 Lazonick's ideas (like those of Piore and Sabel and Best) are underpinned by theories of labour management. Lazonick's 1990 and 1991 books should be read together to get a better, if highly discursive, insight into his general argument. Florida and Kenney (1990) use theories of organisational behaviour to support

an argument similar to Lazonick's in their advocacy of large vertically integrated firms in the United States to overcome Japanese competitiveness. Starting from a Coasean standpoint, Weder and Grubel (1993) find support for the prescriptions both of Lazonick and Piore, and of Sabel and Best.

17 By undertaking similar activities, firms should be able, through economies of scope, to reduce direct costs of production by sharing equipment or skills. Transaction costs, however, refer to the costs of using markets. When transaction costs are substantial, firms may find it cheaper to internalise complementary activities as well.

18 The result could be an increase in modularisation. See Langlois and Robertson (1992).

19 If the firm maintains absorptive capacity in the form of wide-ranging research capabilities, this would be more likely to lead to an increase the number of similar activities than if the absorptive capacity takes the more passive form of aiming for an ability to recognise useful innovations rather than to develop them internally. When the range of fields in which relevant innovations could be developed is a large one a passive stance would probably be a more cost-effective research strategy. In either case, however, similarity in research does not necessarily imply similarity in production capabilities, and a firm may wish to license or otherwise spin off its discoveries that are complementary at the production stage. See, for example, the account in Langlois and Robertson (1989) of how the Ford Motor Company developed designs of machinery for its production line that it then, after the prototype stage, turned over to more conventional machine tool companies.

20 This conclusion is fortified, of course, by the inevitable presence of uncertainty in the innovation process, as a result of which innovations might in fact come from sources that, in an a priori analysis, seem highly improbable.

21 But close complementarity did permit some firms that *used* horses to make the transition to motor vehicles, e.g. the British removal company Pickfords.

22 For a similar analysis using experience curves, see Robertson and Langlois (1994).

23 The views of Stoneman and Diederen are very similar to the attitudes of 'excessive rationality' that are alleged to have led to the relative decline of the British economy after 1870. For a comparative discussion of British, German and American attitudes towards investment and innovation before 1914, see Pollard and Robertson (1979: Introduction).

24 Although Utterback and other writers are certainly sincere, it is worth pointing out that it is much easier to get people to pay attention to (and pay for) ideas that offer them, or their organisations, hope than to ideas that recommend that they be subjected to lingering deaths or euthanasia.

25 There is controversy in the resource-based school of strategy about the extent to which firms should concentrate on developing activities based on their existing capabilities (i.e. concentrate on similar activities) (Kay 1993) and whether firms should develop new capabilities and thus become more flexible in dealing with innovation (Hamel and Prahalad 1989; Prahalad and Hamel 1990). The arguments developed here suggest that Kay is correct in assessing the ability of firms to adjust to radical innovation, but that the policies of Prahalad and Hamel (which are related to suggestions that absorptive capacity be increased) would be of use in adapting better to incremental innovations.

REFERENCES

Abernathy, W. and Utterback, J. M. (1978) 'Patterns of industrial innovation', *Technology Review* 80(7): 40–7.

Baden-Fuller, C. and Stopford, J. M. (1992) *Rejuvenating the Mature Business: The Competitive Challenge*, London: Routledge.

Best, M. (1990) *The New Competition: Institutions of Industrial Restructuring*, Cambridge, Mass.: Harvard University Press.

Chandler, A. D., Jr (1962) *Strategy and Structure: Chapters in the History of Industrial Enterprise*, Cambridge, Mass.: MIT Press.

Clark, K. B. (1985) 'The Interaction of Design Hierarchies and Market Concepts in Technological Evolution', *Research Policy* 14: 235–51.

Cohen, W. M. and Levinthal, D. A. (1989) 'Innovation and learning: the two faces of R&D', *Economic Journal* 99: 569–96.

—— (1990) 'Absorptive capacity: a new perspective on learning and innovation', *Administrative Science Quarterly* 35: 128–52.

David. P. A. (1991) 'Computer and dynamo. The modern productivity paradox in a not-too-distant mirror', *Technology and Productivity: The Challenge for Economic Policy*, Paris: OECD.

Davies, P. (1995) *The Cosmic Blueprint: Order and Complexity at the Edge of Chaos*, London: Penguin. (Originally published in 1987.)

Dosi, G. (1982) 'Technological paradigms and technological trajectories: a suggested interpretation of the determinants and directions of technical change', *Research Policy* 11: 147–62.

Florida, R. and Kenney, M. (1990) *The Breakthrough Illusion: Corporate America's Failure to Move from Innovation to Mass Production*, New York: Basic Books.

Grossman, G. M. and Helpman, E. (1991) 'Trade, knowledge spillovers, and growth', *European Economic Review* 35: 517–26.

Hamel, G. and Prahalad, C. K. (1989) 'Strategic intent', *Harvard Business Review* (May–June): 63–76.

Hayek, F. A. von (1937) 'Economics and knowledge', *Economica* NS 4: 33–54.

—— (1945) 'The use of knowledge in society', *American Economic Review* 35: 519–30.

Henderson, R. M. and Clark, K. B. (1990) 'Architectural innovation: the reconfiguration of existing product technologies and the failure of established firms', *Administrative Science Quarterly* 35: 9–30.

Iansiti, M. (1995) 'Technology integration: managing technological evolution in a complex environment', *Research Policy* 24: 521–42.

Kay, J. (1993) *Foundations of Corporate Success: How Business Strategies Add Value*, Oxford: Oxford University Press.

Kirzner, I. M. (1973) *Competition and Entrepreneurship*, Chicago: University of Chicago Press.

Langlois, R. N. and Robertson, P. L. (1989) 'Explaining vertical integration: lessons from the American automobile industry', *Journal of Economic History* 49: 361–75.

—— (1992) 'Networks and innovation in a modular system: lessons from the microcomputer and stereo component industries', *Research Policy* 21(4): 297–313.

—— (1995) *Firms, Markets and Economic Change: A Dynamic Theory of Business Institutions*, London: Routledge.

—— (1996) 'Stop crying over spilt knowledge: a critical look at the theory of spillovers and technical change', paper presented to the MERIT Conference on Innovation, Evolution and Technology, August 25–27, Maastricht, the Netherlands.
Lazonick, W. (1990) *Competitive Advantage on the Shop Floor*, Cambridge, Mass.: Harvard University Press.
—— (1991) *Business Organization and the Myth of the Market Economy*, New York: Cambridge University Press.
Marshall, A. (1890) *Principles of Economic Growth*, London: Macmillan.
Metcalfe, J. S. (1994) 'Evolutionary Economics and Technology Policy', *Economic Journal* 104: 931–44.
Mowery, D. C. and Rosenberg, N. (1989) *Technology and the Pursuit of Economic Growth*, Cambridge: Cambridge University Press.
Mytelka, L. K. (1992) 'Dancing with wolves: global oligopolies and strategic partnerships', paper presented to the Conference on Convergence and Divergence in Economic Growth and Technical Change: Maastricht Revisited', December 10–12, Maastricht, The Netherlands.
Nelson, R. R. (ed.) (1993) *National Innovation Systems: A Comparative Analysis*, New York: Oxford University Press.
Nelson, R. R. and Winter, S. G. (1982) *An Evolutionary Theory of Economic Change*, Cambridge, Mass.: Harvard University Press.
Nohria, N. and Eccles, R. G. (1992) *Networks and Organizations: Structure, Form, and Action*, Boston, Mass.: Harvard Business School Press.
Pavitt, K. (1986) 'Technology, innovation and strategic management', in J. McGee and H. Thomas (eds) *Strategic Management Research: A European Perspective*, Chichester: Wiley.
Piore, M. J. and Sabel, C. F. (1984) *The Second Industrial Divide*, New York: Basic Books.
Pollard, S. and Robertson, P. (1979) *The British Shipbuilding Industry, 1870–1914*, Cambridge, Mass.: Harvard University Press.
Prahalad, C. K. and Hamel, G. (1990) 'The core competence of the corporation', *Harvard Business Review* 68(3):79–91.
Richardson, G. B. (1960) *Information and Investment: A Study in the Working Of the Competitive Economy*, Oxford: Clarendon Press.
—— (1971) 'Planning versus competition', *Soviet Studies* 22(3): 433–7; reprinted as Annex II in G. B. Richardson (1990).
—— (1972) 'The organisation of industry', *Economic Journal* 82: 883–96.
—— (1990) *Information and Investment: A Study in the Working Of the Competitive Economy*, 2nd edn, Oxford: Clarendon Press.
Robertson, P. L. (1981) 'Employers and engineering education in Britain and the United States, 1890–1914', *Business History* 23: 42–58.
Robertson, P. L. and Langlois, R. N. (1994) 'Institutions, inertia and changing industrial leadership', *Industrial and Corporate Change* 3(2): 359–78.
—— (1995) 'Innovation, networks, and vertical integration', *Research Policy* 24: 543–62.
Romer, P. M. (1990) 'Endogenous technological change', *Journal of Political Economy* 98(5), part 2: S71–S102.

Rosenberg, N. (1963) 'Technological Change in the Machine Tool Industry, 1840–1910', *Journal of Economic History* 23(2): 414–43.

Sabel, C. F. (1989) 'Flexible specialization and the re-emergence of regional economies', in P. Hirst and J. Zeitlin (eds) *Reversing Industrial Decline? Industrial Structure and Policy in Britain and Her Competitors*, Oxford: Berg.

Sabel, C. F. and Zeitlin, J. (1985) 'Historical alternatives to mass production: politics, markets, and technology in nineteenth-century industrialization', *Past and Present* 108: 133–76.

Saxenian, A. (1994) *Regional Advantage: Culture and Competition in Silicon Valley and Route 128*, Cambridge, Mass.: Harvard University Press.

Schumpeter, J. A. (1950) *Capitalism, Socialism and Democracy*, New York: Harper.

Smith, A. (1976) *The Wealth of Nations*, Glasgow edition, Oxford: Clarendon Press.

Sterling, C. H. (1968) 'WTMJ-FM: a case study in the development of broadcasting', *Journal of Broadcasting* 12(4): 341–52; reprinted in L. W. Lichty and M. C. Topping (eds) *American Broadcasting: A Source Book on the History of Radio and Television*, New York: Hastings House.

Stigler, G. J. (1951) 'The division of labor is limited by the extent of the market', *Journal of Political Economy* 59(3): 185–93.

Stiglitz, J. E. (1987) 'Learning to learn, localized learning and technological progress', in P. Dasgupta and P. Stoneman (eds) *Economic Policy and Technological Performance*, Cambridge: Cambridge University Press.

Stinchcombe, A. L. (1990) *Information and Organizations*, Berkeley and Los Angeles: University of California Press.

Stoneman, P and Diederen, P. (1994) 'Technology diffusion and public policy', *Economic Journal* 104: 918–30.

Thompson, G. V. (1954) 'Intercompany technical standardization in the early American automobile industry', *Journal of Economic History* 14(1): 1–20.

Thompson, J. D. (1967) *Organizations in Action: Social Sciences Bases of Administrative Theory*, New York: McGraw-Hill.

Tushman, M. L. and Anderson, P. (1986) 'Technological discontinuities and organizational environments', *Administrative Science Quarterly* 31: 439–65.

Utterback, J. M. (1994) *Mastering the Dynamics of Innovation: How Companies Can Seize Opportunities in the Face of Technological Change*, Boston, Mass.: Harvard Business School Press.

Weder, R. and Grubel, H. G. (1993) 'The new growth theory and Coasean economics: institutions to capture externalities', *Weltwirtschaftliches Archiv* 129(3): 488–513.

INDEX

Abernathy, W. 277
absorptive capacity 271–3, 275, 280, 283
academic search processes 30–4
ad-hocery 147–8
'Adam Smith on competition and increasing returns' 4, 5
adaptability 244
administrative decision 66
adverse selection 244
Aftalion, A. 116
agents; global markets 98, 100; independent 90; individual in Andrews and Richardson 92–7; inter-individual consistency 86; and markets 84–92; rationality and ad-hocery 147; transaction-cost theory 191
Airbus Industrie 235
Alchian, A.A. 79, 190–1
alliances 222, 230–9, 240
allocation 147
allocative efficiency 2, 5, 64
Anderson, P. 280
Andrews, P.W.S. 6, 15, 16, 17, 31; anthropological research strategy 143; competition 105, 116, 142; global markets 97–101; individual agents 92–7; markets 131, 134; normal cost theory 123; post-Marshallian 139, 141, 142; supply curve 128; theory of markets 121; see also markets: Marshall, Andrews and Richardson on
anti-competitive agreements 131
anti-trust legislation 277
Aoki, M. 220

Archibald, G.C. 70
Arena, R. 6, 31, 83–101
Arrow, K.J. 26, 83, 107, 166, 244
Asian Tigers 273
asset; specificity 153, 189, 190–4, 196; see also complementarity; information, similarity, complementarity and innovation
Australia 270–1
Austrian and post-Marshallian economics 138–58; economic organisation and flexibility 155–6; information and investment 145–7; institutions 148–50; Malmgren: Richardsonian arguments and the firm 153–5; Marshall and Hayek 144–5; Marshall and new theory of value 140–1; organisation of industry 151–2; planning and investment 150–1; rationality and ad-hocery 147–8; rearguard actions 141–2; subjectivism and economic change 142–3; summing-up 143–4, 152; theory and empirical reality 143; theory of the firm 152–3
Austrian tradition 2, 7, 8, 11, 84, 110; competition 112; entrepreneur 111; information, co-ordination and competition 134; information and investment 116
Automatic Selection 130–1

Baden-Fuller, C. 279
balance of power, internal 211–13
Baltazzis, N. 21, 29
Baranzini, M. 84
Barzel, Y. 191

INDEX

Baudier, E. 25–6
Baumol, W. 78
Becker, G. 166
behavioural rules 96
Berg, S.V. 229
Best, M. 276, 277
biotechnology 230–2
Blois, K.J. 19
Borch, K. 26
Bowmar (company) 197
Boyle, S.E. 229
Bradbury, F. 172
Breusch-Pagan LM test 254
British Electrical and Allied Manufacturers' Association 3
British Monopolies Commission 3
Brunner, E. 93
Buchanan, J.M. 194
Buckley, P. 227
Burchardt, F. 16
business cycle theory 149–50

Cantillon, R. 185
capabilities 8, 11, 22, 56; Austrian and post-Marshallian economics 139; co-operation 47; co-ordination necessity 44; collaboration clusters 222; firm as microeconomy 52; innovation 278, 279
capabilities concept 163–81; competitive advantage 171–7; decision-making 178–9; direct 'knowledge how' 167–70; division of labour and organisation of knowledge 164–7; evolution 179–81; indirect 'knowledge how' 170–1
capabilities and theory of the firm 183–200; modern transaction cost theory 188–93; production costs: Pigovian price theory 184–5; production costs redux 193–7; transaction costs 185–8
career of Richardson and literature of economics 14–41; Aberdeen University 15; and Andrews 17; applied studies 17; behaviour of economists 14; Chief Executive, Oxford University Press 14, 44; co-ordination 17–18, 19, 20, 21; 'co-ordination of complementary investment' 18; competition problem *see* information and co-ordination in effective competitive process; competitive process 127–32; criticism of general equilibrium 106–7; Debreu and *Information and Investment* 24–9; Economic Development Committee 14; economic organisation principles 44–61; economic papers at Oxford 15; *Economic Theory* 21; employment 15; firm 153–5; Foreign Service 18; *Future of the Heavy Electrical Plant Industry* 150; global markets 97–101; government service 18; heavy electrical plant industry 17, 29; increasing returns 19; individual agents 92–7; institutional arrangements 21; interpretation of Marshallian competition 112; Keble College, Oxford 14; limited impact 20–4; link with Hicks 16–17; mathematical training 16; Monopolies Commission 14, 17; networks, institutions and academic search processes 30–4; Nuffield College 17; Oxford 15, 17; path to economics 15–18; 'Planning versus competition' 21, 150; primacy 19; research co-ordination problem 18–20; research style 17; Rockefeller Foundation fellowship 32; Royal Commission on Environmental Pollution 14; St John's College, Oxford 14, 17; Univeristy Reader in Economics 14; university education 15; view on restraints to growth 244–6; *see also* markets: Marshall, Andrews and Richardson on; *see also* 'organisation of industry; 'Planning versus competition'; *Information and Investment*
cartelisation 6, 104, 105, 110, 113–15, 117, 132
Casson, M. 9, 32, 204–21, 227
central planning 115, 116, 132, 261–2
centralisation 55, 276
Chamberlin, E.H. 93, 105, 108
Chandler, A.D. Jr 156, 264, 276
Charbit, C. 6, 83–101
Chicago school 185
Chiron (company) 232, 238
Ciba-Geigy 238

INDEX

circularity 106–7
Clark, J.B. 70
Clark, J.M. 19, 134
Clark, K.B. 264, 279
Clarke, R. 23
club or network 236, 237, 238–9, 240
co-operation 55, 56, 76; agents and markets 89; boundaries 78; cartelisation 114; co-ordination necessity 44; collaboration clusters 222, 223; communications, scale and structure 55; consolidation costs 58; firm as microeconomy 51; global markets 101; individual agents 96; information, knowledge and co-ordination 69; inter-firm 75, 77, 78; market 96; nature of industry and competition paradox 77, 78; necessity 47–8; non-market 96; organisation of industry 151, 152; paradox 79; transaction-cost theory 192
co-operation and competition paradoxes 63–80; information, knowledge and co-operation 64–9; nature of the firm and co-operation paradox 70–4; nature of industry and competition paradox 75–8
co-ordination 3–9, 11, 17, 19–22, 25–7, 29, 55; Austrian and post-Marshallian economics 139, 142, 145; and capabilities 1–11, 179, 197; cartelisation 114–15, 115; co-operation and competition paradoxes 64; collaboration clusters 224; of commitments 194; communications, scale and structure 54; competition and theory of the firm 184; consolidation costs 57; costs, internal 72; direction 49, 50, 51; external 72; firm 59; global markets 101; horizontal 276; industrial 68, 74, 76; information costs 206, 207, 208; information and investment 116; institutions 149–50; internal 73; of investment 18, 129–30; nature of industry and competition paradox 77; necessity 44; planning and investments 150; pricing within a firm 53; of production 194, 245; production costs 196; productive 68, 71; qualitative 10, 188–9; resource 222; social rules 175; theory 63, 64; theory of the firm 154; through direction 58; transaction-cost theory 189, 191, 192; -type games 154; and uncertainty 261
'co-ordination of complementary investment' 18
Coase, R.H. 6, 32, 116; boundaries of the firm 183; co-ordination 187; consolidation costs 57; factors of production 67; institutional structure of production 63; knowledge 170–1, 173; markets 184; 'nature of the firm, The' 48–9, 65–6, 69, 70, 71, 72–3, 74, 75, 153, 154; organisation of industry 64, 79, 139, 155; price mechanism 52; 'Problem of Social Cost, The' 4–5; qualitative co-ordination 8; theory of boundaries of the firm 63; transaction costs 186, 188, 190, 191
cobweb theorem 27, 111
Coddington, A. 109, 113, 117
codification 172–3, 267–8, 274
Cohen, W.M. 172, 273
collaboration clusters 222–41; evolution 223–6; evolution in diversified firm 226–9; strategic business alliances 230–9
collusion 29, 261–2
communication 54–5, 56, 282–3; diffusion and absorptive capacity 272; firm's growth rate 250; information 207, 274–5; innovation 274–5, 280; Japan 78; organisational form 275; process model 264–8
communication gaps 268–74; diffusion acceleration and absorptive capacity increase 271–3; entrepreneurship 268–9; standards 269–71
comparative advantage 75, 217
comparative efficiency analysis 67
competition 3, 4, 5, 6, 56; actual 105, 107, 113, 116; agents and markets 88; Austrian and post-Marshallian economics 141; collaboration clusters 224; consolidation costs 58; firm as microeconomy 51; free 45; genuine 105, 111; global markets 99; industrial 105; information and investment 109; monopolistic 122; organisation of industry 152;

population ecology of the industry 123; pure 98; short-run 114; theory 127; *see also* co-operation and competition paradoxes; imperfect; perfect
competitive activities 47
competitive advantage 171–7
competitive process 127–32; co-ordination of investment, competitive and complementary 129–30; competition, selection and market discipline 130–2; market co-ordination of investment 128–9
complementarity 6, 9–10, 29, 56, 283; co-ordination 67; collaboration clusters 222, 223; communications, scale and structure 54; consolidation costs 58; direction 50; economic organisation and flexibility 155; firm as microeconomy 52; information, knowledge and co-ordination 68, 69; innovation 278, 282; institutions 149–50; invisible hand 46, 47; production costs 196; theory of the firm 154; *see also* information, similarity, complementarity and innovation
consolidation 76; costs 57–8
consultation 205, 211–13
consumption functions 164
contestability theory 29
contracting, relational 22
convex adustment costs 251
Cook, P.L. 27, 28
Cournot, A. 90
Creative Destruction idea 123, 125
Crisis in Economic Theory 29
Cubbin, J. 246
cumulative causation hypothesis 252
Cyert, R. 15

Daimler Benz 230, 232
Darwin, C. 140
David, P.A. 235, 270
Davidson, W.H. 225
Davies, P. 268
Davies, S. 23
Debreu, G. 24–9, 30, 83, 147
decentralisation 53, 55, 56, 148
decision-making 21, 49, 55, 178–9, 206
decisiveness 211–13

decreasing returns to management 72, 74
Delapierre, M. 230–2, 235, 237, 239
demand and supply 93, 97, 98, 107, 111, 117, 124, 128–9, 205, 206
Demsetz, H. 151, 154, 186, 190–1
Devine, P.J. 23
Diederen, P. 262, 281–2
diffusion 269, 271–3, 281–2
direction 44, 48–51, 56, 57, 58, 72, 223
dislocation effects 117
distributing functions 59
diversification 226–9, 232, 235, 237–40, 278
division of labour 55; capabilities 178, 180; co-ordination necessity 44; competitive advantage 173; direction 49; firm as microeconomy 52; individual agents 94, 96; information costs 207, 208; institutional 78; nature of industry and competition paradox 75, 76; and organisation of knowledge 164–7; production costs 193–4
Dobb, M.H. 19
Dobson, S. 246
dog oligopoly theory 106–7
Dosi, G. 280
Downie, J. 7, 15, 31, 139, 141, 142; population ecology of the industry 122–7; *see also* competitive process; information and co-ordination in effective competitive process
Drucker, P. 8
dual control system 225
dual sourcing 205
Dunning, J.H. 230

Earl, P.E. 4, 6, 14–41, 140, 142, 143
economic organisation principles 44–61, 155–6; cardinal principle 46–7; co-operation, necessity for 47–8; co-ordination, necessity for 44; communications, scale and structure 54–5; consolidation costs 57–8; direction, necessity for 48–51; firm as microeconomy 51–2; firm, other functions of 58–9; invisible hand 45–6; pricing within a firm 52–4
economies of scale 49, 54, 55, 56, 57, 277, 278

INDEX

Eddy, A.J. 115
Edgeworth, F.Y. 45, 105, 108, 112
Eltis, W. 117
endogenous economic growth theory 45
entrepreneur 111, 155, 268–9
equilibration theory 7
equilibrium 45, 66, 108, 110, 122–3, 128, 134, 146; static 72; *see also* general equilibrium; partial
Europe 226, 272
European Union 271, 272
evolutionary theory 7

factor prices 113, 116
Ferranti, S. de 17
firm; Austrian and post-Marshallian economics 141; behaviour 140, 143–4; formal theory of 68; as microeconomy 51–2; Richardsonian arguments 153–5; size 278; theory 64; *see also* capabilities and theory of the firm; firm's growth rate; nature; theory
firm's growth rate 71
firm's growth rate, limits to 243–59; contemporary evidence 246–52; Richardson's view on restraints to growth 244–6; trade-off relationship 252–6
Fisher, F.M. 83, 146
flexibility 8, 155–6, 194–5, 224, 245
Ford, H. 125
Fordism 156
Foss, N.J. 1–12, 28, 31, 134, 138–58
Fransman, M. 78
Friedman, M. 117, 148
Friedman, P. 229
Frydman, R. 148
Fuchs, V.R. 65
Fuller, M.B. 230

game theory 26, 67
Genentec 232, 236, 238
General Economic Equilibrium 83, 84–6, 91, 97, 100
general equilibrium 2–3, 6–7, 24–5; Austrian and post-Marshallian economics 141, 146, 147; competitive process 130; information and investment 104–5, 109, 117, 145; invisible hand 45; knowledge 108; planned economy 115; Representative Firm and costs 113; Richardson's criticism 106–7
George, K.D. 23
Georgescu-Roegen, N. 68
Germany 272, 273, 274
Geroski, P. 78
Gerrard, B. 246
Ghamawat, P. 148
Gilbert, R.J. 22–3
global markets in Andrews and Richardson 97–101
Goffe, W.L. 32
goodwill 90, 94, 99, 131
government 10, 271, 272, 273, 275, 279, 283
Goyder, D.G. 115
Grant, J. McB. 28
Greer, D.F. 23
Grossman, G.M. 265
Grossman, S. 190
Guesnerie, R. 83

Haberler, G. 116
Hahn, F.H. 26, 107, 109, 146, 166, 170
Hall, R. 122
Hall-Hitch model 92
Hannah, L. 31
Harrell, C. 25
Harris, L. 27
Harrod, R. 16, 21, 122
Hart, O.D. 190, 191
Harvard system of referencing 30–1
Hay, D.A. 23
Hayek, F.A. von 2, 44–5, 110, 141, 154, 168, 180, 189, 271; business cycle theory 150; competition 3, 4, 184; 'Economics and knowledge' 144; evolutionary psychology 8; firms 151–2; general equilibrium 115, 146, 147, 164; knowledge 7, 21, 68, 69, 94, 153, 173; market 142, 149, 155, 156; price system 116; scientism 108; *Sensory Order* 167; social rules 175
heavy electrical engineering industry 17, 29
Heiner, R.A. 195
Helpman, E. 265
Henderson, R.M. 279
Hennart, J.-F. 227, 228, 229

INDEX

Hicks, J.R. 2, 6, 16, 17, 27, 32, 85, 86, 145
hierarchy 56, 58, 205, 208, 220, 249, 250; collaboration clusters 224, 225, 230, 231, 238
Hirschman, A. 24
Hoffman-La Roche 232
Hoffman-La Roche-Kodak-Cetus 236
Holmstrom, B. 139, 153, 154
Hughes, A. 33
Hurwicz, L. 25
Hutchison, T.W. 68

Iansiti, M. 279
IBM 197
IBM-Motorola-Apple 235
ICI 232
ignorance 262–4, 265, 274
imperfect competition 83, 91, 94, 107, 109, 122, 127, 131
increasing returns to scale 19, 45, 77–8
industrial districts 277
Industrial Organisation 64, 65, 68, 69, 77
industry; equilibrium 108; maturity 278–82; population ecology of 122–7; *see also* nature; organisation
information 9, 22, 64–9, 283; agents and markets 91; agreements 115; alternative welfare economics 132; Austrian and post-Marshallian economics 139, 145–7; competitive process 128, 129, 132; diffusion and absorptive capacity 273; global markets 98, 100, 101; horizontal 107; impactedness 188; imperfect 46, 83; innovation 282; Japan 78; population ecology of the industry 126–7; quality 204, 213–16, 219–20; quantity 204, 217–20; tacit 207–8; technology 232; vertical 107
information and co-ordination in effective competitive process 121–36; alternative welfare economics 132–4; Downie's population ecology of the industry 122–7; Richardson's competitive process 127–32
information costs and organisational structure of multinational enterprise 204–21; decisiveness, consultation and internal balance of power 211–13; general principles 206–8; information quality 213–16; meta-rationality: minimising risk of mistakes 209–11
information and innovation 262–75; communication gaps 268–74; communication process model 264–8; information, communication and investment 274–5; uncertainty and ignorance 262–4
information and investment 104–18; cartelisation, defence of 113–15; entrepreneur 111; general equilibrium: Richardson's criticism 106–7; investment emphasis 111; knowledge, origins of problem of 107–8; markets as information mechanisms 110–11; perfect competition shuffle 110; planned economy 115–16; Representative Firm and costs 112–13; Richardson's interpretation of Marshallian competition 112; time 109–10
Information and Investment 1–7, 10, 14–18, 22–4, 26–8, 31–3; cartelisation 113, 115; co-ordination of complementary investments 187–8; competition, selection and market discipline 130; competitive process 128; division of labour and organisation of knowledge 164; imperfect knowledge and investment 261; information and co-ordination 122; information, knowledge and co-ordination 68; invisible hand 45; markets 83–4; planning and investments 150; production costs 194–5, 195; research co-ordination problem 18; transaction-cost theory 191
information, similarity and complementarity 275–8; innovation internalisation 277–8; innovation and organisational form 275–6
innovation 6, 8, 11, 283; alternative welfare economics 134; collaboration clusters 224; communication 269; diffusion and absorptive capacity 272; and industry maturity 278–82; internalisation 277–8; mechanism 7, 123, 125, 132, 133, 134; and organisational form 275–6;

294

population ecology of the industry 125; systemic 276; *see also* information and innovation
inputs 52
institutions 8, 30–4, 148–50
integration 52, 196, 237; horizontal 278; vertical 69, 114, 154, 197, 278
inter-firm transactions 5–6
Internet 32
investment 282; alternative welfare economics 132; Austrian and post-Marshallian economics 145–7, 150–1; co-ordination 96, 129–30; competitive 150, 151; competitive process 132; complementary 151; emphasis 111; general equilibrium 107; and imperfect knowledge 261; information and innovation 274–5; market co-ordination 128–9; population ecology of the industry 122; *see also* information and investment
invisible hand 45–6, 59
Italy 276, 277

Jacobson, L. 247
Jacquemin, A. 78
Japan 78, 220, 226, 236, 272; *keiretsu* 276
Jenkins, F. 183
Jevons, S. 183
Johnson, B. 165
Johnson-Johnson 238
joint subsidiaries 114
joint venture 222, 224–30 *passim*, 233, 239, 240
Joll, C. 23

Kaldor, N. 4, 19, 29, 71, 72, 84
Kanter, R.M. 204
Kay, J.A. 1, 22, 31
Kay, N.M. 9–10, 32, 222–41
Kelly, G.A. 168
Keynes, J.M. 16, 20, 153, 183
Kirzner, I.M. 110, 111, 140, 141, 152, 177, 268–9
Klein, B. 189
Knight, F.R. 70, 71, 72, 73, 149, 153, 184
knowledge 5, 6, 10, 11, 64–9, 107–8, 283; Austrian and post-Marshallian economics 139, 141, 152; capabilities and theory of the firm 197; collaboration clusters 222; communication process 268; competitive advantage 174; costs 69, 153; direct 165, 171, 175; dispersed 145, 153; division 94; economic 69; firm as microeconomy 52; general equilibrium 85, 106; generation and communication 264; growth and co-ordination 79, 139; imperfect 101, 261; indirect 165, 175; information and investment 116, 117; innovation 196, 282; institutions 149; nature of industry and competition paradox 78; objective 173; organisation 7, 164–7; organisation of industry 151; perfect 27, 107; planned economy 115, 116; production costs 195; role 68; scientific or technological 69, 173, 273; specific 280; subjectivism and economic change 142; tacit 194; uncertainty and ignorance 263
'knowledge how' 165, 166, 172, 173, 175, 176, 177, 178; direct 167–70; indirect 170–1
'knowledge that' 165, 166, 168, 169–70, 172, 177, 178
Kodak 232
Kopple, R.G. 156, 185
Kuhn, T. 23, 109, 141

Lachmann, L.M. 141, 143, 149, 154, 155
Laffont, J.J. 83
Lamberton, D. 31, 32
Lamfalussy, A. 29
Lancaster, K. 107
Lange, O. 115
Langlois, R.N. 3, 31, 283; capabilities and theory of the firm 5, 8, 183–200; firm 153, 154, 155, 156; knowledge 194; managers 245; standardisation 270
Lardner, D. 183
Latin America 273
Lausanne School 85, 107, 115
Lavoie, D. 143, 145
Lazonick, W. 156, 276
Lee, F.S. 15, 17, 93, 142, 143
Leech, D. 246
Leijonhufvud, A. 31, 33, 105

295

INDEX

Leontief, W. 106
Lerner, A.P. 107
Lester, R.A. 143
Levinthal, D.A. 172, 273
Leyland, N.H. 243, 247, 255
limited liability company 58
liquidity theory of money 155
Loasby, B.J. 28, 31, 33, 104, 117, 139, 156, 184; Austrian economics 152, 153; capabilities 163–81; co-ordination in capabilities 1–12; 'Counterfactual history of twentieth century economics' 138; economists' behaviour 20; firms 140; investment co-ordination 19; knowledge 69; and Richardson's critique of general equilibrium 24–5
long-term contracts 187–8, 189
Lucas, R.E. 143
Lundvall, B.A. 165

McCulloch, J.R. 114
McFetridge, D.G. 225
MacGregor, D.H. 95, 139
McGuinness, T. 23
Machlup, F. 143
MacKie-Masson, J.K. 32
McNulty, P.J. 64, 184
macroeconomic theory of growth 122
macroeconomy 53, 56
Malmgren, H.B. 24, 32, 94, 153–5, 156
Malthus, T. 183
marginal theory of prices 94
marginalist theory of the firm 142
marginalist theory of value 70
market; co-ordination of investment 128–9; competitive 98; consumers 98; discipline 130–2; general 98; as information mechanisms 110–11; relations 99; share 117, 255–61; specific 91, 98, 99, 100; transactions 44, 45, 48, 55, 58, 75, 76, 77, 223
markets: Marshall, Andrews and Richardson on 83–101; agents and markets in Marshallian perspective 86–92; general economic equilibrium: agents and markets 84–6; global markets in Andrews and Richardson 97–101; individual agents in Andrews and Richardson 92–7

Marschak, J. 210
Marsh, J. 15
Marshall, A. 2, 16, 144–5, 156, 184, 252, 276; agents and markets 86–92; anti-Walrasian opposition 138; 'Business chivalry' 88; capabilities 179, 180; co-ordinating production 70; competition 112; deductive system 93; division of labour 169; economic freedom 45; entrepreneur 111; external organisation 5; firm 173; general equilibrium 105, 109, 128; industrial districts 277; *Industry and Trade* 65, 89, 91, 92; information 125; knowledge 11, 116, 164, 177; long-run supply curve 129; market 131, 134; markets 6; and new theory of value 140–1; *Principles* 47, 89, 91, 97, 98, 99, 168, 245; Representative Firm 110; technology 178; *see also* markets: Marshall, Andrews and Richardson on
Marshallian 7, 8, 15, 139, 152, 156
Martin, S. 22
Marx, K. 276
mechanical theory of equilibrium 140
Menger, C. 6, 16, 138, 139, 140, 141, 155, 156, 176
Mercantilism 271–2
mergers 223–9*passim*, 231–3, 238, 240
MERIT-CATI data base 230–1
Merk-Chiron-Ciba-Geigy 236
Merrett, D. 32
meta-rationality: minimising risk of mistakes 209–11
Metcalfe, J.S. 1–2, 127, 262–3
microeconomics 53, 56, 57, 58, 83, 96
Miles, C. 29
Milgrom, P.R. 139, 153, 154, 213
Minkler, A.P. 153, 156
Mintzberg, H. 180
Mises, L. von 116, 119, 138, 143, 149, 153, 155, 156
Mitsubishi 230, 232, 238
monopoly 77–8; rents 265
Monsanto 238
Moore, G.E. 21
Moore, J. 190
moral hazard 190–2, 245
Morgenstern, O. 26, 146, 147
Morris, D. 23

INDEX

Moss, S. 184
multinational enterprise *see* information costs and organisational structure
Muth, R.F. 27
Mytelka, L.K. 230–2, 235, 237, 239, 272

National Economic Development Office 115
nature of the firm and co-operation paradox 70–4
nature of industry and competition paradox 75–8
Neale, A.D. 115
NEDO-type activities 115
Negishi, T. 86
Nelson, R.R. 24, 148, 153, 165, 166, 176, 178, 180, 264, 275, 280
networks or clubs 30–4, 222, 276
niche market 255–6
Nightingale, J. 7, 31, 121–36
Norburn, D. 176
normal cost theory 123

O'Brien, D.P. 1, 6, 7, 104–18, 141, 143
O'Driscoll, G.P. 143, 152
oligopolistic market 134, 142
Olsen, C.P. 175
Opie, R. 109, 111
opportunism 188, 190, 191, 194, 224, 235, 236
organisation; firm as microeconomy 51; of industry theory 79; of knowledge 164–7; production costs 193–4
organisation of industry 151–2
'organisation of industry, The' 5, 6, 8, 17, 24, 150–1, 277; co-ordination necessity 44; production costs 196; transaction costs 186, 195
organisational form 275–6
organisational structure *see* information costs and organisational structure
over-investment 111
overlapping firm boundaries 225
Oxbridge resistance 117

Pareto Optimality 107, 115–16
Pareto-improving 186
partial equilibrium 105, 112, 113
partitioning 206

partnerships 10, 222, 248, 249, 251, 252
Pasinetti, L.L. 84
Pavitt, K. 280
Penrose, E.T. 10, 15, 31, 32, 139, 141, 143; capabilities 3; Effect 244, 246, 254; firms 20, 75, 153, 154, 166, 177; knowledge 5; perfect competition 142; production costs 195–7
perfect competition 7, 46, 68, 71, 72, 112; agents and markets 90, 91; Austrian and post-Marshallian economics 144–5; general equilibrium 84, 106, 107; information and investment 105, 116, 117; institutions 148–9; knowledge 108; nature of the firm and co-operation paradox 73; planned economy 115; rejection 142; Representative Firm and costs 113; shuffle 110; time 109
performance-related pay 214, 216
Phlips, L. 22
Pickering, J.F. 23
Pigou, A.C. 84, 92, 93, 107, 108, 128, 140, 194; price theory 184–5
Pigou-Clapham 'boxes' debate 140–1
Piore, M.J. 275–6, 277
planned economy 115–16
Planned Selection 130–1
planning 6, 29, 105, 113, 115, 150–1
'Planning versus competition' 21, 29, 150
Polanyi, M. 172, 194, 207
Popper, K.R. 64, 69, 71, 77, 78, 170, 171–2
population ecology of the industry 122–7
Porter, M.E. 22, 175, 230
Posner, R.A. 185
post-Marshallian economics *see* Austrian and post-Marshallian; information and co-ordination in effective competitive process
posted-price markets 133
power 9; *see also* balance
Power, J.H. 26, 28
Presley, J.R. 116
price/pricing; agreements 132; determination theory 94; expectations 85–6; fixing,

297

oligopolistic 117; mechanism 28–9, 48, 49, 52, 69, 70; notification schemes 3; system 66; theory 73; within a firm 52–4
primacy of exchange theory 64
principal-agent relationship 153
principal-agent theories 67
private company 10, 248, 249, 251, 252
problem-holders 265–6, 269
production; co-ordination 193; competitive 46; costs 8, 184–5, 186, 193–7; functions 112, 163, 171; information, knowledge and co-ordination 67; planning 67; process 271; techniques 86; theory 64, 66
profitability 52–3, 93, 253, 255, 282
profitability/growth trade-off 246, 247, 251, 252
progress theory 7
property rights 190, 224

quasi-rents 189, 190, 191, 192

Radner, R. 83, 207, 210
Raffaelli, T. 169
rationality 89, 147–8; bounded 188, 190, 204, 205; cognitive 85; complete 205; economic 86, 94, 97; individual agents 94; instrumental 85; perfect 84–5
Ravix, J.-L. 5, 6, 63–80
re-contracting 45, 108
Reid, G.C. 10, 23, 32, 243–59
Reinganum, J.F. 148
rent-seeking behaviour 188, 190
replication of reporting 214, 216
Representative Firm 108, 110, 112–13, 128
research 134; co-ordination problem 18–20; and development 265, 274
residual rights 190
resource allocation 66, 122, 224, 230
resource linkages 232
resources, ownership of 9
restrictive agreements 133
restrictive trade practices 3, 129
Restrictive Trade Practices Act 1956 113
Ricardo, D. 138
risk 59, 117

Rizzo, M. 143, 152
Robbins, L. 16, 66–7, 105, 107, 113
Roberts, J. 83, 213
Robertson, D.H. 70, 92, 105, 116
Robertson, P.L. 10–11, 32, 154, 155, 194, 197, 261–85, 270, 283
Robinson 125
Robinson - which one? 125
Robinson, A. 64, 71, 72, 73
Robinson, J.V. 20, 27, 107, 108, 140, 141, 146
Robinson-Chamberlin-Machlup synthesis 122
Romer, P.M. 265
Rosenberg, N. 165, 166, 167, 277
Ross, D. 23
Rumelt, R.P. 227
Russell, B. 21
Ryle, G. 8, 165, 166–7, 176, 180

Sabel, C.F. 275–6, 277
Savage, L. 117
Saxenian, A. 276, 277, 279
scale 54–5
Scazzieri, R. 84
Schelling, T.C. 194
Scherer, F.M. 23, 24, 115, 117
Schmalensee, R. 23
Schnaars, S.P. 197
Schoenberg, R. 176
Schumpeter, J.A. 123, 125, 131, 178, 179–80, 197, 262, 276, 279
Scitovsky, T. 24
selection 59, 130–2
Sestokova, Madame 21
Shackle, G.L.S. 32, 72, 108, 109, 165
Shove, G. 105
Silicon Valley 275–6, 279
Silver, M. 154, 155, 197
similarity 6, 283; economic organisation and flexibility 155; innovation 278; *see also* information, similarity and complementarity
Simon, H.A. 15, 178, 179, 188
simultaneous equation system 10, 254–6
size and growth of firm 57, 71, 72, 73, 248, 249
small business enterprises 247, 248, 250, 251, 252, 253, 254
Smith, A. 171, 185, 277; co-ordination 170; division of labour 49, 164,

180–1; economic development theory 165; endogenous growth 8; knowledge 11, 116, 173; market transactions and 'invisible hand' 45, 59; Richardson on 7; technologies 178
Smith Kline 236
Social Sciences Citation Index 23–4, 33
sole proprietorship 10, 248, 249, 251, 252
Solow, R.M. 170
solution-holders 265–6, 269
Sonnenschein, H. 83
Sony 125
specialisation 56; collaboration clusters 224; communications, scale and structure 54, 55; consolidation costs 57, 58; division of labour and organisation of knowledge 164–5; flexible 156; innovation 278; production costs 194–5
specific markets 97
specific rights 190
Spencer, H. 140
Spiethoff, A. 116
Sraffa, P. 3, 105, 141, 147, 153
stakeholders 206
standardisation 270, 271
static equilibrium 72
Steindl, J. 123
Sterling, C.H. 271
Stigler, G.J. 15, 65, 66, 108, 277
Stiglitz, J.E. 134, 273
Stinchcombe, A.L. 191, 264
Stoneman, P. 262, 281–2
Stopford, J.M. 279
Streissler, E. 140
structure 54–5
subjective value theory 138
subjectivism and economic change 142–3
Swann, D. 104, 111, 114, 115
Switzerland 273, 274

tâtonnement 83, 108
technical conditions 86
Teece, D.J. 1, 24, 32, 183, 196, 223
theory of the firm 75, 140, 152–3
Thomas, B. 140
Thompson, G.V. 270
Thompson, J.D. 264

time 7, 104–5, 107, 109–10, 111, 112, 132
Tirole, J. 22
trade barriers 205
trade-off relationship 252–6
traditional price theory 184
transaction costs 79, 185–8, 193, 194; competition and theory of the firm 183–4; direction 49; firm's growth rate 248–9, 250–1; information costs and multinational enterprise 204; information, knowledge and co-ordination 69; innovation 278; modern theory 188–93; nature of the firm and co-operation paradox 71, 72, 74; nature of industry and competition paradox 77; production cost 197; theory 67
transfer mechanism 7, 123, 125, 126, 129, 130, 132, 133
Tremblay, P. 26
triads 236
Triffin, R. 108
Tushman, M.L. 280
twinning agreements 234–5

uncertainty 83, 262–4; agents and markets 89; Austrian and post-Marshallian economics 147; cartelisation 113; and co-ordination 261; competition 112, 132; endogenous 147; general economic equilibrium 85–6; individual agents 94, 95; information costs 206; information and investment 117; innovation 282; planned economy 115; strategic 96–7; systemic 94; transaction-cost theory 191
unit costs 245
United Kingdom 270, 273, 274
United States 115, 131, 138, 225, 226, 263, 270–4; *see also* Silicon Valley
Utterback, J.M. 277, 279, 281, 283

value theory 92–3, 140–1
Varian, H. 32
Vaughn, K.I. 138
Vickers, J. 78
Viner, J. 84, 140
Voltaire 52

Wagner, L. 21, 29
Walliser, B. 85
Walras, L. 16, 92, 145; adjustment and time 112; auctioneer 45, 148; general equilibrium 108; Lausanne School 85
Walrasian 2, 3, 84, 85, 86, 89, 91, 146, 147
Ward-Perkins, N. 16
welfare economics 107, 108
welfare economics, alternative 132–4
Western Europe 263
Whitehead, A.N. 169, 183
Wicksell, K. 85
Wicksell init. 85
Williams, B.R. 19–20
Williamson, O.E. 6, 24, 32, 72, 75, 154, 248–9; asset specificity 245; inhospitality tradition 185; merger 224; opportunism 5; transaction-cost theory 67, 74, 79, 188–90, 193, 248–9
Willig, 23
Willig init. 23
Winter, S.G. 148, 153, 165, 166, 173, 176, 178, 180, 280
Wolfe, J.N. 32
Woo, H.K. 169
Woodward, S. 79, 191

Young, A. 19
Young, W. 15

Zajac, E.J. 175
Zeitlin, J. 276, 277
Ziman, J.M. 169